The Bubble Economy

The Bubble Economy
Is Sustainable Growth Possible?

Robert U. Ayres

The MIT Press
Cambridge, Massachusetts
London, England

MIT Press books may be purchased at special quantity discounts for business or sales promotional use. For information, please email special_sales@mitpress.mit.edu.

This book was set in Sabon by the MIT Press. Printed and bound in the United States of America.

Library of Congress Cataloging-in-Publication Data

Ayres, Robert U.
The bubble economy : is sustainable growth possible? / Robert U. Ayres.
  pages cm
Includes bibliographical references and index.
ISBN 978-0-262-02743-4 (hardcover : alk. paper) 1. Power resources—History.
2. Financial crises—History. 3. Sustainable development—History. I. Title.
HD9502.A2A958 2014
338.5'4—dc23
2013041748

10 9 8 7 6 5 4 3 2 1

Contents

Preface

There is a crisis in academic economics, though many senior economists at the great universities don't yet realize it. The problem is, simply, that standard theory, from textbooks, explains less and less of what is going on "out there." I think the problem, in very few words, is that the textbooks tend to treat economic variables like "supply," "demand," "utility," "goods," and "services" as abstractions. But the abstractions are not the reality. Theory assumes that "economic agents" maximize "utility" (or profits), whereas in reality they rarely do so. Much of what has happened to the global economy in recent decades is attributable, at least partly, to weaknesses in economic theory. However, this book is not about theory, or how to fix it. It is about the real world and how it turns.

Yes, I work as an economist (of sorts), but I came to the field a little later than most. My boyhood ambition was to walk in Albert Einstein's footsteps and create a "theory of everything." When I got to college (the University of Chicago), majoring in mathematics and physics, it became obvious that "everything" (even in strictly physical terms) is rather more than I could aspire to grasp in one lifetime. Other needs and interests took over. Several years passed. I wrote a few physics papers, but the available topics seemed irrelevant to the "theory of everything."

Rather suddenly, in the spring of 1962 I was invited to take a temporary job (for a contractor to the DOD) at an atmospheric nuclear test. It was to be held that summer in the Western Pacific. It was a chance to do something different and "real," which was important to me at the time. Based on that experience, I was hired by the Hudson Institute (led by Herman Kahn) to do a study of the economic and environmental consequences of a global nuclear war. I spent three years on that topic, and duly wrote a three-volume report for the Office of Civil Defense. But for some reason I didn't want to make a career of studies of nuclear Armageddon. My newly acquired environmental qualifications impressed a think tank called Resources for the Future (RFF) where I was surprisingly invited to lead a new program on environmental economics. I sensibly declined, for lack of formal economics training, though my report to the Office of Civil Defense did incorporate some economic considerations. Anyway, RFF thought I had something to offer, and I spent a year there (1967), working with a real economist named Allan Kneese. We became good friends and colleagues. He was a pioneer in environmental economics, and my economics mentor.

About then, I met a fellow-physicist, Theodore Taylor, who was worried about nuclear proliferation, and how to stop it. With help from an investor (EG&G) we created a consultancy together, with the grandiose name of International Research and Technology (IR&T). For the next ten years (1968 to 1978) I continued to collaborate with Kneese at RFF, as well as on a series of projects related to environmental economics, energy, transportation, what we now call "life-cycle" analysis (LCA), and environmental statistics.

In 1979 I moved to one of the few interdisciplinary academic departments in the world, as Professor of Engineering and Public Policy.[1] There (as I was told later) the engineering professor who interviewed me said "he might be good economist but he's not an engineer." The economics professor said exactly the same thing, in reverse. Those two non-recommendations seem to have canceled each other out. I was hired. I was lucky.

My point is that very few of us are given the opportunity to do serious interdisciplinary research, even though the need is great. Deep questions cross disciplinary boundaries. For instance, where will the inhabitants of the Maldives and other island countries go when the sea level rises another meter? Will the Arctic Ocean be ice free and open for oil drilling in the coming decades? What are the implications of rising sea levels and increased storminess for coastal regions? Can coastal areas be protected by dikes? How will the dikes be financed? What are the implications for the insurance industry? The questions go on and on, and almost nobody at senior levels in business or government is thinking about the answers. The vast majority of professional and academic economists have no training in physical science, ecology, or engineering. The majority of engineers have no training in environmental science, social science, or economics.

Law schools teach neither science nor economics. Business education (where I have worked for the last twenty years) covers topics like leadership, entrepreneurship, marketing, strategy, technology management, HR management, business economics, and finance. But physical science and environmental science are entirely absent, at least in the business schools I have encountered.

Fortunately, interdisciplinary subjects like "ecological economics," "industrial ecology," "environmental science," and "sustainability" have sprung up and thrived, mainly because of interest by young people. Privately funded nongovernment organizations (NGOs) like the Sierra Club, the Environmental Defense Fund, and the World Wildlife Fund provide a few jobs in those fields. Yet the departmental structures of most universities have not changed or accommodated ecological studies. The US Council of Economic Advisors is recruited from the mainstream university economics departments where science is not taught (or well understood) as are the staffs of the Federal Reserve, the European Central Bank, the IMF, the World Bank, the OECD, and the International Energy Agency. Bankers, nowadays, come from finance departments of business schools. Legislators in the United States are overwhelmingly from law or business backgrounds, not science or engineering. (China and Germany both have more scientists and engineers at top leadership levels than the United States.)

This book started several years ago as an almost visceral reaction to the superficiality of media coverage of issues like climate change, energy security, the financial crisis, job creation, and economic growth. For instance, in the last few years some Anglo-Saxon economists and commentators had been saying that Humpty Dumpty (I mean the eurozone) was about to fall and shatter. That was when the nonfinancial media started to talk a lot about the Greek financial crisis. I was especially taken aback by the sniping of some British Tory politicians who radiated satisfaction that Britain was safe, thanks to not having joined the eurozone in the first place. "Super Mario" Draghi put it nicely when he pointed out that bumblebees are supposed to be aerodynamically incapable of flying. But the bumblebees don't know that, and they fly just fine. Doing away with competitive devaluations between European countries was (I thought) one of the reasons for adopting the common currency in the first place. I still believe that the European experiment will succeed if German domestic politics doesn't go off the rails.

OK, the bumblebees are a digression. My point is that there are lessons yet to be learned. Uncritical belief in oversimplified economic theories, such as the wonders of "capitalism," "free trade," and the "free market" have much to answer for. I think it is important for media to point out that the global financial system is not inherently stable. It is not "self-organizing," to use a word out of the natural sciences. A self-organizing system is inherently self-correcting; it is inherently stable and cures itself from momentary disturbances. The market for agricultural products, for instance, may be self-correcting in that sense. The financial system is only self-correcting by the mechanism of creating and destroying financial bubbles.

Apart from the financial crisis, there is a surprising lack of awareness among financial writers, and economists generally, of the role of natural resources in general, and energy in particular, as drivers of economic growth. I have a hunch—more than a hunch, really—that the price of oil is an important clue, not only to explaining the past but as a guide to the future. Neither labor nor capital can produce anything without natural resource (energy) inputs and waste outputs. The inescapable implication of this fact is that useful energy[2] is a "factor of production" as fundamental as labor or capital. The notion taught in many textbooks is that energy is an intermediate product, "produced" by some combination of labor and capital. This is based on the allocation of payments in the national accounts, either to labor or to capital but not to "nature" or "resources." This notion is misleading insofar as it misidentifies the true sources of productivity. Useful energy is essential to economic growth and will be essential to economic recovery from the present malaise. Energy resources are also a significant component of financial wealth. Energy prices have contributed to financial bubbles. Unfortunately, mainstream economic models still undervalue energy.[3] This has led to economic policy recommendations that will not work. Another justification for this book is to shed light on that blind spot in economic theory.

But, while energy is necessary, some kinds of energy are useful and others (like waste heat) are not. Moreover the by-products of obtaining useful energy from carbon-based fossil fuels are toxic for our home planet, "Gaia," as Lovelock put it poetically some years ago (Lovelock 1979). I argue in this book that long-term habitability for the human race requires a massive global "de-carbonization" program: "re-inventing fire" in the words of Amory Lovins (Lovins 2011). This means ending the global addiction to fossil fuels and the technologies (especially internal combustion engines) that depend on those resources. This in turn means that alternative noncarbon energy resources, namely "renewables," must be developed more quickly. That project has enormous financial consequences. The need for investment in new technology and capital equipment is only one side of the coin. There is a corresponding need for disinvestment in obsolescent technologies, with financial consequences that have scarcely been noticed.

My arguments didn't really hang together for a while, even as I wrote and rewrote. This book went through at least four drafts, plus a lot of tinkering, none of which satisfied me or the colleagues with whom I have shared some of this. There were too many moving parts, too much happening, too many different actors. But finally I realized what one common theme must be: the (comparatively) simple world of Adam Smith and Thomas Jefferson is long gone. Markets in the twenty-first century are not like village markets in which both buyer and seller expect to be better off as a result of every exchange, while third party effects are negligible. A well-known phrase from Adam Smith that captures some of the flavor of early economic theory is "the invisible hand." That phrase reflects the observation that trade is good for everybody, so more trade is even better and trade is the source of the wealth of nations. But trade in the financial markets, even between supposedly sophisticated parties, is not always good for everybody. The invisible hand is not always beneficent. Sometimes it can be more like a fist wearing brass knuckles. The year 2008 was one of those times.

My point is that financial transactions on Wall Street are not like exchange transactions in a village market. The pain on Main Street can far exceed the gains on Wall Street. Part of the reason for this book is to explain why that is so, and what can and should be done about it. It is very important for the future of our society (and of capitalism) that the negative externalities in finance be understood, avoided, eliminated, or compensated by appropriate government intervention. I know the word "externality" is unfamiliar, but it is the right word. I will explain later.

Yes, I do mean government intervention, but not government ownership of the "means of production," as Marx and Engels proposed. That version of socialism has been thoroughly discredited. The government is not the best producer of goods or services (unless regulation is a service). Government is the defender of *rights* (including, but not limited to, private property), the regulator of economic actions, and the umpire of conflicts. The financial markets need to be regulated actively in the sense of leaning "against the wind," mainly by using both monetary and fiscal policy tools. (Of course, rules have a place, and when clear rules are trashed again and again by bankers "too big to fail," there must be real punishment for the perpetrators (and their enablers). It seems blatantly wrong that when an individual embezzles money from his employer, he may go to jail and will certainly lose his job. But when Goldman Sachs does something that costs clients billions and adds billions to its own profits (as it has, repeatedly), the worst that can happen is a virtually unnoticeable fine from the SEC.

President Reagan's notion that "government is the problem, not the solution" is itself part of the problem. Conservative members of the US Congress, along with some in other countries, are now firmly convinced for ideological reasons that "big government" is "too much government" (and too much taxation) and that their primary agenda must be to "shrink" government by cutting taxes. Lobbyist Grover Norquist has made a career getting Republican candidates to sign a pledge, known as "The Pledge," never to vote to raise taxes or allow any change in the tax code that would increase government revenues. Every Republican member of the Congress elected in 2010 had signed that pledge. The 2012 presidential election was framed by the Republicans in exactly in those terms. Consequently the regulatory bodies that exist today have been throttled and emasculated by congressional Republicans since the 1980s. Their explicit goal has been to "starve the beast" by which they mean defunding everything except the (so-called) defense sector. Mr. Norquist frequently jokes that he wants to reduce the size of the government "down to the size where we can drown it in the bathtub." That is a bad and foolish idea.

Let me be clear: I am prepared to say at the outset—in agreement with US Republicans and direct opposition to many of my "green" colleagues—that, on the one hand, most OECD governments, including the US government, today are too big, too bureaucratic, and should be downsized in terms of direct employment and spending in coming decades. On the other hand, *to reduce the size of the bureaucracy does not mean to reduce its role*. It does not mean "deregulation" as the term is used on the political right. It does mean cutting bureaucracies and using economic incentives much more than overdetailed rules written by lawyers. (The Dodd–Frank rules now allegedly amount to 1,000 pages. That is about ten times too much, in my view.) And, having said that, I do not rule out some other drastic interventions, such as enforced breakups of too-big-to-fail (TBTF) banks, or even temporary nationalizations. Such interventions may be an inevitable accompaniment of fractional-reserve banking. If the term "fractional reserve" is unfamiliar, read on. It is crucial.

Hardly anybody, even in the finance departments of business schools or in the executive suites of the towers on Wall Street, is aware of all of the problems in the financial sector per se, not to mention the relevance of peak oil, climate change, and economic growth or how they all interact. Citizens of the United States of America and other democracies really need to get much better educated. Democratic government will fail unless a lot more of the citizens know a lot more about how the economic and financial system works and how it failed and may fail again—and how that system interacts with the larger physical world. Only then will they elect leaders who can make the right decisions. This book is my attempt to help with the public education process.

Oh yes, one last comment seems appropriate. I have seen several rather "blue-sky" studies of how to make the global economy "green." I find myself in agreement with many of the specific proposals in those studies. Some of them I make, for my own reasons, in this book. But a major component of any "green economy" proposal is investment. I am prepared to say, in advance, that the investments that need to be made will have to be made by the private sector, not by governments struggling to balance their budgets. And that in turn means that the investments will have to be both low in risk and more profitable than other long-term investments that offer themselves. This requirement will not be easy to meet, but I think it can be met.

My reason for writing this book can finally be summarized in a few sentences. Most people on Main Street know about one or two of the key factors leading up to the financial crisis of 2008 to 2009 and the recession that followed (which is not over yet). Everybody has heard about the problem of government debt, though few have a clear idea of what it means for them. Some know about the problem of "peak oil" but many are persuaded that it isn't serious or immediate. Most have heard of "global warming" (a misnomer), but thanks to a flood of disinformation from the energy industry, many are skeptical whether it is really happening. (After all, we still sometimes get cold winters.) Most people on Main Street know about subprime mortgages without knowing how they were sold and who bought them, or why. Most know something about "renewables," but not much about the actual options out there. Hardly anybody knows about thermodynamic efficiency. A lot more people need to know about all of these things and their interlinkages.

Acknowledgments

This book, possibly my last, is the product of a lifetime of fifty-plus years of interaction with other scholars, far too numerous to list in full. Yet some important influences I must mention, including those with whom I disagreed. The list starts (chronologically) with Richard Tredgold at the University of Maryland; Phil Wyatt at the University of Chicago; Herman Kahn at Hudson Institute; Allen Kneese and Ronald Ridker at Resources for the Future; Pradeep Rohatgi, Ted Taylor, Jim Cumming-Saxton, and Martin Stern from my years at International Research and Technology; and Granger Morgan, Lester Lave, Francis McMichael, and Joel Tarr in the Department of Engineering and Public Policy at C-MU. More recently (and alphabetically) I have learned much from personal conversations with Ken Arrow, Edward Ayres, Christian Azar, Jeroen van den Bergh, Tom Casten, Colin Campbell, Marina Fischer-Kowalski, Michael Kumhoff, Landis Gabel, Arnulf Grubler, Ludo van der Heyden, Paul Horne, Jean-Charles Hourcade, Reiner Kümmel, Arkady Kryazhimskiy, Skip Laitner, Dietmar Lindenberger, Skip Luken, Kati Martinas, Lou Munden, Nebojsa Nakicenovic, Philippe Pichat, Harry Plant, Lee Remmers, Adam Rose, Bio Schmidt-Bleek, Uwe Schulte, Gerry Silverberg, Udo Simonis, Jim Sweeney, Luk van Wassenhove, Kimon Valaskakis, Gara Villalba, Vlasios Voudouris, Ingo Walter, Ben Warr, and last but not least, Ernst von Weiszaecker. I have also learned from interactions with my students and postdoctoral fellows, especially Rob Axtell, Ike Ezekoya, Geraldo Ferrer, Jeff Funk, Roland Geyer, Xue Lan, Steve Miller, Andre Cabrera Serrenho, and Laura Talens. Above all, completion of this work is indebted to my super-editor Dana Andrus of the MIT Press and to my wife Leslie, who has provided not only useful criticism but also a fund of computer-related skills that I lack.

1

Background

Chapter 1 begins with a brief tribute to Senator Carter Glass, the man with fingerprints both on the creation of the Federal Reserve System and the Glass–Steagall law of 1933 that prevented commercial banks from engaging in trading and investment banking activities. This is followed by a brief look at the Russian émigré novelist and political theorist, Ayn Rand and her ideas. Ayn Rand is interesting both because she was the primary inspiration for modern libertarianism, as well as the chief mentor of Alan Greenspan as a young man and the chief inspiration of today's Republican leadership.

The rest of chapter 1 explains, in ordinary language, some important economic ideas, including the importance of markets, the notion that an exchange implies that both parties expect to be better off, (or there would be no trade) the origin of economies of scale, and the importance of specialization. There is a discussion of fundamental concepts, especially the notions of self-interest, rationality and equilibrium (self-correction). It points out that many transactions in the real world have consequences affecting persons or firms that had no say in the decision. (These are called externalities.) It notes that financial markets are inherently unstable hence prone to creating externalities ("bubbles"). Thus almost any given policy or practice generates unintended and unexpected consequences that can be either positive or negative. Finally, it discusses the role of energy in the economic system, both in standard neoclassical growth theory and in more recent theory where energy has a much greater importance.

In Memoriam: Senator Carter Glass (1858–1946)

There are few heroes in this story, but Carter Glass was one. He was an old-school southern Democrat, from Lynchburg, Virginia, with a frail physique, strong convictions and a famously sharp tongue. He began as a newspaper reporter, later editor and owner, before his election to the State Senate in 1899. In December 1902 he resigned to run for a vacant congressional seat. He was re-elected nine times, until he resigned for the last time in December 1918 to become Secretary of the Treasury for President Wilson. He only served one year in that job because he was appointed to a vacant senatorial seat, which he took in February 1920. Thereafter he was re-elected in 1924 and every six years thereafter until his death in 1946. He was, throughout his career, a Jeffersonian Democrat and (in Roosevelt's words) "an unreconstructed Rebel") meaning that his sympathies were Southern to the core.

Some give him credit for inventing the Federal Reserve System. Glass himself credited Woodrow Wilson. In any case, they worked closely together on the legislation. After the stock market crash in 1929 he fought for reform legislation, including the Glass–Steagall (Banking) Act of 1933, the Reconstruction Finance Act of 1933, the Securities Exchange Act of 1934, and the Banking Act of 1935. He opposed the creation of the Federal Deposit Insurance Corporation (FDIC). Roosevelt offered him the job of Secretary of the Treasury, but he turned it down, partly for health reasons but probably (reading between the lines) because he didn't trust Roosevelt. He disagreed with much of the "New Deal" and especially opposed "unconstitutional" federal interference in private affairs. He fought for a balanced budget in 1936 (which turned out to be a bad mistake). On civil and voting rights he was a reactionary. Truman wrote in a letter to Mrs. Glass after her husband's death that "to the end he glorified in the title of 'Unreconstructed Rebel.'"

I attach one of the pseudo-quotes from McAfee's 1997 article, written 50 years after his death, below (McAfee 1997).[1]

Q. The FRB is currently dismantling the Glass–Steagall Act's walls between commercial and investment banks. As one of the architects of those walls, do you regret the changes?
G. Our subcommittee did not act out of any prejudice or in a whimsical or inadequate way. We consulted practical bankers and experts extensively. We did everything but sleep with experts, and we learned that national banks had created affiliates as a way of doing precisely those things that the National Bank Act prohibited them from doing. Apart from Edge Act corporations and that sort of thing, affiliates were the slippery conjurations of lawyers. Shrewd men operated them and entwined the parent banks in great difficulties. Banks lent their names, prestige and tradition of sound banking operations to these affiliates, and on that

basis did people invest and transact business with them. When calamity struck, not all bankers felt a responsibility to the citizens they had enticed. Not all bankers could afford to. We hoped those measures would answer the public's loss of confidence, protect depositors and investors, and help prevent Federal Reserve facilities from being used in support of stock and commodity gambling, which had brought on the Depression and about which I had been warning for 14 years or more, though I was never simple enough to think I could end gambling. If I may speak personally, I think commercial banks should stick to commercial banking, if that is still feasible. The Board seems to be trying to accomplish many of the same goals as we were, except of course that it does not seem to mind stock gambling as it should and as we did, and it must protect the deposit guaranty fund [FDIC], which we lost no sleep over. . . .

Several direct quotes from Senator Glass can be found later in McAfee's section about the stock market crash of 1929. They are entirely consistent with his scathing view about banks and bankers, as expressed above.

Ayn Rand and Friends; Origins of Libertarianism

Ayn Rand was born Alisa Rosenbaum in Saint Petersburg, Russia. She was the daughter of a well-to-do Jewish merchant family that was impoverished by the 1917 Bolshevik Revolution. Despite her family's reduced circumstances she graduated from the University in Saint Petersburg. Moreover she managed to emigrate from Russia in 1926 and came to the United States. Along the way she changed her name to Ayn Rand. She went to Hollywood where she wrote and sold several movie scripts and a novel, *Anthem,* that was later made into a movie. Its anti-collectivist Orwellian theme was a love story set in a society where individualism no longer existed. In her story all communication was impersonal. Writings and verbal messages (except by the hero) always used the word "we" instead of "I."

Rand also became politically active especially in opposition to Franklin Roosevelt's "New Deal," which she (and others) considered to be the first step toward a collectivist, totalitarian society similar to Marxism-Leninism as then practiced in the Soviet Union. Needless to say, she had no sympathy for the nuanced view of the Bolshevik Revolution, as expressed by Boris Pasternak in *Doctor Zhivago.*

Later (1943) she wrote a more serious novel, *The Fountainhead,* about a free-thinking individualistic architect—possibly modeled on Frank Lloyd Wright—who had to fight constantly against conventional (collectivist) wisdom (Rand 1943). It was a best seller, with worldwide sales of 6.5 million copies, and was made into a successful movie that made the author both famous and wealthy.

In 1950, still living in California, Rand and her husband, Frank O'Connor, met with an admirer of *The Fountainhead* and student of psychology named Nathaniel Brandon, and his (then) girl-friend Barbara Weidman. They all became friends. But two years later, Rand split with O'Connor and moved from Los Angeles to New York City. In Manhattan she initiated a French-style "salon" where political-philosophic-economic issues were discussed with a group of youthful, idealistic followers, one of whom was Alan Greenspan.

Rand's primary motivation, throughout her life, was fierce defense of individualism and opposition to "collectivism" in any form. The positive aspect of her thesis is that all human wealth, apart from natural resources, has been created by a relatively few creative geniuses (all capitalists, of course). I would set the role of natural resources higher and the role of invention somewhat lower than she did, but so far I mostly agree. Rand believed that invention is essentially associated with individualism, whence it cannot prosper in a "collectivist" society. There, too, I tend to agree. But Rand interpreted any government intervention in the idealized "free market" as collectivism, and there I part company with her. In her view, pure "capitalism is the only system geared to the life of a rational being and the only *moral* political economic system in history" (Rand 1967).

Her core idea, later adopted by the Libertarians, was that "every person owns his or her life, and no person can own any other person's life." Her philosophical rejection of collectivism and totalitarianism morphed into a rejection of "socialism" and any social programs that involved any redistribution, namely the use of taxes to help the less fortunate—the "moochers"—at the expense of the creative and productive individualists whom she so admired. She viewed voluntary altruism as harmless but involuntary income redistribution through the tax system as morally wrong. In her view, each person should do with his life whatever he or she wants, without any restriction except that he or she causes no harm to others (a sentiment similar to the Hippocratic Oath).

Alan Greenspan appeared on the scene in 1952 about the time Rand came to New York. As a young man in the 1940s Greenspan had studied music at the Juilliard School in Manhattan. He did not serve in the military during WWII. He played the saxophone and clarinet and briefly toured with a swing band. In 1944 he enrolled at NYU and got a BS in economics in 1948 and an MS in 1950. He started in the PhD program at Columbia University, but dropped out in 1951 for lack of money for tuition. In 1952 he married painter Joan Mitchell, who introduced him to Ayn Rand. (The marriage to Mitchell only lasted a year.) The young and ambitious Greenspan became fascinated with Rand's ideas and joined the regular Saturday evening salon at her apartment in Manhattan. (In 1954 Alan Greenspan joined ex-bond-trader William Townsend to become a partner in an economic consultancy, which changed its name to Townsend-Greenspan and Company (TG&C). In 1958 Greenspan's partner William Townsend died and Alan Greenspan became sole owner of TG&C, which seems to have specialized in regulatory issues. During the next decade it picked up some influential clients, including JP Morgan and US Steel.

Together with Branden[2] and Greenspan, Ayn Rand tried to create a consistent intellectual framework, which they called "objectivism." In 1957 Ayn Rand's third novel *Atlas Shrugged* was published. It was quickly dismissed by reviewers who objected to both her romantic style and her radical ideas. *Time Magazine* called it "a nightmare." Sidney Hook, a well-known philosopher, panned it in the *NY Times*. (Alan Greenspan wrote a letter to the *NY Times* defending *Atlas Shrugged* from Sidney Hook's review. Her hero, a mysterious personage called "John Galt," makes a fifty-page speech in the novel that achieved some notoriety among conservatives. It launched Ayn Rand's entry into intellectual ultra-conservatism through a lecture series that became influential in the 1960s.

In 1958, after the publication of *Atlas Shrugged*, Ayn Rand and Nathaniel Branden created an institute (the Nathaniel Branden Institute) for the propagation of her ideas by means of taped lectures. They also jointly published the *Objectivist Newsletter*. The institute operated successfully from 1958 to 1968 with representation in as many as 60 cities until an acrimonious breakup in 1968 that was explained differently by the two parties. Yet after Rand's death, Nathaniel's wife Barbara Branden wrote her biography (Branden 1986).

The wreckage of the Nathaniel Branden Institute eventually led to the formation of the Libertarian Party. Its first candidate for the presidency of the United States (1972) was one of Rand's most loyal followers. He was John Hospers, a philosopher at Brooklyn College whom she met on the occasion of a lecture there (Burns 1997). The Libertarians got 8,715 popular votes and one electoral vote from a Virginia Republican who split with his party and four years later ran for president as the Libertarian candidate. After the 1972 election Hospers moved to California where he became chairman of the Philosophy Department at the University of Southern California.

In 1968 it seems that TG&C was having financial difficulties. At any rate, its principal, Greenspan, took a job with the Nixon presidential campaign as director of policy research. In 1974 Nixon appointed Greenspan as head of his Council of Economic Advisors. (Ayn Rand attended the White House dinner). He stayed on as chairman of President Ford's Council of Economic Advisors, during the brief Ford presidency (1975 to 1976), but went back to TG&C when Jimmy Carter was elected in 1976. In 1977 NYU gave him a PhD in economics without requiring a thesis. As soon as the Carter administration ended, Greenspan went back to Washington.

On February 10, 1982, President Reagan appointed Alan Greenspan to his Economic Advisory Board. On December 16 of that year Reagan appointed Greenspan as chairman of his Commission on Social Security. When Volker resigned from the Fed in 1987, Reagan appointed Greenspan to be his replacement.

While *Atlas Shrugged* was not admired by academics during its first decade, it still sells 200,000 copies per year and is now widely used in classrooms. (In fact Paul Ryan, head of the House Budget Committee and 2012 vice presidential candidate, is an open follower of her theories. Indeed he allegedly requires every one of his staffers to read the book.)

Personalities apart, Ayn Rand's ideas are based on a very selective reading of the ideas of early economists, including Adam Smith ("self-interest"),[3] David Ricardo ("free trade"), J. B. Say ("laissez faire"), and John Stuart Mill (Smith 1976 [1776], Say 1821 [1803], Mill 1848). Mill wasn't much of a writer of quotable text. However, he wrote in his famous essay *On Liberty*: "The sole end for which mankind are [sic] warranted, individually or collectively, in interfering with the liberty of action of any one of their number, is self-protection." But he went on to write that we should be "without impediment from our fellow creatures *so long as what we do does not harm them*, even though they should think our conduct foolish, perverse or wrong" (Mill 1869). The italics are mine. The problem with that statement by J. S. Mill is that the possibility of *unintentional harm* (in the form of externalities) is not considered. The very existence of externalities in economics was in fact not really acknowledged by theorists until the emergence of welfare economics as a minor topic within the field in the 1920s, and even then, only in terms of rather trivial examples (Pigou 1920; see also (Kapp 1950; Baumol 1967).

Ayn Rand's first nonfiction book was *The Virtue of Selfishness*, a paean to unfettered pure capitalism (Rand 1964). In that book she saw no need for social norms or a society of any kind. It was as though every person could (and should) be an independent, self-sufficient pioneer or rancher in the wilderness, but that the cavalry should always be near at hand to drive off the Indians. Later she edited a collection *Capitalism, the Unknown Ideal* including a number of her own essays, along with three essays by Alan Greenspan and two by Nathaniel Branden (Rand 1967). In one place she recapitulated Mill, again without considering the possibility of externalities and unintentional harm:

The proper functions of a government are: the police, to protect men from criminals, the military forces to protect men from foreign invaders and the law courts, to protect men's property and contracts from breach by force or fraud and to settle disputes among men according to objectively defined laws. (Rand 1967, p. 47)

In other words, Rand saw no need for a society that would offer public services such as roads, public health, education, or research. In her view and that of the Libertarians, all of those services are either unnecessary and should be eliminated, or should be privatized or voluntary. She has no explanation of how the public health service or the public school system could be privatized, or how it could have been created in the first place. It is no coincidence that her emphasis on the legitimacy of military force to protect men from foreign invaders is now applied by the United States to terrorists and jihadists located in countries far away. "Defense" has morphed into the use of force to kill "enemy combatants" and "protect American interests" around the world.

A few pages later (p. 49) she says that "the most infamous piece of legislation in American history" is the Sherman Anti-Trust Act (1890).[4] She (and others, including Greenspan) criticized the legislation for ambiguity as to what is, and what is not, legal behavior. The fact that the law in its original form had almost no applications (except against a labor union, the "wobblies," i.e., the International Workers of the World) testifies to that weakness. In the next few pages she cited a number of inflammatory statements (all by corporate lawyers) as to theoretical possibilities. For instance, she suggested that an executive might be put in jail for setting his prices too high, according to "some bureaucrat" ("intent to monopolize"), too low ("unfair competition"), or for selling at prices exactly the same as competitors ("collusion" or "restraint of trade"). Why so much venom directed at a law with so little practical effect? Why the total lack of any recognition on her part that monopolies do cause harm (by keeping prices too high), as all economists know or should know? Why no recognition that "restraint of trade" can actually hurt people? Why is it that, in her imaginary world, only the tycoons deserve legal protection but not the little guys they ran over on their way to the pinnacles of success?

The Anti-Libertarian Case

Rand's criticism (and that of Greenspan) of legal ambiguity is perfectly valid. She is right that laws should be clear and objective. (The same criticism is being made today with respect to current legislative attempts to fix some problems in the financial industry, notably the Dodd–Frank legislation.) But of course the Sherman Antitrust Act did not give any bureaucrat the power to tell any executive what to do, still less to put any executive in jail, as she imagined. The courts and the Congress have been re-writing and re-interpreting the antitrust law ever since 1890, successively weakening it, to the point where only the most egregious antitrust cases are ever prosecuted and even fewer prosecutions have succeeded.

Over and over in her books Ayn Rand states explicitly *that the only purpose of government, in a capitalist state, is to protect private property.* This justifies taxes to pay for defense, police and a justice system, but nothing else. (And who will serve in the police or the military without submitting to coercive rules and regulations imposed by others?) Education and health care, in her view, must be private goods, to be provided by private companies and paid for by the beneficiary or by private insurance. Regulation of any kind (except within the military) is anathema. She and her acolytes apparently would not have built the dams that protect Holland from North Sea storms. They would not have built the harbor that gave her birthplace, Saint Petersburg, access to world trade. They see no benefit in a public health service, notwithstanding that it was to prevent outbreaks of typhoid fever and cholera in London that its first sewage system had to be built by the city. Without sewers and sewage treatment and water treatment, all by public agencies, those diseases would still be rife.

The Environmental Protection Agency (EPA) was created (by conservative President Nixon) to deal with a host of environmental pollutants, such as mercury (the cause of Minimata disease in Japan that killed scores of fishermen), smog (responsible for an epidemic of asthma, heart disease, etc.), and lead in children's bones (from old water pipes, gasoline additives, paint, etc.). She and her followers don't like the Food and Drug Administration because it imposes costs on drug companies. They ignore the fact that the FDA also prevents unscrupulous companies (or careless ones) from selling drugs that don't work or may even kill people. Does anybody remember the stunted and twisted limbs of the children whose mothers had been given a wonder drug called thalidomide?

Ayn Rand and her Libertarian followers, such as Alan Greenspan, Ron Paul, and "Tea Party" activists like Michelle Bachman and Paul Ryan, presumably think fire protection should be privatized, just as it was before the Great London Fire of 1666. They apparently don't see the need for a weather service that helps farmers decide when to plant and when to harvest, helps airliners avoid dangerous storms, and alerts people on the ground to prepare for hurricanes, tornados, blizzards, and floods. They don't see the need for a Federal Aviation Agency (FAA) to assure aircraft safety, pilot training and to keep planes from colliding with each other in mid-air. They deplore the Federal Communications Commission (FCC), which allocates electromagnetic bandwidth to communications systems of all kinds, including military and police as well as radios and televisions. They see no reason to have a Federal Power Commission (FPC) to license utilities and supervise the operations of the electrical grid. They see no reason for an Interstate Commerce Commission (ICC) or a Securities and Exchange Commission (SEC), or a Geological Survey, or a Bureau of the Census (in the Commerce Department).

The Libertarians, in the name of liberty, would also prefer to get rid of agencies like the Treasury (and the IRS), the Department of Housing and Urban Development (HUD), the Department of Transportation (which is responsible for interstate highways as well as railroads), the Interior Department (which is responsible for mine safety and allocates mining leases and oil drilling leases, as well as managing the Forest Service), the

Agriculture Department (which manages soil conservation and the agricultural extension/ advisory service, as well as subsidies to farmers), the Department of Energy (which manages energy conservation and efficiency programs), the Department of Health, Education and Welfare, and so on. OK, I realize that Libertarians know that most of their privatizing (or eliminating) preferences along these lines cannot be accomplished in the real world. Only 47 percent of the population may not pay federal income taxes, but probably 97 percent depend directly, or indirectly, on the services of one or more of these government agencies.

The point is that some of the services in question may not be doing much good, and some could probably be provided more efficiently. A few, but very few, of them restrict the range of options available to business, except where the businesses in question are extractive industries such as logging or mining, or emitters of toxic or otherwise dangerous pollutants. The bureaucrat putting business men in jail for violating some vaguely defined law is simply imaginary. No such bureaucrat exists or ever did. When there is a possible violation of federal law, it is the task of the Federal Department of Justice to collect the evidence and, if necessary, to make a case to prosecute. When there is an apparent violation of state law, the Attorney General of the state has the responsibility to collect the evidence and prosecute the case. Unfortunately, the regulatory agencies, such as the Justice Department and the SEC, have been starved for funds and consequently unable to enforce many laws adequately. (They never got around to investigating Bernie Madoff, despite strong indications that something was wrong.) The number of businessmen who have been convicted and actually gone to jail for something like fraud or insider trading in US history is minuscule, compared to the magnitude of their cumulative misdeeds.

However politically attractive Ayn Rand's ideas have been to some free market idealists, it is important to identify the underlying economic assumptions. Very briefly, she rejected or did not understand the fact that real goods and services are not abstractions, as they are often characterized in speeches or novels. *In the real world many, if not most, human activities, including economic transactions, have real impacts on other people who are not involved in the activity or transaction.* Sometimes those external effects of market failures can be very harmful or even lethal, yet quite unintentional. John Stuart Mill implicitly allowed for this possibility of unintentional harm to others in *On Liberty* but Ayn Rand (and her followers) seem to be amazingly blind to it.

Virtually all production activities based on physical materials (including fuels) generate wastes that must be disposed of and pollutants that can in fact cause illness or death if not captured and treated. Some wastes, like cadmium, mercury, chromium-6, lead, or carbon monoxide, are so toxic that people die. The award-winning movie *Erin Brokovich* recounts what really happened to several hundred people in California due to groundwater contaminated by ultra-toxic chromium-6 from an electrical utility facility. Health costs due to coal smoke, to take another example, are known to be far greater than the profits of the industry creating them.

Until recently there were no costs to industrial waste producers for the disposal of wastes, and in some cases the costs are still borne by taxpayers or, if unpaid, by society as a whole in terms of degraded health, reduced life expectancy, or degraded environmental resources. The most harmful of all the unintended consequences of using fossil fuels may be climate change in the coming decades from rising sea levels, starvation from extended droughts, more intense storms, and epidemics of diseases and pests. (I said "may be" because there are noisy skeptics in the Republican Party, led by Oklahoma Republican Senator Inhofe, who claim that "climate warming" is a liberal hoax. I think he and Fox News are the hoaxers.)

Finally, as discussed later in this book, financial activities that appear to be entirely private deals, between "consenting adults" or sophisticated institutions can have unintended effects on people who had nothing to do with those specific transactions. The obvious example, but by no means the only one, was the creation and sale of subprime mortgages in huge numbers, many of which were certain to default as soon as housing prices stopped rising. The intended consequence was a decline in mortgage costs allowing more people to own their own homes than ever before. The unintended consequence was an escalation, followed by a sharp decline, of home prices that has left much of middle-class America much poorer than before, and a large slice of that group "under water" in the sense that their homes are now worth less than the mortgages on them. In short, a large profit for the financiers was gained at the expense of a much larger cost to homeowners and taxpayers, without even mentioning the costs of lost economic growth.

As mentioned earlier, there are crucial "common property" resources such as clean air and fresh water, as well as other species of plants and animals, and the electromagnetic spectrum that cannot be owned or exchanged in markets and must therefore be "owned," if at all, by human society, or by a local community. Environmental problems arise when individuals or organizations with a short-term perspective, invoke the "law of capture." What follows is desertification where forests once flourished and oceans with no more fish. Too much of the world is already seriously degraded. Some have argued that this is an argument for private ownership, but it is an even stronger argument for strict regulation.

The phrase "greed is good," spoken so convincingly by the character Gordon Gekko in the movie *Wall Street*, has reverberated around the world. Is it just another way of saying that the driver of economic growth is *self-interest*, as Adam Smith, and virtually all the classical economists pointed out? Or is it a moral statement? More important, perhaps, do the hedge fund managers and private equity funds that Gordon Gekko supposedly represented on film see it as a moral justification for their actions? (It is interesting to note that Michael Douglas, who played the Gekko character, made his own film recently to explain to the public that greed is *not* good after all.) It is a troubling question. But I think the crucial point is that the phrase asserts a causal connection by means of the "invisible hand" between personal selfishness and beneficent societal outcomes. One of the key points of *this* book is that "the invisible hand" is just another word for the external effects of market transactions. They may be positive or negative.

In fairness, there is a powerful argument for private ownership of some finite common property resources such as grazing land or fisheries: the so-called tragedy of the commons (Hardin 1968). This refers to the irreparable losses that are caused by overexploitation of common property resources. When a resource belongs to everybody the "law of capture" applies and the "winner takes all." In fact, the sushi-lovers of Tokyo will probably pay millions of yen for a bite of the last bluefin tuna in the ocean. Future fishermen and tuna lovers are part of the economic transaction between catchers and buyers that does not allow for conserving a viable reproductive base. But they (and the tuna population) suffer a loss of options that can be described as an inherent externality of the fishing business.

The central problem of the commons is that nobody has any incentive to conserve for the future. If *A* doesn't catch the last whale or tuna, *B* will. As a species of fish or birds or large jungle cats approaches extinction, the market price per specimen, paradoxically, goes up. Examples have been discussed in the Sahel, in ocean fisheries, in freshwater resources, oil and gas drilling, and even the earth's pollution "detoxification" capability (Bergh and Verbruggen 1999). In contrast, when the property (e.g., grazing land) is privatized, there can be an incentive for more sustainable exploitation. It may not be effective, but the difference between the two situations is quite evident.

Having said this, it must also be said that the problems of securing long-term availability for the future does not justify private exploitation of the last redwood forests, or the Grand Canyon, or national parks, or beaches. There is a public interest in those things that needs to be protected. Similarly a "public" utility should not use the "right of eminent domain" build a dam to convert a valley into a lake, in order to generate electricity, without consideration for the losses imposed on other users of the valley, from spawning fish to wild animals. In all these cases government regulation to compare the benefits and the costs of alternative policies is essential. The fact that regulatory bodies have often been corrupted or just incompetent does not alter the fact that they play an essential role. The days of the "cowboy economy" where a rancher or farmer in the wilderness could do anything on his own land, without hindrance from neighbors or government, are gone.

Ayn Rand's defense of private enterprise, and her scornful rejection of government regulation, utterly ignores the adverse consequences of unbridled competition based on the law of capture. She had nothing negative to say about the evils of slavery, share-cropping, child labor, usury, or racial discrimination not even about discrimination against women. She saw nothing wrong about abusive monopolies, as long as they were private. She and her protégé, Alan Greenspan, did not believe that financial fraud in the market-place was a problem. One wonders what she would have said about Bernard Madoff who cheated hundreds if not thousands of investors of their savings. *Caveat emptor?* What would Rand and Greenspan say to justify lack of regulation regarding "identity theft" and a variety of fraudulent uses of the Internet? Actually there is no need to wonder. Greenspan, who is still alive, has simply ignored the problems.

Ayn Rand's libertarian view of capitalism is as an externality-free competition between profit-seeking innovators like her heroic characters in *Atlas Shrugged* versus a government dominated by collectivist "moochers." OK, she might have agreed that some small externalities exist, like a fire set by a wind-blown spark, or trash left on the street by careless neighbors. Large externalities, such as inflation, unemployment, inequality or climate change, did not exist in her worldview. That view is quite compatible with the view of a lot of Wall Street denizens, such as hedge fund managers, today. Probably most of them read *Atlas Shrugged* in their youth. (I read it when I was 16 years old. I thought it was great!) Having read a few quotations from *The Wealth of Nations*, they imagine that the "invisible hand" guarantees that financial innovation is just as socially beneficial as technological innovation in Silicon Valley. They have persuaded themselves, and too many politicians, that the invention of a subprime mortgage, a collateralized debt obligation (CDO), or a credit default swap (CDF) is comparable in terms of social benefit to the invention of electric light or the telephone, or the Internet. I can imagine a Gordon Gekko (or Dick Fuld) looking at the Manhattan skyline out of the window of his top floor office at Lehman Brothers and saying "I built that." But the reality is that these financial inventions, in an unregulated marketplace, have enabled a few individuals in Wall Street to make obscene profits for themselves resulting in losses of jobs, savings and homes by millions of people on Main Street.

Is Capitalism Itself the Problem?

For the first time in several decades, capitalism is being questioned by some thinkers, and not only by left wing socialists and members of the "occupy Wall Street" movement. For an example of only one among several I refer to David Korten's book *The Great Turning* (Korten 2006). Let me say in advance that if capitalism is defined as a system that offers the possibility of reasonable rewards for taking reasonable risks, I doubt that capitalism per se is the problem. The danger today is that too many clever folks working on Wall Street have figured out how to take risks with other people's money, privatizing the profits and "socializing" those risks.

Worse, the games they play with other people's money are essentially unproductive, contrary to popular ideology. While the bankers claim credit for the success of our economic system as a whole, their ancient function of allocating capital to productive activities is now largely a fiction. Today they allocate capital increasingly to an activity that can only be called gambling. The fact that money moves makes it look like ordinary economic activity and it shows up as a contribution to GDP. But buying and selling financial instruments, whether stocks and bonds, or derivatives, or whole companies, is not putting money to work producing goods and services for society as a whole. The capitalism of Wall Street is a system that enables the wealthy to get richer at the expense of Main Street, partly by exploiting the existing rules and partly by manipulating the political process that makes and enforces those rules.

I think the Wall Street version of capitalism is very sick, much sicker even than most critics would acknowledge. What happened in the summer–fall of 2008 was a "near-death" experience for the global economy. It would have been an amplified version of the Great Depression of 1931 to 1933, on a larger scale in a more integrated world. If the global economy had truly collapsed, there is no knowing what might have taken its place.

Nevertheless, capitalism, in its pure form, has beneficial incentive features. The problem is to adjust the real political-economic system of the West to take advantage of the beneficial features that have made us wealthy while modifying the dangerous elements that threaten the entire global system. At the same time it is clear from past experience that anything like a violent revolution on the eighteenth- or nineteenth-century model would only make everything worse. The only solution to the current malaise is a step-by step approach, focusing on solving one problem at a time, without forgetting that every change in a complex system is likely to initiate other changes that may lead to quite unanticipated consequences.

The sickness of capitalism is what has led us (again) to the edge of a precipice, where the "system" seems to be breaking down and the people supposedly in charge are not taking responsibility for either the past or the future. For some years after the collapse of the Soviet Union in 1989, a ridiculous notion like "The End of History" could be taken seriously for a while in intellectual circles. Francis Fukuyama's (Fukuyama 1992) thesis was that US style political democracy and capitalist economic liberalism had reached a natural and permanent accommodation. After the bursting of the real estate bubble, in 2008, this attractive notion no longer makes any sense. Even the conservative *Financial Times* has recognized that capitalism is in deep crisis.

Apart from the straightforward "risk-reward" formulation it is helpful to clarify what "we" (meaning the folks on Main Street) understand by the word "capitalism."[5] It is one of those loaded words that mean different things to different people, and for some, is almost a matter of religion. I was struck by an exchange back in 2012 on one of the financial programs on TV, during which the subject seemed to be which of the Republican presidential candidates in the United States was the most committed to the principles of capitalism. The issue was framed in terms of faith, rather than facts. Each candidate seems to be saying that he is more committed to capitalism than the other guy. It reminded me of the religious controversies that destroyed much of Europe in the seventeenth century. Religion, in the sense of doctrinal beliefs supposedly from God (via an intermediary with a long beard), is at the bottom of conflicts that almost any time could explode yet again in the Middle East or elsewhere.

Why is there a religious flavor in most public discussion about capitalism? I don't really know; but the desire for assurance, in the form of unquestioning acceptance of simplistic doctrines from authority figures—with or without long beards—may be a factor. Part of the problem may also be that there is no accepted definition of what capitalism is. The ultra-capitalists are much clearer about what they oppose, namely "socialism." Socialism in turn is identified (by them) with welfare states in Europe, Stalinist central planning, regulation and government ownership of the means of production and control over the individual. Some associate capitalism with "laissez faire," meaning noninterference by government in economic matters. Others equate capitalism with "free enterprise," meaning much the same thing in ordinary English. A surprisingly dominant aspect of the popular definition of capitalism is opposition to taxes, or more generally, to any regulatory or other constraints on the making of money. I will return to that point later, because it is based on a fundamental misunderstanding of reality. (It is surprising, by the way, how little the capitalist elite seems to worry about the revelations of Edward Snowden about the electronic snooping activities of the NSA.)

The other prominent feature of most definitions is "freedom." In economics, freedom is only relevant to the range of available choices, where and how to invest, what career to choose, what products to consume and so on. From the ivory tower it appears that regulation merely reduces the "option space" for those heroic entrepreneurs so admired by Ayn Rand. For most entrepreneurs the option space is actually restricted by other barriers and forces, mostly related to competition. Government regulation in modern democracies is mostly passive, and related to land use, health, and safety. It is rarely a major constraint on economic growth. In the financial arena, regulation may be more restrictive. For a few super-bankers like Sandy Weill of Citigroup in his heyday or Jamie Dimon of JPMorgan Chase today, there is no real competition from peers, and government regulation may indeed reduce their option space. If Jamie Dimon wants to swallow Deutsche Bank (or Citigroup), only the government might stand in his way. Some extremists—likely the same ones who think that the weak banks in 2008 should not have been saved—probably think that this would be an outrageous interference in the free market.

In the late nineteenth-century monopolies (combinations of firms in the same business controlled by a "holding company") were called "trusts." John Pierpont Morgan was a great believer in trusts to minimize what he called "destructive competition," and his views were widely shared by the investor class. In a way, they simply recognized the obvious: that large-scale eliminates duplication of functions and reduces unit costs. Hence monopolies are much more profitable than small firms operating in a competitive marketplace would be. The incentives favoring the creation of trusts were precisely that *competition in a static market is inefficient.* It was inefficient to build two railroads or two pipelines between the same cities when one could handle all the traffic. It was inefficient to build a dozen small blast furnaces in different locations when one big one could produce the same amount of steel at lower cost per ton. It was inefficient to have a lot of small oil refineries when one big one could do the same job at lower cost per barrel. Competition evidently did (and does) involve duplication of activities and of facilities. This is the motivation for mergers and acquisitions today. It is also why some businesses, especially those involving networks, are thought to be "natural monopolies."

The argument against trusts and monopolies then, and now, is two-fold. On the one hand, monopolies are able to raise prices much higher than competitive firms, in order to increase their profits, thus penalizing consumers. Consumers don't like that, and they can vote against it. Competing firms, on the other hand, want to minimize prices (in order to gain market share), rather than maximize them. That is the rationale for Walmart. Consumers vote for that. The second argument, which may be the more important in the long run, is that competition promotes innovation whereas monopoly does not. There is no theoretical reason why monopolies should not also be innovative (as AT&T once was), but the weight of historical evidence says that monopolies are not innovative because they don't have to be. In fact some virtual monopolies, such as ALCOA, US Steel, AT&T, IBM, and Microsoft, have been broken by pressure from smaller but more innovative rivals.

Many politicians and some economists have linked capitalism and political freedom. Three well-known past examples of authors who made that link are Hayek (1944, 1960), Schumpeter (1943), and Friedman (1962). It is worth mentioning that Hayek's 1944 book *The Road to Serfdom* sold over 2 million copies worldwide and had a huge impact on modern libertarianism. It was originally an attack on writers who argued that fascism was a natural reaction to Marxist communism. Hayek argued that fascism and communism were both from the same roots, namely central planning and state control over the economy. This part of Hayek's argument seems a trifle quaint, today, given the obvious economic success of Singapore, China, and Vietnam despite their single-party communist governments.

For the majority of Americans, as I say, capitalism is contrasted with "socialism," which is widely (mis)interpreted by the conservatives and libertarians as high taxes, government ownership of key sectors (e.g., airlines, railroads, utilities, and telecoms) and bureaucratic control (regulation) of the rest. Most Americans think Europe is "socialist" thanks to its welfare programs. That is a view not shared by any actual socialist. In part this is because the left wing parties in Europe are mostly called "social democrats" or "labor parties," and labor unions are still fairly strong. However, the European reality "on the street" is much closer to the American reality except for a few cultural differences. (I have lived in France for the last twenty years.)

What, then, is capitalism? I think it is essentially the system we live in, warts and all. It is a system where almost all of the productive component of the economy is privately owned and managed. It is also a system where investors take risks in exchange for rewards (called profits). Finally, it is a system where firms compete with one another for investors, access to resources, and markets. The role of government, in our capitalist system, is to create and enforce the rules that govern competition and trade. Government provides protection for law-abiding persons and their private property, via the police and courts. Most governments also perform other functions, including the provision of public services (defense, public health, education), and the protection of certain established "rights" (e.g., free speech). But those supplementary functions are outside the realm of capitalism, except insofar as they have to be paid for by tax revenues.

Capitalism has many variants today. The kind of vertically integrated manufacturing company, such as Singer Sewing Machine, Ford, or Eastman-Kodak, that emerged in the nineteenth or early twentieth century has either become a conglomerate like GE or the hub of a global supplier network of suppliers like Apple or Boeing. There is an argument for vertical integration, in some industries, but even the big auto companies are outsourcing more and more functions, not only to China. This is the top-down "franchise model," originated by automobile manufacturer-dealership networks, that now dominates much of the retail "space." There is a central HQ that controls engineering and product design, central purchasing, marketing strategy, brand differentiation, and so on. But Walmart stores, McDonald's restaurants, Starbuck's coffee shops, and Coca Cola bottlers are locally owned, thus giving them a strong incentive to manage efficiently within the legal limits of the franchise.

Consumer cooperatives are an alternative that still exist, and have thrived modestly in some places. But they have not done well in competition with the likes of Walmart or K-Mart or Target due to inadequate access to finance (and skeptical bankers) but most likely due to excessive internal democracy and consequently weak management. Would it make sense to allow a large number of small entrepreneurial firms in the same service business, but different localities, to combine in order to achieve economies of scale? This has been the argument for universal banking, for instance. I wonder if there is room for a bottom-up (inverted franchise) structure based on local entrepreneurs in a specific activity, each free to innovate unlike McDonalds, Starbuck's, Coca-Cola bottlers, or bank branches but able to benefit from a centralized supply-chain structure? I will say a little more about this in connection with energy-service companies (ESCOs) in chapter 9.

Most of the former centrally planned economies around the world have now adopted some version of capitalism, without necessarily adopting the forms of political government that have evolved in Europe and in the former British colonies (including the United States). China is not a democracy, but it is certainly capitalist, and its current form of centrally controlled and supervised capitalism is arguable more successful (so far) than the US or European versions.

Some critics will equate capitalism with consumerism and the glorification of consumer choice. The more important consequence of consumption is that it is in conflict with saving and investment. Income spent on current consumption is not saved or invested. But the rich OECD countries, especially North America and Western Europe, have been consuming more than they earn, by borrowing. Borrowing for purposes of consuming goods or services produced within a country can be justified to a degree, insofar as the spending by borrowers is income for production workers and interest payments on debt by borrowers is a return on investment to lenders. But borrowing from other countries for purposes of consuming goods produced elsewhere is much riskier proposition. The United States, in particular, has been playing that game, with an ever-increasing imbalance of trade combined with an ever-increasing foreign debt. This imbalance may still be tolerable for a time, as long as the debt is in dollars, but it cannot continue forever. The fact that there is no automatic mechanism to prevent or compensate for imbalances such as this one is a fundamental weakness of capitalism as it now exists.

Economic Background: The Incentive Structure

I hate to start with the dismal science, but some of what follows really must be said, and perhaps we'd better get it over with. This section and the next two discuss a few core ideas of economic theory, and how they have evolved since the eighteenth century. These ideas, and the history behind them, are quite important today, sometimes in unexpected ways. Whatever you think about John Maynard Keynes, he was unquestionably right when he said: "Practical men, who believe themselves exempt from any intellectual influence, are usually the slaves of some defunct economist" (Keynes 1935, p. 383). So I summarize below a few of the key ideas of (mostly) defunct economists.

Perhaps the first truly original insight in the field was Adam Smith's observation that the operation of markets exhibits a "win-win" pattern (to use modern terms), which he characterized memorably as the beneficent action of an "invisible hand." Virtually all of the writings of the classical economists, beginning with Adam Smith and David Ricardo, focused first on markets and trade, and only later on production. A major part of the writings of generations of economists since Smith's time has focused on understanding the mechanisms and conditions, such as "comparative advantage," underlying the phenomenon of exchange.

When the subject was first discussed in Western Europe in the eighteenth century, there was long-distance trade in metals, wood for shipbuilding, "naval stores" and luxury stuff such as silk, cotton cloth (calico, muslin), wine, tea, tobacco, and spices (and slaves). However, most trade took place in village or town marketplaces. The archetypical exchange transaction in that marketplace was a purchase by an individual customer of some tangible product, such as a loaf of bread, or a pair of shoes, from another individual or shop, at an agreed price. The medium of exchange was money in the form of coins made from copper or silver. (Gold coins were much scarcer.) For larger transactions metal coins were occasionally backed up by a "bill of exchange" issued by a reputable banker (or a goldsmith). To be sure, there were trading companies, such as the Muscovy Company, the Hudson Bay Company, or the East India Company, but such entities accounted for a small fraction of total trade.

The essential feature of exchanges in village markets (or any transaction between two individuals, for that matter) was that *both buyer and seller expected to be better off after the exchange*. To clarify this point, consider that purchase of a loaf of bread. The baker has more bread than he can eat, whereas with the money he gets for the sale, he can buy flour and have something left over (profit) that can be spent on other goods. The customer wants the bread for dinner at the agreed price, more than she wants to keep the money. So both parties consider themselves better off after the exchange than before. Otherwise, no such exchange would occur. Hence the very existence of trade meant that the people engaging in it were increasingly prosperous.

An Austrian economist, Carl Menger ([1871] 1994), was the first to define precisely the conditions for a market exchange. The market price of a product (good), according to Menger is the point where the seller *A marginally* prefers an additional increment of money to an increment of the good, while the buyer *B marginally* prefers an increment of the good to an increment of money. This is now called *utility maximization.* Incidentally, the definition above applies only to the case where neither buyer nor seller cares about the past or the future (no memory, no foresight). When there is a long-term relationship between them, as in a village market, short-term utility maximization may not always be appropriate. For instance, if the seller is a farmer in trouble temporarily (e.g., due to bad weather), the buyer may want to keep him in business as a supplier by sacrificing short-term profits. Or the buyer may be temporarily in difficulties, but the seller may decide to allow credit, for the same reason. There are many variants of these themes.

Of course, you knew all that. But saying it in that particular way was very helpful to nineteenth-century economic theorists. Notice the terms "increment" and "marginal" in Menger's definition. They are important because it turns out that they are the key to introducing differential calculus into economics. That was actually a revolution in the history of thought because it invited quantification of notions like the declining marginal return on investment or consumption. Not surprisingly, it is called the "marginalist" revolution.

Exchange transactions can be looked at in another way, as *games,* because bargaining is a sort of contest of wits. The money-for-goods transactions mentioned above, where both parties expect to be better off as a result of the exchange, can be thought of as a win-win game. The gaming aspect is the negotiation about price. For a simple loaf of bread, the price in supermarkets or bakeries today is likely to be fixed because individual negotiation about pennies is too time-consuming and the potential gains or losses are not worth the time. However, for larger transactions, such as the sale of a house or of a business, bargaining is much more important, and the gaming aspect is much more central.[6]

It can be shown, subject to a few assumptions, that the optimum outcome of a bargain is the one that maximizes the total combined utility of the two parties (Ayres and Martinás 2006). This happens when the buyer and the seller split the difference between the prices that would maximize their respective gains. For instance, if seller *A* wouldn't sell at less than 50 while buyer *B* wouldn't buy at more than 100, the best outcome for both is to sell at 75. Of course, in real life neither party knows the other's internal valuation, which is why negotiation is a skill, not an exercise in simple arithmetic.

As it happens, not all economic transactions are win-win games like trade in village (or national) markets. There is a theory of games (von Neumann and Morgenstern 1944) that has led to some interesting insights into real economic behavior and negotiation. (No less than eight Nobel prizes in economics have been given to game theorists, and their progenitor, John von Neumann, died too soon to get one). There are a lot of variations: games can be symmetric or not, moves can be simultaneous or not, they can be cooperative or not; the players can have memories or not; the outcomes can be win-win or "lose-lose." This is short for saying that the sum of the winner's gains is equal to the sum of the other player's losses. Poker is a zero-sum (win-lose) game. So is stock-market trading. Unsuccessful revolutions or wars (e.g., the intifada or the Vietnam conflict) can be thought of as lose-lose for obvious reasons.

I am not a game theorist, so my insight is untrustworthy. But my hunch is that win-win outcomes generally require cooperation between the players, based on trust (supported by the memory of previous games), while lose-lose outcomes are the most likely result of distrust, short-term utility maximization and even betrayal of prior agreements, in the name of self-interest. Of course some games are "win-lose" by virtue of their structure and rules. For instance, changes in the structure of firms on Wall Street in the past generation (e.g., corporatization) have tended to erode the former role of cooperation and trust.

The distinction between win-win and lose-lose is not just theoretical. It can be illustrated by the famous "prisoner's dilemma." In this example, prisoners A and B both face a situation in which there is a possibility to win or to lose, and the outcome for A depends on what B does. The classic version is where two prisoners who committed a crime together are in jail, in separate cells so they cannot communicate. If neither confesses they both will be set free because there is no evidence. But if only one confesses, the other will be punished severely and the confessor will be punished less severely. The reward for collaboration (both remaining silent) may, or may not, be greater than the reward for betrayal. If each accuses the other, they will both be punished, but not as severely as the worst case where only one accuses the other. The problem is that remaining silent may be the best option for both A and B, but only if they both remain silent. But it is the worst option for *A* if he remains silent but *B* defects, and vice versa. So, if utility maximization means avoiding the worst case outcome, the safest strategy for both is to accuse the other.

The difference between win-win and lose-lose, in the Prisoner's Dilemma is trust (or lack of it). If the players can trust each other to abide by previous agreements, they can both achieve the best outcome, which is to be set free without penalty (i.e., maximize utility). If they do not trust each other, the best they can do individually is to avoid the worst outcome. This simpler situation seems artificial. However, in the real world, bargaining with minor villains to procure the convictions of bigger ones is an important strategy of prosecutors in criminal cases or counterintelligence authorities. For the same reason, criminal gangs (or sports teams bent on cheating) may force all members of the group to commit serious crimes (or take EPO or steroids) in order to ensure that all will be punished if any one decides to confess. Confession is less likely if all who know the truth are themselves guilty. (Incidentally, as you might have noticed, the outcome in this example depends on the details. If the gains from remaining silent are greater for each individual than the payoff for defecting, the outcome will be win-win rather than lose-lose.)

Another important insight from the nineteenth century is that in a static exchange economy with production and consumption (but no banks) there exists an equilibrium solution with a set of prices such that all markets "clear" (Walras [1874] 1954). In other words, it is possible, in such an idealized situation, to achieve an outcome where there are no surpluses, no shortages and no unemployment. (The theoretical existence of such a solution was only proved much later for special cases; see Wald 1936; McKenzie 1954; Arrow and Debreu 1954.) A related economic conjecture, following Walras, is that there is a tendency in pure static exchange markets (which means the number of chips on the table is finite and not growing) to approach an equilibrium condition, called the "Pareto optimum" (Pareto 1906). This is a state where no agent can improve his or her situation by trade, except at the expense of another agent. This is a zero-sum outcome, like poker but in a different context.

Since 1960 so-called computable general equilibrium (CGE) models have been developed, both static and dynamic versions, mainly for national economies. They generally assume that economic growth occurs in Walrasian equilibrium. For realism they may allow deviations from some of the standard equilibrium assumptions such as exogenous taxes, government demands, unemployment, monopoly pricing, or pollution. Unfortunately, the CGE models all have a fundamental weakness, namely the inherent assumption of equilibrium itself. This makes them essentially useless for predicting financial instability (e.g., bubbles) or analyzing the impact of financial stabilization policies.

The emerging theory of nonequilibrium dynamics, applied to finance, is discussed in the next section. A short digression may be helpful to those who have not studied economics. The idea of equilibrium, and its relationship with prices, is conveyed in economic textbooks by means of a simple diagram (figure 1.1) with prices on the vertical axis and demand on the horizontal axis. On the one hand, it is intuitively obvious that the lower the price of a good or service, the greater the demand is likely to be, so this relationship is expressed by means of a curve that declines from upper left to lower right. The slope of that curve is called the price elasticity of demand.[7] The different demand curves represent different situations, such as different income levels. In words, it is the percentage demand increase (decrease) for a 1 percent price decrease (increase).

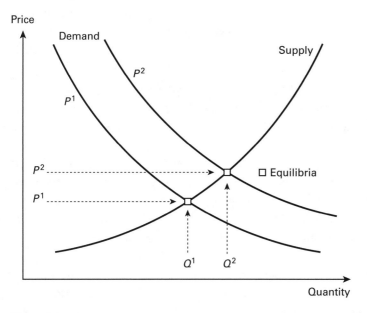

Figure 1.1
Supply/demand equilibria

On the other hand, the diagram always shows a cost curve that increases from lower left to upper right, as demand increases. This curve means that each additional *unit* of output costs a little more than the last one. Somewhere in the middle of the textbook diagram, the declining curve and the rising curves must meet. If the curves can be considered as representing the whole output of the economy, rather than a particular commodity, the crossing point of the two curves will be the center of a small region where the idealized economy supposedly operates. The *equilibrium point* is where the marginal cost reduction due to increasing demand is overcome by the marginal cost increase of supply. *Economists generally assume that the real economy is always at, or at least near, such a point.*

The increasing demand for goods as prices fall is easy to understand from everyday experience with respect to luxuries. As your income rises, or as prices fall, you will probably spend more on cars, houses, and vacations. But how realistic is the rising cost curve? In the real (material) economy unit costs of production of goods and services typically *decrease* as output increases, since fixed costs and overhead can be shared among more and more units of output. The unit cost of production also declines, thanks to economies of scale and experience (learning). The only time the marginal supply cost curve increases is when it gets very close to a capacity limit. In other words, as long as there is excess productive capacity, the marginal cost curve declines, rather than increasing. The cost of money (i.e., interest rates) to finance increased output will also rise as output approaches capacity limits *if (and only if) the money supply is limited and consequently rationed* (e.g., by the gold standard or something equivalent).

Even if one accepts the assumption of a rising cost curve, and that an equilibrium point exists in principle, that does not mean that the equilibrium will be stable. Economists normally assume stability. But in the real world there are systems that are absolutely stable, others that are quasi-stable (for small perturbations) and still others that are absolutely unstable.

In graphic terms, a stable, resilient system might be represented by a Mexican "jumping bean" in the bottom of a big bowl, such that no conceivable jump will take the bean out of the bowl (figure 1.2a). But the simplification of the financial system by globalization and consolidation makes the size of the jumps greater with respect to the size of the bowl or reduces the height of the sides of the bowl (figure 1.2b). It is no longer inconceivable that the bean could jump out of the bowl. From a static perspective, the financial system is really unstable (figure 1.2c) because there is no automatic stabilizing mechanism to keep the bean in the bowl. (There is no bowl.)

How stable is the world economy? Experience of booms and busts suggests that it is not as stable as the Mexican jumping bean in a big bowl. Nor is it absolutely unstable, like a stationary bicycle. The moving bicycle analogy is better. However, there are degrees of instability depending, (as in the case of ecosystems) on diversity and complexity. Complex ecosystems are generally more stable (resilient) than simple ones.

One aspect of economic complexity is the existence of a wide variety of products and services to serve a wide variety of tastes, ages, and incomes. Another is interdependence. In prehistoric times (and much more recently in some countries) people lived in small groups (tribes) or villages, far from central government. As recently as the early twentieth century the economies of different countries were relatively independent and disconnected. Financial troubles in one country did not necessarily affect other countries with different economies (and different currencies). Apart from some well-known exceptions (e.g., the Credit Anstalt case in 1931), there was little or no problem of "contagion" until recently.

Globalization has simplified the world of trade, investment, and money. The international agreements on "free trade" have reduced trade barriers. This is a simplification. The dominance of the US dollar as the

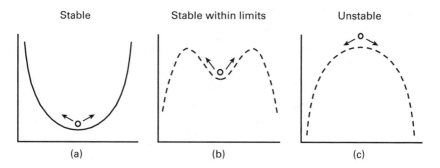

Figure 1.2
Stability/instability

global reserve currency is another aspect of this simplification. Moreover the number of competing independent banks within countries has declined dramatically. The financial world is now dominated by a few dozen very large banks that are so tightly interconnected that trouble for one is instantaneously transmitted to others. It is not too far off the mark to say in fact that the global financial system, outside of Asia, underwent a "near-death experience" in September and October of 2008. Money moves at the speed of light today. (In 2007 the trading volume on foreign exchange markets was $3.2 trillion *per day*, plus $2.1 trillion in currency derivatives; see (Lietaer, Ulanowicz, and Goerner 2009). Those numbers are higher today.

This simplification of the global economy, in the name of efficiency, has also reduced the stability (resilience) of the global financial system. The "globalization" trend has a downside that is far from beneficial. It has moved production and production-related income away from the rich countries, especially the United States, while not reducing domestic consumption. The excess consumption increases GDP, but that increase is based on spending borrowed money (borrowed from the net exporters). In the thirty years between 1981 and 2011 spending for consumption in the United States increased by $8.2 trillion (in 2011$) but the output of internationally tradable goods and services increased by only $600 billion (Morgan 2013). The difference was borrowed and added to US foreign debt.

If the lost jobs in the United States were immediately replaced by better ones, and if the increased imports were balanced by increased exports, as free-trade proponents always argue (and trade theory assumes) there would be no big problem apart from the excesses of consumerism per se. But when the lost production is not replaced by other production, lost jobs are not replaced by better ones, the system is unstable, and it cannot survive long, still less prosper. The notion of dynamic equilibration by regulation (riding the bicycle) makes more sense than the idea, shared by many conservatives, that the solution is to reduce the role (and size) of government drastically. That would have no effect on the trade deficit; it would make regulation more difficult and thus make the instability worse.

It is time to talk about companies and organizations (as contrasted with individuals). The fact that traders expect to gain from trading implies that two or more traders in the same business can gain even more as a coordinated group than they can gain as individuals. The reason is that an individual trader has to be a "jack of all trades," whereas a group (or firm) can take advantage of the different skills or characteristics of its members ("division of labor" as characterized by Adam Smith). The main characteristic of a firm is that it is an organized group of cooperating individuals with a common purpose. The cooperative aspect is central, because it allows the group to be more successful (i.e., productive) than its members could be on their own. But mere aggregation also introduces all sorts of possibilities for noncooperation (competition, rivalry) within the firm. To minimize these "centrifugal" forces, discipline is needed. Eventually the need for discipline seems to evolve into some sort of hierarchical structure. Such structures probably have an evolutionary origin.

Real firms are often linked by biological forces, starting with sex and kinship. The multigeneration family is a social group built around sexual relationships and their evolutionary purpose, which is reproduction of the species. Tribes evolved from families and tribal interactions, usually competition for land and resources, that eventually resulted in higher order social structures, such as armies, towns, nations, and empires. Of course, agriculture, homemaking, and government also involve many different skills, so a large farm, factory, or household will also have specialists to do different jobs. The same is true of military and civic society. The phenomenon of specialization or *division of labor*—makes it productive and profitable to combine individuals with different skills in a single organization. This is a win-win game where everybody is better off working together than independently. Diversity and specialization are a source of efficiency and productivity. Economies of scale make it profitable for small communities and small firms to cooperate and perhaps to merge.

In short, firms (like families) exist to take advantage of the division of labor allocating different tasks to specialists. The earliest trading companies had to buy ships and finance long voyages. A trading voyage to the Indies also required an organization: a ship with a captain, mates, and a crew with various occupational specialties. Financing such a trip was too costly for most merchants or even wealthy nobles on their own. So they got together and shared the risk, and the profits. Later single ships were seen as too risky, so trading companies acquired more ships and shared overhead expenses to cut unit costs and risk. The same incentives to get bigger apply everywhere in the business world. Small firms were (and are) swallowed by larger ones to exploit economies of scale. Bigger is often "fitter," in Darwin's sense and more efficient in the economic sense. In fact economy of scale (cooperation and specialization) is a primary driver of economic growth.

Of course, the little fish, and the small firms, try to avoid being swallowed by bigger fish and bigger firms. They adopt a variety of strategies for survival, but one of them is to get bigger as fast as possible. Thus faced with a choice between investing in growth, vis-à-vis investing in energy efficiency (say), a firm will almost always opt for growth. This is one of the reasons why companies do not always take advantage of profitable opportunities to save energy, as standard economic theory would predict. I will return to this point later.

The world we live in today has little or no resemblance to Thomas Jefferson's ideal society of individual homesteading families or small artisans that still existed in the western United States a hundred and fifty years ago. Today the economic landscape is dominated by large complex conglomerates, multinational companies and giant "universal" banks. Like it or not, these large institutions are very productive, and the high material standard of living the western world enjoys today is largely due to the high productivity resulting from economies of scale. The interactions among these entities also bear little resemblance to the simple exchange relationships of a simple economy of many small firms competing in a "free market"; a condition that much economic theory still assumes.

There is a limit to the economic benefits of large size, however. Bigger seems to be better as long as firms do not become monopolies or oligopolies. Basically the justification for collecting a number of producers under a single roof was (and is) to achieve maximum economics of scale by reducing overheads and "destructive competition" in the words of J. P. Morgan. When they do become monopolies, innovation and growth tend to slow and may stop altogether, as I have noted previously. This is not, so far as I can see, a "law" of economics. But it seems to be a fact. The reason is probably that innovation is difficult and even destructive, so companies rarely undertake changes that are uncomfortable for the incumbents. Why compete against one's existing business? They do so, in general, only when there is no choice, and they almost always wait too long. IBM missed the PC; Kodak missed the digital camera.

A company nowadays takes one of two legal forms. The first and oldest is a partnership. Most law firms, doctors' group practices, and accounting firms today are partnerships. A partnership's earnings after costs are distributed among the partners, according to some agreed rule, and each partner is personally responsible for his or her share of partnership investments. The other type of company is a corporation, which is a "legal person" but with limited liability for the actual persons in case things go wrong. Managers may or may not be owners; if not, they are "agents" for the owners, with fiduciary responsibility but no legal liability for losses except in the case of criminal behavior. This means that corporate executives are able to take more risks (with the owner's money) than members of a partnership. This distinction has been very important in the history of finance.

Perhaps the most important point about corporations from a theoretical perspective is just that they are legal persons, not really "owned" by anyone, not even shareholders. A new branch of economics has appeared since the 1980s dealing with "principal-agent" theory (Jensen and Meckling 1976). That theory, or parts of it, seems in fact to have justified the extreme emphasis taught in most business schools in recent years on "maximizing shareholder value" as measured by share prices (Hansmann and Kraskman 2001). According to this doctrine, neatly summarized by Milton Friedman (*New York Times Magazine* September 13, 1970), "the social responsibility of business is to increase its profits."

According to the believers, it is the fiduciary duty of senior executives to maximize share value, regardless of the interests of other stakeholders from employees to customers, suppliers, or the natural environment. This assumption, in turn, has seemingly justified colossal pay packages for CEOs linked to short-term stock-market performance, and indirectly to large bonuses for traders who maximize short-term profits and move on to other targets of opportunity. I say "assumption" above because it is actually untrue. An eminent legal scholar, Lynn Stout, has recently pointed out that there is no such fiduciary responsibility on managers of public companies to maximize shareholder value (Stout 2001). In case after case, courts have decided that boards of directors have the last word, and that they are constrained only by the "business judgment rule," which allows them to allocated corporate resources however they think the long-term interest of the firm will be best served, whether to R&D, new product development, employee salaries, employee health care, community service, or even environmental protection.

Of course, it is true that profit-seeking short-term investors have argued the converse, and their arguments have been widely accepted by the financial community and by academia. Since the 1980s well-financed corporate "activists" (e.g., Carl Icahn or KKR) have succeeded in forcing corporate boards to adopt "shareholder-friendly" policies, such as large stock buybacks. They have made many hostile takeovers, replacing recalcitrant boards via leveraged buyouts (LBOs) and other devices. A large number of firms in the United States (and elsewhere) have been subjected to "financial re-engineering," which invariably involves cutting "unproductive" activities, cutting long-term projects, cutting employee benefits, squeezing the workers, and so on. The re-engineered firms, with reduced costs (but increased debts), are often relabeled and sold to the public via public share offerings (IPOs).

This outcome is often contrary to the real interests of long-term owners, as opposed to speculators, because cost-minimizing strategies that maximize profits in the short term are likely to be inconsistent with investment strategies that would maximize long-term growth. It can in fact be argued that "shareholder-value" thinking on the part of investment bankers and short-sighted insurers (e.g., AIG) was largely responsible for the subprime mortgage crisis that nearly destroyed the global economy in 2008. However, the principal-agent "shareholder-value" conundrum is a digression from my primary concern, which is instability and disequilibrium.

Money, Banks, and Financial Bubbles

The textbook explanation of economic equilibrium between the supply and demand for goods (figure 1.1) in the last section ignores money, except insofar as the idea of prices implies the existence of some medium of exchange. Before the "monetarists" (especially Milton Friedman) came along and tried to explain economic growth in terms of the money supply (Friedman and Schwartz 1963), economic theory neglected the idea of money as a commodity or as a store of wealth. Yet money is necessary (like physical capital) in production but is conserved in the short run (like energy) in the production process (Friedman and Schwartz 2008). Money may not be a "factor of production" in the same way as capital, labor, or energy and materials, butwithout money (actually, credit), barter can occur but production and consumption in the modern world cannot take place.

Now, in the context of *bubbles*, which this book is (partly) about, it is important to recognize that for money (credit and debt) *there is no automatic equilibrium between the supply and demand*. The demand for particular goods like cars at any given time may be limited. But there is no natural and inherent upper limit to demand for money as credit. Perhaps more to the point, there is no natural limit on the supply of credit by banks.

While the supply of credit by lenders is not self-limited, the other side of credit is debt. And the magnitude of debt that can be carried by borrowers (the money supply) is definitely limited. Indeed, from a certain perspective, it is the mismatch between *credit creation* by lenders and *debt creation* by borrowers that is dis-equilibrating. Credit is a necessary concomitant of economic growth but debt is a growth inhibitor (or growth stopper). It is true that all debts are assets for the lenders, but it is not necessarily true that, like the US war bonds of WWII, "we owe it to ourselves." As pointed out in the preface, there is an important asymmetry between credit and debt. Society, at present, cares more about protecting creditors than debtors, even though the banks are able to increase credit without effective restraint and with minimal risk to themselves.

Most people think finance is the business of banks. But in reality, banks are only the most visible part of it. The best way to think about the financial system is by analogy with the metabolic circulatory system in the human (or any animal) body. The circulatory system has active and passive components. The passive components are blood vessels, temporary storage (the spleen), and the blood itself. The most obvious of the active components is the heart, but the leg muscles also help to pump the blood back to the lungs from the lower extremities, the lungs serve to re-oxygenate it, and the bone marrow replaces the worn-out blood cells. When the body is physically active, the function of the circulatory system is to carry oxygen to the muscle cells (and others), where it reacts with molecules of sugar (glycogen), generating mechanical power and motion.

The oxygen in the blood is a little like the money supply of the economy. The circulation of blood is analogous to the system of payments in the economy, whether by cash, checks, or bank transfers. The more active the body, the more oxygen (blood) is needed to feed the muscles and other organs. Similarly the money supply expands or contracts according to the activity of the economic system. Moreover the conversion of oxygen to carbon dioxide in the body is analogous to the relationship between credit and debt in the economic system. Credit is active, like oxygen; debt is the accompanying waste product, like carbon dioxide. Too much debt, like too much carbon dioxide, is lethal to the organism. (How much debt is too much? Opinions among economists differ widely. I'll get to that later.)

Of course, the analogy has flaws. In the human body, oxygen is literally consumed by muscular activity, and carbon dioxide is literally exhaled. In the financial system, credit is "consumed" in the process of creating goods and services. But debt can accumulate if the creation of goods and services yields a return (profit) insufficient to repay on a current basis. Here the analogy between physical and financial metabolism is imperfect. But it does make the point that the financial system is a lot more than a system of payments, though the payments are essential. *It is the system of payments that the banks are uniquely able to perform.* And it is the system of payments that bank regulators must secure and protect above all else, just as the first priority of the surgeon in an ER is to keep the patient's heart (and lungs) pumping.

The economy of capitalist countries has been characterized by a sequence of booms and busts. The boom typically involves an asset price bubble or a resource price spike (exaggerated by speculators), followed by a "crash" followed by a recession. This sequence, except for the specifics of the asset price bubble, seems to have repeated itself with remarkable regularity since the industrial revolution, and probably earlier (e.g., see Kindleberger 1989; Reinhart and Rogoff 2009). Historically there have been bubbles in a number of different asset categories: for example, tulip bulbs (Netherlands), shares in various trading monopolies (Mississippi, South Seas), Oklahoma land, Florida land (more than once), oil drilling in the Rockies, gold, silver, common stocks (several times), "old masters," dot.com companies, and (most recently) house prices.

But the crucial point is that *steady growth-in-equilibrium exists only in textbooks.* Yet most financial economists still believe in it because it is consistent with the Walrasian equilibrium discussed in the previous section and the standard assumption of rational economic behavior (e.g., Solow 1970; Bernanke 2000). Schumpeter (1928), Minsky (1982), and

Kindleberger (1989, cited above), and Keen (2011) are among the few who have argued, as I do here, that the financial system is inherently unstable. Even the most influential gurus of market rationality have begun to have doubts (Fama and French 2004). For some thoughts from a financial genius on why financial markets don't equilibrate, see Soros (1988)

A bubble occurs when the rising prices of a particular asset class attract speculators who have no desire to own or use the asset per se, but simply want to make money by selling again at a higher price. Today this phenomenon is called "momentum." In Adam Smith's terminology, an asset bubble occurs when investors are interested only in *exchange value*, but not in *use value*. The bubble phenomenon assures high, but unsustainable, rates of return for early investors. The rational speculator will sell when the costs of holding the asset exceed the present value of expected price increases. Looking at the bubble phenomenon from a distance, it is easy to say "I'm too smart to fall for a swindle like that." Maybe you are. But think again. The trouble is deep seated: people really want to believe in winning the lottery. And even ultra-smart investors like Warren Buffet sometimes have difficulty distinguishing a bubble from a long-term trend. Most people never know that a bubble is not a trend, until afterward.

The prices do stop rising eventually when buying slows down and rational investors start to sell. The bubble then collapses when the irrational speculators take alarm and all try to get their money out at the same time. That triggers the crash. Late investors, who were fooled into thinking it could go on forever, lose their shirts (or even their jobs and homes). This often causes another economic recession. The crash invariably leaves a lot of devalued debt. Some of that devaluation applies to the bank's capital base. What follows is that banks then reduce lending by many times (depending on their leverage) more than their losses and that is what stops economic growth. Keen has shown, empirically, that the reduction in "bubble debt" (he called it "Ponzi debt") associated with the subprime mortgage crisis is correlated with reduced aggregate spending. He explains both the Great Depression and the financial crisis of 2008–2009 based on this hypothesis (Keen 2012).

Suppose that the financial system were, as it pretends to be, imply an aggregation of pairwise contracts between lenders with "liquidity" (i.e., cash) and borrowers with some assets or means to repay. Suppose the lenders have access to information about the would-be borrowers enabling them (the lenders) to evaluate the riskiness of each loan. (This is what the ratings agencies are supposed to do.) In such a case the lenders will charge higher interest for the riskier loans. The lenders will also want to allocate the available funds among as many borrowers as possible, so as to minimize the loss if any one of them should default. (Bankers who loaned money to kings, in the past, rarely got paid in coin and sometimes, like the Templars who were bankers to King Philip "the Fair" of France in 1307, they got a different sort of payoff.)

Up to this point, the lender could be anybody with more money than needed for everyday expenses. Suppose that the moneylender is you. Each loan you make decreases your liquidity by that amount, while increasing the (temporary) liquidity of your borrower by the same amount. Of course, you will demand security for your loan, in the form of some asset that can be sold if necessary. Debts and assets balance. There is no overall change in the money supply of the world. The difference between you (as hypothetical moneylender) and a bank is that when the bank makes a loan in the form of credit, it simultaneously creates an asset for itself, *without any loss of liquidity*. The bank can continue to lend, thus increasing the world's money supply, without limit—unless the central bank imposes a limit. The usual limit on total lending is set as a multiple (called "leverage") of the bank's "capital base." That capital base consists of liquid assets: cash or securities that can be turned into cash immediately. In general, the client's security, such as a house or a vineyard or a shop, is not liquid. That is why the size of the (liquid) capital reserve is important.

The obvious risk for a bank that lends more than it holds in reserve (its capital base) is that for some reason (perhaps only a rumor) a lot of depositors may decide to withdraw their money at the same time. This phenomenon, a "run on the bank," was once rather commonplace among small local banks. If there is no rescue from outside, such as a loan from a larger bank, many depositors and shareholders, alike, may be ruined. It was for this reason that the Bank of England (founded in 1694 to make a large private loan to the government) became the official banker of the UK government and the clearinghouse for other banks. It became the controller of the money supply (tied to the gold standard) in 1844 and the "lender of last resort." It was finally nationalized in 1946.

The US Federal Reserve Bank (actually a network of regional banks) was created in 1913 to perform the same functions for the same purposes.

The European Central Bank (ECB) was created in 1998 for the seventeen countries in the eurozone to be the "hub" of a network of existing central banks in Europe. In reality the ECB is being forced more and more to behave like a supernational central bank, though it is still not clear who would be responsible in case of a major European bank (or country) default.

The other, less obvious risk for a bank is that its liquid reserve (cash, securities) can lose in market value. Securities like stocks and bonds do change in value daily. Central banks that bought gold recently, thanks to a rule change in Basel, have suffered up to a 25 percent drops in their asset values. Currency can lose value in relation to the international reserve currency; only the reserve currency—such as the US dollar—is safe from that particular hazard. Still, there is nothing, not even gold or diamonds, that can be regarded as an absolute "store of value." Value is always relative.

A key sub-thesis of this book is that the financial industry (Wall Street) has become increasingly adept at creating bubbles for its own benefit. Schumpeter noticed long ago that banks create money endogenously (Schumpeter 1934), contrary to standard general equilibrium theory. His student, Minsky, elaborated it into a theory to explain the Great Depression. The theory has been further developed by Keen to explain the more recent crisis (Minsky 1982; Keen 2011). The Minsky–Keen model has not yet been widely accepted, but I rather like it. In principle, rising prices should be a signal to the central bank to raise interest rates, but this is painful and pressures to let the good times keep rolling can be enormous, as we saw in 2006 to 2007.

What the invisible gnomes at the Bank for International Settlements (BIS) in Basel, Switzerland, have been doing since 1988 is, among other things, to fix risk-weights for different kinds of assets in a bank's capital base. The capital base of a bank is weighted in proportion to the riskiness of the assets (Bank for International Settlements (BIS) 1988, 2006). Cash and investment-grade bonds were originally counted at full nominal value. Bonds rated less than triple A and other assets like mortgages, business loans, and commodities are now counted at less than full nominal value according to ratios determined by the BIS. Business loans are considered to be riskier than government debt or mortgages, for instance. This is one reason why lending to small business has lagged. Since risk weights differ from one asset class to another, the mix of assets (loans) determines the bank's leverage. After the first risk-weighting (1988), US banks began making fewer business loans and buying mortgage-based bonds because they were regarded as less risky and therefore required less capital to be held in reserve. This increased their leverage and hence their lending capacity (and profits).

The idea that a bank or insurance company is "too big to fail" (TBTF) means that failure would have dangerous and unacceptable impacts on other banks and on the rest of the economy. The word used nowadays to convey this idea is "contagion." If the payment system stopped working, the economy would literally collapse. Imagine a world with no cash machines, no bank transfers, and no checks. This very nearly happened in the fall of 2008. One among several ways contagion can occur is currently on show in Europe. Conservatives and libertarians worry that if bankers know they will be bailed out (too big to fail), they will engage in riskier behavior. This behavioral phenomenon is called "moral hazard" for some, less than obvious, reason.

Regarding contagion, if the assets of a bank are suddenly downgraded by the ratings agencies (reacting to the markets) the capital base needs to be upgraded to compensate. Hence, if a country (or a big bank) were to default and be unable to pay its debts, its bonds would decline in value, or even become worthless. In that case all the other countries, and banks, that have bought those bonds in good faith would suddenly be in trouble. The monetary loss to the banks is less important to the economy by a large factor than the impact on leverage and lending. When the bank's capital base is cut by a dollar, it can lend (depending on the leverage) as much as 30 dollars less. In that case, all the small businesses dependent on a line of credit from the bank are in trouble, and some of them will fail also. The fractional reserve system is a system based on leverage. It is sometimes forgotten that leverage works both ways. It multiplies profits, and losses.

What, then, are the requirements for *sustained* economic growth-in-equilibrium (assuming, for the moment, that such a thing is possible)? Clearly, one requirement is continued availability of both credit and liquidity. Another requirement, still not widely accepted among mainstream growth theorists but no less valid, is availability of physical resources and especially energy. But still another requirement for sustainable growth is *stability*, namely to avoid bubbles. One way, perhaps the only way, to avoid bubbles is to restrict or ration credit. This is what the central bank is supposed to do to calm "irrational exuberance" (Alan Greenspan's words) or in the words of an earlier Fed chairman (William McChesney Martin), "to take away the punch bowl just as the party is starting to roar."

Before the final closing of the US "gold window" in 1971, there was such a restriction on money supply, or people thought there was. But recent history suggests that without the gold standard, or belief in it (or an equivalent), the supply of credit also seems to increase with increasing credit demand. In fact, as Schumpeter noted in his 1934 book, banks were creating credit endogenously during the lead-up to the Great Crash (Schumpeter 1934). The central banks can manipulate demand (within limits) by manipulating short-term and overnight interest rates. In the United States this is done by the Federal Open Market Committee (FOMC), which is a committee within the Federal Reserve System.

Of course, a few defaults among a large number of small borrowers are much easier to tolerate than a default by a single large borrower. But in a modern bank, power goes first and mostly to the deal-makers (or "rainmakers"). Risk management is somebody else's responsibility, and that person, or department, rarely has enough power to do the job properly. There is often a department devoted to shifting risks to other organizations that may have no clue as to what they are taking on. Consequently protection against defaults by spreading risk has become a central theme of the financial industry in recent years. When risk is shifted to society as a whole, the impact on the rest of the society can be much greater than might otherwise have been the case.

An artificial limit to credit creation, or its associated risk, is therefore essential. In the last century the amount of credit created by banks was rationed by law (e.g., by convertibility to gold).[8] Today it is achieved (in principle) by strict regulation of the fraction of assets that need to be held in reserve. But surely the cost of risk insurance should increase progressively with the magnitude of the damage that would be done by a default. To achieve a textbook supply versus demand equilibrium, *the economy needs a mechanism to increase the cost of credit as bank leverage increases.* The monetary authority with the task of adjusting the cost of credit in response to certain trends in the economy is the central bank. I defer further discussion of possible ways and means to chapter 8 of this book.

Externalities and Market Failures

As pointed out earlier, economics back in the eighteenth and nineteenth centuries was really built around the idea of a market consisting of a collection of pairwise exchange transactions (between a seller and a buyer or a borrower and a lender). The key point was that both parties in any pairwise deal expect to gain; otherwise, there would be no point in the exchange. Most transactions are exchanges of money for goods or services. The service category includes promises of future gain, such as shares or other securities. But in all these cases it remains true that both parties expect to be better off as a result of the deal. It may not work out that way, for any of a variety of reasons, but expectation is what matters. In economics 101 financial transactions between two parties are presumed to be win-win (i.e., beneficial to both). One of the "wins" from trade is economic growth itself. This is what I suppose Adam Smith meant when he wrote about "the invisible hand."

Externalities were not explicitly recognized by economists until the twentieth century. The formal definition of an *externality* is a cost (or benefit) incurred by a party who did not agree to or participate in the action causing the cost or benefit (a third party). In the older literature (Pigou 1920; Marshall 1930) an example of a negative externality might have been a fire in a farmer's haystack caused by the sparks from a passing steam locomotive. A positive externality might be the pollination services the bees of a beekeeper perform for neighboring farmers. Today there are no steam locomotives, hence no sparks, and the bees are having trouble reproducing themselves for reasons nobody quite understands but that may well be consequences of an externality (environmental pollution).

When a few economists began to think along these lines nearly a century ago, they assumed that the externalities were minor and that the harmful consequences, if any, could be compensated by legal processes (torts), if legal costs were negligible (Coase 1960). But the realities of the legal process make legal remedies difficult or impossible for an individual to achieve against a giant corporation. (It is no accident that the vast majority of inventors have died poor, while some of their bankers have made large fortunes.) Thanks to some episodes (like smog or Minimata disease or *Silent Spring*), economists in the 1960s began to realize that externalities are not necessarily small and unimportant (Kneese, Ayres, and d'Arge 1970). Climate change wasn't on the environmental agenda at the time.

Some externalities are very positive (win-win). For example, the actions of an inventive entrepreneur like George Westinghouse (or one of Ayn Rand's heroes) may create a new industry. Similarly a chance discovery (e.g., of penicillin) may save many lives. It is not too far off the mark in fact to say that "Schumpeterian" economic growth is really based on positive externalities (also called "spillovers") from business innovations (Schumpeter 1912, 1934). These spillovers are in turn results of investment in education or R&D. The "learning curve" that brings unit costs down is also a kind of externality. It results from the accumulation of production experience, none of which was undertaken for the purpose of social or private learning. Yet the declining cost of production leads to increased demand for the product, more employment, and higher GDP, whence the whole society benefits.

Some externalities involve very serious damages to millions of people, and the environment (Kneese 1977). Rachel Carson's *Silent Spring* told the story of how pesticides used by farmers to kill destructive insects and increase food output also killed the birds that ate the insect eggs and grubs (Carson 1962). The additive, tetra-ethyl lead (TEL), that enabled gasoline engines back in the 1920s to operate at much higher compression ratios (and increased both power output and fuel efficiency) turned out to be so harmful to the environment and human health that it had to be banned. The use of fluorocarbons as propellants in spray cans and as refrigerants has caused an "ozone hole" in the stratosphere. That phenomenon sharply increased the level of dangerous ultra-violet (UV) radiation on the ground, especially in the arctic and Antarctic regions. Fluorocarbons have had to be been sharply restricted for this reason. Oil spills, like the recent one in the Gulf of Mexico, are becoming more dangerous and costly as drilling goes into deeper waters.

The most dangerous externality of all is probably the increasing concentration of so-called greenhouse gases (carbon dioxide, methane, and nitrous oxide) in the atmosphere.[9] This buildup is mostly due to the combustion of fossil fuels. It has the potential for changing the Earth's climate in ways that would harm people in large parts of the world. Powerful storms hitting coastlines in unexpected places may be only the first hint of what is coming.

In order to make rational decisions about policy, there is a need to put a price on such externalities because it is not enough to say that a landscape or a coral reef is "priceless" in a world where funds for environmental protection are limited. More specifically, it would be very helpful for governments to know the external cost of pollution or GHG emissions. The obvious example is coal combustion. A recent study at the Harvard Medical School gave low, medium, and high estimates of the unpaid social costs, mainly health related, of coal combustion. Their "low" cost estimate was $175 billion per year (Epstein et al. 2012).

This calculation has been criticized on the basis that it includes some future climate costs that are controversial because of the underlying assumptions about discount rates. I think the "low" estimate is really too low. But another study entitled "Hidden Costs of Energy" by the US National Academy of Sciences–National Research Council did not include any allowance for GHG emissions, mercury emissions, higher food costs, or national security issues. It still set the cost of coal combustion on human health at $53 billion a year, mostly from sulfur oxide and microparticulate (smoke) emissions (NAS/NRC 2005).

These numbers, which are conservative, compare with the total *revenues* of the US coal industry, which are around $25 billion per year (Heinberg 2009). If these unpaid costs were added to the price of electricity, even taking the too-low NAS/NRC estimate, they would just about double the price per kilowatt. Moreover, if the situation is bad in the United States, it is far worse in coal-burning Asian countries such as China and India. A recent Chinese study pointed out that exposure to coal smoke has cut two to three years from the average life span of workers in north versus south China. Unfortunately, there are a number of other examples of comparable market failures in the economy. However, my point is simply that market failures, generally related to negative externalities, are far from small.

Environmental economists usually propose that unpaid social and health costs should be "internalized" by adding them to the price of coal. If that were done (by means of a tax or penalty), coal would cost several (from 3 to 20) times as much as it does today, and the industries that use it would be far more inclined to support the development of other sources of energy, such as renewables. This has not happened to date because of the enormous political power of the coal-mining and coal-using industries (e.g., electric power companies with old coal-fired plants). So the market failure continues. The "brass knuckles" of the invisible hand are quite clear in this case.

There are many other examples, where some economic activity has turned out to be harmful to other people, or firms, or to the common environment. It is now very clear that externalities associated with waste and pollution are an unavoidable consequence of a simple fact: that our economy is based on extracting raw materials from nature, processing them and producing material goods that ultimately become wastes soon after use (Ayres and Kneese 1969). With few exceptions, services require goods of some sort, whether the scissors of the barber, the CAT scanner in the hospital, or the jet plane. This material dependence is a direct consequence of the first and second laws of thermodynamics. (The slogan "zero pollution" widely employed by politicians and advertisers selling "green" products is a thermodynamic impossibility; it is akin to perpetual motion.)

What I am saying here is that economics in the real world is as much about externalities as it is about what happens in hypothetical "free" markets where goods and services are treated as abstractions. Yet the market concept remains central to economics today. Most people who talk about economics (or finance) assume that markets exist and function reasonably well. The second part of this assumption—that markets are working well—is dangerously simplistic.

One main point of this book is that financial activities can, and do, create negative externalities. Indeed the losses to third parties can be far greater than the gains from the original exchange transaction(s). To cite one example: during the years 2003 to 2007 house prices in the United States rose much faster than previously because demand for housing was artificially increased by bank lending to people who would not normally qualify for a mortgage. This was a *positive externality*, presented as a government intervention to compensate low-income people for being unfairly priced out of the homeownership market. It worked for several years. But many homeowners saw a way of converting equity to cash by refinancing, and speculators saw opportunities to buy houses in a rising market, with no cash down payment. When the boom ended in 2007 and the bust followed, the debts remained and virtually all buyers who had taken out mortgages in the rising market suffered when prices fell. This was a *negative externality*. This sort of negative externality is associated with many bubbles, and I believe it is inherent in the structure of the global financial system.

Energy in Economics

So far I have barely mentioned energy. I discuss energy from an historical perspective in chapter 2. The main point I need to make here is that energy has been neglected in economics, except as a commodity, until quite recently. As a consequence its importance has been seriously neglected. This is probably because energy was not understood, even by physicists, back when economics was a new subject that was essentially about trade. Energy is understood better by physicists today, but most economists have not studied engineering or science.

Economic growth is not automatic; it never was. Growth before the eighteenth century was hardly noticed, and not at all understood. Things changed between 1700 and 1750 for a variety of reasons. One was the political settlement in Europe (Peace of Westphalia, 1648) that ended the religious wars and simultaneously cut religious influence (and later, privilege) in national governments. Government gradually became more secular.

One consequence of growth was increasing political complexity, accompanied by growing bureaucracies. Another was progress in military technology (due to the wars), and its application to colonization in Africa, India, and the New World. A third was deforestation due to population growth and forestland clearing, especially in England. The latter triggered the discovery and utilization of coal to replace charcoal. The technological and economic consequences are worth a separate chapter.

In a nutshell, the increasing availability of high-quality energy from hydrocarbons, at an ever-decreasing cost (until recently), has been a primary driver of economic growth in the industrial countries since the industrial revolution. By the middle of the nineteenth century, economists finally realized that the British economy was entirely dependent on coal (Jevons [1865] 1974). That continued until oil and gas came along. The same could be said of most countries, except the few that were blessed with significant hydroelectric resources. Throughout the nineteenth century coal was king. But oil from the Persian Gulf, and from Texas, and development of the internal combustion engine, changed that situation. Nuclear energy was supposed to be the next step, but after several accidents at nuclear power plants, the future of nuclear energy is now in doubt.

However, this section is about energy in economic theory. The neoclassical theory of economic growth began (more or less) with the two great papers by Robert Solow (1956, 1957). It assumes that economic growth is driven mostly by exogenous forces (known as "technical progress" or "productivity improvement") that are continuing but unexplained features of the economy. But the theory regards the demand for energy (and other resources) as a *consequence*, not a cause, of economic growth. This implies that resources are essentially *created* by some combination of capital and labor (Solow 1956, 1957).[10] This theoretical oxymoron is unfortunately embodied in virtually all large economic forecasting models used by governments and international agencies today. Neoclassical theory seriously underestimates the importance of energy as a factor of production.

A brief digression here is unavoidable, since most PhD economists will not accept the statements in the last sentence without a fight (figuratively speaking, I hope). The reason that neoclassical economics is wrong about the importance of (useful) energy or work is because of a theorem that is taught early in every graduate-level macroeconomic textbook. The theorem says, in simple language, that the importance of each "factor of production"[11] is necessarily *exactly equal to its cost share in the GDP*. The cost share of energy, defined as the revenues of energy companies in most OECD countries, has been somewhere in the neighborhood of 4 percent (it is a little larger now). From this it seems to follow that energy is not very important. For this reason most mainstream economists have no trouble believing that economic growth can continue at more or less current rates for the next hundred years (or forever) without increasing energy availability at constant or declining prices. It is that ideological belief in the (relative) unimportance of energy that lies behind statements about getting the economy "back on track."

But suppose that energy (useful energy) is really the "lifeblood" of the economy, as I believe. Suppose that labor is productive if, and only if, there is a flow of useful energy (as food) to activate the workers. Human (and animal) labor has been largely displaced by machines that do physical work much faster than either humans or horses. But machines without a flow of activating useful energy (fuel) can do nothing and produce nothing. Now suppose that energy is a third "factor of production" in addition to capital and labor. Suppose also that there are physical relationships between those three inputs. For example, suppose that capital is unproductive without a certain labor input and that both capital and labor need a certain energy input based on the design of those machines.

These relationships can be expressed as mathematical constraint equations. The constraints, in practice, allow only a limited range of *combinations* of capital, labor, and useful energy. When these limits are taken into account mathematically, it turns out that the cost share theorem is wrong (Kümmel, Ayres, and Lindenberger 2010). More precisely, it is inapplicable because the model economy on which it is based is much too simplified and the simplifications have made it irrelevant to the real world. To be specific, the conceptual model on which the original theorem was based is an economy consisting of a large number of small enterprises ("price takers") using rented capital and rented labor to produce a single product ("GDP") that is both a consumption good and a capital good. It was also assumed that the capital and (undifferentiated) labor inputs are independent of each other, in the sense that any combination can be used to produce GDP, although one particular combination probably turns out to be the best (most productive).[12]

The formal disproof of the neoclassical cost share theorem as it applies to more realistic models of the economy (more than one sector, more than two factors, etc.) is quite mathematical and need not be reproduced here (Kümmel, Ayres, and Lindenberger 2010; Kümmel 2012). The practical implication of the formal mathematical disproof, and follow-on econometric analysis, is simple: *energy is much more important than its cost share implies, whereas undifferentiated labor is less important.* In other words, a scarcity of useful energy is far more difficult to overcome than a scarcity of labor. Here I need to remind you that by introducing the notion of "division of labor," Adam Smith long ago showed, perhaps without realizing it, that undifferentiated labor is essentially meaningless. But the theory and the models based on the theory still use it. (Today it is painfully obvious that education and training to improve the quality of the labor force are crucial to economic growth—but so is useful energy.)

Another implication of the disproof is that the economy in the future will not depend on the *size* of the future labor supply but on its education and skills (i.e., its *quality*). Hence politicians worried about low birthrates are not thinking straight. Low birthrates will make it easier, not harder, to cope with future environmental problems, and even future economic problems, in a society where most of the work is done by machines and computers, not people. A third implication is that economic growth is by no means automatic—as I said at the beginning of this chapter—and that our great grandchildren may not be much richer, or even as rich, as we are today. In fact I expect growth (in the industrialized countries) to slow down considerably, or even go negative for a while, at least until the global addiction to fossil fuels is finally cured.[13]

A fourth implication is that macroeconomic policy makers have been basing their policy prescriptions on a fundamental misunderstanding; namely that undifferentiated spending on goods and services is the key to growth and employment. Indeed central bankers depend quite a lot on the prescription for setting short-term interest rates known as NAIRU (nonaccelerating inflation rate of unemployment) and the "Taylor rule" (Taylor 1993). NAIRU means the lowest rate of unemployment that doesn't accelerate inflation. The Taylor rule (a successor to the old Phillips curve) relates short-term interest rates to price inflation and the GDP growth gap between actual and "potential" growth rates. Unemployment is one measure of that gap.

Unfortunately, potential growth is currently taken to be an extrapolation of past growth adjusted for inflation. In other words, it assumes that the future will be like the past and that either energy doesn't matter or that it will continue to be available in unlimited amounts at constant or declining (relative) prices. But the Taylor rule takes no account of the possibility of an actual slowdown in growth due to higher energy prices (Warr and Ayres 2006). If potential growth is really much lower than historical growth (as I argue) the gap is much smaller than it appears to be. This suggests that the Taylor rule is now telling central bankers to keep their short-term interest rates lower than they should be. Perhaps the rule needs to be revised. This point is discussed again in chapter 7.

2

On the Role(s) of Energy in the Economy

This chapter explains why the discovery of huge fossil energy resources (coal, petroleum, natural gas) kicked off the fastest period of technological innovation and economic growth in history. It turns out that those resource stocks have acted as *technology incubators* on a vast scale. The need for pumps to keep mines dry led to steam engines that, in turn, enabled railroads, metallurgy (iron, steel), steam boats, gas light, and steam turbines to make electricity. The discovery of petroleum in the mid-nineteenth century led on to internal combustion engines, autos, airplanes, plastics, and synthetic fibers. The substitution of machines for human and animal muscles has been the active driver of economic growth. Human labor is unproductive without useful energy (food) to activate it. Capital goods also need useful energy to function. Hence energy is a "factor of production." Future economic growth depends on the availability of useful energy as fossil fuels, or substitutes.

Energy from Natural Resources as the Driver of Industrialization

There was very little "industry" in the modern sense, before the nineteenth century. Manufacturing was largely restricted to guns, ships, textiles, ceramic tiles, bricks, and brewing. Whereas in the older, mostly agricultural societies almost everybody was engaged in activities related to food production or animal husbandry, machines released people to do other things. The early water mills and windmills took care of labor-intensive grinding operations (to make flour) or irrigation. Later they powered simple machines such as looms to make cloth or sawmills to cut wood. Iron smelting and other metalworking were very minor and remote activities, except for blacksmiths serving local demand for horseshoes, pots and pans, nails, and the like.

Money also played a role, of course. Money in the Middle Ages was mainly coinage from copper, silver, or gold. The Swedish military conquests of the sixteenth and seventeenth centuries were partly financed by the "copper mountain" at Falun. The Spanish Empire in the sixteenth and seventeenth centuries was originally financed by silver from the Joachimstal mine in Bohemia or gold looted from the Aztec and Incan civilizations, but later by silver from the mines of Potosi in Peru (now Bolivia). However, Sweden and Spain did not use the metal money for productive investments. It was used for conspicuous consumption by the aristocracy and the Church, or for paying mercenary soldiers to fight their wars. Those payments to soldiers increased the money supply, without increasing output, and consequently led to inflation.

Coal, by contrast, could not be converted directly into money like gold or silver. It had value only in use. That simple difference made all the difference. The fuel used by most of the manufacturers was charcoal. In northern Europe the price of charcoal was rising from the fifteenth century on due to deforestation. The importance of wood and charcoal as fuel declined after coal began to be mined in quantity. In Great Britain and continental Europe the switch from charcoal to coal began on a small scale in the sixteenth century and accelerated in the eighteenth century. In Eastern Europe and North America the switch took place a century later, because wood for charcoal was still plentiful.

Coal was increasingly needed as a substitute for scarce charcoal. But as coal near the surface was removed, the mines got deeper, and as they got deeper, they were flooded by groundwater. Getting that water out of the mines was essential. From a technology perspective, the Industrial Revolution began in 1711. That was the year Thomas Newcomen installed his first steam engine—really a simple pump—in a coal mine. It consisted of a single large vertical cylinder in which there was a piston attached to a rocker arm. The piston moved up when steam was injected into the cylinder. It moved down, pushed by atmospheric pressure (and gravity) when the steam was condensed by a jet of cold water, leaving a partial vacuum.

This bulky machine did not resemble the steam engines that came later. But it was able to replace a team of horses that had been harnessed to a wheel to pump the water out of a flooded mineshaft. This was the origin of the unit of measure "horsepower." Newcomen's invention solved a serious problem. During the next fifty years, seventy-five of these engines were installed in coal mines all over England. James Watt realized that Newcomen's engine wasted a lot of heat. By saving the condensed steam (which was still hot water) in a separate chamber, much less fuel was needed to turn it back into steam. Watt joined forces with Matthew Boulton to manufacture the new "condensing" steam engines. Until the end of the eighteenth century all Watt & Boulton steam engines operated at atmospheric pressure and steam temperatures barely above the boiling point of water.

In 1803 the first self-propelled steam-powered traction vehicles—called locomotives—were built for coal mines, using new high-pressure steam engines developed by a Cornish engineer, Robert Trevithick. His engines were more compact and more powerful than the Watt & Boulton engines. They were used in the mining industry and became the basis of George Stevenson's first operating railway (Stockton to Darlington, 1825). The next two decades saw a huge railway building boom in England and some other countries.

The first railway investments produced high financial returns, commonly returning 10 percent or more per annum on their capital (Taylor 1942, p. 23). This attracted more capital to the industry. In the second boom period, 1844 to 1846, new railway companies were formed with an aggregate capital of 180 million pounds. This boom virtually consumed all the financial capital available for investment at the time (ibid.). Returns began to fall when the main lines were finished and railway service was being extended into smaller towns by 1860 (in the United Kingdom) and by 1890 in the United States.

The next major application of steam power was in textile manufacturing. The power loom, introduced in the late eighteenth and early nineteenth century, converted a cottage industry into a factory-based industry. (The East India Company played its part in creating markets for the machine-made products from Manchester by effectively destroying the Indian textile industry of Calcutta.) In the words of historian Paul Kennedy:

What industrialization, and in particular the steam engine did was to substitute inanimate for animate sources of power; by converting heat into work through the use of machines—rapid, regular, precise, tireless machines. Mankind was thus able to exploit vast new sources of energy. The consequences of introducing this novel machinery were simply stupendous: by the 1820s someone operating several power-driven looms could produce twenty times the output of a hand-worker, while a power driven "mule" (or spinning machine) could produce two hundred times the output of a hand-worker. A single railway engine could transport goods that would have required hundreds of pack-horses, and do it far more quickly. (Kennedy 1989, p. 145)

Steam power was soon applied to ships and riverboats, especially in the United States, with its large territory and big rivers. Steamships began to displace sailing ships as early as the second decade of the nineteenth century, although the sailing ships later made a comeback. But it was the spread of the railways that created the first major market for wrought iron and later, steel. (Early cannons and rails were made from cast iron.)

Iron was very expensive until the Industrial Revolution because of technological and resource constraints on the size and temperature of blast furnaces. The larger the blast furnace, the higher the temperature it can reach. But larger furnaces also needed larger quantities of fuel to keep going. More fuel means longer distances over which fuel wood or charcoal had to be transported. Thus in the Middle Ages it was more advantageous to produce iron in small, decentralized furnaces scattered around in the forests, which were still plentiful. But the annual iron output of a small, charcoal-fired blast furnace in one year was less than what a twentieth-century steel mill produced in a single day. The advent of large-scale iron smelting had to await efficient coal mines and railroads to carry the coal and the ore.

Thanks mainly to declining iron prices (thanks to coal), demand for wrought iron (especially for rails) increased and English iron production grew from a mere 68,000 tons in 1788 to 500,000 tons in 1825 and then jumped to 1 million tons in 1835, 2 million tons in 1848, and 3 million tons in 1855. Because of the new uses of coal (and coke), English coal production grew spectacularly from 6.4 million tons, in 1780 to 21 million tons in 1826 and 44 million tons in 1846.

Steel, which usually contains between 0.2 and 2 percent carbon, is much stronger and tougher than iron. Steel was the industrial material of choice (as it still is). But steel is much more difficult to produce in quantity than pig iron, or cast iron, partly because it melts at a much higher temperature than pig iron. The problem of making liquid steel directly from molten pig iron was finally solved in the middle of the nineteenth century (independently) by Henry Bessemer in Wales and William Kelly in the United States, during the period 1858 to 1864.

Their innovation was to blow air through a big pot of molten iron, from the bottom. The oxygen in the air combined with the dissolved carbon, creating spectacular fireworks and a lot of air pollution, and heated the molten mixture to the higher temperature at which steel remains liquid. After that, steel could be poured and cast, or rolled into plates and sheets while hot. Bessemer got his name on the process, which was rapidly adopted around the world because it brought the price of steel down to a point where it could be used for almost anything, from rails to machinery, ships, barbed wire for fences, wire cable for bridges, and girders for bridges and skyscrapers. The coal-based iron and steel industry was also very profitable in the nineteenth century, and those profits not only paid for the expansion of the industry but also provided excess profits for investment in other sectors.

Of course, the burgeoning steel industry needed large quantities of coke, which is made by heating bituminous coal to drive off the volatiles (including sulfur, as mentioned earlier). The coke ovens that sprang up around the world's steel centers, such as Sheffield and Birmingham in England, the Ruhr Valley in Germany, and Pittsburgh in the United States also generated a valuable by-product called "coke-oven gas" (quite similar to natural gas in composition) that soon found several new markets.

Starting in 1876 and through the 1880s coke-oven gas also provided the fuel for the first commercial 4-stroke "Otto cycle" internal combustion engines, commercialized by Nikolaus Otto with Gottlieb Daimler and Wilhelm Maybach (based on prior work by Lenoir and Beau de Rochas). Otto's gas-fired internal combustion engines soon began replacing the small steam-engines in German factories, partly because the fuel was cheap and partly because they could be started and shut down more easily. Several hundred thousand of Otto's gas engines and others from imitators were sold during those years.

By 1890 Daimler and Maybach went on to reduce the size and increase the power of the Otto 4-stroke engine. They reduced its size and weight by increasing rotational speed (rpms) and compression ratio. Daimler also invented the carburetor, which allowed the use of liquid fuels with low boiling points, originally benzene distilled from wood, but later gasoline derived from crude oil. In fact gasoline was originally a low value by-product of the petroleum industry, whose main product at the time was "illuminating oil" (kerosene) for lamps. Daimler and Maybach joined carriage- maker Karl Benz to found the Daimler-Benz Company. That partnership gave birth to the world's largest manufacturing industry, the auto industry.

Two other energy-conserving inventions are worth mentioning. One was Rudolf Diesel's pressure-ignition engine, which was heavier but operated at much higher pressure ratios and correspondingly higher efficiency. The engineering and manufacturing difficulties were very difficult to solve, and the earliest uses were just on ships, followed gradually by railways, trucks, and buses. Diesel engines for cars only arrived in the 1970s.

The other important energy saving invention for internal combustion engines was the "antiknock" additive, tetra-ethyl lead (TEL), discovered in the early 1920s. At the time, gasoline engines could not operate with compression ratios above 4 to 1, because of pre-ignition or "knocking." The addition of TEL—marketed as "ethyl" gas—enabled gasoline-powered automobile engines to operate at compression ratios as high as 12 to 1, although 8 or 9 is more common today. The higher compression ratios (as with the diesel engine) that became possible and normal after 1930, increased fuel efficiency of cars by more than 50 percent. However, it also created a lot of toxic air pollution until TEL was banned in the United States in 1969 and subsequently in most of the world.

In summary, coal was the great technology "incubator" of the eighteenth and nineteenth centuries. It provided the motivation to pump out flooded mineshafts, and it provided the fuel required to make the steam power. It motivated canals and fueled the steam locomotives that carried the coal from mine to factory. The use of coal (as coke) for iron production changed that industry. Coal as "town gas" was used for lighting. And finally coke-oven gas powered the first internal combustion engines. By the end of the nineteenth century, electricity produced by high-speed steam turbines was taking over, and the nights were no longer dark, both outside in the streets and indoors. All railroads used coal for motive power throughout the whole of the nineteenth century, and well into the twentieth century. Coal is still the major fuel for electric power plants in many parts of the world, including the United States, China, and India. Coal is also the primary fuel for Portland cement production—the essential ingredient of concrete—and the source of coke for the global iron and steel industry.

Meanwhile the discovery of large reserves of petroleum and natural gas under the ground in the nineteenth century subsequently "incubated" a host of new technologies, starting with fractional distillation in refineries and followed by all of petrochemistry. Liquid fuels from petroleum are now the basis for all surface and air transport (except electrified railways), as well as off-road construction and agricultural machines, not to mention chemicals. The investments that have created these machines and infrastructures mostly came from the profits of coal mining and petroleum drilling, and their numerous industrial "spin-offs."

Evidently neither coal nor rock oil was especially valuable as such, unlike gold and silver. But, unlike gold and silver, they were powerful technology incubators that created far more wealth than all the gold in Fort Knox.

The Search for Black Gold

The 1850s saw the beginnings of the global petroleum industry. It began due to a shortage of sperm whale oil, used for oil lamps. The whales were being hunted close to extinction for their blubber, but by the 1840s the source of supply was obviously failing. Other sources of animal fat were tried, notably from meat packing plants in the United States, but the oil did not burn as cleanly as whale oil and it smelled. The answer turned out to be "rock oil," which was found in many parts of the world but had never been utilized extensively for several reasons, mainly the lack of suitable distillation facilities for separating the usable "fractions." The fractional distillation process was developed in 1854 by Benjamin Silliman, professor of science at Yale University, for a banker named James Townsend. He was the person who organized and financed the Pennsylvania Rock Oil Company (capitalized in 1855 at $300,000 [$8 million in 2011 dollars], with 12,000 shares sold to the public).

Petroleum leaks were already well known, so crude oil was quickly found by the drillers under "Colonel" Edwin Drake. The first well produced 500 barrels a day. The crude oil was sold for $0.80 ($17_{2011}$) per barrel, at the wellhead. A refinery based on Silliman's design was soon built to separate the fractions with different boiling points. In the years after 1859 the US oil industry expanded rapidly, starting in western Pennsylvania. (Pennsylvania Rock Oil Company, later Seneca Oil, failed during the first "oil glut" in 1863.) The most important distillate fraction then, and for the next half century, was "illuminating oil" (kerosene). This rapidly became the dominant global fuel for lamps, replacing whale oil and animal fats.

John D. Rockefeller, with his brother, William Flagler, and Samuel Andrews, created the Standard Oil Company of Ohio in 1870. Headquarters were in Cleveland because it was near the Pennsylvania oilfields, with good rail service already available. Rockefeller concentrated on acquiring refineries and shipping. When he started there were 250 other refiners in the United States. By 1873, using cutthroat methods to destroy or absorb competitors, he controlled 80 percent of the Cleveland refining capacity, which was a third of the US total. There was a deep recession in that year (that lasted six years), which he used to buy or destroy more competitors. By 1878, after eight years in business, he controlled 90 percent of all US refining capacity. Standard Oil of Ohio was originally financed by the National City Bank of Cleveland, a Rothschild bank. The Rothschild banks were major backers of the Rockefeller empire from its beginning.

By 1880 Rockefeller group also controlled the Pennsylvania Railroad and other feeder railroads. Standard Oil Trust was formed in 1882. Its profitability encouraged others to follow its business model during the last two decades of the nineteenth century. Trusts (monopolies) were established in nearly 200 industries, of which the largest were AT&T, US Steel, and Union Pacific Railroad. Other trusts were established in sugar, tobacco, and meatpacking.

During the twenty-five years, from 1882 through 1906, the Standard Oil Trust made net profits of $838,783,800 ($20 billion$_{2011}$) of which $290,347,800 ($7 billion$_{2011}$) was reinvested in the company. The rest was distributed as dividends to the shareholders. That dividend money was re-invested in railroads, electric lighting, gaslight (Consolidated Gas Co. of NY), as well as copper (ASARCO), US Steel, and Corn Products Company In fact the sale of Carnegie Steel to J. P. Morgan for $300 million ($7.8 billion$_{2011}$) in 1901 to create the "steel trust" (United States Steel Corporation) was triggered by John D. Rockefeller's attempt to buy Carnegie Steel a few years earlier.

But Andrew Carnegie inflicted on Rockefeller one of his few (temporary) defeats. He threatened to build his own railroads from Pittsburgh to Lake Erie, and from Pittsburgh to the Atlantic coast, thus by-passing the Pennsylvania Railroad, also controlled by Rockefeller interests. This threat tripled the price tag when J. P. Morgan came calling at Rockefeller's behest. Morgan did not even haggle. Morgan and his associates capitalized the steel trust (US Steel) at $1.4 billion (*$36 billion$_{2011}$*). Less than half of that total was attributable to properties actually owned by the trust. The rest was "water" representing expectations of future profit. The shares were bought by the public, based on a propaganda blitz not too different from the one that accompanied the recent "Facebook" IPO. (The word used by bankers to characterize the suckers, who bought their "watered" shares, was "gudgeons"; Myers [1909] 1936).

From 1881 on, the newly created "trusts" received a great deal of adverse attention due to unfair monopolistic profit-maximizing business practices, such as rate discrimination by the railroads, that punished the farmers. The Interstate Commerce Commission (ICC) was established in 1887 to deal with that problem by fixing rates, but others continued. In 1890 came the Sherman Anti-Trust Act, which supposedly outlawed monopolies. Unfortunately, the Act was not as effective as it should have been because of ambiguous language. In 1892, the Ohio Supreme Court declared that the Standard Oil Trust was an illegal monopoly and ordered its dissolution. The trustees complied, on paper, but they continued to run the subsidiary companies by virtue of their seats on the individual Boards of Directors.

It was President Theodore Roosevelt, elected in 1900, who made the difference. He persuaded the US Congress to create Departments of Labor and Commerce. He had the Department of Commerce create a Bureau of Corporations to collect evidence against the trusts. Then he instructed his Attorney General to initiate 44 prosecutions of trusts for violation of the terms of the Sherman Act and its later revision. The Clayton Act of 1914 finally clarified the situation by defining the specific actions of the trusts that were prohibited.

This period became known later as the era of "muckraking." Over a thousand articles were printed during that decade, attacking corruption, environmental degradation, and predatory business practices of the trusts. The exposés were published by magazines like *Atlantic Monthly*. The biggest target of all was the Standard Oil Company of New Jersey, and the principle accuser was journalist Ida M. Tarbell, who wrote a series of influential articles starting in 1902 that were later collected and published in book form as *The History of the Standard Oil Company* (Tarbell 1904).

In fact Rockefeller interests still have large or controlling stakes in all the big Standard Oil spin-offs, plus Marathon Oil, Freeport McMoran, several airlines (United, Delta, Northwest), ITT, Xerox, Westinghouse, Honeywell, Hewlett-Packard, Motorola, Monsanto, Pfizer, General Foods, Quaker Oats, Union Carbide, International Harvester, and International Paper (Henderson 2012). Those stakes came from oil profits.

Meanwhile the oil industry was growing outside the United States. In 1871 an expert commission of geologists had concluded that the Ottoman territory between the Tigris and Euphrates rivers was likely to be a good source of high-quality (easy to refine) petroleum. This report triggered an exploration race. However, transportation was poor, and this fact was one of the incentives for Germany to invest in the region. German railway engineers were hired to build railways in Turkey. The Anatolian Railway Company was formed by Deutsche Bank and Württembergische Vereinsbank in 1888. The rail line from Istanbul to Konya at the Syrian border was complete by 1896. In 1898 the Ottoman government awarded a contract to complete the line from Konya to Baghdad. It was incomplete by 1914, and was only finished finally by the Iraqi government in 1940.

After Pennsylvania, the next major source of petroleum was near the town of Baku, in Azerbaijan on the Caspian Sea. There, Robert Nobel (older brother of Alfred), started developing an oil industry in 1873 (when Rockefeller was just beginning). By the end of the nineteenth century, the Rothschild banking family had joined the Nobels in Azerbaijan, still an Ottoman province. For some years it was the primary oil producer in the world, albeit landlocked and increasingly dominated by neighboring Russia.

In 1892 Marcus Samuel, a London merchant, persuaded the Rothschilds to finance a new venture, to sell "Russian" kerosene in the Far East in competition with Standard Oil of New Jersey. It is referred to as the "Coup of 1892." He created Shell Oil Company, which later merged with Royal Dutch to create the basis of the modern behemoth. The Rothschilds and Nobels were driven out of Russia—but not out of the oil business—during the 1905 anti-Czarist revolution. (Azerbaijan was briefly independent after 1918 but became part of the USSR in 1920.)

A 1901 German report said that Mesopotamia sat upon a "veritable lake of petroleum" constituting an inexhaustible supply, which Germany was anxious to dominate. In the same year, after a long search, oil was found in Iran by British geologists, and the Anglo-Iranian Oil Company, with an exploration license, was formed to control it. That company later became British Petroleum.

After 1903 the British government took official notice of the pending Berlin-to-Baghdad railroad project. On completion, it would have given Germany rail access—by-passing the British-controlled Suez Canal—to the Persian Gulf and the Indian Ocean. It would also have given Germany easier access to its colonies in East Africa (present-day Ruanda, Burundi, and Tanzania), as well as German Southwest Africa (now Namibia). Quite apart from this, it would have given Germany access to the oil that had recently been discovered in Persia, near the Gulf, where more discoveries followed rapidly.

However, without overland transportation access, the Persian Gulf was effectively monopolized by British interests, supported by the British Navy. The Iranian resource assumed greater importance when the British Navy, urged by First Sea Lord Winston Churchill, switched from coal to oil as fuel for its ships after 1911. The advantages were that oil-burning ships had longer range, and needed to carry fewer men. Also there was no source of coal to be found in the Middle East, whereas there was plenty of crude oil (from Persia) at the time. The possibility of a German port on the Persian Gulf, and possibly German warships in the neighborhood, was also seen by some in London as a potential threat to British interests in India. The British played "hardball." One consequence was the 1914 semi-nationalization of Anglo-Iranian Oil and the forced marriage of Shell with Royal Dutch, in both cases due to British Admiralty concerns about assuring fuel oil supplies for their navy and merchant marine.

However, after 1901 the center of gravity of world oil production moved to Texas, thanks to the huge "Spindletop" gusher, and its accompanying boom. The Texas field around Spindletop was rapidly being developed by Texaco and Gulf Oil Co. In 1910 there was a big discovery in Mexico, where the Potrero del Llano 4 well was soon producing 110,000 bbl/day, making it the most productive well in the world (Yergin 1991, p. 231). The following year major deposits were discovered under Lake Maracaibo in Venezuela. Then Southern California joined the party. By 1921 Mexico was the second largest producer in the world. Oil was being found everywhere and overproduction (glut) was soon to become a problem.

Standard Oil Trust was finally convicted by the US Supreme Court and was ordered to break itself up. This was done in 1911, resulting in the spin-off of a number of vertically integrated oil companies. (Eight of those spin-offs retained the name "Standard Oil"). The result was surprising: the stockholders especially Rockefeller came out of it richer than before because the whole trust turned out to be worth much less than the sum of the individual parts.

By 1925 several of its daughters became internationally important, including Standard of New Jersey (ESSO), Standard of New York (Mobil), and Standard of California (SOCAL, now Chevron). Together with Texaco, Gulf, BP, and Shell, these firms became known as the "seven sisters." The "seven sisters" met secretly at a castle in Scotland in 1928 to agree on a joint policy to restrict output to avoid glut. But in 1930 there was another find in Texas creating an even worse glut. The huge East Texas field was discovered by "Dad" Joiner and his backers, notably H. L. Hunt (who created Humble Oil Company, later bought by ESSO). Oil discoveries in the Persian Gulf area were continuing. Meanwhile major oil discoveries had also been made in other parts of the world.

By 1913 the use of petroleum-based fuel for motor vehicles had resulted in such a radical increase in the demand for fuel that the oil companies (mostly the spin-offs of Rockefeller's Standard Oil of New Jersey) had to develop new "cracking" technologies to convert heavier fractions of petroleum into more volatile fuel (gasoline). The market for illuminating oil for lighting was declining, thanks to electrification, but the market for gasoline was growing faster. A new technology was created for "thermal cracking" of heavy molecules in the crude oil to increase the share that could be used in gasoline engines.

The first US patent for thermal cracking technology was awarded to W. M. Burton of Standard Oil Company of Indiana in 1913. (A Russian engineer, V. Sukhov, had patented essentially the same technology in 1891, but the Standard Oil Trust had refused to pay the Russians.) Thermal cracking doubled the yield of gasoline from crude oil. After the Standard Oil breakup of 1911, the need to pay newly independent Standard of Indiana large royalties kicked off a technological competition. That race resulted, at last, in the continuous catalytic cracking process now used around the world, invented (mainly) by Eugene Houdry in the 1930s (Enos 1962)

In 1917 the state of Texas gave authority to regulate pipelines to the Texas Railroad Commission (originally created to regulate freight rates). This was followed two years later by authority to deal with the problem of petroleum overproduction, which was driving prices down. One of the reasons for this regulatory initiative was the "law of capture," which meant that wells were routinely drilled close together to grab as much oil as possible, without any concern for maximizing the life or total output of the resource. Early oil fields tended to be very crowded, with as many as ten wells per acre. This mode of production was terribly inefficient, as geologists pointed out, but it took the industry some time to see the need to let the government (instead of a cartel) regulate output.

A re-allocation of concessional arrangements followed the breakup of the Ottoman Empire and its territories. US Secretary of the Treasury Andrew Mellon succeeded in muscling into Kuwait on behalf of "his" oil company, Gulf Oil. In 1934 the Kuwait Oil Company was established as a joint venture between Gulf Oil Co and British Petroleum.

In fact the concessions of the old Turkish Petroleum Company—without the German banks, whose shares had been confiscated by the Treaty of Versailles—were re-allocated among five stockholders in 1928. The division was 23.75 percent to each of the four "majors," namely Anglo-Persian (later British petroleum), Royal Dutch Shell, Compagnie Française du Petroles (now Total), and Near East Development. The latter was a consortium of five US oil companies, several of which were among the "seven sisters" created by the breakup of Standard Oil in 1911.

Behind the symbolic Berlin-to-Baghdad railroad lay a much bigger concern. Back in 1912 Calouste Gulbenkian, an Armenian entrepreneur with Turkish connections (who had helped in the creation of Royal Dutch, back in 1902) organized the Turkish Petroleum Company (TPC). It had rights to oil exploration in what is now Iraq. Before the war, TPC was owned 47.5 percent by Anglo-Persian (now BP), 22.5 percent by Royal Dutch Shell, and 25 percent by Deutsche Bank, with 5 percent (nonvoting) reserved for Gulbenkian himself. After WW I, the German banks were dispossessed by the Versailles Treaty, but Gulbenkian was not.

The secret Sykes–Picot agreement of 1916 (before the United States entered the war) would have awarded Palestine and Iraq to Britain, Syria and Kurdistan (including oil-rich Mosul) to France and Constantinople, and some coastal territory on the Anatolian side of the Black Sea to Russia, as well as giving Greece the islands or the Peloponnese and parts of Thrace (Izmir) on the west coast of Turkey. This plan fell through when the Bolsheviks took over Russia in 1917 and rejected the deal, along with the Russian debts. Needless to say the "Young Turks" under Kemal Ataturk also did not agree to dismemberment of post-Ottoman Turkey in favor of Russia (or Greece). Anti-Bolshevism helped their cause. However, while Istanbul and the outlet of the Black Sea remained Turkish after the war, the Versailles Treaty retained most of the other features of the secret treaties. In particular, Britain kept Iraq, with its oil, as a mandated territory, under the newly created League of Nations (Yergin 1991).

The sixty-year period between 1928 and 1968 was dominated by depression and several wars. WWII was at least partly driven by concerns about oil, since both the German tanks and the German air force needed fuel. The small Ploesti field in Romania was the only one in Western Europe at the time. Was Rommel's North Africa campaign intended not only to cut the Suez Canal but also to secure overland access to the Persian Gulf? Was the German invasion of Russia really aimed at the oil province of Azerbaijan? The German submarine fleet was certainly aimed at the oil tankers from Texas and Louisiana that were keeping Britain in the war.

Meanwhile, beginning in 1933, engineers from Standard Oil of Californian (SOCAL) began exploring in Saudi Arabia under license. Huge discoveries followed quickly. In 1936 SOCAL sold a 50 percent interest to Texaco. The name was changed to Arabian American Oil Company (ARAMCO) in 1944. By 1945 the Ras Tanura refinery was the largest in the world. In 1948 ESSO joined the consortium. In 1950 the consortium got a tax break from the US government equal to 50 percent of its profits. By 1956 ARAMCO confirmed that it had the largest off-shore field (Safaniya) and the largest on-shore field (Ghawar) in the world. ARAMCO was nationalized in 1980, though its shareholders retained international marketing rights. Saudi Arabia currently has the largest proved reserves and the largest daily output of petroleum.

The west Texas fields were already in decline by the 1950s, and the US output of crude oil reached its all-time peak in 1969. The United States had already become a significant importer (from Venezuela) in the 1950s and the import share of domestic consumption was rising inexorably. In 1960 the Oil Minister of Venezuela persuaded other exporters to organize themselves into a cartel, the Organization of Petroleum-Exporting

Countries (OPEC) in order to control output and raise prices, on the pattern of the Texas Railroad Commission. For the next decade OPEC was not very visible, or very effective, because not every producer was in it, and the United States was still the gorilla in the room. That changed in 1971.

The "Oil Shocks" of 1971 and 1981

The first "oil shock" was triggered by the three-week Yom Kippur war of October 5 to October 26, 1973. The conflict was between Israel and a coalition of Arab states led by Egypt and Syria. The Arabs, led by Gamal Abdel Nasser, attacked first. Urged by Secretary of State Henry Kissinger, President Nixon decided to support Israel with a huge airlift of military supplies. This allowed Israel to inflict a devastating military defeat on the Arabs, resulting in Israeli occupation of the Sinai, Gaza, the Golan Heights in Syria, and the West Bank.

The war itself ended quickly. But OPEC, dominated by Arab countries, suddenly woke up. On October 16, 1973, OPEC announced a unilateral 70 percent price increase of $5.11/bbl ($20_{2011}$). This was to be followed by a series of incremental reductions in output until market prices reached the level desired by OPEC. The Arab members of OPEC simultaneously declared an embargo against the United States, the United Kingdom, and the Netherlands and to a lesser extent other countries that supported Israel. And, to drive home the point, Saudi Arabia "acquired" 25 percent of ARAMCO at that time. The embargo was effective. It didn't end until March 1974 when the Israelis (under US pressure) withdrew from the Sinai desert and much of the Golan Heights overlooking the Sea of Galilee.

There was a sharp increase in the price of oil starting in October 1973 from around $19 per barrel to more than $43 per barrel (2013 price equivalent, see figure 2.1) in less than six months. The price spike was partly caused by the embargo. But the embargo was possible because of a confluence of two other factors: (1) OPEC countries had seen their revenues decline in real terms because of an inflation driven depreciation of the dollar in the 1950s and 1960s and (2) the increasing dependence of the Western countries on imported oil from OPEC countries. In the 1960s US domestic oil production was approaching its peak (1969 to 1970). It was this that gave OPEC bargaining power vis-à-vis the international oil companies.

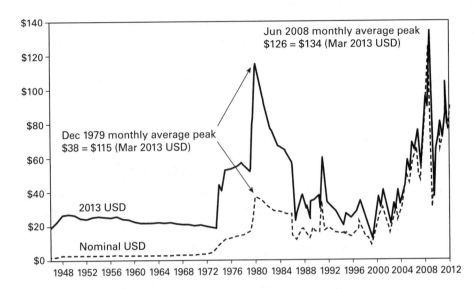

Figure 2.1
Monthly average US domestic crude oil prices, 1946 to 2012. Prices from US Energy Information Agency.

When oil prices tripled in 1974 there was a tremendous flow of money to the exporting countries (figure 2.2). The oil revenues, *all of it in dollars,* flowed initially to the USSR (Russia), the Middle East, North Africa, Nigeria, Venezuela, and Mexico. The big oil exporters got rich very suddenly, and the opposite happened to oil-importing countries. In 1974 the United States experienced a deep recession and a stock market crash. The "excess" oil revenues (based on prices above today's equivalent of $30 per barrel) that moved to the oil exporting countries between 1973 and 1985 added up to about $3 trillion (constant 2006 US dollars). The United States, being the biggest importer, probably accounted for a third, or around $1 trillion of that financial flow.

Sadly, that windfall was not used productively in the exporting countries. Hardly any of the recipients were democracies; many were military dictatorships or absolute monarchies. The Soviet Union's share of the windfall was partly used to finance money-losing left-wing regimes abroad, notably Cuba and Angola. In other exporting countries some was used to purchase weapons, as well as private jet aircraft, and luxury goods for the elites. Some was used to finance grandiose projects such as real estate developments, as in Abu Dhabi, featuring skyscraper hotels, golf courses, and yacht harbors.

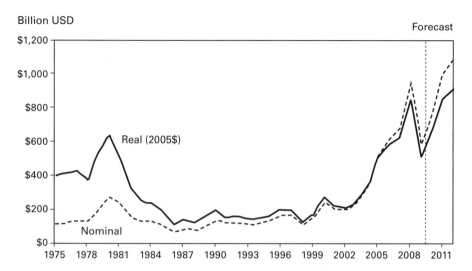

Figure 2.2
OPEC net oil revenues. Data from US EIA, Short-Term Energy Outlook, 2009.

The Iranian revolution in 1979 cut off Iranian oil exports briefly and doubled international oil prices again, to a peak over $40/bbl ($100_{2011}$) in 1980 before beginning a decline that finally reached bottom in 1986 (see figure 2.1). The high oil price has been attributed to fears that the trouble would spread. It did trigger an immediate but deep recession, especially due to its impact on the US auto industry, where a large number of jobs disappeared. Meanwhile, an Islamic Republic was declared in Iran on April 1, 1980, with Ayatollah Khomenei as the Supreme Leader. This enabled the Shiite majority to institute an anti-Western theocracy that still remains in power. In November 1980, Islamic militants attacked the US embassy and took fifty-two Americans as hostages in an attempt to force the United States to extradite the Shah back to Iran for trial. They did not succeed in that, but they did help Ronald Reagan defeat Jimmy Carter. Then in 1980 Iraq attacked Iran, hoping to annex some territory and access to the Gulf while Iran was in a state of turmoil.

That resulted in yet another deep economic recession as credit, especially for small and medium-size businesses, dried up. The price of oil started to drop during that recession, and kept going down through the first Reagan years. Overall, it fell dramatically from about $40/bbl in 1980 to around $13/bbl in 1986 (from $114 to $22 in 2012 dollars).

This was probably a predictable consequence of the recession as some did predict it, but other theories are out there. One theory attributes the extraordinary price decrease to a "price war" in OPEC. There is another more interesting (but unproved) theory that the US government conspired with the Saudi government to cut prices so as to deprive the Soviet Union of hard currency. Whether that was the intention or not, the USSR was hit hard. Those low prices may have triggered the end of the cold war and the leadership change that finally led to the breakup of the USSR and the Warsaw Pact.

An accounting identity says that *every dollar that flows out of the United States eventually returns in some form,* either as payment for manufactured goods, services, or assets. Some was spent on US manufactured products, such as aircraft and computers. Some was spent on tourism and college fees for the children of the OPEC elites. But since the United States already had a trade deficit, a lot of the return flows of petrodollars had to end up as investments in US assets, notably Treasury bonds. In effect the United States purchased oil from the oil exporters—and still does—with borrowed money.

But some of those petrodollars were deposited in US bank accounts, where they could be re-loaned to other oil-importing countries. The US money-center banks stepped in to "help" by lending money to the less developed countries to enable them to buy oil and keep their economies going. Over $350 million ($900 million$_{2011}$) went to Latin America, mainly to Argentina, Brazil, and Mexico. The banks (backed by the US government) were also eager to finance US exports to those countries. Latin American banks were obliging. They borrowed heavily (mostly recycled "petrodollars"), increasing their country's total indebtedness fourfold from $75 billion ($250 billion$_{2011}$) in 1975 to $315 billion ($640 billion$_{2011}$) in 1975 to $315 billion ($640 billion$_{2011}$) by 1982.

Thanks to this borrowing, the second oil shock in 1979 to 1980 triggered a financial crisis in Latin America. Countries that had borrowed US dollars to pay for oil since 1974 were now faced with still higher prices for the oil, plus rising interest rates being charged by the US banks due to rising domestic inflation. Latin American debt service had been $12 billion ($40 billion$_{2011}$) in 1975. It rose to $66 billion ($135 billion$_{2011}$) in 1982, which was impossible to meet. The consequence was a formal bankruptcy of Mexico in August 1982 and major bank failures in Argentina, Brazil,

Chile, and Mexico. The cost of the IMF bailouts has been estimated at between 4 and 55 percent of GDP for Argentina. For Chile the range of estimates was from 29 to 41 percent of GDP (Reinhart and Rogoff 2009, tab. 10.9). The economic crisis brought on by the successive oil price spikes may well bear some responsibility for the collapse of civilian government in several Latin American countries.

From 1982 to 1985 US banks collected $108 billion ($225 billion$_{2011}$) in repayments from Latin America. The economic damage to Latin America is hard to measure exactly, but it was immense. However, it was not all due to bad behavior by the US banks. The Latin American elites who diverted public money to their private accounts must bear quite a bit of the blame, along with banks in Switzerland and other places that have actively solicited "hot" money, which is attracted by "privacy" laws designed for that precise purpose.

Iraq, under Saddam Hussein, invaded Iran in November 1980. The main purpose of the invasion was to annex the oil-rich province of Khuzestan and its oil port on the Persian Gulf. However, the Shia-led revolution in Iran was encouraging Shia militants in Iraq, and there was a spate of attacks and assassination attempts aimed at officials of Saddam's Ba'ath party in Baghdad. The Iraqi attack contributed to worries about the security of global oil supplies, and thus to the high price of oil in 1980 to 1981. Iraqi attack bogged down into a stalemate. While over half a million soldiers and civilians lost their lives on both sides, the international price of oil began to decline in 1982.

During the period 1974 to 1985 the United States produced, on average, only a little more than half of the oil it consumed from domestic sources. Given that excessive US payments to oil exporters in those years were of the order of $1 trillion, there was another similar or larger shift of wealth from consumers to domestic producers spread over twelve years or so. Call it $1.5 trillion. Most of it was paid out as dividends to the shareholders of oil companies or used to buy back shares. None, or very little, was spent on developing alternative sources of energy.[1]

In 1979 to 1980, thanks to the high price of oil (due to the Iranian revolution), there was a short-lived boom in oil and gas exploration in the western United States. Many small investors lost money in dry holes, as prices dropped. One episode had longer lasting financial consequences. The Penn Square Bank, in Oklahoma, failed in July 1982. The failure was due to a large number of nonperforming loans to oil and gas prospectors, collateralized by leases and drilling permits that never produced anything. Penn Square, in turn, owed a billion dollars to the seventh largest bank in the United States, Continental Illinois National Bank (CINB).

When the link to Penn Square became known to the CINB depositors and shareholders (along with other troubles), there was a loss of confidence in CINB itself. Big depositors began to move to other banks. Finally, in May 1984 there was a run on the bank. The Federal Deposit Insurance Corporation (FDIC) was forced to treat CINB as being "too big to fail" for fear of a domino effect bringing down more of the US financial system. To do so, the FDIC paid out $4.5 billion ($8 billion$_{2011}$) for redeeming depositors, of which only $3 billion ($5.1 billion$_{2011}$) was insured by the FDIC (Federal Insurance Deposit Corp. 1997). That precedent has also changed the way in which bank shareholders think about risk.) In the aftermath, Continental Illinois was taken over by Bank of America. This episode raised the concern, which has become more acute in recent years, that in the event of failure big banks will always be treated better than smaller ones, and better than their customers.

Apart from all else, there was lost economic growth during the oil recessions of 1974 to 1975 and 1979 to 1981. I won't attempt to estimate the costs of lost growth and lost jobs (an estimated one million jobs were lost in the US auto industry, just in 1979), but it was significant. Admittedly, the lost growth was due to many causes and only partly due to the oil price spikes. However, the high price of oil in those years was certainly a factor.

Drilling for Oil on Wall Street

In the years between 1982 and 1985, Texas oil-man T. Boone Pickens invented a new strategy, later termed "green mail." He began by using the assets of his small exploration and drilling company, Mesa Petroleum, as collateral for loans he used to take buy a controlling interest in Hugoton Production Co. (which was thirty times larger than Mesa). He then used the assets of Hugoton as collateral for borrowing still more money (from Milken and Drexel) to buy stock in other oil companies, such as Phillips Petroleum, Unocal and Cities Service. The purpose was simply to drive up their stock prices, which were normally based on proved reserves. Pickens created in effect his own "bubble." It was called "drilling for oil on Wall

Street" because new oil discoveries had been declining since 1960, as seen in figure 2.3.

Pickens greatest "coup" was an attack on Gulf Oil, one of the "six sisters" in 1985. Again, he used junk bonds from Drexel. The attack was especially effective then because the price of Gulf stock had been depressed due to nuclear fuel problems at a subsidiary, Gulf-General Atomic. The outcome was that Gulf Oil Company, one of the industrial stalwarts of Pittsburgh, was forced it to sell itself to a "white knight" (Chevron) for $13.2 billion (*$24 billion*₂₀₁₁).

That was a tragedy for Pittsburgh, where Gulf had its corporate headquarters and R&D facilities (where my uncle once worked), all of which were shut down. It was quite a bargain for Chevron and Christmas in July for Pickens. Pickens made a personal profit of $400 million (*$740 million*₂₀₁₁) on his stock holdings in Gulf Oil Company. It is interesting that Mr. Pickens is still playing the same game, now promoting shale gas ("The Pickens Plan"). He has had some success.

An economically significant, energy-related incident occurred on March 28, 1979. There was a nuclear accident at Three Mile Island, near Harrisburg, Pennsylvania. Nobody was killed, but the cost of cleanup was high and the intensity of public concern was even higher. That was primarily because the cause of the accident was not completely understood and the

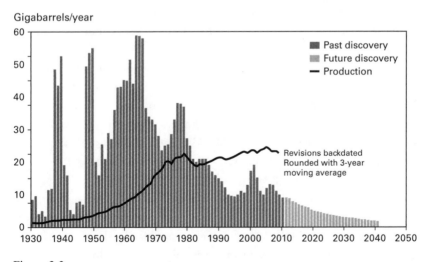

Figure 2.3
Growing gap between oil production and oil discovery

assurances by experts that reactors were completely safe was clearly shown to be unjustified. As a consequence no new reactor has been commissioned in the United States after that date. The later accident at Chernobyl in Ukraine led to even more intense opposition. The end of nuclear power (in the United States) resulted in a return to coal-burning power plants, and the resulting pollution and atmospheric buildup of "greenhouse gases."

Oil and the Collapse of the Soviet Union, 1986 to 1989

The price of oil declined rather rapidly after 1982 as OPEC production, combined with Soviet (Russian) production, increased faster than global demand. The price reached a low point in 1986. (That low point corresponded exactly with the low point in unemployment during the Reagan administration.) Of course, high oil prices of the early 1980s also induced new entrants to the oil export market, especially from West Africa. Saudi Arabia also ratcheted up its output, temporarily. That in turn led to a new oil glut.

During the early 1980s oil production in the Soviet Union had reached a peak and stabilized between 4.0 and 4.5 billion barrels per year. There was a slight dip in 1985, followed by a slight increase, but Soviet production then dropped precipitously after 1987 and fell to under 3 billion barrels in 1996, before climbing again (Reynolds and Kolodziej 2008). In contrast, global production soared in the years after 1986, keeping prices low.

The low prices during the oil glut of 1986 to 1988, combined with reduced Soviet output, cut the hard currency oil revenues of the USSR. As a result the USSR could no longer finance its satellite in Cuba, the left-wing regimes in Nicaragua and Angola, the war in Afghanistan, the Warsaw Pact and its other foreign adventures. This loss of hard currency revenues may even have triggered the internal changes ("perestroika" and "glasnost") that ended the cold war in 1989 and permitted Eastern Europe to join the growing European Union.

A CIA plot to cut oil prices in the late 1980s has been suspected, though I am skeptical. If so, the plot worked remarkably well, and the USSR collapsed in 1989 to 1990, without a shot being fired. Still, there were those in power in the United States, including Vice President George Bush, who might have wanted to take credit for such a plot to further an election campaign, even if there was no actual plot. We may never know.

The Iraq Wars, 1991 and 2003

During 1989 to 1990 the emir of oil-rich Kuwait was overproducing crude oil, according to OPEC quotas. At any rate, Saddam Hussein, the dictator of Iraq seems to have been a believer in the CIA "plot" theory mentioned above. He claimed that Kuwait's overproduction cost Iraq $14 billion. He demanded compensation from Kuwait. None was offered. On August 20, 1990, Saddam Hussein invaded Kuwait, which had no real defenses, and "annexed" it. His excuse was that Kuwait was Iraq's "thirteenth province" and that it should never have been given its independence in the first place. (He had a fairly good case in law but did not choose to resolve it peacefully. Probably he assumed, correctly, that there was no court with jurisdiction and thought that a *fait accompli* would be accepted.)

This gave Saddam control over 20 percent of the world's oil reserves. According to published accounts, he then moved his army (eleven combat divisions, including the elite Republican Guard), to the Saudi Arabian border. This story is disputed by others, some with insider knowledge. King Fahd allegedly asked President Bush for military help, although there are people who believe that he did so reluctantly under pressure by US Secretary of Defense Dick Cheney. Both Cheney and Bush seem to have been very keen for an excuse to invade Iraq, probably to secure future access to the undiscovered oil thought to be under the Iraqi desert.

Anyhow Bush and some European partners sent ground forces under the name "Operation Shield" to defend Saudi Arabia. In January 1991 US and other coalition forces initiated "Desert Storm," starting with an intensive air attack. Iraq deliberately caused a huge oil spill in the gulf (estimates range from 2 million to 6 million barrels) either as a defensive measure or to prevent the US forces from confiscating it. US marines moved back into Kuwait and easily defeated the Iraqi army. But President Bush announced a cease-fire (February 28, 1991) and did not move on to Baghdad or depose Saddam. The Gulf War caused another oil price spike to $35/bbl ($60_{2011}$) due to fears that the Iraq war would cut supplies. That spike was also accompanied by a recession (1990 to 1991) that cost George H. W. Bush his job. Bill Clinton was elected to the US presidency in 1992.

Oil prices recovered a little between 1991 and 1996, but during 1997 and 1998 the price of oil dropped back to around \$20/bbl (\$29$_{2012}$), the lowest point since 1973. Thanks to cheap oil, the US economy boomed. (That was also the brief period of US budgetary surplus.) Then the dot. com recession hit, starting in March 2000, and after the destruction of the World Trade Center buildings by Muslim extremists on September 11, 2001, the price of oil rose again to \$30/bbl (\$40$_{2012}$). After that it dropped back a little briefly during the post dot.com (and 9/11) recession.

Thanks to the beginning of the second Iraq war, starting in March 2003, oil prices started to climb again, and fast. There was a slight setback after the price hit \$80 in early 2007. But then it continued up like a skyrocket until the West Texas crude spot price hit \$145.31 on July 3, 2008, and a number of analysts were predicting \$200 oil, or more. The next and much deeper recession began in 2007 and lasted through 2008 into 2009 and after. The crash was responsible for the dramatic fall in West Texas crude oil to a low of \$30.28 per barrel on December 28, 2008. (The price recovered after that, almost as fast as it had fallen. It reached \$100/bbl again in 2011 and has hovered around that level since then.)

To be sure, the recession of 2008 to 2009 was attributed mainly to the subprime mortgage crisis, and not to the price of oil. I have much more to say about that in subsequent chapters. More important for the thesis of this book, however, the United States has allowed itself to get much too dependent (George W. Bush used the word "addicted") to imported oil from politically unstable countries. "Protecting," if that is the right word, those countries has been considered a fundamental US strategic interest. Certainly the US Sixth Fleet, physically based in Bahrain and patrolling the Indian Ocean and the Persian Gulf, is devoted to that task. The two wars in Iraq were partly, if not largely, about US access to Iraqi oil, whatever high sounding excuses the two Bush presidents, father and son, used to justify them.

In fairness, imported oil is not the only cause of the long-running ever-increasing US trade imbalance. Part of it stems from the post–WWII recovery period when Europe, benefiting from low (relative) wages and US military protection, began to export its manufactured products back to the United States, as Japan and South Korea did later. Whole industries, from watches, cameras, bicycles, motorcycles, radios, and TVs moved away from the United States during those postwar years. But the major factors were the costs of the Korean and Vietnam wars, which were largely borne by the United States, notwithstanding nominal contributions from NATO allies. Finally, the enormous US "defense" expenditures supporting military bases and fleets around the world, amounts to a significant dollar outflow. Moreover defense spending contributes little to future productivity, which is one of the reasons US manufacturers today prefer to outsource as much as possible. However, the important point I need to make here, and again, is that these imbalances are not self-correcting.

3

A Brief History of Bubbles and Busts through 1933

This chapter is essentially economic history focused on the role of finance. It recounts the origin of the gold standard and some of the problems resulting. It recounts the development of trusts (and antitrust laws) followed by the creation of the US Federal Reserve system to provide a backstop against runs on the bank. It follows the post–WWI reparations negotiations, the German hyperinflation, the Dawes plan (and bonds), the creation of the Bank for International Settlements (BIS), the US stock-market "bubble of 1928 to 1929 and its aftermath, the Great Depression, leading to the nationalization of gold and the Glass–Steagall Act of 1933.

Economic History, pre-1913

In "the olden days," say before the sixteenth century, economic growth was financed mostly from personal savings and enterprise profits (e.g., from a trading voyage) reinvested. Borrowing was only possible with established security, such as land or gold, or perhaps a crop or a mine claim, although some payments were made by means of gold equivalents (bills of exchange based on receipts from a depository, often a goldsmith). Modern banking began in the Italian city-states, Florence, Genoa, and Venice in the fourteenth century, in support of long-distance trade. The early banks were family affairs (Bardi, Peruzzi, Medici). The Fuggers and Welsers joined the fraternity in the fifteenth century and dominated German finance in the sixteenth century.

Banking moved to Amsterdam in the sixteenth century and to London in the seventeenth century. It spread to seventeenth-century London when goldsmiths, who often acted as custodians for bullion or coins, noticed that much of the gold in their vaults was never withdrawn because their customers were using bills of exchange for most purposes. Some crooked financial genius began the practice of lending money at compound interest based on fictitious gold deposits (but not without demanding collateral; see Werner 2005, ch. 12). This was the beginning of fractional reserve banking, and it is the mechanism whereby banks today are able to "create" money (as credit).

Early in the eighteenth-century John Law, a Scotsman, had the idea of creating a bank whose capital consisted of paper (bonds) based on hypothetical future profits from some trade monopoly. This idea was proposed at first for Scotland and rejected, but was later accepted in France where the government was insolvent due to profligate spending by the "sun king," Louis XIV. There it became the basis for the Banque Générale and the Mississippi Company (later "Mississippi Bubble"), which sold shares to the public based on greatly exaggerated profit expectations. It collapsed when the number and value of the shares issued far exceeded the unrealistic revenue expectations that had been fed by rumors. John Law was (perhaps unfairly) discredited by the bubble's collapse. He had to flee from France.

But the idea had already crossed the English Channel. A similar bubble, also based on a private trade monopoly, the "South Sea bubble," started in 1711. Again, the shares were sold to the public based on unrealistic expectations of monopoly profits from trade with Chile, Peru, and the "antipodes." The profits were supposed to pay off the English public debt. But in fact the "dividends" to early investors were paid from the money received from later investors. Those shares were (briefly) treated as currency. After the collapse of this "Ponzi" scheme[1] (1720) the privately owned Bank of England (the official banker and gold depository for the British government at the time) bought the South Sea bonds for silver. This coup also made the BoE the official lender to the government.

By the middle of the eighteenth century it needed taxes to pay the interest owed to the Bank of England. The need for gold as a monetary base for the pound sterling drove the so-called "mercantile" policy, under which England exported manufactured goods to its colonies in exchange for payment in gold. In 1764 Parliament passed the Currency Act forbidding the American colonies from printing their own money and requiring all taxes to be paid in gold or silver. Mercantilism was ruinous for New England, which had no gold or silver mines and had to compete in export markets with the mother country itself. This foolish policy was the principal underlying cause of the American Revolution of 1775 to 1778.

In 1844 the Bank Charter Act gave the Bank of England (still private) the exclusive right to issue paper money, but only in quantity equal to the amount of gold it held in reserve. This restriction, the "gold standard," kept the money supply from exploding, prevented inflation, and made the English pound sterling the de facto reserve currency of the world. Japan adopted the gold standard in 1872, for instance. Other countries gradually switched from a silver standard to a gold standard in the following decades. China and Hong Kong were the last to switch, after 1908.

It is a widely ignored fact that national debts—in the past in Western Europe at least—have been almost entirely due to wars and military spending. The period since WWII is not typical. There have been many periods in history when expenditure on war exceeded government revenues for significant periods, resulting in the need to borrow from banks or proto-banks. In some cases the banks were ruined when the borrower couldn't (or wouldn't) repay. This was the fate of the Fugger bank of Germany, when Philip II of Spain suspended interest payments on loans in 1575.

Despite its enormous annual income in the form of silver from the Potosi mine in Peru, the Spanish-Hapsburg government defaulted on its debts a number of times, entirely due to the huge costs of war, often on four fronts. The most expensive were the wars against the Dutch (1567 to 1607, 1621 to 1654). During those years Spain received shipments of silver worth 121 million ducats from its American colonies, but its army in Flanders alone cost 218 million ducats. (The costs to the rebellious United Provinces were less, but still very large.) Spain was also fighting against England or France much of the time and against the Ottoman Turks most of the time. When Philip II died in 1598, he left a national debt of 100 million ducats, and the interest payments amounted to two-thirds of Spanish crown revenues (Kennedy 1989).

In the 1540s Henry VIII of England fought a series of wars against France and Scotland, costing over 2 million pounds, over ten times the normal revenues of the crown. King Henry obtained additional income from confiscating Church lands and property to pay for these wars. Queen Elizabeth, by contrast, avoided wars and kept the national debt comparatively small. Her successors did not. During the five wars from

1688 through 1783, ending with the war against the United States (1776 to 1783), the British government spent altogether 606 million pounds against revenues of only 405 million pounds, the difference being made up by 230 million pounds in loans (Kennedy 1989, tab. 2, p. 81). (I have rounded the totals, but I cannot explain the discrepancy in Paul Kennedy's numbers). The costs to England of the Napoleonic wars (1793 to 1815) were vastly greater: 1,658 million pounds, compared to revenues of 1,218 million pounds (ibid.). Again the difference of 440 million pounds was made up by borrowing. (Luckily the English government was able to borrow from its own people, unlike the governments of many other countries.) The rapid economic growth during the industrial revolution made it possible for England to pay off that debt rather easily.

Speaking of background, I think it is interesting to recall the long contest between Alexander Hamilton and Thomas Jefferson during the formative years of the United States of America. Hamilton wanted to industrialize the country, and he was prepared to borrow money to invest in infrastructure. Jefferson, by contrast, envisioned a country of small self-sufficient farming communities, and he didn't like debt.[2] He once said:

I place economy among the first and most important virtues, and public debt as the greatest of dangers. . . . We must make our choice between economy and liberty, or profusion and servitude. If we can prevent the government from wasting the labors of the people under the pretense of caring for them, they will be happy.

The tension between those, like Hamilton, who see credit as a tool for enabling investment for growth and those, like Jefferson, who see debt as a sort of immorality, if not sin, remains today. It is interesting that Jefferson also saw "economy" (in the sense of industrialization and growth) as being incompatible with "liberty" (self-sufficiency and freedom of choice). Ayn Rand and her present-day followers see "liberty" (i.e., no government interference or regulation) as the *precondition* for growth.

Anyhow, after Jefferson and his successor (John Quincy Adams) had paid off the costs of the Louisiana Purchase, the new forty-ship navy, bribes to the Barbary pirates, paying for the War of 1812 and rebuilding the city of Washington, DC, the federal budget went into surplus. The surplus was due to selling off public lands west of the Appalachians. The federal budget remained in that blissful state from 1816 until 1836 (Malkin 1988). Then the supply of land available for sale began to run out. There were a few other budget surplus years in the late 1880s, but deficits dominated after that until the Harding and Coolidge administrations in the 1920s.

The Westward Expansion of the United States, 1870 to 1913

After the Civil War (1861 to 1865), the United States began expanding rapidly westward, and large investments were needed to build railroads and other infrastructure. The limited supply of precious metals was an effective limit to the US money supply and hence to economic growth. The gold discoveries in California in 1849 triggered massive westward migration and caused inflation, but did not add to the government's gold stock.

The great transcontinental railroads were successfully financed by land grants and selling bonds to foreign investors through the New York stock exchange, based on the expectation of future profits. These projects were mostly successful. The oil industry, the steel industry, the telephone industry, and the electrical industry were all funded initially by banks, who were repaid (as underwriters) by the sale of bonds and equity shares to the public.[3]

Much of that investment came from Europe, since the United States had a large and constantly growing trade surplus, partly in agricultural products such as grain, in "illuminating oil" after 1870, and also in manufactured products like agricultural machinery and electrical goods. In effect these shares also became fungible assets for the shareholders, either as security for margin loans or (if retained by the issuing bank) used as bank reserves to justify lending still more money. The fungible shares not only added to the money supply, they had a multiplier (leverage) effect on the banks assets and bank-lending capacity.

However, the big banks were not much interested in financing small business, then or now. Farmers had good markets for export to Europe. Farms also needed finance. This became a major political issue in the 1890s (and again later). The Benjamin Harrison administration (1889 to 1893) was somewhat spendthrift, by the standards of the time. The "billion dollar Congress" of 1889 to 1891 provided a pension for disabled Civil War veterans. It also provided for other public works and naval ships.

The Sherman Silver Purchase Act of 1890 committed the Treasury to buy 4.5 million ounces of silver per month from the western silver mines at market prices. Payment had to be in gold, of course. This depleted the US Treasury (of gold) and also caused the price of silver to fall. By the time Grover Cleveland took office in 1893 the Treasury surplus had fallen below \$100 million (*\$2.6 billion*$_{2011}$)[4] for the first time since 1873 and the decline accelerated. The Panic of 1893 started with the failure of the Reading Railroad. This in turn led to the failure of thousands of small businesses and hundreds of banks in the area served by that railroad. The local recession morphed into a major nationwide depression that spread to Europe and did not end until 1897. US unemployment reached 4 million at its peak.

But the panic also caused a lot of people to hoard gold. It was effectively a "run" on the Treasury. By 1895 the federal government was literally almost out of gold. That would have prevented the US government from paying its bills. President Cleveland asked J. P. Morgan to organize a consortium to lend \$62 million (*\$1.75 billion*$_{2011}$) in gold to the Treasury. (It is alleged that this gold was provided by the Rothschilds.) This enabled the treasury to issue \$7 million (*\$200 million*$_{2011}$) in "gold certificates" to its creditors. That saved the day.

President Cleveland was heavily criticized for this move by populist William Jennings Bryan, a fellow Democrat, who advocated silver as a basis for money and complained in a famous speech that farmers were being crucified "on a cross of gold." Consequently Cleveland lost the 1896 election to Republican William McKinley, who was strongly supported by J. P. Morgan. Some have said that McKinley was a mere puppet, entirely controlled by the great financial magnates. The "Wizard of Oz" was a political satire; the "yellow brick road" was a fairly obvious reference to gold politics. (But some say that Morgan himself was merely a Rothschild agent; see Kolko 1963; Mullins 1983.)

The need for the US Treasury to borrow gold in 1895 was ironic, since the United States was accumulating gold from Europe at the time, to compensate for its continuing and growing trade surplus. By 1914 the US Treasury was sitting on about a third of the world's total gold supply (Kennedy 1989, p. 248).

Toward the end of the nineteenth century, big banks began to finance the cartelization of large-scale industry. Edison's electrical inventions were commercialized by companies financed by J. P. Morgan, and after many mergers eventually resulting in the creation of General Electric Company and a number of electrical utilities. The House of Morgan (backed by the Rothschilds) also financed the formation of AT&T, GM, and DuPont. The creation of US Steel, mentioned previously, was a merger of Carnegie Steel Co. with other smaller steel companies, also financed by the Morgan Bank. Union Carbide was the result of such a merger of companies manufacturing calcium carbide (the basis for acetylene, widely used for lamps).[5] AT&T was created by mergers of a large number of local telephone companies with a manufacturer, Western Electric Co.[6] Gulf Oil, ALCOA, Koppers Coke, and the Carburundum Company, all in Pittsburgh, were financed and partly owned by the Mellon Bank. General Motors was another creation by mergers, financed partly by banks and partly by wartime profits of E. I. DuPont de Nemours.

Europe experienced similar creations of industrial behemoths, often as "national champions," by bank-financed mergers, although the bank role was often less than the government role. Such was the case in the creation by mergers of Anglo-Persian Oil Company (eventually British Petroleum) and Royal Dutch Shell.

The major industrial mergers, financed by banks like the House of Morgan, were financial investments that paid off in the short to medium term, thanks to economies of scale and monopoly profits. The breakup of Standard Oil Co. in 1911 was a lone exception to the general trend toward cartelization, or "trusts" as they were known at the time. See box 3.1. The dominant business plan of great nineteenth-century financial magnates has been characterized as follows: There were two major stages. The first was to obtain often by bribery of corrupt politicians exclusive rights to some component of the public domain, often a monopoly or land, timber or mineral rights (Myers [1909] 1936).

The second stage was to organize an operating company (e.g., the Union Pacific Railroad) and a separate holding company (e.g., Crédit Mobilière). The holding company was created to build the railroad for the operating company. Shares of the operating company would be sold to the public at high prices based on anticipated future (with large immediate profits for the underwriter) and a sizable fraction of the shares would be retained by the financiers to assure continuing representation on the board of directors.

Shares of the holding company would be divided among the same group of financial entrepreneurs who would also get large dividends based on the profits from selling overpriced construction services to the operating company. But the construction was actually performed by subcontractors employing Italian, Irish, Chinese, or Philippino immigrant-workers paid a minimum or sub-minimum wage.

In short, a very large part of the funds received by selling shares in the railroad (or other enterprise) was actually kept by the bankers. This pattern, in some form, was repeated many times by the "robber barons" of the age.[7] The creation of industrial trusts (monopolies) by mergers, organized by banks, with "value added" by reorganization and later resale to the public at high prices, as in the case of the steel trust, was also carried out at least 200 times with minor variations.

The issuance of railroad bonds was the main and lucrative business of three investment banks J.P. Morgan, Kuhn-Loeb, and Speyer & Company. Kuhn-Loeb financed E. H. Harriman's takeover of Union Pacific and his attempt to merge it with Central Pacific. (That was frustrated by the US Antitrust Division of the Justice Department.) These firms constituted an oligopoly that kept out interlopers like the newer Jewish investment

Box 3.1
Sherman Anti-Trust Acts of Congress

Sherman Anti-Trust Act of 1890, during the Harrison administration, was introduced by Senator John Sherman of Ohio. The act declared simply that "restraint of trade" was illegal. Penalties included a $5,000 ($126,000_{2011}$) fine and/or a year's imprisonment. However, the language was vague and "restraint of trade" was subjective. In 1894 Attorney General Richard Olney used the Act against the American Railway Union, during the famous Pullman Strike. (The union president, Eugene Debs, was convicted of contempt of court, and imprisoned.) However, thanks in part to the "muckrakers," such as Ida Tarbell, the Sherman Act was the basis for several lawsuits against Standard Oil, beginning in 1892. They eventually forced the breakup of Standard Oil into 34 companies, including Standard Oil of New Jersey, Standard Oil of New York (which became Socony-Vacuum after a merger with Vacuum Oil Company), Standard Oil of Ohio (SOHIO), Standard Oil of Indiana, and Standard Oil of California (SOCAL).

The Sherman Act was clarified and improved by the Clayton Act (1914), which prohibited agreements between companies to control prices in order to reduce competition. It also forbade directors to serve on the boards of competing companies.

banks Oppenheimer & Co, Lehman Brothers, Salomon Brothers, and Goldman Sachs (Ellis 2009).

By 1913 the public lands in the United States had been largely allocated by corrupt politicians or preserved (like national parks). The major industries of the time had already been reorganized as trusts or legal monopolies under holding companies. A new source of profits for financiers was needed. The war in Europe offered plenty of profitable opportunities, both for industry and agriculture. After the war, a new money-spinning scheme emerged: the sale of common stocks to ordinary citizens using borrowed money (i.e., buying "on margin").

J. P. Morgan died in 1913, just before the start of WWI. The other significant financial event of that year was the creation of the Federal Reserve Bank (FRB) by the Federal Reserve Act. It was a modification of the so-called Aldrich plan introduced the previous year, which would have created a sort of banking cooperative, owned by the big New York banks. The Aldrich plan was a scheme to keep the whole system in (very few) private hands. It was too blatant. President Teddy Roosevelt killed it. He said:

The issue of currency should be lodged with the government and be protected from domination by Wall Street. We are opposed to . . . provisions [that] would place our currency and credit systems in private hands. Quote cited by Lietaer, Ulanowicz, and Goerner (2009)

The Aldrich plan was rejected by the US Senate, partly because the senators from outside of New York had no part in it (Ahamed 2009). A new plan was mooted. It created regional branches of the Fed. But Wall Street pushed back. President Roosevelt finally had to compromise. Senator Carter Glass of Virginia played a very important role, along with Woodrow Wilson who had succeeded Teddy Roosevelt. Doubtless they all deserve some of the credit (or blame). Wilson said, of Glass, that he "snarled the Federal Reserve Act through Congress, out of one side of his mouth." After the law's passage Carter Glass was jubilant:

The thing which has been vainly discussed and intermittently attempted for 20 years has finally been accomplished.

The final bill was signed by President Wilson on December 23 of 1913; see box 3.2. He didn't like it either; he said:

I am a most unhappy man. I have unwittingly ruined my country. A great industrial nation is controlled by its system of credit. Our system of credit is concentrated. The growth of the nation, therefore, and all our activities, are in the hands
of a few men. We have come to be one of the worst ruled, one of the most completely controlled and dominated Governments in the civilized world, no longer a
Government by free opinion, no longer a Government by conviction and the vote
of the majority, but a government by the opinion and duress of a small group of
dominant men. Cited by Lietaer, Ulanowicz, and Goerner (2009)

Carter Glass's contribution has been summarized (by Milton Friedman) as substituting decentralized private control for centralized private
control by the New York banks, as proposed by the previous Aldrich
plan. But Glass rejected that interpretation as "a total misunderstanding" and said that "no greater misconception was ever projected in this
Senate Chamber." Perhaps he exaggerated. But today, a century later, it
appears that he was mostly right and Friedman was wrong. The modified version of the Aldrich plan still left control of the NY Fed (by far the
largest and most important of the twelve regional banks) firmly in the
hands of the five big Wall Street banks. But the NY Fed does not dominate the system today.

The Post-Morgan Era, 1914 to 1933

Most popular histories seem to believe that WWI was a consequence of
Serbian nationalism, supported by Czarist Russia (with French financial
backing) and opposed by Austria, supported by Germany. Much has been
written about how treaty obligations between the nations were invoked
one after the other and nobody had an exit strategy (Tuchman 1962;
Kennedy 1989).

Another factor often cited is the undoubted fact that land-locked Germany had been largely excluded from the colonization of Africa, and the
resulting access to cheap resources. Germany wanted its "day in the sun"
and meant to get it. However, behind the scenes, I believe that oil was a
major factor. The German ambitions in Mesopotamia symbolized by the
Berlin-to-Baghdad railway were also important insofar as they clashed
with British-French interests in the region.

At the beginning of the 1914 to 1918 war most governments in Europe
suspended gold convertibility (i.e., abandoned the gold standard). They
did it in order to print money to pay for the war. At the beginning of the
war Great Britain was the banker for the world, controlling $20 billion

Box 3.2
Federal Reserve Act

The Federal Reserve Act (1913) created the Federal Reserve System. The Act, proposed by Senator Carter Glass, created the present structure of twelve regional reserve banks ruled by a central board of members appointed by the President. The Glass bill gave the Federal Reserve authority to regulate the nation's banks, but not the brokers and stock-exchange activities "except as speculative activities might relate themselves to the facilities of the Federal Reserve banks." That omission had serious consequences in 1929. The five New York banks that owned "class A" stock in the New York Federal Reserve bank were Chase-Manhattan, First National City Bank (now Citibank), Morgan Guaranty Trust, Chemical/Manufacturers Hannover, and Bankers Trust. Chase and Morgan Guaranty have since merged, while Bankers Trust was acquired by Deutsche Bank. The stock was "sealed" in 1914 and has not been publically traded since. The five banks had interlocking directorates with the "seven sisters" of the oil industry.

($410 billion$_{2011}$) in foreign investments; France had $9 billion ($180 billion$_{2011}$) in foreign investments, of which $5 billion ($100 billion$_{2011}$) were in Russia. (Those Russian debts were repudiated by the Bolshevik regime that took power in October 1917.)

The costs of fighting WWI have been tabulated by Paul Kennedy (1989, p. 274, tab. 25). Based on US dollars at 1913 prices the allies (Britain, France, Russia, Italy, and the United States spent altogether $57.7 billion ($1.2 trillion$_{2011}$), as compared to $24.7 billion ($520$_{2011}$) spent by Germany and Austria-Hungary. Costs to the British Empire were $23 billion ($474 billion$_{2011}$), France $9.3 billion ($193 billion$_{2011}$), Russia $5.4 billion ($112 billion$_{2011}$), Italy $3.2 billion ($66 billion$_{2011}$), and the United States $17.1 billion ($353 billion$_{2011}$). Britain, France, and Italy had to borrow from the United States much of what they spent, as noted in connection with gold in an earlier section. The national incomes of the major countries in 1914 were $11 billion ($230$_{2011}$) for Britain, $6 billion ($122$_{2011}$) for France, $4 billion ($82 billion$_{2011}$) for Italy, $7 billion ($32$_{2011}$) for Russia, $12 billion ($250$_{2011}$) for Germany, and $3 billion ($62 billion$_{2011}$) for Austria-Hungary. The examples above are among the relatively few for which data is available.

By the end of the war, the United States was owed $12 billion ($150$_{2011}$) by all countries, of which $5 billion ($62 billion$_{2011}$) was from Britain and $4 billion ($50 billion$_{2011}$) was from France. Britain in turn was owed

$11 billion (*$130 billion* ₂₀₁₁) by seventeen other countries, of which $3 billion (*$37 billion* ₂₀₁₁) was from France and $2.5 billion (*$31 billion* ₂₀₁₁) from Russia. In effect, Britain borrowed from the United States in order to lend to others. These were war debts, mainly to US banks (led by the House of Morgan) and payable in gold. The Europeans wanted the war debts and reparations to be combined, and they pressured the United States to forgive most of those war debts, on the moral ground that it had entered the war too late, just in time to pick up the pieces and make big profits (Ahamed 2009). There was truth in that accusation, but banks are not moral entities.

At the beginning of the Great War the four "Great Powers" had total gold reserves of about $4.7 billion(*$97 billion* ₂₀₁₁), with Germany and the United Kingdom each having about $800 million(*$17 billion*₂₀₁₁), France with $1.3 billion(*$27 billion* ₂₀₁₁) and the United States had about $1.8 billion(*$37 billion* ₂₀₁₁). By the end of the conflict, Germany's reserves were depleted to $150 million (*$1.8 billion*₂₀₁₁), the United Kingdom had the same as before, France was down to about $650 million (*$8.1 billion*₂₀₁₁), and the United States was up to nearly $4.2 billion (*$52 billion* ₂₀₁₁), and still rising. In response, one strategy employed by all the Europeans was to outlaw gold coins and withdraw them from circulation (Ahamed 2009) p.162.

Looking ahead from that point in time, the US gold reserves remained roughly constant until 1928 and then declined somewhat. Germany regained some gold reserves between 1923 and 1928 (after the hyperinflation was stopped), but there was a sharp decline in late 1930. French gold reserves increased steadily until 1932, when they stabilized at about $3.3 billion (*$46 billion* ₂₀₁₁). US gold reserves fell slightly after 1923, then rose and reached $4.2 billion (*$47 billion* ₂₀₁₁) in early 1930 and continued to increase throughout the rest of that year. Reserves fell by nearly $1 billion (*$12 billion* ₂₀₁₁) in the first months of 1931, stabilized temporarily, then dropped again at the end of 1931.

In 1913 Britain had a money supply (currency in circulation and bank deposits) of $5 billion (*$104 billion* ₂₀₁₁). This was backed by $800 million (*$17 billion*₂₀₁₁) in gold, of which only $150 million (*$3.1 billion*₂₀₁₁) was in the vaults of the central bank BOE). The rest was in the form of coins or bullion held in other banks. During the war the money supply increased to $12 billion (*$200 billion*₂₀₁₁) whereas the gold supply did not change. Britain spent $50 billion (*$850 billion* ₂₀₁₁) on the war itself, largely by selling its overseas investments. Domestic prices increased by a factor of two and a half. The problem for the Bank of England was what to do about the gold standard and the reserve status of the pound sterling. France spent $30 billion (*$500 billion* ₂₀₁₁) on the war, of which only 5 percent was paid for directly by French taxes. Half was covered by war bonds sold domestically and $10 billion (*$170 billion* ₂₀₁₁) came from loans by the US banks or British banks. The Rothschilds were centrally involved. This left an unpaid gap of $2.5 billion (*$42 billion*₂₀₁₁) that was filled by printing money. As a result the currency in circulation in France tripled and prices rose accordingly (Ahamed 2009). France subsequently introduced an income tax to pay for (part) of the war costs.

Immediately after the war ended, the Banque de France reasserted its independence and limited the amount of currency in circulation to 41 billion Francs. With a semi-stable currency recovery made headway, by means of a weak franc and being the only country of Europe not on the gold standard, until 1925 when a scandal (*l'affaire des faux bilans*) at the Banque de France caused the institution to lose trust and caused the government of the day to fall. The scandal together with the floating currency led to a fiscal crisis and a very uncertain exchange rate. French investors began pulling their money out of the country and sending it to safer havens. Finally, all the high officials contaminated by the scandal were kicked out and the situation stabilized to some degree. But it was not until war debt agreement of 1926 that France achieved a modicum of stability.

At the beginning of the Great War a gold mark was fixed at 4.1 marks to the US dollar, but by the end of the war it was 8.91 marks per dollar. By the end of 1919, it was 47 marks per dollar, and by November 1921, it was 300 marks per dollar. The "London ultimatum" of May 1921 insisted that the reparations be paid in gold or dollars at the rate of 2 billion gold marks per year, plus 26 percent of German exports. By 1921 Germany was collecting just 10 marks in taxes for every 100 marks of expenses, and had lost all but $120 million of its $1 billion (*$17 billion*₂₀₁₁) of its prewar gold reserves. A significant part of the cause was the reparations to France and England, which accounted for a third of the German budget deficit during those years. But, while the domestic deficit could have been dealt with by borrowing from the Treasury (as the Japanese do now), the foreign debt had to be paid in gold or hard currency. This left the Reichsbank of the Weimar Republic no choice (in the opinion of its president-for-life, von Havenstein) but to issue unbacked paper money to purchase foreign currency.

The hyperinflation took the value of the gold reichsmark from 4.2 to the dollar in 1914 to 11 trillion to one dollar in 1924 as shown in figure 3.1. But Gustav Stresemann, and his newly created commissioner Hjalmar Schacht, did an end-run around the Reichsbank. What they did was to create a new currency, the *rentenmark*, backed by land rather than gold. The trick was to limit the total number of rentenmarks in circulation to 2.4 billion, worth about $600 million. The new currency circulated alongside the old one. The exchange rate was fixed by Schacht at 1 trillion old reichsmarks to 1 rentenmark. Amazingly, the old currency meanwhile regained some value (from 11 trillion to the dollar, back to 4.2 trillion to the dollar). The currency had been stabilized. At that point, the German government was able to pay off all of its internal debts, which were valued at $30 billion (*$370 billion in 2011 dollars*) in old marks for 190 million in rentenmarks or $45 million (*$0.55 billion$_{2011}$*); see Ahamed (2009, p.189). The Stresemann government also cut costs and carried out a number of fiscal reforms, resulting in a balanced budget by summer 1924.

In 1925 Britain, under Chancellor of the Exchequer Winston Churchill, ceased the production and use of gold coins, although it still retained the so-called gold bullion standard for its money supply. But, influenced by Bank of England chief Montagu Norman, Churchill returned to the prewar gold standard at the symbolic prewar exchange rate of $4.86 dollars to the pound, up from $4.40. That exchange rate may have been a matter of pride for the British who were hoping the regain for London the financial primacy it had had before the war. But the exchange rate was too high by at least 10 percent. Exports were weak and domestic agriculture struggled against imports. Indeed the social consequences led to so much discontent among the blue-collar workers that the General Strike in 1927 united all the unions and led to a near- revolution.

The question of German war reparations dragged on for years. This was partly due to deliberate German negotiating strategy. But it was partly because the numbers first proposed by the allies were so high that the German economy could not possibly support them. The Reparations Commission, established in Paris in 1919, set the total at $33 billion

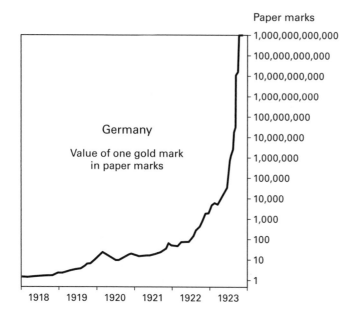

Paper marks

1,000,000,000,000
100,000,000,000
10,000,000,000
1,000,000,000
100,000,000
10,000,000
1,000,000
100,000
10,000
1,000
100
10
1

Germany

Value of one gold mark
in paper marks

1918   1919   1920   1921   1922   1923

Figure 3.1
Hyperinflation in Germany, 1918 to 1923

(*$360 billion in 2011 dollars*) to be paid in gold. (There wasn't enough gold in the world for that.) Keynes objected and resigned from the British delegation to Versailles After the war he wrote:

> Will the discontented peoples of Europe be willing, for a generation to come, so to order their lives that an appreciable part of their daily produce may be available to meet a foreign payment . . . that does not spring compellingly from their sense of justice or duty? On the one hand, Europe must depend in the long run on her own daily labor and not on the largesse of America; but on the other hand, she will not pinch herself so that the fruit of her daily labor may go elsewhere. In short, I do not believe that any of these tributes will continue to be paid, at the best, for more than a few years. Keynes (1920) cited by Malkin (1988 p. 96)

The British came up with a new reparations figure of $10.5 billion (*$110 billion*$_{2011}$, equal to the prewar GDP). But, as Keynes predicted, only a tiny fraction was ever paid.

In 1922 the US Congress created a Commission on War Debts led by banker Andrew Mellon. The commission was told not to offer anything better than 90 cents on the dollar to the British. Americans wanted to be paid in full for war debts but did not demand any reparations from Germany. They thought this offer was generous. In fact the Europeans thought otherwise; after all, they had suffered enormous casualties and property losses, while the United States had profited from the war. As ex–Prime Minister David Lloyd-George later wrote:

The World War, prolonged over four years on a more intense and destructive scale than human imagination had ever previously conceived possible, left all belligerent nations at its close deeply impoverished, burdened with immense debts. . . . The people of the United States are no better off . . . that their customers throughout the world cannot afford to buy their goods. Lloyd-George (1932) cited by Pollock (2012)

William McAdoo, who had been President Wilson's Secretary of the Treasury, and who had been in charge of making the loans, had a very different view:

Since it fell to my lot to initiate the policy of foreign loans, I know, perhaps better than anybody else, the origin of these loans. . . . I have heard, at times, arguments to the effect that the money we advanced to friendly governments during the war were not loans at all, except in form, that they were in reality gifts or contributions. . . . These arguments have no basis in fact or in anything but the imagination of those who make them. . . . Every borrowing government understood that it was receiving loans, not gifts, and that it was expected to repay them. . . . The obligation further provides that the principal and interest thereon shall be paid in gold coin of the United States without any deduction. McAdoo (1931, p. 414) cited by Pollock (2012)

So the United States came to be known during those negotiations as "Uncle Shylock." The English negotiators, including Stanley Baldwin, hoped for a settlement at 60 cents on the dollar. After painful negotiations with the Mellon Commission, the Bonar Law government in Britain agreed very reluctantly to a settlement at 80 cents on the dollar. France held out and later (1926) settled for 40 cents on the dollar, while Italy did even better, also in 1926, at 24 cents on the dollar (Ahamed 2009).

The outcome of the negotiations about war debts was the so-called Dawes plan of 1924, named for Charles Dawes. Dawes was elected to the position of Vice President of the United States, under Coolidge, later that year. In 1925 he was awarded the Nobel Peace Prize for his plan. He should have got the booby prize. Under that plan German reparations payments were reduced and restructured. The French occupation of the Rhineland was ended. The Reichsbank was to be supervised by foreign creditors.

The Dawes plan, in operation between 1924 and 1929, enabled German firms and institutions (e.g., towns) to issue bonds, sold to US citizens, that would be "senior" to the official reparation payments, hence first in line. This trick enabled Germany to import a great deal of capital during those years to cover both its domestic deficit and its annual reparations payments (Ritschl 2012). The Dawes bond, backed by war debt, paying 7 percent with twenty-five-year maturity, was a great success at first. However, the consequence was that German domestic debt increased substantially during those years, culminating in a crisis. In 1929 another commission, let by Morgan banker Owen D. Young, cut the German reparation still further and stretched them over fifty-nine years. A new set of bonds was issued to help Germany pay off its Dawes bond debts. The other significant outcome of the Young Commission was the creation of the bank for International Settlements (BIS) in 1930 (see box 3.3). The BIS's ostensible purpose when it was created was to funnel German reparations payments back to France and England and thence, indirectly, back to the United States. I will say more about its role in financing German rearmament later.

The US government had spent $30 billion (*$500 billion*$_{2011}$) on WWI, of which $10 billion (*$170 billion*$_{2011}$) was loans to other countries. That money was borrowed from US banks that expected repayment in full. They dumped most of their risk on the public, through the sale of Dawes bonds, which were supposedly backed by gold. For the US taxpayer, WWI was expensive, increasing the national debt from just over $1 billion (*$20 billion*$_{2011}$) in 1914 to $25.5 billion (*$280 billion* $_{2011}$) at the close in 1918. But, for the next eleven years the federal budget was in surplus, reducing the debt by 36 percent. In 1930 the US public debt was down to $16 billion (*$180 billion* $_{2011}$).

The Stock-Market Crash and Its Immediate Aftermath

WW I was a source of huge profits for some US companies, especially in steel (for armor plate), vehicles, guns, oil, and chemicals (for explosives). US Steel and DuPont were among the biggest winners. Most of the US loans to Britain and France were for armaments and supplies purchased from the United States, so the dollars came back as payments. These profits were available for reinvestment in the same or other industries after the war. DuPont invested its war profits from munitions in William Durant's merger of Buick, Cadillac, Chevrolet, Oldsmobile, and Pontiac that became General Motors (of which DuPont interests eventually owned 25 percent;

see Lundberg 1968). And there was plenty of money to pay for roads, long-distance telephone lines (AT&T) and the radio start-up (RCA).

The 1920s were a time of great US national prosperity, financed to a considerable extent by wartime profits and the collection of war loans to the European countries that had fought each other from 1914 to 1918. But most of all, the prosperity was due to domestic factors, especially the electrification of industry, the new technology of mass production, the construction of roads to open up the hinterlands, the mechanization of farm-work that released labor for the factories and simultaneously increased food grain for the market (because it was no longer necessary to feed the horses). Then too there was a hot new technology: radio and radio broad-casting, as well as some useful household inventions like vacuum cleaners ("Hoovers"), refrigerators, and washing machines (without spin driers).

During the Coolidge administration, the federal revenues grew and grew, faster than any apparent need for them. The head of Coolidge's Bureau of the Budget, General H. M. Lord complained in 1927:

Despite consistent efforts to reduce revenue by cutting taxes . . . we seem helpless in the face of the country's continuing prosperity. Reduction in taxes has come to be almost synonymous with increases in public revenues. At the end of each year we are called upon to decide what to do with the surplus millions. Lord cited in Malkin (1988, pp. 50–51)

Deciding how to spend that money was a tough job, but someone had to do it. No wonder Ronald Reagan idolized "Silent Cal" Coolidge and kept his picture on the wall of the Oval Office.

The US stock-market bubble of 1925 to 1929 was driven at first by the postwar industrial growth. The Federal Reserve's Index of production rose from 67 in 1921 to 126 in June 1929. The American auto industry sold 5,358,000 cars in that year (Galbraith 1954, p. 7). To finance their rapid growth, many companies had issued shares, which were traded on the New York Stock Exchange. During the 1920s demand for short-term corporate loans declined substantially, possibly due to the accumulation of profits during the war, together with unprecedented growth of the re-tail stock market. During this period the big banks increased their hold-ings of equities and long-term bonds. Those holdings constituted a time bomb that contributed to the events of 1929 to 1930.

In 1927 Britain, France, and Germany sent a joint delegation to Wash-ington to try to persuade the Federal Reserve to cut the rediscount rate for borrowers (i.e., themselves). The Fed also bought US government bonds from the private sector (a policy now known as "quantitative easing"), thus providing the sellers with both cash in hand and low interest rates. Many of them used this cash to purchase common stocks on margin.

The business model of the investment banks was to issue shares of existing companies or, leveraged investment trusts, while the commercial banks promoted margin loans[8] to brokers. The commercial banks made their profits from lending to brokers based on the "rediscount rate" set by the Federal Reserve. Speculative margin buying increased demand, which drove up prices. Rising corporate profits (which were real) also led to rising share prices. This encouraged still more margin buying, much of it in so-called "bucket shops" operated by fast-buck artists to take advantage of the ignorant "suckers," of which there were many.

However, as Senator Carter Glass warned the Senate in February 1929:

The great corporations of the country have acquired the habit of throwing their surplus funds into the vortex of stock speculation, instead of distributing them among their stockholders in the nature of dividends, and individuals are doing the same thing. . . . Member banks of the system have manipulated their deposit accounts so as to transfer from the demand deposit account, requiring a reserve of 7 percent, to the time deposit account, requiring a reserve of only 3 percent, thereby releasing enormous funds to be thrown into the maelstrom of stock speculation. When I presented a bill here last week to restore the reserve behind time deposits to the . . . original set up, banks all over the country began writing letters of protest. That [bill] alone would withhold from those speculative activities at least $300,000,000 [$3.2 billion$_{2011}$]; but banks are not willing to desist. SEMP (2007)

In the same speech, Senator Glass attacked Charles E. Mitchell ("Sunshine Charlie"), who was the head of the largest bank in the United States, National City Bank:[9]

As I pointed out publically six or eight weeks ago, when an outstanding director of the New York Federal Reserve Bank (FRB)–the president [Mitchell] and of the largest bank in the Western Hemisphere defied the board and publically avowed that his obligation to the stock gamblers was superior to his obligation as a sworn officer of the Federal Reserve System, what the board should have done was to have incontinently kicked that fellow out of his position before noon of the day upon which he made that announcement. SEMP (2007)

On another occasion, Senator Glass discussed the advisability of regulation with the head of a New York Investment banking organization. Senator Glass wanted a 5 percent tax on investments held less than sixty days, to curb speculation. The following conversation ensued:

Banker: That would ruin the market.
Senator: Supposing it does; it is better to ruin the market, as you say, than to ruin the country, as will surely happen if this gambling fever continues to spread.
Banker: My own opinion, Senator, is that the people of this country are just beginning to realize on the prosperity to which they are entitled.
Senator: I hope you are right, but common sense tells me that you are wrong. The day of reckoning for gambling cannot be escaped. It must come. I think something must be done to deprive people of the privilege of mortgaging their homes and their futures to buy stocks on margin and to keep blowing up bubbles that are certain to break in their faces. SEMP (2007)

Another financial innovation of the pre-1929 period was the highly leveraged investment trust. Investment trusts were initially created back in 1880s specifically to invest in operating companies, on behalf of a group of investors. The trust was mainly a device to keep control over a number of companies in the hands of a few financiers. Such trusts only invested in stocks, not in real productive assets. (The first example was the Standard Oil Trust, mentioned earlier.) Trusts were able to sell their own shares to the public. They left all decision-making authority in the hands of their sponsoring investment banks. The sponsoring banks were paid a management fee as well as receiving income from the purchase and sale of trust shares.

The number of such investment trusts in the United States before 1921 has been estimated as about 40, of which US Steel was the most outstanding. But the number grew much faster than the prices of stocks. There were 160 such trusts at the beginning of 1927 and 300 or so a year later. In 1928, 186 additional new trusts emerged, and in 1929 another 265 were created. The sale of shares in trusts during 1927 was $400 million ($5 billion$_{2011}$). In 1929 the NYSE finally allowed the trusts to be listed. The value of shares in investment trusts sold to the public reached $3 billion ($32 billion$_{2011}$), which was at least a third of all capital funds raised during the year. By the time of the crash in October, the trusts had total assets of more than $8 billion ($85 billion$_{2011}$) (Galbraith 1954, pp. 45–55).

Some investment trusts employed leverage, usually by selling bonds and preferred stock as well as common stock. In these cases a rise in the value of a common stock in trust *A* would increase the value of *A* since the value of the bonds and preferred shares would not have changed. It would also increase the value of trusts *B* and *C* that held shares of *A*. Thus the gain is multiplied. This fact enabled speculators to multiply their paper gains in trusts by investing in each other's trusts. One extreme example was the so-called American Founders Group, organized in 1921 for a total investment of only $500 ($5800$_{2011}$). It grew mainly by virtue of creating new trusts within trusts, acquiring companies by using stock in a rising market, and maximizing leverage. It finally encompassed a group of thirteen companies with total market value by October 1929 of $686,165,000 ($7.5 billion$_{2011}$), of which $320,000,000 ($3.5 billion$_{2011}$) was invested in other companies in the group. When that house of cards collapsed it was later found to have owned virtually nothing at all of any enduring value (Galbraith 1954, p. 64). Money was making money from money (and then losing it) with no substance at all.

A series of activities by Goldman Sachs, beginning on December 4, 1928, epitomizes what was going on (Galbraith 1954, pp. 66–67). Actually the driving force was a senior partner named Wadill Catchings. On that day the firm issued shares for an investment trust called Goldman Sachs Trading Corporation, with an initial capital of $100 million ($1.06 billion$_{2011}$). Goldman then resold 90 percent of the shares to the public for a total of $93.6 million ($1 billion$_{2011}$), leaving it with a net investment cost of $6.4 million ($60 million$_{2011}$), and total control of a subsidiary with $100 million ($1 billion$_{2011}$) in cash at its disposal. Goldman Sachs Trading Co. then bought back 560,724 of its own shares in the market (over half) at a cost of $57 million ($600 million$_{2011}$), from this cash, leaving $43 million in cash.

Meanwhile the market price of the remaining shares rose from the original $104 to $222.50 by February 7, 1929. On February 21, Goldman Sachs Trading Company acquired another investment trust, called Financial and Industrial Securities Corporation bringing the combined nominal assets of the Goldman Sachs Trading Company to $235 million ($2.5 billion$_{2011}$). Some of those shares it sold to William Durant (the founder of General Motors) who then resold them at a profit, driving prices still higher.

Then in the summer of 1929, the Goldman Sachs Trading Company, in partnership with investor Harrison Williams,[10] launched two new investment trusts, by name Shenandoah and Blue Ridge, within a month. The total stock sales for these two trusts were, respectively, $177 million ($1.9 billion$_{2011}$) for Shenandoah and $142 million ($1.5 billion$_{2011}$) for Blue Ridge, for a total of $319 million (Galbraith 1954). The trading company still had most of its $235 million in cash in the bank, minus a few million for expenses. The money was then used to buy small companies at inflated prices. But prices stopped rising and started down in October 1929. By 1931 losses by Goldman Sachs Trading amounted to 70 percent of all the losses by fourteen leading investment trusts (Ellis 2009, p. 28). A few years later, the value of the Goldman Sachs Trading Company had fallen from a peak above $250 per share in February 1929 to a low of $1.75 per share.[11] Leverage works both ways.

Leverage through trusts magnified the monetary losses when buying enthusiasm waned and prices began to fall. By October 1929 there was over $8 billion (*$85 billion$_{2011}$*) in broker's loans outstanding. The loans to the brokers constituted a significant fraction of the assets of many banks. These "margin calls" drove prices down and triggered still more margin calls. The "crash" in October 1929 led to a flood of margin calls as brokers sold into a declining market. That triggered what has been called "a race to the bottom. It hurt many brokers and banks, as well as millions of ordinary citizens.

By 1929 the United States was by far the leading industrial country in the world (thanks to the Great War in Europe) and the dollar had become the effective world reserve currency, because high interest rates attracted foreign investments. The US money supply was fixed in terms of the gold supply, with 40 percent gold coverage of Federal Reserve notes. (In September 1931 the British abandoned the gold standard, in order to increase public spending.) But US investors were free to buy foreign assets with gold. Thanks to the stock market crash, which destroyed a lot of (spendable) paper wealth, the Federal Reserve, following conventional wisdom, refused to supply liquidity. Instead, it tightened the money supply by raising interest rates (Temin 1976; Kindleberger 1989). Real interest rates reached nearly 13 percent in 1931 (Reinhart and Rogoff 2009, tab. 15.1). This was partly to prevent too much of the gold from leaving the country. That misguided policy of cutting the money supply certainly contributed to the "great contraction" as Milton Friedman called it (Friedman and Schwartz 2008).

The "laissez faire" approach was originally based on ideas formulated by the French economist J.-B. Say early in the nineteenth century (e.g., that "supply creates its own demand"). It was accepted by most economists and businessmen, including the US Secretary of the Treasury,

Andrew Mellon (a very wealthy banker). Mellon's advice to President Hoover was a classic exposition of the laissez faire philosophy:

... liquidate labor, liquidate stocks, liquidate farmers, liquidate real estate. It will purge the rottenness out of the system. High costs of living and high living will come down. People will work harder, live a more moral life. Values will be adjusted and enterprising people will pick up from less competent people ... Hoover (1951 p. 30)

Incidentally, Andrew Mellon spent most of 1930 and 1931 overseas trying to persuade the Europeans to repay their war debts to the United States.

The stock-market crash at the end of October 1929 weakened the capital base of all the US banks. About 40 percent of all US banks failed during the next few years, in contrast to Canada and Australia, where no banks failed. The reason (according to some) is that Canada and Australia had only a few large "universal" banks, according to the British pattern. But the US bank failures were probably not due to their holdings of long-term bonds and equities, as alleged by some (Saunders and Walter 2011, p. 4). The immediate problem was drastically reduced credit availability to businesses. Businesses had to cut back, laying off workers and cutting bank deposits. The unemployed workers had no incomes and could not spend, while the banks could not lend. This further cut into business revenues, resulting in more layoffs, worse business conditions, and a downward spiral with no mechanism in place to stop it. Much the same downward spiral is observable in parts of Europe today.

The dominant "laissez faire" ideas shared by most economists at the time were best articulated by Friedrich Hayek (1931). They were challenged by John Maynard Keynes in response to the rampant unemployment he saw in Britain and America. Keynes famously recommended deficit spending, even if only to hire men to "dig holes and fill them in," in order to create demand for goods and services (Keynes 1935). His advice was controversial and not taken seriously by the establishment, at least in the United Kingdom and the United States. In the 1930s the United States did very little deficit spending. (Hitler, in contrast, used deficit spending on autobahns and a military buildup to recover from the depression.) Germany escaped the 1936 to 1937 recession (Ritschl 2012).

President Hoover saw the problem of the banks, but he didn't believe the federal government should intervene directly. The Fed wasn't able to help the small banks because they were mostly local and not members of the Federal Reserve System. He created the National Credit Corporation (NNC), a cooperative, to make loans to troubled banks. However, the NNC demanded too much collateral and was ineffective. So in January 1932 Congress created the Reconstruction Finance Corporation (RFC) to make loans to businesses, but mainly to banks. It had initial capital of $500 million ($6.5 billion$_{2011}$) and the right to borrow more from the Treasury, but authorization had to be renewed a year later by the next administration.

The RFC did help matters somewhat during its first year (Butkiewicz 2002). However, a controversy arose regarding some loans. A new law in July 1932 required the RFC to provide information on all loans to Congress. Then the Speaker of the House, John Nance Garner, demanded that the RFC publish the names of all banks receiving loans. This deterred some banks from asking for help for fear that depositors would assume that the bank was in danger of collapse, thus causing the panic that could ruin them (Butkiewicz 2002).

From 1930 to 1933, during President Hoover's administration, the US economy went from bad to worse: the GDP was down 15 percent, with over 30 percent unemployment at the bottom, in 1933. Over the three years from October 29 until the winter of 1933, investors lost 89 percent of aggregate stock-market wealth, measuring from intra-day highs to intra-day lows. In practice, cutting the money supply meant letting many farms, small businesses, and banks fail. That is what Friedrich Hayek and Andrew Mellon (and most economists) advised, and it is what happened.

Meanwhile the income tax rate under Hoover quadrupled, albeit from a very low level. Not only that, it was made retroactive, which forced a lot of people to take their savings out of the banks. That contributed to the bank failures (Malkin 1988, p. 52). One out of every five banks had failed by the time Roosevelt took office. At the same time house prices were down 80 percent, and roughly 50 percent of all mortgage debt was in default (Lewis 2010, p. 55). In 1932 the last US Congress during the Hoover administration enacted the Federal Home Loan Bank Board (FHLBB) to supervise housing loan guarantees. That was the predecessor of the Federal Housing Administration (FHA).

FDR and the New Deal, 1933 to 1946

In January 1933 Congress re-authorized the RFC and passed the Gold Reserve Act, which authorized the President to close the banks for a "bank holiday" of one week—which he did—and to nationalize the US gold supply. The President did so, by executive order, a month later. Individuals, firms, and banks were obliged to sell all privately owned gold to the Treasury, except for $100 ($1440_{2011}$) per person in coins and some exemptions for industrial use. It was reimbursed at the price of $20.67 ($300_{2011}$) per ounce. This Act also established a requirement that Federal Reserve notes had to be 60 percent backed by gold.

The Emergency Banking (Glass–Steagall) Act of March 1933 gave the RFC the power to buy bank stocks. It also created the Federal Deposit Insurance Corporation (FDIC) to protect small depositors from losses due to bank failures. The Act (regulation Q) also enabled the Federal Reserve to regulate interest rates on savings accounts. (That provision was repealed by the Depository Institutions and Monetary Control Act of 1980.) The Glass–Steagall Act also separated investment banking (underwriting the issuance of shares in companies) from commercial banking, so as to prevent investment banks from gambling with FDIC insured depositor's money. This restriction was repealed by the Gramm–Leach Bliley Act of 1999.

The National Housing Act was passed in 1933. It created the Federal Housing Agency (FHA) and the Federal Savings and Loan Insurance Corporation (FSLIC) to insure deposits in S&Ls. In 1938 Congress amended the National Housing Act to create the Federal National Mortgage Association (FNMA) to create a secondary market for mortgages insured by the FHA, to allow the banks to increase their lending for housing.

In 1934 silver was also nationalized and the dollar was devalued again, by 41 percent, to a price of $35 ($477_{2011}$) per ounce. This permitted the Treasury to issue another $3 ($41_{2011}$) billion in bonds, thus increasing the money supply as a growth stimulus. It agreed to exchange dollars held by foreign central banks for US gold at the rate of $35 per ounce. Thereafter, the dollar was backed only partly by the gold in Fort Knox, but increasingly by the "faith and credit" of the US government.

In January 1933, congressional hearings were organized by the departing Republican chairman of the Senate committee on banking and currency, Peter Norbeck. He hired Ferdinand Pecora, an assistant district attorney from New York, as the committee's Chief Counsel. When the change of congressional leadership occurred, Pecora asked the new chairman, Duncan Fletcher, to permit an additional month of hearings. Chairman Fletcher kept Pecora on.

The Pecora investigation continued even longer, and during its life it uncovered a number of abuses, including the fact that members of the Morgan Bank's "preferred list" (including ex-President Calvin Coolidge and Supreme Court Justice Owen Roberts) had got into major IPOs at steeply discounted rates. More serious, National City Bank was found to have sold packages of bad loans to Latin American countries. Senior figures from Wall Street—including Richard Whitney, head of the NYSE; George Whitney, a Morgan partner; investment bankers Thomas Lamont (Morgan Bank) and Albert Wiggin (Chase National Bank); and Charles Mitchell of National City Bank—were interrogated. In some cases, they were later prosecuted.[12] Carter Glass's *bête noir*, "Sunshine Charlie" Mitchell, was indicted and prosecuted by future governor Thomas E. Dewey for tax evasion. He was not convicted of the criminal charges, but the government later won a civil suit against him for a million dollars.

The Reconstruction Finance Corporation (RFC) was re-authorized immediately after FDR took office, with added powers. There was an immediate problem, which began in Detroit when the RFC offered a loan to Union Guaranty Trust, in which Henry Ford had a deposit of $7 million (*$100 million*$_{2011}$). Governor Couzens insisted that Ford should subordinate his debt to that of the other depositors, meaning that everyone else would get paid first. But Ford refused. The resulting conflict led to a panic, which Governor Couzens stopped by declaring a "bank holiday" (Butkiewicz 2002). Several states followed, and FDR then made it national.

The bank holiday lasted a week and gave President Roosevelt some breathing time to allay the panic. (Senator Glass, a Democrat, declined Roosevelt's offer to be Secretary of the Treasury, because of doubts about the constitutionality of the "bank holiday"; SEMP 2007.) Throughout his tenure, President Roosevelt was bitterly opposed by congressional Republicans as well as some Democrats. Some of them objected to his policies on constitutional grounds. Some Republicans thought FDR was a communist, or the nearest thing to it.

When FDR took office the federal debt was $20 billion (*$280 billion*$_{2011}$), which was 20 percent of the US GDP in that year. By 1936 it had increased to \$33.7 billion (*\$450 billion*$_{2011}$) or 40 percent of GDP, thanks to a series of budget deficits ranging from 2 to 5 percent per annum. The RFC borrowed \$1.5 billion (*\$21 billion*$_{2011}$) from the Treasury in 1932, \$1.8 billion (*\$25 billion*$_{2011}$) in each of the 1933 and 1934 before cutting back the rate of expenditure to around \$350 million (*\$4.5 billion*$_{2011}$) per annum until 1941. The depression began to abate in 1934, partly due to Roosevelt's "New Deal" policies, which included some job creation by federal government spending on capital projects, mainly the construction of roads, dams (Hoover and Grand Coulee), the Tennessee Valley project (TVA), and rural electrification. The US GDP rose 20 percent in that year, and continued to recover in 1935.

The Reconstruction Finance Corporation (RFC) was a significant factor in stabilizing the financial situation from 1933 through 1935. In those years it purchased \$782 million (*\$10.5 billion*$_{2011}$) in preferred stock from 4202 individual banks and \$343 million (*\$4.6 billion*$_{2011}$) in capital notes and debentures from 2,910 banks. Altogether nearly 6,800 banks were helped, and bank failures nearly ceased during those years (Butkiewicz 2002). By 1936 the US economy was finally beginning to recover, and President Roosevelt, who was still under the influence of conservative bankers, thought it was time to balance the federal budget again. The result was another recession.

Unemployment was still 15 percent as late as 1940. It did not fall to 1920s levels until after 1941, when re-armament was under way and many young men were taken out of the workforce by the military draft. Public debt in 1941 was 46 percent of the GDP. It peaked at 120 percent of GDP in 1945 financed by War Bonds and Victory Bonds, paying 3 percent, bought by the public largely for patriotic reasons, but also because there was a shortage of consumer goods to buy. The debt was down to 70 percent of GDP by 1950 (Malkin 1988). Nobody was worried about the threat of too much debt at the time. Economists pointed out that both buyers and sellers were Americans. "We owe it to ourselves" was the mantra.

The creation of the Bank for International Settlements (BIS) in 1930 was mentioned earlier. By 1938 it was effectively controlled by the Nazis, even though the President was an American, Thomas Harrington McKittrick. When the war started (1939), the directors (apart from McKittrick) included Hermann Schmitz, head of IG Farben, Baron Kurt von Schroder, head of JH Stein Bank of Cologne (and also a Gruppenfuhrer in

Himmler's Gestapo), Dr. Walter Funk, head of the Reichsbank, and Emil Puhl. Puhl was vice president of the Reichsbank and personal representative of Hitler. The two British directors were Montagu Norman (a Nazi sympathizer) and Sir John Simon, Secretary of the Exchequer.

After the Anschluss the gold reserves of Austria in 1938 were immediately deposited in BIS vaults. It was then transferred to the Reichsbank, under Funk. When the Germans moved into Prague, they ordered the directors of the Czech National Bank (at gunpoint) to deliver its $48 million ($630 million$_{2011}$) gold reserves to the Reichsbank. The storm troopers were told that the gold had already been transferred to BIS, with instructions from the Czechs to forward it to the Bank of England. The Germans told the then BIS president, the Dutch banker J. W. Beyen, to instruct Montagu Norman (head of the Bank of England) to return the gold to the BIS. He immediately complied. The gold was then sent to Germany (Mendez 2001).

During the war, some US corporations were actually sending critical materials to Nazi Germany, by way of Fascist Spain, with finance arranged by the BIS. In the year 1944 the United States was shipping 48,000 tons of oil and 1,100 tons of wolfram (tungsten ore) to Germany per month (Mendez 2001). (Somehow the ships carrying those shipments were not attacked by German submarines.) Later, in 1944, the Reichsbank sent $348 million ($3.7 billion$_{2011}$) in gold looted from the national banks of Austria, Holland, Belgium, and Czechoslovakia, plus gold stolen from Jewish victims in concentration camps to BIS to be made available for later use by well-connected senior Nazis, who knew they were losing the war (Higham 1983).

Much of the material in the paragraphs above (and a good deal more) was not known until after the war, but some of it was uncovered by a journalist-economist, Paul Einzig, who brought it to the attention of British Labor MP George Strauss. News reached Secretary of the US Treasury, Henry Morgenthau, who tried to get a straight story from Sir John Simon, who had been a BIS director before the war. But Simon evaded the questions and lied about it, as did others. One of the other liars was Morgenthau's representative in Basle, Merle Cochran, who was also a secret Nazi sympathizer.

Finally, Morgenthau was convinced that the BIS had been essentially a Nazi bank that was helping to finance the German war effort. But there was a concerted (and effective) cover-up by powerful bankers and others to deny the truth of BIS wartime activities. Morgenthau tried to get the Bretton Woods delegates to close down the BIS, but its "friends," such as Winthrop Aldrich of Chase-Manhattan Bank, Edward Brown of First National City Bank, Sir Anthony Eden, and even Lord Keynes (after some arm-twisting) managed to veto that effort and keep the BIS going after the war. The likely reason, apart from burying the past, was that the extraordinary treaty status it enjoys (see box 3.3) would be very hard to renegotiate.

However, the BIS now has a different official purpose. It was repackaged as a central bank for the central banks, intended primarily as a coordinator of financial policy pertaining to exchange rates and (more recently) risk-weighting of assets and loans. It was also intended as a venue for a policy discussion group among central bankers. The BIS has always kept a low profile, and up to 1977, it was almost invisible even to the people of Basel, where it is located. In that year it built a new headquarters building in Basel. However, when it was created (more accurately re-created) back in 1946 its member banks controlled 95 percent of the "movable" (i.e., lendable) currency in the world. This fact alone makes it much more important than is commonly realized.

Incidentally, the so-called Dawes bonds, created in 1924 and backed by German reparations and commercial debt, were defaulted in 1934 by the incoming Nazi regime under Hitler. The direct loss to US bondholders (including many small banks) was around $10 billion (*$120 billion*$_{2011}$). Of the roughly one million bearer bonds issued (with a face value of $1,000), 300,000 bonds were sold by US bondholders after 1934 for pennies on the dollar. Later most of those bonds were bought back by Nazi agents and, still later, secretly resold for 40 or 50 cents on the dollar in Switzerland. Those funds, funneled through the BIS, helped finance German rearmament (Higham 1983).

The Dawes bonds were never canceled, so there is a potential liability still remaining. After the war (1953), West Germany offered to pay principal and accumulated interest on those bonds, except for the 300,000 bonds that were sold by Americans (and bought back by Nazi agents) in the 1930s. The German government did not want to acknowledge what had really happened, so it claimed that those bonds had been kept in the Reichsbank and stolen by the Russians, during the initial Russian

Box 3.3
Bank of International Settlements (BIS), 1930

The BIS was chartered in Switzerland and located in Basel, on the border between France and Germany. It was organized as a commercial bank; its shareholders were the major central banks of Europe, plus Japan and Canada. Central bank deposits are used for short-term loans to governments. Profits suffice to finance all activities of the BIS. Central bankers meet there ten times a year to settle questions pertaining to exchange rates, gold shipments, and capital ratios. It is a major gold repository. The US participation was originally unofficial (because of congressional isolationism) but is now official. The American shares are by First National City Bank (now Citibank). The BIS received an extraordinary immunity from government interference and taxes, in both peace and war. This immunity was guaranteed by a treaty between the founding nations signed in The Hague, in 1930 (Epstein 1983, no. 7343).

---

occupation of Berlin. There are cynics who doubt this story. The very few bondholders who could prove where their bonds were in 1945 (i.e., not in Berlin) were offered "conversion bonds" with a forty-one-year maturity. This was a trick to cut actual payments, since most people could not prove where their bonds had been kept. The US government did not complain about this scheme, at the time. The conversion bonds that were issued by West Germany in 1953 finally matured in 1994.

After ignoring the issue for half a century, the US government (SEC) finally decided to disallow the German gimmick for reducing its liabilities (by requiring proof that the bonds were not in Berlin in 1945) on constitutional grounds, thus supporting the surviving US bondholders. People who did not accept the conversion bonds in 1953 are now legally entitled to claim recompense, although it will not be easy. It is a big deal. The total liability of the German government, in current dollars, could theoretically be as much as $600 billion, although it is probably much less. No doubt there is a class action suit winding its way through the courts.

Two new financial institutions were created by the Bretton Woods Conference. The two new ones were the International Bank for Reconstruction and Development (IBRD, now informally known as the World Bank), and the International Monetary Fund (IMF). The World Bank was intended to finance reconstruction, mainly in Europe, while the IMF was intended as a kind of financial doctor, to step in as a lender of last resort when a national economy got sick from gorging on too much rich food (hard currency loans) and couldn't repay. The IMF has been quite busy in recent decades.

Ratification of the Bretton Woods treaty was not easy or automatic. President Charles de Gaulle of France was not happy with the treaty and he was only persuaded to ratify by a $1 billion (*$10 billion*$_{2011}$) loan. The United Kingdom refused to ratify until it got a $4.4 billion (*$44 billion*$_{2011}$) loan. But the Bretton Woods treaty was finally ratified by all the signatory countries in 1946.

4

Post–World War II

The post–WWII period starts with the Bretton Woods conference (1946), which established the US dollar as the world's reserve currency. The dollar inflation caused by two wars ("guns and butter") enabled the creation of OPEC and forced Nixon to close the "gold window." Thereafter currencies floated. Then came the oil price "spike" of 1974 to 1975, establishing OPEC as the global "swing" supplier. The Iranian revolution followed along with a second oil price "spike." The accumulation of "petrodollars" was loaned many countries to finance development, but the high US interest rates of 1980 to 1982 caused several bankruptcies. Starting in 1982, the Reagan administration encouraged deregulation while increasing money in circulation. This was followed by a series of financial innovations and changes on Wall Street, including securitization of mortgage-based bonds, corporatization of investment banks, "junk bonds," LBOs hedge funds, derivatives, and so on.

Recent history, starting with the "dot.com" bubble and the subsequence "subprime mortgage" bubble is described in some detail. The crisis of 2008 has multiple sources. But excessive deregulation starting in the 1980s, coupled with "risk-spreading" (from the banks to their clients and the taxpayers), plus structural weaknesses resulting in instability have played a big part. Recent experience suggests *that the negative externalities of universal banking and mega-finance now can (and did) outweigh the efficiency benefits.*

The Postwar Recovery, 1947 to 1970

After 1946 the British had tried to retain a system of trade preferences within the so-called Sterling bloc (the former British Empire countries).

But that was prevented by the Bretton Woods system, strongly enforced by the US government, which wanted free access for American exporters to the former British (and French) colonies around the world. The Attlee government of the United Kingdom, which succeeded the wartime Churchill government, broke the new rules almost immediately by a 40 percent devaluation of the pound sterling, which had been set at $4.86 per pound by Montagu Norman back in 1925. The new exchange rate was $2.80 per dollar. This move was economically justified by the postwar situation in Great Britain, which had lost fully 25 percent of its national wealth in WWII, and whose (relatively undamaged and consequently not rebuilt) export industry was no longer competitive.

The Marshall Plan was initiated in 1947 and began functioning in 1948, along with the European Cooperation Act (ECA) and its subsidiary, the European Payments Union (EPU), created in 1950. The US occupation of Japan began to restructure the Japanese economy, and one of its first actions was to enforce a version of the Glass–Steagall Act in that country. The EPU funneled money to European countries through the BIS. This put the BIS at the heart of European integration process, which began with the six countries of the European Coal and Steel Commission (ECSC) in 1950, the predecessor of the European Union.

The flow of US capital to Europe continued for four years through 1952. Western European countries received $13 billion (*$104 billion*$_{2011}$) over that period, in addition to $12 billion (*$96 billion*$_{2011}$) contributed by the United States via other recovery and defense programs. This capital flow helped Europe to recover industrially and, incidentally, to reduce and finally reverse its postwar trade deficit with respect to the United States.

The Korean War (1950 to 1953) started when North Korea, backed by the People's Republic of China and the Soviet Union, invaded South Korea in a surprise attack on June 25, 1950. The United Nations, primarily based on US military power, defended South Korea. In exchange for military basing privileges during the Korean War, Japan also obtained preferential access to the US market that was not reciprocated. This gave Japan an economic boost in the 1970s and 1980s.

The Korean War ended in a military stalemate in the summer of 1953, but there was no peace treaty. Roughly 30,000 US soldiers are permanently stationed in South Korea near the border. In addition there are major bases for the US Marines and Air Force facilities in Okinawa. The economic costs of the Korean War, and its aftermath, to the United States (but not Europe) were, and are, significant.

In 1953 President Eisenhower thought that the Reconstruction Finance Corp was no longer needed. In that year it ceased lending. It was wound up in 1957. During the life of the RFC it borrowed $51.3 billion from the Treasury and $3.1 billion from the public, all of which was used to bolster the banks.

In 1957 the six-country European Coal and Steel Commission (ECSC) was broadened to become the European Economic Community or EEC (better known as the "Common Market"). At the same time other European countries formed the European Free Trade Association (EFTA), which was led by the United Kingdom. In 1967 the European Community (EC) was formed by a merger of the EEC and Euratom. Britain finally joined the EC, and EFTA disappeared.

In the 1950s, thanks perhaps to the apparent success of Roosevelt's New Deal, some steps were taken to strengthen the Glass–Steagall Act of 1933. Resistance to regulation was then at low ebb in the United States (see box 4.1).

In civil society there was an innovative new device for allowing people to go into debt without posting security. At first, it was just a new and beneficial service for the well-to-do. The Diners Club card, the first credit card, appeared in 1950. It allowed businessmen to eat and entertain at twenty-seven prestigious restaurants around the country, with bills presented monthly. The American Express green card first appeared in 1958. Bank of AmeriCard was introduced in California the following year. It

Box 4.1
Tinkering with Glass–Steagall

In 1956 the Bank-Holding Company Act was passed by Congress to prevent bank-holding companies that owned two or more banks from crossing state lines or engaging in non-banking activity. This was done to close a loophole in the Glass–Steagall Act of 1933.

In 1960 Congress explicitly required the regulators to apply Regulation Q (the anti-usury law) to S&L loans. The interstate provisions of the Bank-Holding Act were repealed by the Riegle–Neal Interstate Banking and Branching Efficiency Act of 1994 as part of the slow demolition of Glass–Steagall.

later became VISA and is now the most widely used card in the world. In 1966 MasterCard was introduced by the City Bank of New York, also initially for customers with good credit ratings. It was advertised as the "everything card" with a new feature: revolving credit. For the first time it was not necessary to pay off the balance each month. This was the first true credit card.

Today MasterCard is the main rival of VISA. More to the point, US credit card debt is now enormous, $19,000 per household in January 2009, declining to around $15,000 currently (2013). Most people have several cards. Some use them indiscriminately, as though the thought of repayment never occurs to them. The banks have discovered that credit card owners are easy targets. Interest rates on unpaid balances are far higher than mortgage interest rates, and late payments are routinely punished by heavy fees. Credit cards constitute a major source of profit for banks.

The credit card enables users to spend future income before it is earned. Families have been able to consume more than they can afford. Everybody knows the rules and the risks of being labeled a poor risk. But for society as a whole, it is doubtful whether consuming sooner, with borrowed money, rather than later with earned money, is truly a social benefit.

The first hint of changing public attitudes toward deregulation and privatization came in 1963 when Congress reversed the 1934 law nationalizing silver. But 3.2 billion ounces of silver still remained in Fort Knox. In 1967 the government stopped selling silver from the stockpile at $1.29 ($7.00₂₀₁₁) per troy ounce. In 1968 came a bigger step when gold was denationalized, without retaining any explicit linkage to the money supply. In 1974 President Ford signed a bill permitting US citizens to own gold coins again for the first time since 1933. Now anybody can buy gold, in any form. It has become a favorite investment of people who worry about inflation. It started at $37 ($165₂₀₁₁) per troy ounce in 1971 and peaked at $860 per ounce ($1,720₂₀₁₁). Then it declined steadily until the latest inflation panic, starting in 2008. The peak in 2011 was $1,908 per ounce. The most recent (2013) gold price has dropped again (to about $1,400/oz).

From 1965 through 1968, thanks to the Vietnam war, US military expenditure rose 41 percent while taxes did not (Malkin 1988). The war costs were not paid for out of taxes, but mostly by borrowing. The

Vietnam war did little for US nonmilitary industry but added significantly to the national debt and to domestic inflation. There was a modest income tax surcharge in 1969, but it was too late. Johnson's "Great Society" program was seriously wounded by the enormous diversion of resources to the war effort.

In 1968 the Federal National Mortgage Agency (Fannie Mae) was privatized and made into a profit-making company, albeit still government sponsored and still entitled to borrow money from the Treasury at rates lower than the commercial banks. This removed most of its debts from the official national accounts. This entitlement seemed to the markets like an implicit guarantee. However, a small spin-off, the Government National Mortgage Agency (Ginnie Mae), was reserved for veterans and some other government employees.

In 1970, two years later, during the Nixon administration, Fannie Mae was split to spin off a junior brother, also profit-making, known as Freddie Mac. This was supposed to encourage competition. At the same time the two entities were allowed to buy private mortgages not insured by the FHA from banks and other mortgage companies. This kicked off the mortgage bond business that, years later, dominated Wall Street. Ginnie Mae started to explore with Salomon Brothers the possibility of selling off bundles of mortgages as bonds.

The project was stopped temporarily by the partner in charge of government bond-trading at Salomon Brothers, William Simon (later Secretary of the Treasury from 1974 to 1977) on the ground that mortgages could not be sold as bonds because of inherent uncertainty about the length of maturity. "Who wants to buy a bond if he doesn't know when he might get his money back?" was Simon's question. The problem was that home mortgages can be paid off at any time, and this is likely to happen any time interest rates fall, allowing borrowers to refinance at lower rates and consequently reducing the income stream for the bondholders.

Nevertheless, a year later (1971) Freddie Mac issued its first "participation certificate" consisting of a package of mortgages suitable for sale to a bank or other investor. Mortgage bonds became big business a few years later when William Simon's objection to bonds was resolved by a clever fix.

In 1970 there was a financial disaster that almost, but not quite, caused a financial crisis and almost destroyed Goldman Sachs. It came about because Penn Central (result of the merger of the two biggest railroads in the United States, the New York Central and the Pennsylvania Railroad) suddenly declared bankruptcy despite having enormous, but illiquid, real estate assets in midtown Manhattan and elsewhere. This left a large number of institutional investors holding commercial paper from Penn Central that had been issued by Goldman Sachs.[1] All of the investors wanted their money back. But the total added up to $87 million (*$400 million*$_{2011}$). Goldman Sachs' total capitalization (the personal wealth of the partners) was only $57 million (*$260 million*$_{2011}$). Worse, when Penn Central went bankrupt, hundreds of other holders of commercial paper, nearly $3 billion (*$14 billion*$_{2011}$) from other issuers, also wanted their money back.

It was like a run on a bank. Issuers of commercial paper had to borrow money from their banks to pay for the commercial paper they had to buy back, and the Federal Reserve had to lend the banks $1.7 billion (*$8 billion*$_{2011}$) to re-liquefy them (Ellis 2009, ch. 7). The banks were all "made whole" by the FRB, which bought their worthless Penn Central paper at par value. National City Bank was the first in line. But smaller firms were left to "twist in the wind" (to paraphrase Nixon's hatchet man, John Ehrlichman).

One victim was Commercial Credit Corporation, in Baltimore, which had had issued several hundred million dollars of commercial paper. The firm was nearly put out of business when all its clients wanted their money simultaneously. The firm had to go to the banks to cover their outstanding loans. The banks (who were all fully reimbursed later) paid Commercial Credit only 80 cents on the dollar to take over these loans, nearly bankrupting a firm that had nothing whatever to do with Penn Central (Malkin 1988, pp. 86–87). It was a good example of a negative (pecuniary) externality.

That story had a happy ending. Commercial Credit was subsequently bought by Control Data, the computer company in Minneapolis. Control Data later sold it to Sanford Weill (who had just resigned from American Express). Weill did a financial engineering job on the company. After a successful IPO, it became the basis of a series of acquisitions in the insurance industry culminating in Weill's takeover of Travelers Group in 1993. Travelers merged with CitiBank in 1999.

All of the owners of worthless Penn Central commercial paper sold by Goldman Sachs sued, and the SEC issued a report strongly condemning the firm for failing to convey to its clients important information that they had about the bad financial condition of Penn Central. This information had actually been hidden from Penn Central shareholders and top management by the CFO, David Bevan, until shortly before the collapse. But the Goldman Sachs partner who worked with Bevan knew most of the bad news much sooner than the owners of commercial paper. Worse, he used that information to protect Goldman Sachs, rather than the poor suckers who had bought their commercial paper.

Some of the Goldman clients were willing to settle for 20 cents on the dollar, but some wanted full restitution and the trials continued until November 1974, when Goldman Sachs lost several court cases. Their argument, as usual, was *caveat emptor*: that is, the buyers were sophisticated investors and should have done their own "due diligence" before buying. But when it was revealed to juries that Goldman had known about the problems and didn't tell their clients, the firm had to pay out $30 million (*$125 million*$_{2011}$) in cash from its capital base, spread over several years (Malkin 1988). That saved Goldman, but most of its clients, who lost money, having bought highly rated securities from a reputable investment bank, were never reimbursed.

The Commercial Credit debacle seems to have triggered a major internal re-structuring of Goldman Sachs during the 1970s, led by partner John Whitehead. In the older system, senior partners had long-term personal relationships with clients, and they were personally responsible both for selling and delivery of all services, large or small. Whitehead's idea was to separate the selling of financial products from the delivery of services. This structural shift was eventually imitated by all the other firms. It helped propel Goldman Sachs from the second tier of investment banking to the top of the table.

Real growth in Europe after the war was driven initially by reconstruction, paid for in part by the Marshall Plan, and open access to the US market. The German "economic miracle" of the 1950s and 1960s was based largely on exports of traditional engineering products, including cars, machinery, electrical goods, and chemicals, made with relatively low-cost skilled labor in newly rebuilt factories.

By the end of the 1960s Western Europe had recovered to a large extent. Japan was beginning its economic boom, with annual growth rates of 8 to 10 percent, fueled to a large extent by exports of consumer electronics, cameras, and motorcycles, followed shortly by cars. US manufacturing exports were increasingly outpaced by manufacturing imports. In 1970 the US balance of trade, which had been positive for fifty years, became negative for the first time since WWII (Arnold 2000).

There was no dominant business model in the finance sector during the postwar period, except perhaps the conglomerate theory that became influential in the 1960s. Pepsico, a merger between Pepsi-Cola and Frito-Lay, is an example of one of the few successful conglomerate mergers of the period. The theory was explained most succinctly, if retroactively, by the Boston Consulting Group (BCG). It was expressed as a 2 by 2 "growth share matrix" for portfolio management: one axis is the growth rate and the other axis is market share. The four boxes are labeled *stars* (high market share and fast growth), *cash cows* (high market share, low growth), *dogs* (low market share, low growth), and *question marks* (low market share, high growth).

The key insight was that "dogs" should be sold or spun off while "cash cows" should be used to support growing businesses ("question marks" in need of capital) or to acquire others. This approach did seem to retroactively justify a number of unlikely conglomerate mergers profitable for the investment banks and brokers involving different and unrelated businesses. Possibly the best example was Warren Buffet's successful investment fund, Berkshire Hathaway, originally a New England shirt company.[2] However, there was no convincing economic argument for conglomerate mergers in the first place.

The question left unanswered was why a fast-growing "star" should be financed by a "cash cow' belonging to a parent organization managed by another business, rather than utilizing the financial services of specialist investment banks to raise capital for growth. The main argument for conglomerate mergers at the time was that companies within a conglomerate could perform services for each other and share overhead expenses. Unfortunately, these hypothetical synergies rarely happened in practice and most of the conglomerates created in the 1960s and 1970s were not successful. When broken up, the value of the parts often turned out to be greater than the value of the whole. Most of the conglomerates created in the 1960s and 1970s were later dismantled, after takeovers and IPOs of the separate spin-offs.

But there were no major financial crises during the New Deal period or the postwar recovery years. The Glass–Steagall Act was still working.

The Nixon-Carter Period, 1970 to 1981

By 1970, inflation had become endemic, thanks largely to Lyndon Johnson's "guns and butter" policy (the Vietnam war). By 1974, inflation reached 5.74 percent per annum. Inflated dollars were worth less, year by year, but payments for imported commodities denominated in dollars, like oil, were not increased to compensate. This hurt the oil exporters, in particular. (Recall the discussion in chapter 2 on the "oil shocks.") Meanwhile gold coverage for the US sovereign debt (to foreign central banks) had declined from 100 percent in 1963 to 22 percent by 1971.

In early 1971 there was a run on the dollar due to European worries about the US willingness to convert eurodollars to gold. The US money supply (M2) jumped 10 percent in a few months. The dollar declined by 7.5 percent against the Deutschmark (DM) in that year. According to classical economic theory, embodied in the Bretton Woods system, President Nixon should have raised interest rates to strengthen the dollar and attract foreign capital flows, or Germany should have reflated its currency to attract more imports. Germany and Switzerland were unwilling to do that. Rather suddenly, both countries unilaterally withdrew from the Bretton Woods system, followed by France. Switzerland and France both also exchanged a lot of eurodollars for gold, at $35 ($155₂₀₁₁) per troy ounce as permitted by the Bretton Woods rules. President Nixon had to do something, or at least so his advisors said.

What he should have done is a matter of debate. What he did is history. On August 15, 1971, President Nixon unilaterally closed the "gold window" and revoked the US promise to exchange gold for dollars, although he kept the price fixed at $35 ($155₂₀₁₁) per ounce. (A year later, he raised the price of gold to $42.22 ($180₂₀₁₁) per ounce, effectively devaluing the dollar by 20 percent.) He also imposed a price freeze and an import surcharge. It was the end of Bretton Woods.

Thereafter the United States was free to "print" money by issuing treasury bonds (T-bills) backed only by the "faith and credit" of the US government. Moreover the banks were also suddenly free to create money by making loans, subject only to the amount of leverage they were allowed (by the FRB and the Bank of International Settlements) to apply. Starting in that year, the fraction of liquid assets the banks were required to hold in reserve—against possible runs on the bank—(the "fractional reserve requirements") began to decrease gradually. The Fed became increasingly compliant (or complacent) about the stability of the financial system.

Another event occurred in 1971 that had long-term consequences. The investment bank, Donaldson, Lufkin and Jenrette or (DLJ), which had been founded in 1959, achieved full membership in the circle of insiders, when Lufkin was elected to the Board of Directors of the NYSE. At the first meeting he attended, in 1970, he announced that DLJ was about to launch an initial public offering (IPO). This was in contravention of the Exchange rules at the time. But only one of the board members objected. In short, DLJ was allowed to convert from the traditional partnership structure to a corporate structure without fuss or discussion. Others followed very soon. Merrill Lynch was the next to go public, in 1972, and the rest of the partnerships followed by 1990. (Goldman Sachs was the last.)

Michael Lewis thinks that it was John Gutfreund's decision to turn Salomon Brothers from a partnership to a corporation in 1981 that really changed the culture of Wall Street. In fact he thinks the events of 2003 to 2008 can be traced to that IPO. He says:

The moment Salomon Brothers demonstrated the potential gains to be had from turning an investment bank into a public corporation and leveraging its balance sheet with exotic risks, the psychological foundations of Wall Street shifted from trust to blind faith. No investment bank owned by its employees would have leveraged itself 35:1, or bought and held $50 billion in mezzanine CDOs.[3] I doubt any partnership would have sought to "game" the rating agencies, or leapt into bed with loan sharks, or even allowed mezzanine CDOs to be sold to its customers. The short term expected gains would not have justified the long-term loss. (Lewis 2010, pp. 258–59)

The meaning of this change was not only that the former partners would receive a lot of money, overnight, with no responsibility to keep it invested in the business. The subtler implication was that they were no longer individually responsible for the risks undertaken by the firm. Whereas a partner was taking risks with his own money (and that of the other partners), a corporate officer could and did take risks with shareholders and even clients' money. The degree of risk aversion declined significantly in later years.

In an attempt to encourage competition in the financial industry, and hopefully to attract more investment (and savings) by ordinary investors, and more trading by mutual funds and pension funds, the SEC took another step toward deregulation of finance. It announced that brokers would no longer be permitted to charge fixed rates on the sale or purchase of stocks. This announcement occurred on May 1, 1975, and it is remembered by the financial community, without pleasure, as "May Day" because that was the day that ended the stockbrokers traditional relationship with clients. Low-cost brokerages like Charles Schwab appeared and forced the established mainstream brokerages to compete on prices. It put them out of the business of providing free research and advice to retail clients.

Also in 1975 the SEC did something else. For reasons that were never explained well, if at all, the SEC gave the three existing ratings agencies, Moody's, Standard & Poor's, and Fitch, all private corporations, effective protection from competition. In other words, they were given oligopoly status as nationally recognized statistical rating organizations (NRSROs). The SEC said that only ratings by these three NRSROs would satisfy the many requirements for "investment grade" and higher ratings that had been imposed on banks, S&Ls, pension funds, endowment funds, and insurance companies since 1936. It would be hard not to believe that this protection from competition had something to do with the accuracy of their later ratings (Friedman and Kraus 2011, pp. 3, 104).

There was a major oil discovery in the Gulf of Mexico in 1976, the Canterell field (named after its discoverer). It was developed in the late 1970s by PEMEX, Mexico's national oil company. The field qualified as a "supergiant," one of the last such large discoveries, and created an oil boom in Mexico. The US banks, led by Bank of America, loaned PEMEX $2.5 billion ($7.5 billion_{2011}$) without any credit (or other) "due diligence" check (Malkin 1988, p. 102).

In those years US banks, such as Citibank and Chase-Manhattan were very active in soliciting business from third-world countries. They called it "go-go banking." This change in lending practice (and standards) was justified by the notion that governments would not default. Besides, it was easier to deal with a dictator than a gaggle of individual enterprises. One Latin American Finance Minister said later: "I remember how the bankers tried to corner me at conferences to offer me loans" (Makin 1984, p. 147). Here is a quote that tells the story succinctly:

Latin American technocrats, the best of them trained at some of the same (or better) economics faculties of Harvard, MIT or Chicago, as the bankers, offered a one-stop service. Instead of sending out costly specialists to evaluate individual projects, the banks left that to the local governments. They [the countries] borrowed the money in their own name and parceled it out to nationalized and private enterprises. They had been freed from the tiresome inhibitions imposed by traditional banking agencies such as the World Bank. . . . For the Latin American elite, the money was the realization of a dream: foreign investment without foreign control or a foreign lien on the profits. Malkin (1988, p. 101)

Little did they know. The US money-center banks did very well, if not by doing much good. Half their profits came from foreign business by 1979. The Latino elites did well too. Much of that money went straight to Swiss and other tax-haven bank accounts. It is estimated *ex post* that one-third of the money loaned by American banks to the countries south of the border between 1979 and 1983 came right back as "flight capital." There are no exact figures, of course, but detailed examination of published data (a form of double-entry bookkeeping) tells part of the story (Walter 1985). In the case of Brazil, the leakage rate was modest, a mere 10 percent. But 40 percent of Mexico's borrowing, 60 percent of Argentina's, and 100 percent of Venezuela's loans went to Switzerland or came right back, often to other departments of the same banks (e.g., wealth management) that had made the loans (Malkin 1988, p. 107).

The dark side of that lending spree was that when US interest rates rose sharply in 1980 to 1981, the countries that had borrowed in dollars couldn't repay. Then the IMF would step in and enforce "structural adjustment" policies on the countries, but nothing was done to recapture funds from the dictators or their cronies. Those "reform" policies made sense to conservative office-bound academic economists (the so-called Washington consensus). But those structural adjustments meant ending subsidies for basic foods and other social services. Structural reforms almost literally took food from the mouths of children. The IMF is still enforcing these "austerity" policies.

Jimmy Carter was elected in 1976, largely due to the poor state of the US economy due to the recession of 1974 to 1975. The first two years of Carter's administration (1977 to 1978) were characterized by rapid economic recovery, sharply declining unemployment, and real economic growth. But inflationary pressure did not abate. In fact it accelerated. During the Carter presidency inflation became self-propelled because the economic system began to adjust to it. People began *expecting* higher prices, and factories started buying some commodities in advance of actual needs, thus pushing prices up. Wage negotiations with unions began to include automatic adjustments to the consumer price index. Pensions and social security payments were indexed to inflation.

Wage inflation in response to rising prices pushed some people into higher tax brackets, resulting in increased pressure for wage increases (and tax decreases). US inflation was 5.8 percent per annum in 1976 (the same as in 1970), but up to 7.77 percent in 1977, and 11.3 percent in 1979 when the second (Iranian) oil price shock occurred. The Fed tried to counter the inflation by clamping down on the money supply. This pushed interest rates up but merely added to price inflation. The term "stagflation" was coined at that time to describe low growth with high inflation.

During 1979 to 1980 the US inflation got worse. T-bills rose to 15.5 percent in March 1980, fell back to 7 percent because of the 1979 recession, but rose again to 15.7 percent in December 1980. This series of economic disasters probably resulted in the election of Ronald Reagan. The Fed, under Paul Volcker, kept on tightening the money supply to kill inflationary expectations until the prime rate reached 24 percent in the spring of 1981.

It is important to note that the inflationary pressures were much more severe outside the United States virtually everywhere except the major exporting economies like Germany and Japan. The hardest hit were the countries that had borrowed a lot of recycled "petrodollars" from US banks to finance recovery and growth after the first oil shock. When US interest rates rose sharply in the late 1970s, and especially during Volker's "inflation killer period" (1980 to 1981), the Latino debtor countries could not pay and needed IMF bailouts. Of course, those bailouts come with tough conditions. The conditions for emergency loans almost always involve cuts in food and fuel subsidies, and cuts in other public services that hurt the poor. Moreover, whereas the hyperinflation in Germany and Central Europe in the 1920s ended quickly after national budgets were balanced, this didn't work in Latin America. While inflation was reduced by the IMF interventions, it never stayed down.[4]

The political backlash to the oil embargo also enabled the Carter administration to introduce some energy-saving initiatives, such as the

CAFE standards for automobiles, the utility deregulation act PURPA, and several abortive programs to make the US energy independent. The latter initiatives never went anywhere, due to the political power of the oil lobby.

In 1976 the firm of Kohlberg, Kravis and Roberts (KKR) was formed when the three partners left their previous employer, Bear-Stearns. KKR was, and still is, one of the most important players on Wall Street, especially during the Reagan years, in the business of organizing management buyouts, takeovers, and mergers.

The first mortgage-based securities (MBSs) were created by Lewie Ranieri of Salomon Brothers and Larry Fink of First Boston. They solved the problem cited by William Simon; namely what happens when homeowners sell or refinance? Their scheme strongly resembles the classification of corporate and government debt into bonds, with various degrees of seniority, or "subordination." The subordinate debts are only paid after the "senior" debts. Similarly "preferred" shares are paid before "ordinary" shares. The subordination scheme, which put commercial debt above reparations payments, was in fact the secret of the popularity of the Dawes bonds that paid for German recovery, from 1924 through 1929. That sad episode was discussed earlier in connection with the creation and later the "repackaging" of the Bank for International Settlements (BIS) in Basel.

As applied to mortgage-based bonds, the subordination scheme was to create a "tower" of mortgages with many stories, each consisting of a "tranche" of mortgages. The top tranche was defined, simply, as that segment of the whole pool whose dividend is paid first from the stream of income to the pool of mortgages, and is therefore the "senior" (i.e., safest) by definition. It pays the lowest dividend (or "coupon") to reflect this greater seniority, or safety. Dividends to lower "subordinate" tranches are paid after the higher ones. They pay correspondingly higher dividends (coupons) because they are less safe. Any defaults in the pool as a whole reduce the total revenue for the pool, but the upper tranches are still paid in full whereas payments to the lowest tranches may be cut off. Payments to the bottom "equity" tranche are cut first. Again, the "equity tranche" (so called because the bank normally kept it) was not individually better or worse than the others, in terms of the quality of the individual mortgages, but being the last to be paid, it had the highest risk and paid the highest dividend.

The "top floors" of the MBS "tower" were rated AAA simply by virtue of their position as first in the sequence of payment. Obviously higher floors were quite safe and were rated AAA. Tranches near the bottom got lower ratings of AA, A, BBB, and BB and unrated (called "equity" because they were normally retained by the banks as reserves). However, the AAA part of the tower was usually by far the largest, typically about 80 percent of the pool. The bottom "equity" tranche typically incorporated only about 2 percent of the mortgages in the pool. The subordination scheme turned out to be quite popular with clients, since it enabled them to choose the degree of risk and reward. I mention the system again, later, in connection with a discussion of the rating agencies and their role in the financial collapse of 2008.

In 1978 Salomon Brothers created a Mortgage Department, in parallel with its corporate and government bond departments, and Salomon Brothers finally began selling mortgage-backed securities (MBS). The department was created by Lewie Ranieri, a Brooklyn-born Italian-American bond trader who had started in the Salomon Brothers mailroom. The MBSs were five- or ten-year bonds that could be sold to investors (mostly S&Ls). Salomon created the market and handled the trades. These securities were created in partnership with the Bank of America.

At first the mortgage-based bond business was slow, but after 1981 it accelerated enormously. Ranieri claimed that "securitization" resulted in a sharp increase in capital available for home mortgages, with the result that average interest costs to borrowers were reduced by 2 percent per annum on average. He was probably correct in both claims. From 1980 to 1984, before all the other banks jumped in, Salomon Brothers and First Boston had a virtual duopoly and made enormous profits. (Salomon was in fact paying the young bond traders relatively little compared to the profits being made; that enabled other firms, like Merrill Lynch, to hire away the most talented members of Ranieri's team.) This was a primary cause of Ranieri's eventual split with Salomon CEO John Gutfreund, leading to his departure (Lewis 1989); see box 4.2.

The Savings and Loan banks (S&Ls), hit by the rising inflation, were in trouble because they had been lending long-term at low interest rates but borrowing from the money market at much higher inflation-driven short-term rates. In 1981 the Economic Recovery Tax Act was passed to encourage real estate development. The FLHBB changed its accounting

Box 4.2
First steps toward urban redevelopment

The Housing and Community Development Act (HCDA) of 1977 was signed by President Carter. The Community Reinvestment Act (CRA), title VIII of HCDA) is the antidiscrimination component, intended to help provide the credit needs of low and moderate income communities and to combat credit discrimination ("red-lining") by real estate interests. All banks insured by the FDIC are required to support this effort, and federal regulatory agencies (FHA, etc.) determine CRA compliance. The rules monitored by CRA were modified by Congress several times after 1977.

rules to permit S&Ls to defer accounting for losses from impaired asset for ten years. This made balance sheets look better, though it did not change the causes of the problem.

In 1981 Fannie Mae began issuing "pass-throughs," an early form of mortgage-backed security. A year later the FHLBB reduced the net worth requirement for S&Ls from 4 to 3 percent, and allowed equity capital to be counted as reserve. There were other changes in the law. Effectively S&Ls were now allowed to speculate, not just in real estate per se, but in mortgage-backed securities and corporate "junk" bonds (about which, more later).

The major financial innovations of the 1970s were corporatization, internal specialization, and "securitization," especially of mortgage loans. Ranieri of Salomon Brothers was the pioneer in that area. His innovation made Salomon the star in the investment bank firmament for a decade. That innovation, together with others (derivatives) later contributed to the destruction of an enormous amount of wealth. However, those who paint Ranieri as a villain are far off base. He was in no way responsible for the derivatives later constructed from mortgage-backed securities or the creation of the subprime mortgage industry that nearly sank the global economy in 2008.

Reaganomics, 1982 to 1988

The end of the Carter administration in 1980 marked the low point in terms of US public debt as a fraction of GDP since WWII. However the core inflation rate had been rising since the Vietnam war. The US inflationary spiral reached a peak of 13.5 percent nominal (5 percent real) in early 1981. Something had to be done. The inflationary spiral was finally stopped by the US Federal Reserve Bank (FRB) under Carter-appointee Chairman Paul Volcker. The Fed allowed the "prime" (rediscount) rate to rise, albeit briefly, to 21.5 percent in the spring of 1981 (figure 4.1). This sharp rise in short term interest rates was followed by, a second, even deeper, recession. The US stock market crashed in 1981 to 1982. The Dow-Jones index bottomed at 777 in August 1982.

Thanks to the recession triggered by the second "oil shock" and the Fed's intervention, under Carter-appointee Paul Volcker, the US "core" inflation rate fell sharply, starting in 1982. It was down to 3.5 percent by 1983, and the era of "Reaganomics" began.

The high interest rates of the late 1970s and then 1981 to 1982 were very hard on the savings and loan (S&L) banks, which were financed entirely by small depositors. Part of their problem was that the interest rates they could offer depositors were capped by law (Regulation Q). The S&Ls could only park their deposits in "investment grade" securities, as determined by the three ratings agencies specified in 1976 by the

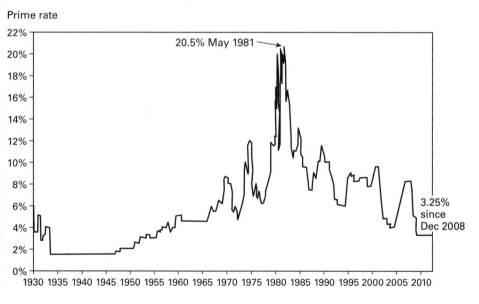

Figure 4.1
US prime rate from 1930 to 2013. Data from US Federal Reserve Bank.

SEC. The S&Ls were losing depositors. During the next two years the Federal Home Loan Board (FHLBB) took a number of steps to deregulate the mortgage business. These included changes in "net worth" rules and accounting changes such as deferral of losses from the sale of impaired (depreciated) assets; see box 4.3.

In response to the partial deregulation of S&Ls in 1981 and 1982 (together with the "securitization innovations by Salomon and First Boston) a new breed of mortgage originators emerged. To attract more borrowers they began offering so-called "adjustable rate mortgages" (ARMs) and other exotic contracts with very low interest rates for the first two years, to

Box 4.3
"Saving" the S&Ls and cutting taxes

The Depository Institutions Deregulation and Monetary Control Act (DID-MCA) of 1980 raised the limit on insured deposits in S&Ls from $40,000 to $100,000 ($80,000–200,000$_{2011}$) and abolished the anti-usury (regulation Q) cap on interest rates chargeable by S&Ls. It also gave banks some incentives to lend to low income people with less than perfect credit ratings.

The Kemp–Roth Economic Recovery Tax Act (ERTA) of 1981 cut individual marginal tax rates by 23 percent over three years, and cut capital gains rates from 28 to 20 percent and cut corporate taxes by $150 ($300$_{2011}$) billion over five years. It created IRAs and extended employee stock ownership program (ESOP) rules. It also cut estate taxes and changed federal regulations to help spark the real estate boom of the next few years by allowing S&Ls to reclaim back taxes for the previous ten years.

The Alternative Mortgage Transactions Parity Act (AMTPA) of 1982 ended the rule that mortgages had to be amortized at a fixed rate. It allowed innovative mortgage types, such as adjustable rate mortgages (ARMs), teasers followed by balloon payments when due, interest only for a few years with a "reset" of the rate after a few years, and "option-ARMs," which allow underpayment of any amount, with the interest added to the principal.

The Secondary Market Enhancement Act (SMEA) of 1984 allows non-GSE firms (like Salomon) to offer mortgage-based securities in competition with the Fannie Mae and Freddie Mac. Lewie Ranieri of Salomon lobbied hard for this.

The Tax Reform Act (TRA) of 1986 disallowed the deduction of interest on consumer loans (credit card, auto, etc.) but allowed the deduction for mortgage loans. This encouraged the use of home equity mortgage loans to pay off consumer loans.

The Real Estate Mortgage Investment Conduit (REMIC) Law of 1986 prevents double taxation of mortgage-based securities.

be followed by floating rates and/or balloon payments later. These ARMs were marketed to people with decent jobs and prospects who could not yet afford a conventional mortgage. The mortgages were then sold either to one of the two government-sponsored mortgage finance entities (Fannie Mae or Freddie Mac) or directly to investment banks. The investment banks (especially Salomon Brothers and First Boston) proceeded to "securitize" these mortgages into mortgage-based securities (MBSs).

In 1983 Larry Fink's group at First Boston created the first collateralized mortgage obligation (CMO), using mortgages from Freddie Mac. These securities, had shorter maturities (and higher returns) than the mortgages themselves. Rated "investment grade," they were then sold to the S&Ls and other long term investors. The extraordinary profitability of the business from 1980 through 1984 was due to the fact that, during those years, it was a virtual duopoly of Salomon Brothers and First Boston. And, for a time, they made enormous profits selling to S&Ls. *Caveat emptor.*

It will be recalled from the previous chapter that, following the big Cantarell oil bonanza of 1976 in the Gulf of Mexico, there was a rush of US commercial bank lending to Mexico and other Latino governments. As already mentioned, a lot of the lending in that period not just to Mexico was channeled to governments, rather than to enterprises, under the impression that governments would not default. That assumption was called into question in 1982, when Mexico declared that it could not pay interest on its debts *because it was completely out of dollars.* This episode bears a curious resemblance to the occasion under the Cleveland administration (chapter 3) when the US Treasury nearly ran out of gold.

The reason for the Mexican dollar shortage (also discussed in the last chapter) was that $11 billion ($22 billion$_{2011}$) in "flight capital" had disappeared from Mexican banks in the previous six months.[5]

Since the "money-center" banks must have had an inkling of the origins of the sudden influx of new deposits in their Mexican branches, one might think that the banks should have alerted the Mexican authorities and helped them recover the money. But banks don't do that. It isn't their business model.

Yet, if Mexico, which owed $85 billion ($170 billion$_{2011}$) to those banks, had actually defaulted—stopped paying interest—the banks would have had to discount the value of those loans to zero. That was a huge fraction of the combined capital of those banks (Malkin 1988, p. 107). Foolishly all the US banks had made those loans (with recycled petrodollars) without credit checking, or collateral, taking the risk (and profits) themselves rather than passing it on to other investors.

It is worth recording that in 1976 Arthur Burns, then head of the Fed, had asked the banks to be more careful about foreign loans and was told—politely, no doubt—that the banks knew more about foreign banking than he did, so please shut up. Later British MP Harold Lever, who was also worried about the bank loans to developing countries, was told by then Secretary of the Treasury, William Simon "Don't teach banks how to run their business."

When Mexico couldn't pay, Walter Wriston of CitiBank engaged in a marvelous cover-up to avoid having to declare to regulators the plain fact that their Mexican loans were "nonperforming." Wriston, in an article for the *New York Times* in September 1982, essentially declared that sovereign countries could never go bankrupt and that the borrowers (starting with Mexico) were welcome to borrow even more money to refinance their debts (Malkin 1988, pp. 108–109). Magic! Paul Volcker and the Fed came through with a new loan package for Mexico. So CitiBank et al., being too big to fail, was rescued by the US taxpayers. It was a dangerous precedent.

The "rescue package" for Mexico, was only the beginning. With oil prices falling after the 1980 peak, Mexico was in deep trouble. All the Latin American countries, and most of the third world, were being pinched badly by the FRB's tight money policy (to kill inflationary expectations). The policy worked but the pain was extraordinary. Overall, GDP in Latin America fell by 15 percent comparable to the Great Contraction the United States in 1930 to 1933. For the next several years Latin America was getting money from the US Treasury, matched reluctantly by the banks, just to pay interest on their debts. Overall, by the end of the 1980s, Latin America had repaid over $100 billion *more* than they had received in the first place. Incidentally, Walter Wriston's successor, John Reed, wrote off $1 billion in third-world debt, a small fraction of his bank's profits from the episode.

One of the things that George H. W. Bush will be remembered for, apart from the first Iraq war, is that in the presidential campaign of 1980, he correctly characterized Ronald Reagan's main thesis—that tax cuts would increase government revenue—as "voodoo economics." He was right, but Reagan won the nomination and the election with Bush as his vice president. Voodoo economics became mainstream. Now it is respectfully called "Reaganomics." Reagan cut the income tax rate for the very rich from 70 to 28 percent (Economic Recovery Tax Act of 1981) but didn't cut taxes for the middle class, who were supposed to benefit from the "trickle down." He cut corporate tax rates from 50 to 38 percent. Profits did increase, which helped to inflate the stock market. But spending, especially for the military, also increased by 40 percent. Hence the federal deficit tripled and the federal debt *increased* by $1.86 trillion during the Reagan years.

At the same time, the Fed was cutting interest rates from the peak of 25 percent in early 1981. Not surprisingly, many investors switched to equities. The long stock-market boom that began in 1982 greatly increased the wealth of the shareholders in general, but especially the professional investors (and raiders), as well as the brokers and investment bankers. This group mostly belongs in the top income decile, and constitutes a large share of the top 1 percent of incomes. Combined with tax cuts that differentially benefited the people with the highest incomes, and especially people with capital gains (from rising stock prices), the rich got a lot richer during the Reagan-Bush years (and since).

From 1982 through 2005 average incomes rose only slightly, but all the gains were only for the top 20 percent, whereas stock prices (as represented by the Dow-Jones average) rose by a staggering 1,400 percent. In the twenty years following, government debt as a fraction of GDP rose every year. During the Reagan administration there was no increase in government tax revenues although the supply-siders had confidently predicted one.

The junk bond market also opened up in 1982. Junk bonds were "high-yield" corporate bonds not rated as "investment grade" by the rating agencies. When government bonds were paying 6 to 8 percent, the junk bonds paid as much as 15 percent or more. They were bonds issued by "fallen angels" (bonds of formerly blue-chip companies in trouble), smaller companies that needed money for growth or acquisitions, or by growing start-ups that banks wouldn't lend to.

Michael Milken, a trader at Drexel, Burnham and Lambert, had made a study of these bonds in graduate school. He realized that despite very low default rates, they were often undervalued because lack of an investment-grade label from the ratings agencies made them seem "imprudent" to most conservative investors. He also noticed that those bonds tended to behave more like equities than like investment grade bonds because, when a company in trouble was near a turnaround, the prices of its bonds rose while the opposite occurred when a company seemed close to default. But when a default did occur, the bondholders could take over the company and make management and other "financial engineering" changes that have become the hallmark of the hedge funds and private equity firms.

Michael Milken had spent years unsuccessfully proselytizing for high-yield bonds but in 1982 the market for these bonds, mainly to S&Ls who needed higher yielding investments, began to boom. During 1981, the value of junk bonds issued was a mere $831 million *($1.6 billion$_{2011}$)*. By 1985, it was $8.5 billion *($16 billion$_{2011}$)*, and in 1987, it reached $12 billion ($21 billion$_{2011}$). The new business plan was "financial engineering." It required minimal equity and a lot of debt, justified by the promoters on the basis that interest on debt was tax exempt for companies, whereas profits paid out as dividends were "double taxed."

Leveraged buyouts (LBOs) became the new money game on Wall Street. The strategy of a "raider" was to buy a company with junk bond money. Once in control, the raider would force the company to take on new debt to pay off the junk bonds.[6] The next step was to sell nonproductive assets like land and buildings, cut costs by laying off older workers soon to be eligible for pensions, cut or eliminate health benefits, cut R&D, and restructure the pension plan by changing from "defined benefits" to "defined contributions." All of these changes would combine to increase short-term profits on the "bottom line." Then the restructured company, with a more attractive balance sheet, could be sold to the public via an initial public offering (IPO) at a much higher price. Needless to say the IPO was arranged with the help of the raider's friendly investment bankers. (The game became known, informally, as "buy, strip, and flip.")

The takeover game actually began with Victor Posner's hostile takeover of Sharon Steel Company, in 1969. But Posner simply "milked" his "cash cows" for his own benefit, by paying himself an enormous salary and selling undervalued assets to other companies that he controlled. Posner did no restructuring. The rebirth of the modern LBO began in 1982 with a new face. Wesray Capital was a limited partnership in which ex-Treasury Secretary and ex-Salomon managing director William Simon, and two partners, invested an estimated $1 million *($2 million₂₀₁₁)* of their own money. Wesray then bought Gibson Greeting Cards from RCA (which had become a conglomerate) for $58 million ($118 million₂₀₁₁) in cash (borrowed, of course) plus $22 million *($45 million₂₀₁₁)* in liabilities. They sold it in a year later in 1983 via an IPO for $330 million *($650 million₂₀₁₁)*. The costs were covered by junk bonds collateralized by Gibson's assets. Simon made a personal profit of $66 million ($130 million₂₀₁₁) from his investment of $333,000 *($675,000₂₀₁₁)*, a return of 2,000 percent. It was a powerful lesson on the miracle of leverage to the watchers on Wall Street.

It was Drexel bonds that financed most of the major corporate raids and raiders of the next few years, although other investment banks entered the arena eventually. The list of raiders financed by junk bonds (in alphabetical order) includes Marvin Davis, Asher Edelman, Sir James Goldsmith (in England), Samuel Heyman, Carl Icahn, Irwin Jacobs, Nelson Peltz, Ronald Perelman, Boone Pickens, Saul Steinberg (Lewis 1989, p. 260), and Ted Turner. Turner used his Turner Broadcasting Company (later CNN) to take over MGM, another merger creation. Both companies were losing money, but Turner succeeded by borrowing $1.4 billion. At one point he bragged that he owed $2 billion and quipped "Today it's not how much you earn but how much you owe" (Malkin 1988, p. 75). (Turner got his money back by selling off MGM's library of 3,800 films.)

All of these LBOs increased the indebtedness of the target firms, which is one of the reasons why corporate debt has grown so much since 1980. The public justification for this debt buildup was (1) that interest costs were tax deductible, in contrast to dividends, and (2) that the need to pay back debt would force "lazy" managers of "sleepy companies" to be more efficient than they had been previously. The US economy is still paying the cost of that mythology.

In 1986 the LBO boom accelerated. Over 3,000 mergers and buyouts took place in that year. Drexel, Burnham and Lambert made a profit of $545 million *($1 billion₂₀₁₁)* for the year, on revenues of $4 billion *($7.2 billion₂₀₁₁)*, making it the most profitable investment bank on Wall Street, for the first time (Lewis 1989). In 1987 Michael Milken paid himself $450 million *($790 million₂₀₁₁)*.

In 1988 the junk bond market was worth $200 billion ($360 billion$_{2011}$), mostly used for stock buybacks or ESOPs. But $44 billion ($77 billion$_{2011}$) was used for LBOs with management consent and $6 billion ($10.5 billion$_{2011}$) for hostile takeovers.

The most famous of the LBO advisors (and promoters) were Bruce Wasserstein and Joe Perella, who made $385 million ($675 million$_{2011}$) fees for their employer, First Boston, in the year 1987. Soon after (January 1988) they formed their own firm, which prospered spectacularly, especially from the RJR-Nabisco food-fag-fight. Wasserstein became famous for his "dare to be great" speech, by which he successfully persuaded many clients to bid more than they thought prudent. It was effective in driving up share prices. Wasserstein and Perella sold out to Dresdner Bank in 2000 for $1.4 billion ($1.8 billion$_{2011}$) a mere two years after forming their firm. Wasserstein's personal estate was worth around $2.3 billion when he died in 2009 (Cohan 2010).

The end of the first phase of the LBO boom was hastened by the October 19, 1987, stock market crash. The NYSE lost 554 points (22 percent of total value) in that single day. Some observers retroactively blame programmed trading, but that doesn't explain similar drops in countries where there was none. Contributory factors included the recent announcement of a US trade deficit at record levels, and the fact that P/E ratios were then much higher (20:1) than the historical average (15:1). Another possible contributory factor was a recent increase in long-term bond yields from 7.6 percent at the beginning of 1987 to 10 percent in the summer, making bonds a more attractive investment than stocks.

But the most likely trigger(s) for the crash were (1) a statement by US Secretary of the Treasury James Baker suggesting that the US dollar needed to fall (because of the trade deficit) and (2) passage of legislation in the House Committee on Ways and Means to disallow the deduction of interest payments on loans for the purpose of corporate takeovers. That legislation was introduced on Tuesday, October 13, and the market began to decline immediately. It passed the committee on October 15. By Friday, October 16, the market was down 10 percent, the largest three-day drop in fifty years.

Then, after the weekend, a lot of investors apparently decided to get out of the market simultaneously a virtual run on the market. The specialists on the floor of the exchange(s) could not match sell orders with buy orders for several hours. Trading had to be suspended on several exchanges to allow a catch-up. Surprisingly, the market bounced back immediately and continued to rise during the remainder of the year. (The anti-takeover legislation in the House Ways and Means Committee that was presumed to have triggered the crash was stripped from the final bill.) Damage outside of Wall Street appears to have been relatively small.

In 1988 the SEC sued Drexel for insider trading and Attorney General Elliot Spitzer of NY State threatened to use RICO, the antiracketeering law, to force Drexel to explain its dealings. Drexel pleaded *nolo contendere* and was effectively driven out of business by the backlash. It closed down in 1990. Milken was indicted by Federal Grand Jury on 98 counts of fraud and racketeering, mainly in regard to insider trading of stocks. (It seems insider trading is not illegal for bonds, but it is a crime for stocks). In April 1989 Milken pleaded guilty to 6 counts and was fined $200 million (*$360 million*$_{2011}$), plus payment of $800 million (*$1.4 billion*$_{2011}$) to Drexel and other investors hurt by his actions. He also spent some time in jail. (However, his net worth was probably $2 billion (*$3.6 billion*$_{2011}$) at the time, so he kept around $600 million.)

In 1989 the default rate for high-yield ("junk") bonds increased sharply from the 2.2 percent average for the period 1982 to 1988 to 4.3 percent in 1989. This triggered a 7 percent spread between the junk bond rates and the prime rate, and made high-yield (junk) bonds much less attractive. That ended the "junk bond" era. But the Dow Jones Industrial Average reached 2,700 by 1990 as compared to 824 in 1980 (and 777 at the lowest point).

In 1986 the FRB "reinterpreted" section 20 of the Glass–Steagall Act to permit Bankers Trust (and later others) to undertake underwriting and other investment activities as long as they remained under 5 percent of revenues. Chairman Volcker objected but was overruled by the Board. He resigned soon after. His replacement as chairman of the FRB was Alan Greenspan. The Bankers Trust decision became the basis for later allowing Chase Bank to underwrite commercial paper. Citicorp, JPMorgan Chase, and Bankers Trust argued for extending this opening to allow underwriting of municipal bonds and mortgage-backed securities.

The key financial innovation of the 1980s was not LBOs or "private equity," although they grew explosively during the Reagan years. Both of those things also happened in the late 1920s under the name of "investment trusts." Hedge funds were another growth sector. The first "hedge

Box 4.4
Closing S&Ls

In 1987 the Federal Competitive Equality Banking Act (FCEBA) created the financing corporation (FICO) to issue bonds to pay for the closure of S&Ls. According to Michael Lewis, William Simon bought a lot of the bonds at low prices and made a personal profit of $1 billion ($1.75 billion$_{2011}$) (Lewis 1989, p. 100).

In 1989 Congress passed the Financial Institutions Reform, Recovery and Enforcement Act (FIRREA). The Act created the Resolution Trust Corp. (RTC) to liquidate insolvent S&Ls.

fund" was formed in 1949, although the rapid expansion began during the Reagan years. Imitations followed. By 1968, there were 140 hedge funds in the United States, according to a survey by the SEC (Patterson 2010). George Soros's Quantum Fund was one of them. By 1990, hedge funds held $39 billion ($61 billion$_{2011}$) in assets (ibid., p. 313). By mid-2012, the hedge fund industry (including funds of funds) controlled $2.4 trillion in assets. However, the main change from the 1970s was "junk bonds" and the LBO phenomenon that increased the use of leverage.

Another key event of the 1980s was the Thatcher administration's "Big Bang" financial reforms in the United Kingdom (October 26, 1986). The previous system in the United Kingdom consisted of four large commercial clearing banks plus a number of "single-capacity" merchant banks, brokers, jobbers, and dealers. The London-based financial sector had been losing ground to New York, in the competitive sweepstakes. The Big Bang cut regulation, permitted brokers and jobbers to merge, and allowed the big banks to become "universal" by engaging in investment banking. It also permitted foreign institutions to compete with the established locals. Thatcherites wanted to put an end to what they thought was over-regulation (by the Bank of England) and to allow unfettered competition and "meritocracy" to flourish. US firms like Salomon Brothers, Goldman Sachs, Citibank, and Lehmann Brothers also flourished in London.

The result was that London's financial center, which had been losing out to competition from Wall Street, regained the international lead (temporarily) by 2000. It was the apparent success of the Big Bang that provided ammunition for Alan Greenspan and the US bankers who wanted to repeal the Glass–Steagall Act. However, while the Big Bang was profitable for London (for a while), it is not clear that the conversion of commercial banks like Barclay's, Lloyd's, Royal Bank of Scotland (RBS), and National Westminster (NatWest) into European-style "universal banks" was a good idea in the long run.

A few years later (1992) the Maastricht Treaty was signed by twelve European countries (E12), since expanded to twenty-seven countries (see box 4.5). The treaty did many things, but one of them was crucial to the financial crisis. It created the exchange rate mechanism (ERM) that was supposed to keep European exchange rates within narrow bands, based on the Deutschmark. The ERM was the basis for the common currency, the euro, which was finally adopted by a seventeen-country subgroup of the EU in 2000. The Treaty specified that Eurozone member countries should keep budget deficits below 3 percent per annum. However, it (mistakenly) allowed those countries to retain full control over their fiscal affairs, with no central mechanism for budgetary discipline, monitoring, or sanctions for violation of the rules. This omission has led to the recent (continuing) eurozone financial crisis.

Box 4.5
Maastricht Treaty

The treaty of the European Union (TEU), also known as the Maastricht Treaty of 1992 (where it was signed) converted the European Economic Community (EEC) from a common market into the European Union. It continued and extended the arrangements agreed in prior treaties, including European membership, common monetary and economic policies, European Central Bank (ECB), European Parliament, Court of Justice, and so on. The treaty also established a common currency, the euro, for seventeen of the European Union members. One of the key conditions was a commitment to keep deficits less than 3 percent per year. An important feature was the so-called exchange rate mechanism (ERM) to govern currency exchange rates in the Union. The euro became operational in 2000. Unfortunately, the treaty did not provide for central supervision with effective sanctions against cheaters, or for central control over fiscal policies. As a consequence a number of southern countries in the eurozone have allowed public debt to grow to unsupportable levels, creating a split between the northern countries in the group, and the Mediterranean countries. Ireland, Greece, Portugal, Spain, and Italy are currently being forced to undertake fairly drastic austerity measures (higher taxes, reduced public spending). Greece may have to leave the eurozone.

In 1992 Britain tried to join the ERM while keeping the pound above 2.7 Deutschmarks. But British inflation was much higher than Germany's and the only way to keep the pound so strong was to keep interest rates high. Yet, to do so hurt the domestic economy, especially the export sector. George Soros's thought the circle could not be squared, so his Quantum Fund made a 10 billion pound bet against the British Pound. The pound was strongly defended by the Bank of England, which spent 3.3 billion pounds in one day buying sterling at par. It was like Canute commanding the tide to go out. The problem was that the British economy was in recession and interest rates needed to come down. (It was the same challenge faced—and failed—by the US FRB back in 1931.)

On "black Wednesday," September 18, 1992, Britain withdrew from the ERM, and George Soros's Quantum Fund came away with an estimated 1 billion pound profit. It made Soros a hero in some quarters and a "vulture capitalist" in others. At present a number of Tory financial gurus are publically giving thanks that Soros did what he did, because it has enabled Britain to devalue the pound and keep its domestic economy growing rather steadily, up to 2008. It is also one of their arguments for remaining outside the common currency (euro).

Housing Policy: From S&Ls to Subprime Mortgages, 1989 to 1997

In January 1989 George H. W. Bush succeeded Ronald Reagan in the White House. Bush announced a program for "rescuing" the S&L industry by liquidating the insolvent thrifts with taxpayer money. The cost was estimated at $30 billion to $50 billion ($50–90 billion$_{2011}$). The Resolution Trust Corporation (RTC) was created to dispose of the assets of the S&Ls to be closed. The RTC was run by William Seidman. His approach, since widely imitated, was to split target institutions into "good banks" and "bad banks," selling off the assets of the latter and allowing the former to survive.

The number of S&L failures, finally, was 747 out of a total of 3,234, and the final cost of the RTC operation to taxpayers was about $40 billion ($60 billion$_{2011}$) through 1999 (McLean and Nocera 2010). The RTC evidently did a good job, given the situation it began with. However, it is worth remembering that the S&Ls were in trouble, in the first place, because they were unable to earn enough by investing their depositor's money in legitimate "investment grade" securities to cover their fixed costs. Hence, when depositors started taking money out for investments with higher returns, the S&Ls were easy targets for investment banks and real estate promoters. Many pension funds and insurance companies are in a similar situation today, thanks to the extremely low returns on Treasury bonds.

Bill Clinton defeated George Bush in the next election of 1992. He took office in January 1993. In that year, in response mainly to pressure arising from the cleanup of the S&L situation, the SEC introduced a new accounting rule applicable to bankruptcies, the "mark-to-market rule" (see box 4.6).

However, the MTM rule has later turned out to be too draconian, at least for banks. It defined in some detail how "market value" was to be calculated in cases where there was no real market. (This would be a major breakthrough in economics.) But lack of a proven methodology has not deterred the rule makers and accountants. Worse, the intersection of capital adequacy rules set by Basel I made MTM into a legal test of whether or not a bank is insolvent (Friedman and Kraus 2011, pp. 88, 147).

The problem was (and is) that "market prices" are not meaningful where the supply and demand for the asset in question is unstable or highly volatile—that is, not in equilibrium—or simply not measurable. Even where there is a secondary mark for illiquid assets, such as uncompleted housing projects, there is plenty of evidence that panics can (and have) reduced the market values of such assets far below any rational level. I do not think this is a problem that can be solved by accountants,

Box 4.6
Mark-to-market (MTM) rule

In 1993 the Securities and Exchange Commission (SEC) enacted an accounting rule via the Financial Accounting Standards Board (FASB): Rule 115. It was intended to increase the transparency of company reports, including banks. The rule, known as "mark to market" or MTM, required all corporations, including banks, to "mark" the assets on their balance sheets based on "market prices." This was intended to protect shareholders and bank depositors against fraudulent or "creative" accounting practices where assets (e.g., mineral rights) might be assessed at unrealistically high values.

Box 4.7
Toward more homeownership

The Federal Housing Enterprises Financial Safety and Soundness Act (FHEFSS) of 1992 required the Government Sponsored Entities (GSEs), Fannie Mae and Freddie Mac to devote a percentage of their resources to "affordable housing" for lower income groups. They were specifically directed to increase pooling and selling such loans. The Office of Federal Housing Enterprise Oversight (OFHEO) was created to oversee them.

In 1992 George H. W. Bush signed the Housing and Community Development Act, which amended the charters of Fannie Mae and Freddie Mac to reflect congressional desires respecting the increased availability of low income housing. "Affordable housing goals" were established, initially at 30 percent of total new housing units. Under the Clinton administration, that goal was raised, step-by-step, to 50 percent. Under the second Bush administration, it went up to 55 percent.

or lawyers. Critics of the MTM rule have been vociferous, and in retrospect, they have a very strong argument (Friedman and Kraus 2011).

In 1990 Fannie Mae lobbyists persuaded Paul Volcker to argue that the government-sponsored enterprises (Fannie Mae, etc.) should not need as much capital base as banks. The purpose was to increasing mortgage-lending capability. In the same year Fannie Mae got a new CEO, Jim Johnson, who engaged in intense lobbying against OFHEO and succeeded in effectively neutering it.

Adjustable rate mortgages (ARMs) had been in the market since the advent of mortgage securitization. The first US *subprime* ARM was issued in 1989 by Guarantee Savings and Loan, quickly followed by Long Beach Mortgage and others. Non-bank mortgage companies such as The Money Store, Famco, Option One, New Century, and FirstPlus entered the market, in competition with Fannie Mae and Freddie Mac. Country-Wide followed soon after and eventually took the lead. In 1991 investment in "private label" subprime mortgage-backed securities was a mere $10 billion ($15billion $_{2011}$). Not for long. In 1994 sales of subprime mortgages reached $40 billion ($57 billion$_{2011}$) mostly by mortgage companies (not banks). This figure grew to $60 billion ($80 billion $_{2011}$) by 1997.[7] The sale of subprime mortgages increased every year thereafter. By 2007 half of all the mortgages in the system (19.2 million) were subprime (McLean and Nocera 2010).

In 1992, the Federal Reserve Board (FRB), under Alan Greenspan, raised the revenue cap for banks to engage in non-bank activities from 5 to 10 percent. JPMorgan Chase was the first to get permission to underwrite securities. It was soon followed by the others.

In 1993, the Boston Federal Reserve Bank (BFRB) published a report "Closing the Gap: A Guide to Equal-Opportunity Lending." It recommended a number of policies to better serve lower income and minority groups. One of its recommendations was to loosen the income threshold for obtaining a mortgage. This report had an impact on the Clinton administration, especially the Department of Housing and Urban Development (HUD).

During the first Clinton administration, HUD was run by Secretary Henry Cisneros. He was a Latino (only the second to achieve such high public office) and former Mayor of San Antonio, Texas. Cisneros focused his efforts, during his four-year term, primarily on revitalizing public housing in cities. By the following year the Clinton administration adopted a formal goal of achieving 67 percent homeownership by the year 2000 (SCIT).

The Riegle–O'Neil Interstate Banking and Branching Efficiency Act (IBBEA) of 1994 repealed the interstate banking provisions of the Bank Holding Act of 1956, which had essentially prohibited banks from crossing state lines.

In 1994, Blythe Masters of JPMorgan Chase sold the first credit default swap (CDS) to the European Bank for Reconstruction and Development. It was to insure Exxon's credit line (loans) from the Morgan Bank. The London-based Financial Products Group (FPG) in American International Group (AIG) the world's largest insurance company took over the marketing of CDSs, and for the next fifteen years it was a money machine. By 2001, FPG accounted for $300 million ($375 million$_{2011}$) or 15 percent of AIG's profits (Lewis 2010, p. 71). These CDSs were essentially bets that the diverse borrowers would not default in concert. The costs of CDSs were based on the ratings (by the credit agencies, Moody's, S&P, and Fitch). AIG mistakenly assumed, at first, that the ratings were meaningful and that the premium payments were like free money.

It is important to know that a credit default swap (CDS) is different from an ordinary insurance policy in several important ways. The most important difference is that a CDS can be purchased by anybody wanting to bet that a firm (or a country) will not be able to pay its debts (Dodd 2004). A CDS is normally created for a bond, but the sum total of all CDS on a given bond, or package of bonds, can (and has) vastly exceeded the value of the bonds. These features made the derivatives tradable, but increased the potential loss to the insurer enormously. Just how much became clear in 2008 to 2009.

Indeed derivatives (not only CDSs) soon became a favorite form of investment for financial speculators in the late 1990s. Warren Buffet called them "financial weapons of mass destruction" in one of his letters to stockholders (Buffet 2002), and so it proved. In 1993 a German firm, MG Corp (subsidiary of Metalgesellschaft), reported a loss of $500 million (*$725 million*$_{2011}$) from speculating in derivatives, and the loss could go higher. But in the same year Chemical Bank reported profits of $236 million (*$340*$_{2011}$) from derivatives trading and JPMorgan Chase beat that with a gain of $512 million (*$740*$_{2011}$) (Watkins 2013).

1994 was the year of formation of Long-Term Capital Management (LTCM), a hedge fund with initial capitalization of $1 billion (*$1.4 billion*$_{2011}$). It was led by John Meriwether (formerly head of arbitrage at Salomon Brothers), with Robert Merton, Myron Scholes, Jon Corzine, and other "quants." Their methodology was based on the Black–Scholes–Merton capital asset pricing model (published in 1973; see chapter 7 for more on the weaknesses of models).

More specifically, LTCM identified pairs of financial assets that should theoretically have had equal value (e.g., long-term bonds with the same expiration date, issued a few months apart or in different places). Then they would look for slight differences in the current prices of those assets. In a rational world, more often than not, the overpriced one will decline and the underpriced one of the pair will increase. So LTCM would "long" the underpriced one and "short" the overpriced one simultaneously, keeping the total net investment near zero to make a tiny profit. But this can become a large profit, thanks to leverage.

In an irrational world the discrepancy between the overpriced and underpriced sides of the supposedly matched pair of assets can increase, rather than decrease, and this can continue for some time. Under these bizarre conditions the fund has to find more money to cover both the long position and the short position simultaneously. In practice, the net cost is no longer zero. As the spread increases, the cost of the bet gets expensive.

Box 4.8
More tax cuts for real estate

The Taxpayer Relief Act (TRA) of 1997 increased the capital gains tax exclusion on house sales (per couple) from $125,000 to $500,000 (*$175,000–675,000*$_{2011}$). This greatly encouraged the purchase of second homes and vacation homes by the well-to-do. It helped to create a mini-boom on the west coast metro areas (California, Oregon, Washington) where inflation adjusted housing prices increased at the rate of 10 percent per year in 1998.

In 1996 the FRB, under Greenspan, lifted the revenue cap for banks to engage in non-bank (i.e., investment) activities from 10 to 25 percent, effectively nullifying a key element of the Glass–Steagall Act of 1933. There was some intellectual backing for this action. For instance, an influential academic book published at that time supported "universal banking" in the United States on the basis of economies of scale, scope, proprietary information, and market power (Saunders and Walter 1994). (The authors have subsequently modified their ideas.)

In the summer of 1997 Sanford (Sandy) Weill, CEO of Travelers Insurance Company, sought to merge with JP Morgan Bank, the merger failed at the last minute. Travelers then bought the brokerage Smith-Barney. Starting in 1998 every large bank acquired its own security underwriting and brokerage department. Bankers Trust purchased investment bank Alex Brown and Co., just before it was acquired, in turn, by Deutsche Bank). It was the first such banker-broker combination. First Boston was acquired by Credit Suisse. Wasserstein and Perella was acquired by Dresdner Bank. Later in the year the FRB, under Greenspan, eliminated many restrictions on "section 20 subsidiaries" and stated that the risks of letting commercial banks into the brokerage business were "manageable."

The stage was set for banks to create and trade securitized assets of all kinds, including (especially) mortgage-based bonds and all the derivatives and swaps based on them. Wall Street cheered. The immediate consequence was a number of other mergers. On May 4, 1998, Travelers Insurance and Citicorp agreed to merge, with a $70 billion (*$92 billion*$_{2011}$) stock swap. The merger was illegal according to the Glass–Steagall Act of 1933, so the FRB, led by Alan Greenspan, provided a one-year exemption to get the law changed. Later in the year Travelers bought Salomon

Brothers for $9 billion (*$13 billion*$_{2011}$). Salomon Brothers then merged with Travelers-owned Smith-Barney to form Salomon-Smith-Barney.

In 1997 JPMorgan Chase created a package of CDSs and called it Broad Index Secured Trust Offering (BISTRO) a precursor for a later invention called a synthetic collateralized debt obligation, or "synthetic" CDO. Since the CDSs are tradable, as noted above, they have market value (in principle) and a bundle of them, constructed from different loans, from student loans, credit card debt, auto loans, aircraft leases, prime mortgages, and, eventually, subprime mortgages can be treated as a forms of wealth. A combination (sum) of a CDO and its synthetic mirror image has a constant value equal to that of the original CDO, so a synthetic CDO is actually the complement of a standard CDO. When the standard CDO loses value, the synthetic mirror image gains value by the same amount. It is the equivalent of a credit default swap for a CDO, and it is constructed from credit default swaps for the underlying bonds. But the interesting (and dangerous) feature of this invention is that synthetic CDOs can also be used as collateral to finance still more real estate (or other) loans, as well as other activities, such as leveraged buyouts (LBOs).

In late 1997 Freddie Mac, with First Union Capital (which later became Wachovia) and Bear Stearns, issued securitized CRA loans for the first time, in the amount of $385 million (*$510 million*$_{2011}$). Those loans were guaranteed by Freddie Mac. They were not subprime, but the proverbial foot was in the proverbial door. The need to meet CRA targets was becoming one of the drivers of GSE (Fannie Mae and Freddie Mac) policy.

In 1998 JPMorgan Chase approached Joseph Cassano, who by then was head of the Transaction Development Group in American International Group (AIG), with a proposal to package credit default swaps (CDS) and sell them, as insurance, to buyers of the mortgage-backed

Box 4.9
Creating a benchmark and a tool for cheaters

The Community Reinvestment Act (CRA) rules were modified in 1995 to break down home loan data by neighborhood, income and race, providing evidence for community groups to complain about discrimination. This was a powerful prod for Fannie Mae and Freddie Mac. It also gave the investment banks data and tools they were able to use, later, for purposes of "gaming" the ratings agencies, as discussed later.

securities already on the market, mainly S&Ls. Cassano agreed to the deal. However, until late 2004, credit default swaps (CDSs) for subprime mortgage-based bonds accounted for a tiny percentage of AIG's sales. The market for these swaps had been exempted from regulation since 1993, although the Commodity Futures Trading Commission (CFTC) claimed jurisdiction as part of its original mandate.

The LBO boom continued and grew since 1992 under the name "private equity," but with less emphasis on quick turnover. The equity contribution to LBOs began to increase from the earlier levels, with somewhat less reliance on debt financing. The totals kept growing. Private equity investment in 1992 was only $20 billion (*$30 billion*$_{2011}$); it increased to over $300 billion (*$385 billion*$_{2011}$) by 2000 (the peak year for that form of investment). The later decline in deal-making may have been due to higher prices and fewer attractive targets, partly because CEOs of target companies had learned ways to fend off corporate raiders, notably by means of stock "poison pills" and "buybacks." But those devices also tended to increase stock prices and corporate debt in tandem.

Basel Backfires: Japan and the Asian Crisis

Japanese banks found a new financial game in 1985 to 1988. They created a bubble of their own by investing massively in Tokyo (and other central city) real estate. In consequence the price of urban land skyrocketed in the late 1980s, accompanied by the Nikkei stock average. Both indexes peaked in 1989, at very high levels. Japanese capital exports also peaked in 1989 when Japanese investors bought Rockefeller Center and other famous US landmarks. At the peak of the frenzy, home mortgages in Tokyo were being issued with 100-plus year repayment schedules. At the peak, Japanese land (mostly commercial property in the major cities) was allegedly worth five times as much as all the land in the United States. It accounted for 70 percent of Japanese net worth (Werner 2005).

The Japanese real estate bubble ended suddenly, almost certainly because of a ruling by the BIS in Basel (usually referred to as Basel I). Before this ruling it was the practice to measure capital adequacy in terms of a simple ratio of total assets (loans outstanding) to capital, regardless of the riskiness of the assets. In June 1988 BIS recommended that all commercial banks in the world should risk-weight their assets and set the ratio of capital base to risk-weighted assets at 8 percent or more (Friedman and Kraus 2011, pp. 62–63). A bank with a lot of risky assets (according to the rating agencies) would need more capital in its base than a bank with safer assets.

All assets were divided by the BIS into four categories ("buckets"). Cash and government bonds were deemed to be "risk free" and required no capital base. Securities from "public sector entities" (e.g., Fannie Mae) were deemed to be a little bit risky, and risk-weighted at 20 percent. Whole mortgages (unsecuritized) were risk-weighted at 50 percent along with gold bullion, and all the rest were considered to be 100 percent risky.[8] An asset in the riskiest (100 percent) "bucket" needed a capital base equal to its value. An asset in the 50 percent bucket needed a capital backing of 50 percent of its value, while an asset in the 20 percent bucket needed a backing of only 20 percent of its value. Adding up the backing needed for all of the bank's assets could not be less than 8 percent of the total, corresponding to a maximum leverage of 12.5 to 1 (Bank for International Settlements 1998, 2006).

Basel I was especially hard on the Japanese banks, which had most of their assets in the riskiest category, resulting in much higher leverage than Basel I allowed (more like 20 to 1; Epstein 1983).[9] To reach the 8 percent level effectively forced them to cut lending by about half. Since then there have been hundreds of thousands of business bankruptcies in Japan. Moreover, after ten years, 25 percent of all Japanese bank loans were still "nonperforming." Japan entered a twenty-year recession, during which neither fiscal nor monetary policy has been effective (Werner 2003, 2005). Japanese land prices and stock market prices declined more or less continuously from 1990 to 2010, even though Japanese exporters have continued to thrive (driving the value of the yen higher and higher against the dollar; the strong yen policy changed in 2012).

Russia and other Asian countries, including Thailand, Indonesia, Philippines, and South Korea but not China, also encountered financial problems during the mid-1990s. However, the timing is essentially coincidental. The causes were different and much more closely related to the Latin American crises of 1980 to 1983. All of those countries (unlike Japan) required IMF intervention; I discuss them in the next section.

The Basel I accord on capital adequacy in 1988 was a game changer in another way. This was because it enabled some would say forced the banks to engage in "regulatory arbitrage." They did this by shifting loans between "buckets" to maximize leverage (and profits) while satisfying the BIS capital adequacy rules. Business loans (with a risk weight of 100 percent) might yield a leverage factor of 10, whereas direct mortgage loans yield a leverage factor of 20 and loans to government sponsored entities (GSEs) have a leverage factor of 50. For a plausible rate of return on lending (5 percent) and interest paid to depositors (2 percent) yielding a spread of 3 percent an average leverage of 20 is needed. Hence low-leverage business loans need to be "balanced" by high leverage loans. Friedman points out that profits are greater by a factor of 5 for loans to GSEs as compared to business loans (Friedman and Kraus 2011, pp. 64–65).

Another, no doubt unintended, consequence of Basel I was that banks could sell "whole" mortgages to Fannie Mae and Freddie Mac (risk-weighted at 50 percent) and buy back securitized mortgage packages (risk-weighted 20 percent). This had the effect of increasing the banks' lending capacity, and profits, by 250 percent. Banks could not afford *not* to play this game, whether or not they maximized leverage to the absolute limit. This was a major reason why Fannie Mae and Freddie Mac ended up with so much government guaranteed debt. A further consequence of Basel I was that when fully effective (after 1992), it resulted in a contraction of credit for individuals and firms, especially small and medium businesses (big firms don't need banks for credit) and an increase in credit for housing. Thus Basel I explains a lot of what was happening later, from 2002 through 2007.

The IMF and the Asian and Russian Financial Crises, 1997 to 1998

In early May 1997 the Southeast Asia financial crisis began with a speculative attack on the Thai currency, thanks to doubts about the ability of Thai borrowers to repay dollar-denominated loans. On May 14, the Thai Central Bank devalued the currency by 20 percent. It wasn't enough. By December, the Thai government agreed to close fifty-six insolvent finance companies; 30,000 white-collar workers were to lose jobs. The trouble spread. The Malaysian Central Bank intervened to prop up the Malaysian currency (successfully). Malaysian Prime Minister Mahathir Mohammad blamed speculators (and Soros's Quantum Fund, in particular). Interest rate speculators using highly leveraged derivatives were certainly at work, but it was not necessarily Soros.

Soon after, the Philippines and Indonesia were dragged into the maelstrom as short-term lenders got nervous. Speculators attacked those currencies. In July, the Philippine peso was devalued and the IMF promised a $1 billion (*$1.3 billion*$_{2011}$) loan, the first use of its emergency funding mechanism. Indonesia widened its trading exchange rate band with a partial flotation. That wasn't enough. A few days later the rupiah was free-floated and declined by 30 percent. Indonesia then asked the World Bank and the United States for help. Meanwhile, in August, Thailand agreed to tough IMF terms for a $17 billion (*$23 billion*$_{2011}$) bailout loan.

Speculators next attacked the fixed exchange rate of the Hong Kong dollar, betting that it could not be kept within the official band. On October 23, 1997, Hong Kong raised bank lending rates 300 percent to stop the threatened run. The H-K stock market index fell 10.4 percent, destroying $29.3 billion (*$4 billion*$_{2011}$) in (paper) wealth. Shorts on the stock market made a fortune. On October 31, the IMF agreed to a bailout loan for Indonesia, that (later) reached $40 billion (*$53 billion*$_{2011}$). The government closed sixteen insolvent banks. On the same day the IMF delayed a previously promised $700 million (*$940 million*$_{2011}$) loan to Russia for failure to implement previously promised reforms. Russia had been borrowing too much abroad and also paying for the Chechen war and reconstruction, at an estimated cost of $5.5 billion (*$7.5 billion*$_{2011}$). Exchange rate speculators then attacked the ruble.

The troubles reached Japan and Korea. On November 3, 1997, Sanyo Securities (Japan) went bust owing $3 billion (*$4 billion*$_{2011}$), due to losses in derivatives. Two weeks later Hokkaido Takshoku Bank (one of the top ten), collapsed due to bad loans and losses in derivatives. On the same day the Bank of Korea stopped trying to support the currency (won), and let it fall below 1,000 won per dollar, a record low. Exchange rate speculators made another killing. On November 21, South Korea requested IMF aid. (The government was heavily criticized by nationalists.) The next day (November 23) President Clinton said that the Southeast Asian economies were experiencing "a few glitches" on the road." On December 3, the IMF quickly approved a $57 billion (*$75 billion*$_{2011}$) bailout package.

On December 18, South Korea elected Kim Dae Jung, the first president from the opposition party. On December 23, the World Bank released the first $3 billion (*$4 billion*$_{2011}$) part of a $10 billion (*$13 billion*$_{2011}$) package, to help the S. Korean, economy. On December 24, the IMF agreed to early payment of another $10 billion to forestall default on long-term debts; South Korea agreed to the IMF conditions, including opening domestic Korean markets to imports. The labor unions were very unhappy about all of it. On May 5, 1998, the unions called a two-day strike.

On January 8, 1998, President Suharto of Indonesia presented his budget. The rupiah dove to new lows. Four days later, Peregrine Investments (Hong Kong), the largest private investment bank in Asia, filed for bankruptcy due to nonperforming Indonesian debts. On January 15, the IMF signed a new agreement with Suharto. Conditions included the elimination of monopolies held by his cronies. Food prices increased 80 percent, and the rupiah hit 12,000 per dollar. On March 11, Suharto was sworn in for his seventh 5-year term. On May 4, the IMF authorized a payment of $1 billion (*$1.3 billion*$_{2011}$). Two weeks later Suharto resigned, after two months of turmoil. On May 22, the IMF suspended payments once again, pending "stabilization."

From October 1, 1997, to August 17, 1998, the Russian central bank spent $27 billion (*$36 billion*$_{2011}$) to buy rubles so as to keep the ruble in the desired band between 5.7 and 7.1 per dollar. The Russian crisis began in early 1998 when reserves began to drop precipitously due to excessive borrowing of dollars. It reached a crisis point on March 23, 1998, when President Yeltsin fired his entire cabinet. On May 27, the Russian Central Bank tripled interest rates (to 150 percent) to avert collapse of the ruble. It was too late. On June 1, the Russian stock market crashed, and Russian hard currency reserves fell to $14 million (*$18.5 million*$_{2011}$).

The contagion finally reached New York. On August 3, 1998, the DJIA plunged 300 points, its third biggest loss. On August 11, the Russian stock market collapsed again, and trading was suspended. On August 17, Russia allowed the ruble to float, and it fell from 7 to the dollar to 21 to the dollar by September 1. The Duma also suspended foreign debt payments for ninety days. Latin American markets plunged again, on fears of further devaluation. On August 31, the DJIA dropped 512 points, the second worst loss in history, apparently due to turmoil in world markets, but especially in Russia. All over the world investors dumped stocks and moved into bonds, especially US government bonds, for safety. Between July 1 and October 1, 1998, the DJIA fell 2000 points (25 percent) and the Nasdaq fell from 2,900 to 1,450 (50 percent), as seen in figure 4.2.

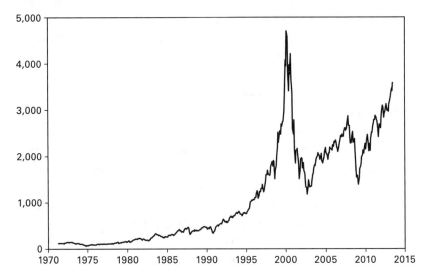

Figure 4.2
NASDAQ-100 from February 1971 to July 2013 (end of month close)

On June 24, Prime Minister Kirienko submitted a new reform plan to the IMF; the IMF released $670 million (*$890 million*$_{2011}$) that had previously been suspended. On July 6, the Russian stock market dove again; the cause was blamed on its failure to privatize the state owned oil company. On July 13, the IMF finally agreed in principle to a package of $23 billion (*$30.5 billion*$_{2011}$) for Russia, and the stock market recovered. On July 17, the Russian Duma approved part of Yeltsin's proposed tax reforms, but the left-wing parties in the Duma rejected higher sales and land taxes. Yeltsin vetoed tax cuts and increased taxes by edict. This persuaded the IMF to give final approval of the $22.6 billion (*$30 billion*$_{2011}$) loan package.

On September 7, 1998, the Russian Duma rejected Yeltsin's prime minister designate and the Russian Central Bank chairman resigned. On September 17, Russian investors and lenders estimated their losses at $100 billion (*$130 billion*$_{2011}$). As it happened, this was the nail in the coffin of Long-Term Capital Management (LTCM), which, but for a timely intervention by Bill McDonough of the New York Fed (mentioned later) nearly triggered a worldwide financial collapse.

On September 23, the Japanese Nikkei declined to a twelve-year low. On November 4, the DJIA dropped another 216 points, and Congress blocked US funding for the IMF. Later it was discovered that $5 billion ($6.6 billion$_{2011}$) of the IMF money designated for Russia had been stolen before reaching its intended destination, just like the funds loaned to Argentina, Mexico, and Venezuela back in the 1980s. Nobody has undertaken a serious investigation of what happened, which is probably all we need to know. According to the World Bank the cost of IMF bailouts in terms of the fraction of GDP lost, were as follows: Korea (60 percent), Argentina (55.3 percent, Malaysia (45 percent), Thailand (45 percent), Chile (44.3 percent), Japan (24 percent), Mexico (19.3 percent), Venezuela (18 percent), and Spain (16.8 percent). In contrast, the United States only lost 3.7 percent of GDP as a consequence of the bailouts of the US thrifts.

The main lesson of the Asia crisis should have been that foreign currency loans to local real estate developers in rapidly growing economies are a sure recipe for disaster. In every one of the countries involved (as well as China) there was a huge disparity between the amount of commercial and residential floor space being planned and under construction and the local demand for housing, hotels, and offices. But the IMF has no authority or jurisdiction over the Western banks making the foolish loans (still without adequate credit checks), even though it is expected to bail them out when the loans go bad. The losers are rarely the banks. They are the local people who lose jobs when foreign financing suddenly disappears and local investors who lose savings when projects are canceled.

A Failed Attempt to Regulate the Derivatives Market

Alan Greenspan and other Wall Street gurus have been great fans of "spreading the risk." That sounds like a good idea. Who could object? The most popular scheme for spreading the risk was to create and sell (or buy) derivatives, such as credit default swaps (CDS) and interest rate swaps. The credit default swap (CDS) was invented by JPMorgan Chase and supposed to be a kind of insurance against the risk of default. However, unlike conventional insurance policies, *there was no requirement that that buyer of a CDS had to be the owner of the asset being insured.* This had two dangerous consequences: (1) it made the CDS derivatives tradable and (2) there is no limit to how many CDSs could be created for a given asset. Some assets (e.g., oil tankers) were "insured" many times over.

That potential amounts to leverage by another name. This means that the market value of the CDSs on a given asset could be many times greater than the market value of the asset itself. Moreover the CDSs—having market value—can be used as collateral for loans. Hence the sale of CDSs and other swaps is a way of creating money by creating a new form of collateral for debt (and potential liability). Since these derivatives are tradable, they are not only traded in enormous numbers; they became objects of speculation and "weapons of mass destruction" in Warren Buffet's memorable words.

In 1997 President Clinton appointed a lawyer named Brooksley Born as the new chair of the Commodity Futures Trading Commission. The CFTC is the federal agency responsible for supervision of the over-the-counter (OTC) futures and commodity options markets. Born had been a senior partner of Arnold and Porter, a big Washington law firm, with a lot of experience in financial fraud cases. She soon became seriously worried about the unregulated market for derivatives, such as the credit default swaps (CDSs) introduced by JPMorgan Chase. It is important to realize that swaps (not only the famous credit default swaps) are *futures*, which, unlike equities, are purchased almost entirely with borrowed money. (The margin required for buying a futures contract is typically in the range of 4 to 7 percent of the nominal value of the asset.)

From the end of 1994 to the end of 1996 the "notional value"[10] of CDS contracts sold increased by 154.2 percent and the number of swaps jumped 46 percent in the first half of 1997 as compared to the previous six months. The rate of growth was scary. Looking ahead from 1997, the notional value of CDSs that existed in 2003 amounted to $2.69 trillion. The notional value of CDSs in mid-2007 was $62.2 trillion, compared to the total value of household real estate in that year, which was $19.9 trillion. The growth rate was truly explosive, a factor of 23 in four years. But that was later.

Here some explanation is needed for the nonspecialist. To some extent the numbers cited above are misleading. They tend to get cited in the media because of their shock effect. Actually the total face (notional) value of all derivatives, not just CDSs, on October 15, 2008, was $596 trillion. This cornucopia consisted of a variety of options such as interest rate swaps and indexes. But the total value of all global financial assets at that time (according to McKinsey) was a "mere" $167 trillion.

How is this possible? The answer is that the notional value of a derivative is the value of the asset on which it is based, not its market value. Derivatives are options. The value of an option is not the same as the value of the asset. Thus the option to buy a tanker of oil at a fixed price is not the same as the value of the oil in that tanker. If the market price is lower than the option price, the option is worth nothing at all. But if the price of oil should happen to spike, the option might be worth even more than the present value of the asset itself. Underlying assets in fact are counted more than once because different derivatives are based on them. Some derivatives are based on the prices of other derivatives. Evidently derivatives are well suited for leverage. Some were undoubtedly created for just that purpose.

During the years 1994 to 1997, there were a number of instances of major losses and bankruptcies leading to lawsuits. The GAO published a report listing 22 major losses involved with derivatives trading (Markham 1997) while another report listed 360 cases of significant end-user losses from derivative transactions (General Accounting Office 1997). In 1994 Orange County, California, one of the wealthiest counties in the United States went bankrupt because the financial officer of the county had speculated with county money in some of these complex derivatives from Bankers Trust that he didn't understand.

Two corporate clients won lawsuits against Bankers Trust in 1995, both claiming that they had not been correctly informed, or could not understand the risks involved. Procter and Gamble (which lost $157 million) obtained 6,500 tape recordings in which there were some embarrassing internal comments by Bankers Trust (BT) employees, such as "we set 'em up." Another described the contract with P&G as "a wet dream." These and other comments were damning evidence that BT salesmen were deliberately misleading their clients. The two cases received a lot of publicity that raised wider concerns about derivatives trading (Kirk 2009). They also supported the argument that the doctrine of *caveat emptor* has limits, even when the client is a large corporation with a presumably competent legal staff.

Then on October 22, 1997, the stock market swooned and lost 522 points, so President Clinton called the President's Working Group together (Kirk 2009). There was a worry that some parties might not be able to meet their margin calls, putting counterparties at risk and resulting in a potential domino effect on the economy (as happened in 1929). The lenders were the big banks, so the question at issue was whether any of the banks were going to be in trouble. The agency legally responsible for regulation of the over-the-counter (OTC) futures market was the Commodity Futures Trading Commission (CFTC) chaired by Brooksley Born. She wanted to do something. There were some disagreements about the jurisdiction of the CFTC. However, Born did not particularly care who did the regulating. She just wanted it to happen.

Early in the sequence, shortly after Born was appointed, she was invited to have lunch with Chairman Greenspan. She had spent several years, during her prior career at the Washington law firm Arnold and Porter, dealing with one of the most egregious cases of fraud in market history, the attempt by the Hunt brothers to corner the silver market. Yet Greenspan insisted that laws against fraud were not needed because "if a stockbroker was committing fraud, the customer would figure it out and stop doing business with that broker." Voila! This was typical of Greenspan's naïveté with respect to the need for regulation. He truly believed that the market for derivatives, like the whole financial market, would be self-regulating. Worse, he was utterly unwilling to let contrary facts affect his core beliefs. The Bernie Madoff revelation was still in the future.

After a long series of losses to nonfinancial clients since 1993, resulting in accusations of fraud and many fines, the CFTC proposed to re-examine its way of regulating the over-the-counter (OTC) market for derivatives. It was planning to issue a document called a *Concept Release,* which was essentially a set of questions that needed to be answered. The ideologically driven de-regulation cabal, Secretary of the Treasury Robert Rubin (ex-chief of Goldman Sachs), SEC Chair Arthur Levitt, and Fed Chair Alan Greenspan wanted to stop the CFTC from publishing its concept release. They called a meeting of the President's Working Group in Rubin's conference room at the Treasury, on April 21. The meeting was very tense "standing room only" according to her assistant, Michael Greenberger, who was with her. The apparent purpose was to browbeat Born into backing off, namely to not issue the proposed *Concept Release* (Kirk 2009).

At the end of the April 21 meeting, Greenberger recalls that Rubin said to Born "I am told that you do not have the jurisdiction to do this." She answered "Well, that is interesting. All my lawyers at CFTC have assured me that we have exclusive jurisdiction to do this." She was, of course, a lawyer herself. Thereupon Rubin replied "Oh, you're listening to government lawyers. You shouldn't be listening to government lawyers. You should be listening to private lawyers. All the private lawyers representing the banks say that you don't have the jurisdiction. Will you assure me that before you do anything about the concept release you will discuss this with the Department of Treasury lawyers?" And she said, "Of course."

But Rubin would not take her calls. Moreover he told his lawyers not to talk with her, hoping that she would get the message and go away. At any rate, after two weeks of waiting for a Treasury lawyer to call and set up a meeting, and after making a number of attempts to fix such a meeting herself, she gave up and went ahead with the release. It was duly printed in the *Federal Register* the morning of May 12, 1998. The gang of four (including Deputy Secretary Summers) immediately issued a joint statement obviously prepared in advance criticizing the CFTC. Their joint statement said:

We have grave concerns about this action and its possible consequences. . . . We are very concerned about reports that the CFTC's action may increase the legal uncertainty concerning certain types of OTC derivatives.

A few days later, Larry Summers, Rubin's deputy at Treasury, called Born and said, according to her memory:

I have thirteen bankers in my office. They say that if you go forward with this you will cause the worst financial crisis since World War Two. . . . Stop, right away. No more!

He went on and on about this so-called problem, and did so in a very rude and bullying manner (Goodman 2008). In retrospect, it appears likely that Robert Rubin was not really thinking about legal jurisdiction. Apparently most of the Wall Street lawyers had assured him, contrary to what he said to Born, that the regulation of financial derivatives was well within the mandate of the CFTC. What Rubin was really trying to do was to humiliate Born and to drive her out of office. A year later Rubin, Greenspan and Summers finally succeeded in that objective.

The bankers and Larry Summers, the famous economist, were evidently blind to the consequences of *lack* of regulation, which turned out (later) to be nothing less than the worst financial crisis since WWII. Then Greenspan, Rubin, Levitt, and Summers proposed a moratorium on the CFTC's plan to regulate OTC derivatives, and they continued their united opposition for months. Greenspan said:

Aside from safety and soundness regulation of derivatives dealers under the banking and securities laws, regulation of derivatives transactions that are privately negotiated by professionals is unnecessary.

Greenspan, like his mentor Ayn Rand was (and still is) unable to see that private transactions can have adverse public consequences affecting people not involved in the transactions. As I have explained earlier, these are called negative externalities. And they are commonplace.

Ironically, the collapse of John Merriwether's Long-Term Capital Management (LTCM) occurred right in the middle of this episode. In May and June 1998 LTCM lost 10 percent—$461 million (*$620 million*$_{2011}$) —from its capital, which had been about $4.7 billion (*$6.2 billion*$_{2011}$) at the beginning of the year. In July and August the losses accelerated, due to panicky stock and bond market reactions to the Asian and Russian crises. The costs of carrying the matched pairs of (supposedly) equal-valued thirty-year Treasury bonds rose dramatically due to freakishly rising yield differentials. LTCM needed to invest more capital, which had to be borrowed. By the end of August the cumulative losses reached $1.85 billion (*$2.4 billion*$_{2011}$). In September LTCM was forced to "unwind" a number of its short positions at a bad time and during the first three weeks of September its capital decreased from $2.3 billion (*$3 billion*$_{2011}$) at the beginning of the month to $400 million (*$530 million*$_{2011}$), less than 10 percent of what it had been in January.

What isn't obvious to the newspaper reader is that LTCM was exceptionally leveraged to 125:1. In other words, for each dollar of invested capital they had borrowed $125 from a bank. In fact they had borrowed from all the big banks on Wall Street, each unknown to the others (Kirk 2009). This means that the counterparties (banks) behind that last $400 million of remaining assets could have lost up to $50 billion in the worst case, if they were not hedged themselves. The nominal value of derivatives on the books of LTCM when it collapsed was in fact $1.4 trillion (*$1.9 trillion*$_{2011}$) (Dodd 2004).

At that point, on September 25, 1998, a bailout of LTCM was organized by Bill McDonough, chairman of the New York Fed. He called in a consortium of commercial banks and told them to take care of the problem. In their own interest, they had to do it because the fund still had $1.4 trillion (*$1.9 trillion*$_{2011}$) in paper on its books, for all of which the banks who had loaned the money were liable if things went more pear shaped.

The consortium raised $362.5 million (*$480 million*$_{2011}$) in exchange for 90 percent of the ownership of what remained of the fund. (The $400 million left to the partners was wiped out by their personal debts.) Merriwether's "quants"—Myron Scholes, Robert Merton, and his core team from the glory days at Salomon Brothers—were suddenly out of business. Later, when the Asian and Russian crises had eased off, the bets on market rationality that LTCM had made began to pay off again. So the deep-pocket banks in the rescue consortium got some (most?) of their money back eventually without suffering further damage (Kirk 2009).

It is ironic, to say the least, that Robert Merton and Myron Scholes (Fischer Black was dead) received the Nobel Prize in Economics from the Swedish National Bank, in 1999, one year after the collapse of LTCM. Nobody on the award committee seems to have noticed that their capital asset pricing model doesn't work when investors who are human don't behave like microscopic-particles engaged in Brownian motion.

On October 1, 1998, Jim Leach, the chairman of the House Banking Committee, held an oversight Hearing on the LTCM collapse. Rubin, Levitt, McDonough, Greenspan, and Brooksley Born were called to testify. Chairman Leach said he wanted "answers" and assurance that it could never happen again. Ironically, Alan Greenspan, the primary opponent of regulation, included this remarkable sentence in his testimony before the Committee:

Had the failure of LTCM triggered the seizing up of markets, substantial damage could have been inflicted on many market participants, *including some not directly involved with the firm, and could have potentially impaired the economies of many nations, including our own.* (Italics are mine)

This was a direct contradiction to his earlier statement justifying his opposition to the efforts of the CFTC to begin to think about regulation of the exploding derivatives market. He acknowledged in effect, without realizing it, that there really are externalities in the financial markets. He acknowledged that the risks taken by LTCM, with its 125:1 leverage factor, might have set off a global panic. You would think this might have encouraged the legislators to pause and think in their headlong rush to get rid of Glass–Steagall. It didn't. They didn't.

At this point the banks created a group called the Counterparty Risk Management [policy] group, mimicking the President's Working Group. The Rubin–Levitt–Greenspan one-year moratorium on regulation of derivatives was passed by Congress in the same month, October 1998. The Treasury produced a report in April 1999 that called for some mild regulation, but not enough. The Bank's group produced their own report two months later, basically to convince everyone that they would take care of the (supposedly nonexistent) problem themselves. The President's Working Group reported a year later in November 1999, after Rubin, Born, and Greenberger were all gone. That report influenced nobody and achieved nothing. Instead, the Gang of Four, plus Phil Gramm, did Wall Street's bidding, in spades.

The Office of the US Comptroller of the Currency issued a working paper in 2000 that defended the Gramm–Leach–Bliley Act on cost–benefit grounds. According to that working paper, "academic research"—probably a reference to (Saunders and Walter 1994) —had "demonstrated" that the "deadweight"[11] costs of regulation to the banks was "as great or greater" than the benefits received by the banks. What they meant by benefits was deposit insurance and the government safety net (the Fed). Looking back, I doubt that legitimate academic research could possibly arrive at such a bizarre conclusion today. Virtually none of the big banks would have survived the crisis of 2008 without that government safety net. Yet regulation is still regarded as a "deadweight loss" by many economists and virtually all bankers. However, as noted, the authors of the 1994 book previously cited have somewhat modified their earlier support for financial de-regulation (Saunders and Walter 2011).

On the last working day of the lame-duck Congress, December 15, 1999, a 262-page OTC deregulation bill was attached to the 11,000-page omnibus appropriations bill. Michael Greenberger, who was there, is convinced that no member of Congress ever read it, and that it was written on Wall Street, because it contains everything the banks wanted, and none of the controls that Brooksley Born's CFTC wanted (Kirk 2009). It became the Commodity Futures Modernization Act of 2000, which formally and totally deregulated the derivatives market (see box 4.10).

The JPMorgan Chase–AIG deal to sell packages of credit default swaps (CDSs) went into high gear at that point in time. Joseph Cassano, the head of the Transaction Development Group in the London-based Financial Products Unit of AIG between 1987 and 2008, was personally paid $280 million in salary plus $34 million in bonuses for his work (*Washington Post*, Business Section, June 30, 2010).

Box 4.10
End of Glass–Steagall

A law (unnamed)—written on behalf of the Gang of Four—was passed by Congress in March 1999 specifically to prohibit CFCT from regulating derivatives exchanged over the counter (OTC). It was aimed directly at Brooksley Born. She resigned three months later.

The Glass–Steagall Banking Act of 1933 was finally repealed by the Financial Services Modernization Act (Gramm–Leach–Bliley Act) of 1999. It was passed by a large majority of both Houses of Congress on November 15, 1999, but senator Phil Gramm of Texas took personal credit for it:. President Clinton seems to have regarded this law as a victory.

The Commodity Futures Modernization Act (CFMA) of 2000 explicitly allowed unregulated trading of credit default swaps (CDSs). The law also contained language written by Enron executives, explicitly exempting its energy trading on electronic markets from regulation (known as "the Enron loophole"). This law was strongly supported by Texas Senator Phil Gramm, whose wife Wendy (formerly chair of the CFTC) was on the Enron Board and who received $1.86 million ($2.4 *million*$_{2011}$) in compensation from Enron for her services. What services and to whom?

Another pertinent event in June 1999 was the issuance of a consultative paper, "A New Capital Adequacy Framework," by the BIS. Part of the motivation for this paper was a concern that the banks were not lending enough to businesses and individuals. It must have been obvious already by then that the Basel I risk-weightings were simplistic, but they were not formally revised at that time. The major innovation suggested then, and implemented later, was to use external credit ratings (from the usual suspects) as a way of classifying risk weights. (Basel II, which formalized this change, was published in draft form in 2004, and finally in 2006.)

The chief result of the consultative paper, and the research that led up to it, was the recognition that the Basel I risk classifications were much too crude, and that there was a need for finer and subtler differentiation. For example, government debt (sovereign bonds) should also be subclassified according to the ratings of external ratings agencies. Having concluded that external ratings should be used to distinguish degrees of risk, it followed that this principle should be applied to the "tranches" within a mortgage-based bond (MBS) from the highest "senior" tranche to the "mezzanine" tranches (both rated AAA), down through the lower (subordinated) tranches to the lowest (unrated) "equity" tranche.

On average, the AAA tranches constituted 79.3 percent of the subprime mortgages in the pool, followed by AA (6.6 percent), A (5.4 percent) BBB (4.3 percent), and BB (2.6 percent), leaving the unrated "equity" tranche (retained by the bank as an additional cushion or "overcollateralization"), which typically constituted 1.9 percent of the total number of mortgages in the pool (Ashcraft and Scheuermann 2008).

As explained earlier but worth repeating, *the credit ratings did not reflect degrees of riskiness of the mortgages within the tranches, but merely the order in which payments from the revenue stream were made.* The ideas set forth in the BIS consultative paper led to a specific change in the rules governing capital adequacy calculations in US financial institutions, known as the "recourse rule," issued in 2001 (discussed later in connection with the real estate bubble).

5

After the End of Glass–Steagall

The Dot.com Bubble, 1998 to 2001

The "dot.com" bubble was a fad, promoted by believers in the new, new digital age, who divided the world into those advanced "new economy" business thinkers who "get it" as opposed to those backward "old economy" business people who were still thinking in old ways. It was a celebration of the "information superhighway" and many of its uses.

The technological drivers of the bubble were microprocessors (notably the Intel 8086) and the high-speed data interchange system among a number of major US universities that was initiated back in the 1970s. It was sponsored by the Advanced Research Program Agency (ARPA) of the US Defense Department. As this Internet technology improved it became the platform for email, and a number of organizations joined the system to exchange data and information and to perform functions such as distance learning.

The next innovation was the World Wide Web (www.) invented by Tim Berners-Lee at the European research center CERN (1991). It is a set of nodes containing information in accessible form that can be accessed directly via the Internet. In 1993 the *Mosaic* web "browser" was released and quickly became a huge success among the digital cognoscenti. The dot.com boom can be dated from April 4, 1994, when the start-up firm, *Netscape* was incorporated by the entrepreneur Jim Clark (the founder of Silicon Graphics) and Marc Andreeson, a dropout from the University of Illinois. It was based on "search engine" software previously developed by Andreeson and others at that university (Lewis 1999). There were 25 million Internet users at the time of the release, and the number was growing rapidly. Predictably, the Netscape IPO was a spectacular success, for a while. Netscape held 90 percent of the browser market in the late 1990s.

The biggest financial winner of all in the 1990s was, of course, Microsoft and its founder Bill Gates. Microsoft (not located in Silicon Valley) and its proprietary PC operating system, *Windows*, dominated the digital ecosystem (until Google came along) by incorporating other software technologies such as *Excel* (spread sheets), *Word* (word processing), *Outlook* (email), and its browser *Explorer*. It was *Explorer* that displaced Netscape's browser and eventually killed Netscape as an independent company.[1] Netscape was eventually sold to America-on-Line (AOL).

More broadly, the dot.com boom was based on the new computer technologies, the World Wide Web (www) and genetic engineering technology. New and promising applications of the new capabilities were being created rapidly, especially in the universities and research centers of Silicon Valley. But from the financial point of view, the dot.com boom/bubble was based on the spectacular success (in a few cases) of a new business model based on the Internet. The business idea was to offer innovative Internet services simultaneously and free to millions of users, allowing markets to grow with unprecedented rapidity. Once a large group of habitual web-users with a specific interest were available, advertisers aiming at that group would sign up. The start-up costs had to be financed by venture capitalists (many located on Sand Hill Road, Palo Alto) and repaid from IPOs.

This was where the financial industry and Wall Street got involved. Jim Clark's next venture after *Netscape* was *Healtheon*, which raised $40 million by an IPO (Morgan-Stanley) in early 1999 (Lewis 1999). The shares were offered at $8, rose to $32 in the first day of trading, and sold at $120 per share in the summer of 1999, when *Healtheon* merged with Microsoft's *WebMD*. The combined firm is still doing well as a service to health professionals, though it has been criticized for favoring drugs sold by pharmaceutical companies that advertise online.

The genetic technology boom started in 1980 with the Genentech IPO (bought by Hoffman-La Roche in 2009), followed by Cetus in 1981(merged with Chiron in 1992, bought by Novartis in 2006), Amgen in 1983, Genzyme in 1986 (bought in 2011 by Sanofi-Aventis), and Gilead Sciences in 1992. Several start-ups every year followed that promising beginning. In 1986 alone, $900 million was raised by biotech start-ups. The 1990s saw even more money invested in the field by venture capitalists. Toward the end of the decade excitement grew to dizzy heights. It climaxed with the announcement of a "working draft" of the human genome in 2000 jointly by Craig Venter and Francis Collins. (The complete human genome was published in 2003.)

Genomics effect on the stock market may be indicated by the history of one IPO, Tularik, which was offered at $14 per share in early December of 1999. By the end of the first day, the price had risen to $20 per share. By the end of the month (and the year), it was above $32 per share. The peak price was $89.62 on February 18, 2000. (In 2004 Tularik was bought by Amgen.) But that was only one stock. Altogether, in the year 2000, 63 genomics IPOs raised $5.4 billion ($7 billion$_{2011}$). It is noteworthy that very few of those start-ups have survived.

Prices of Internet and information technology stocks rose extremely rapidly from 1997 to the peak in 2000, and fell just as rapidly from 2000 through 2002. According to an article in *Barrons* magazine, the stock-market losses from peak to trough were about $5 trillion ($6 trillion$_{2011}$), but most of those aggregate losses were matched by earlier aggregate gains. In that sense it was almost a "wash." However, in this case, too, there was a significant shift in wealth from ordinary Main Street investors to Wall Street. The financial institutions were first to invest as the prices went up and first to unload at the top. The investment bankers contributed significantly to the "hype," and they made money on all the IPOs, of course. The young entrepreneurs who created successful companies in Silicon Valley also made a lot of money. But the vast majority of start-ups (and their investors) did not get rich. In numbers the losers greatly outnumbered the winners. Overall, the top decile got richer (as usual) at the expense of the other investors. However, from the peak in 2000 to the trough in 2003, US household net worth declined from almost $45 trillion to about $41 trillion, a net loss of $3 trillion.

Among the corporate losers in the dot.com debacle in 2000 were the mobile phone companies that had bid much too high for third-generation licenses; the start-up telecom companies, like Global Crossing; as well as communication systems companies like Alcatel, British Telecom, France Telecom, Erickson, Cisco Systems, and Lucent (formerly part of AT&T) and Nortel that invested in high-capacity optical fiber communications channels and other equipment that remained underutilized for many years thereafter. The manufacturers of the optical fiber cables, such as Corning and JDS Uniphase, also suffered huge losses.

So much for the Hi-Tech contributions to the bubble. There was a regulatory contribution as well. The chairman of the Fed, Alan Greenspan, acknowledged that there was an equity bubble building as early as 1996. His famous remark about "irrational exuberance," at a Federal Open Market Committee meeting was in that context. Proposals had been made to tighten margin requirements for investors. Greenspan admitted that proposals to tighten the margin requirements would solve the problem. "I guarantee that if you want to get rid of the bubble, or whatever it is, that will do it." Evidently he didn't want to get rid of the bubble because he opposed tightening the margin requirements and did nothing to stop the bubble. (Later he said in several speeches justifying his non-actions that tightening margins would not have been effective, contradicting his earlier "guarantee" that it would solve the problem; see Blake 2008.) Without fear of regulation of derivatives, or tightening of margin requirements, equity prices "went into orbit" according to at least one critic who was there (Blake 2008).

Many IPOS were sponsored by investment banks, some of which raised money for companies that had no profits and some that had no revenues. *Infospace* and *Excite* were two examples of search engine start-ups that were overtaken by Google. Their struggles to survive led to problems that came to public attention later in the course of a criminal investigation by NY Attorney General Eliot Spitzer. At its peak in 2000, the 130 or so Internet companies that were publically traded had a nominal valuation of $1.3 trillion (*$1.6 trillion*~2011~) (Willoughby 2000). Then the bubble burst as bubbles do. The surviving winners from those days include America-on-Line (AOL, which later merged unhappily with Time-Warner), Yahoo, Google, e-Bay, and Amazon.

WorldCom, led by a charismatic character, Bernie Ebbers, was the result of 65 mergers, ending with the acquisition (for stock) of an established long-distance telephone firm MCI. It was a $37 billion deal, the largest to date in US history. Unfortunately, the management of World-Com was unable to integrate all the different acquisitions effectively, resulting in errors, confusion, duplication, crossed wires, and a poor reputation for customer service. Revenues began to decline around 2000. But the financial structure was a kind of bubble, depending on the rising stock price to secure the bank loans that were financing the growth of the company.

The WorldCom stock price peaked at $60 per share in 1999. Ebbers had used his personal stock to secure private loans of $400,000 and company stock to collateralize a $5 billion bond issue from Salomon-Smith-Barney. When rumors of losses began to leak out, he was in trouble. The full story of WorldCom's downfall is too long and messy to tell here, but in the end it turned out that the company had fraudulently understated debts and overstated assets by $11 billion. The company filed for Chapter 11 bankruptcy in July 2002. Bondholders got 35.7 cents on a dollar, and stockholders got nothing. Ebbers got 35 years in jail.

Enron was another major casualty of the period. It was the result of a 1985 merger of two energy companies. Like WorldCom it depended on hype and a rising stock price to secure its loans. The business plan of the company (energy trading) was greatly admired by some business analysts, and by the business press. It was named "The most innovative company in America" by *Fortune Magazine* six years in a row (1996 to 2001) as well as being named one of the 100 best companies to work for, also by *Fortune*. It was touted by many analysts right up to the day it imploded.

That happened because of a report by another analyst, Daniel Scotto, entitled "All Stressed up . . . and No Place to Go" that encouraged shareholders and bondholders to get out. Once the stock price stopped rising, the game was over. The banks demanded repayment and the money wasn't there. Part of the problem was that money-losing subsidiaries were put into offshore, off balance entities, so their losses, including losses on derivatives based on energy prices, were invisible. As an example, JPMorgan Chase, one of the largest derivatives dealers, had persuaded a group of insurance companies to write surety bonds collateralized by pre-paid natural gas swaps with an Enron special purpose (off balance sheet) entity (Dodd 2004).

The Enron stock price reached $90 per share in 2000, and fell to $1 per share by November 2001. The shareholders lost $11 billion. Like World-Com it resorted to fraud to hide debt in the form of partnerships off the balance sheet, and several executives went to jail, including Ken Lay, the chairman (and major contributor to George Bush's campaign for the presidency), and Jeff Skilling, the CEO. Arthur Andersen was the auditor. After Enron, Arthur Andersen was convicted of criminal behavior and lost its license, though the conviction was later overturned by the US Supreme Court. Before the collapse, on August 14, 2001, Paul Krugman had written a critical column about Enron in the *New York Times*. Ken Lay, the chairman of Enron, replied a few days later in a letter to the editors as follows:

The broader goal of Krugman's latest attack on Enron appears to be to discredit the free market system, a system that entrusts people to make choices and enjoy the fruits of their labor, skill, intellect and heart. He would apparently rely on a system of monopolies controlled or sponsored by government to make choices for people.

Those words could have been written by Ayn Rand herself (perhaps they were).

WorldCom and Enron were not the only companies caught in accounting scandals. Tyco and Adelphia were nearly as bad. Dennis Koslowski and Mark H. Swartz of Tyco also went to prison. There were lesser, but still serious, accounting scandals at other big companies including Health South, Rite Aid, Sunbeam, and even Xerox. The appalling truth was that "creative accounting" had become indigenous in many firms. The accounting firm, Arthur Andersen was broken because of the complicity of its auditors in several frauds.

One good thing that came out of the dot.com bubble and the Spitzer investigation was the Sarbanes–Oxley Law (see box 5.1). Although the law was viciously attacked and mocked by opponents of regulation, none of their predictions of doom came true: corporate profits have soared, and corporate financial reports are now much more trustworthy than they were previously. There have been no recent examples of accounting scandals at large public companies.

The NASDAQ index fell from an intra-day peak of 5,132 in March 2000 to less than a quarter of that level with a loss of $5 trillion in market value less than three years later (figure 4.2).

Box 5.1
Public Company Accounting and Investor Protection Act, aka Sarbanes–Oxley, signed into law July 30, 2002

> The Act created an oversight board and addressed a number of issues, mostly arising from the accounting scandals mentioned above. These issues included auditor independence, enhanced disclosure (e.g., of off-balance sheet transactions), and conflicts of interest by corporate officers and analysts. By far the most important innovation was the requirement that top officers, including CEOs and CFOs, sign the tax returns and personally take responsibility for the accuracy of the data being reported.

The Subprime Real Estate Bubble and the Oil Price Spike, 2000 to 2008

The collapse of the dot.com bubble after March 2000 caused a deep recession. Inflation was obviously not a problem. Control over interest rates is the Fed's primary macroeconomic policy tool. The Fed, still under the sainted Greenspan, cut interest rates eleven times from 6.5 percent (May 2000) to 1.75 percent (December 2001). During the next year several more cuts brought US prime interest rates down to 1 percent in 2002, where they stayed for two years (figure 4.1). Meanwhile the collapse of the dot.com bubble had left a gap in the range of available investments with potentially high payoffs. The huge lending capacity of the US banks needed another profitable outlet. Money couldn't sit in their pockets. It had to go somewhere. Some moved to places like Hong Kong and Singapore, for investment in the recovering Asian economies, and some went to China, which was growing fast. But China hasn't been very kind to foreign investors in terms of bringing profits back home. And the banks were understandably cautious about lending to developing countries after their experiences of 1998. The "answer" during the years 2002 to 2006 was the property boom, largely created by the FRB under Greenspan.

A change in the regulations for calculating capital requirements helped to kick it off. This change had been under discussion within the US regulatory agencies since 1994, but it was greatly accelerated by the previously cited BIS consultative paper published in 1998 (Bank for International Settlements 1998) The so-called recourse rule for capital calculations was, in most respects, the same as the scheme incorporated later in Basel II (Bank for International Settlements 2006). The differences don't matter here.

The real change was that all of the "tranches" of mortgages in a tower of mortgage-based securities (MBS) were rated in accordance with their position in the "tower," or order of payment. The ratings are not based on intrinsic quality but simply on the order of payment. Thus in every MBS there is always an AAA tranche (because it gets paid first), and so forth, down to the lowest "equity" tranche that gets paid last. What the recourse rule did was to cut the risk weight for the higher tranches and increase it sharply (to 100 percent) for the lowest (equity) tranche. This meant that a bank would have to have capital in its base equal, dollar for dollar, to the face value of the mortgages in the equity tranches of any MBS it held.

This was an attention-getter, even though it only applied to a small (roughly 2 percent) fraction of the total pool. It clearly invited risk arbitrage. Hence banks had a strong incentive to sell (i.e., get rid of) these equity tranches, because of the huge impact on capital requirements and consequently on lending and profits. It would have made economic sense for the bank to subsidize the sale in any one of several ways. I have no means of knowing whether this actually happened. What did happen was that from 2000 to 2001 the sale of non-bank mortgage-based bonds doubled and continued to increase every year through 2005 before turning sharply negative in 2007 to 2008 (Friedman and Kraus 2011, p. 69). Friedman thinks that this boom was largely due to the adoption of the recourse rule.[2] I think he is partly correct, though other factors were at work.

On June 17, 2002, President George W. Bush issued his own "Blueprint for the American Dream" as a part of his push for an "ownership society." It set a goal of increasing home ownership by 5.5 million through 2010, to be financed by tax credits, subsidies and $440 billion in Fannie Mae guaranteed loans to establish an entity called NeighborWorks America together with "faith-based organizations." It also encouraged loosening restrictions on home mortgages. One of the restrictions that were loosened was the traditional condition that existed when I was first buying a house, namely that a mortgage applicant should pay at least 15 percent or preferably 20 percent as a down payment. No more. The following year (2003) Alan Greenspan's Fed lowered the prime interest rate to 1 percent, the lowest in 45 years, to help the property boom and the associated construction industry employment, probably looking forward to the election of 2004. In that year US homeownership reached its all-time high of 69.2 percent [SCIT]

Quite apart from the recourse rule, the goal of increasing homeownership fit perfectly with the needs of the banks. To the banks, and the rating agencies (S&P, Moody's, Fitch), housing investments looked like a safe bet in 2002 to 2003. Back in the 1990s the default rate for home mortgages was negligible, and the prices of new houses had never dropped in the country as a whole (since WWII). Sadly a lot of bankers thought that events before WWII were irrelevant.) The prices of secondhand houses tended to follow the prices of new homes, and they were rising (see figure 5.1). Conventional home mortgages were yielding several points above

Sale prices in 1,000 USD

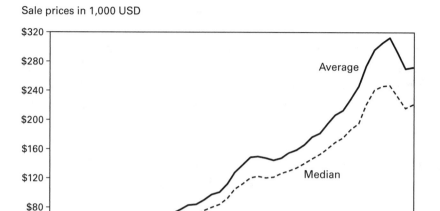

Figure 5.1
Median and average new home prices in the United States, 1963 to 2010. Data from US Census Bureau.

the prime rate at which banks could borrow from the Fed. Mortgage-originating companies sprang up to take advantage of rising prices by selling "adjustable rate" mortgages (ARMs) to marginal buyers with little or no equity to invest.

The most dangerous of the new mortgages, first offered by Quicken Loans in January 2005, were adjustable rate loans that allowed a purchaser to pay zero (actually 0.03 percent) interest for the first six months, later extended to two years, after which the unpaid interest (plus fee) would be added to the principal and the interest rate would revert to "normal." The sales pitch was that meanwhile the buyer's income would have risen enough to cover the difference. Or, if not, the house could be resold at a profit in the ever-rising real estate market. In reality, however, the majority of purchasers of this type of mortgage simply refinanced and then did it again with another two years of zero interest. There was even a variant offered by some mortgage companies where the mortgage price was set even higher than the house's actual value and the purchaser was allowed to take out the difference in cash. After two years the buyer could do it again and take out more cash (based on the higher market price.) It was a "free lunch" by another name.

The most aggressive mortgage sellers were the non-bank "private label" mortgage originators like HFC, Country-Wide, and The Money Store.[3] By 2004 there were a lot of them. A mortgage-originating company didn't care about the creditworthiness of its customers because it just sold the mortgages to one of the banks. (A large number of these mortgages were in fact originated without any credit check on the finances of the buyer.) They were packaged by the bank into mortgage-based securities (bonds) that the ratings agencies conveniently rated (from AAA to "equity"), carrying different interest rates. The bonds were then sold to S&Ls or insurance companies or pension funds looking for higher returns than other AAA bonds available. Of course, it took some time to do this, usually a month, so the banks always carried quite a bit of this paper on their books.

The Federal Reserve, under Greenspan, had no negative or cautionary word to say about the real estate bubble. Greenspan said repeatedly during this period that there was no problem because "house prices do not go down." He did not agree with those who thought a "bubble" was in progress. He called it "froth." Most incredible (to me) here is what he said in April 2005:

The rising prices that drove this money machine were driven, for a while, by excess demand. Where once more marginal applicants would simply have been denied credit, lenders are now able to quite efficiently judge the risk posed by individual applicants and to price that risk appropriately. These improvements have led to rapid growth in sub-prime mortgage lending; indeed, today subprime mortgages account for roughly 10 percent of the number of all mortgages outstanding, up from just 1 or 2 percent in the early 1990s. (Greenspan 2005)

Greenspan's last sentence was true. As for lenders being able to judge credit risks efficiently, and price them appropriately, he must have been seeing things from inside an ideological bubble of his own.

After 2005 the banks, starting with Goldman Sachs, created a new type of security that needs explanation. The equity tranches (combined with BBB and BB tranches) for a lot of mortgage-based securities were bundled together to create something called a "collateralized debt obligation" or CDO. This CDO receives whatever revenues the BBB, BB, and equity tranches of its component securities (MBS) get. (Remember that this group of mortgages is not lower in quality than others, merely last in line in their original securities.) So the new CDO also has an AAA tranche that gets paid first from whatever revenue stream there is, and so on down the line. It should be noted that the AAA tranche in a CDO should not include anything like 80 percent of the mortgages in it, contrary to an assertion by Lewis (2010). The size of the AAA share in a CDO does indeed depend on the assumed revenue stream, which depends in turn on the probability of defaults by mortgages in the original MBSs.

Of course, when the CDOs were first created, a revenue stream had to be assumed, and someone had to make a calculation as to the probability of default. For this they needed to know how the ratings agencies made such calculations. Although the ratings models and algorithms were supposedly secret, the bankers discovered that the ratings agencies were putting a lot of weight on the *average* credit ratings of the owners in each tranche of a pile of mortgages. So Goldman Sachs and the others constructed bonds with just enough mortgages with very high credit ratings so as to balance a number of very low credit ratings and still meet the cutoff. (They called these "barbell" bonds.)

There were other ways of "gaming" the accreditation agencies. This was possible because the rating agencies were using models and assumptions (that turned out to be wrong) and because nobody was really looking at the mortgages inside the bonds. One of their assumptions was that home prices would never decline on a nationwide basis, even though real estate prices had declined by 50 percent or more in the 1930s nationwide. As explained earlier, piles of BBB, BB, and equity bonds now re-labeled as CDOs got re-rated as new bonds, of which some fraction (presumably less than 80 percent) were rated AAA, based on the same argument, namely that their diversity meant that they the individual mortgagees would not default altogether.

As mentioned in chapter 4, it seems that from a cash flow perspective, the credit default swaps (CDSs) for a given CDO behave exactly like the complement, or mirror image, of the CDO. When one goes up, the other falls by the same amount. The owner of the CDS has to pay "insurance premiums" every six months, just as the owner of a CDO like an S&L had to pay interest to its depositors. The complement of the mirror image is a "doppelganger" of the original CDO, known as a "synthetic" CDO.

A synthetic CDO can be regarded as another sort of mortgage bond based on CDSs for a large number of bits and pieces of mortgages. It sounds safer, somehow. The credit-rating agencies in fact thought so too and gave the CDOs and their synthetic twins triple A ratings. That made them salable to clients. Michael Lewis writes that the CDO was "in effect, a credit laundering service for the residents of lower middle class America. For Wall Street it was a machine that turned lead into gold" (Lewis 2010, p. 73).

In 2005 and 2006 Goldman Sachs, followed by the other investment bankers, sold at least $50 billion of collateralized debt obligations (CDOs) to other banks, pension funds, trust funds, endowment funds, or insurance companies. And they persuaded AIG (and others, later) to take the responsibility for their inevitable future failure by selling credit default swaps (CDSs) in the same amounts. AIG sold those SDSs for ridiculously low prices (12 basis points or 0.12 percent of the face value), being under the illusion that a designation of AAA actually meant what most people on Wall Street assumed that the chances of default were 1 in 10,000 per year, while AA meant the chances of default were 1 in 1000, down to BBB, 1 chance in 50 (Lewis 2010, p. 51). Goldman made a profit off the top of these transactions of the order of $1 billion, and the creation of CDOs (and "synthetics") removed any limit on the magnitudes of the trades that followed because so little cash had to change hands (Lewis 2010, p. 77).

Meanwhile Fannie Mae and Freddie Mac (government-sponsored but private companies) were competing for market share with the non-GSE mortgage originators who were actively promoting subprime mortgages totally without regulation. In 2000, non-GSE subprime lenders sold $130 billion worth of mortgages, of which $55 billion was packaged as mortgage-based bonds. By 2004, the non-GSE mortgage sellers had automated the approvals process, essentially not bothering to do credit checks or income checks. By 2005, $625 billion of subprime mortgages were sold, and $507 billion of that total was re-packaged as mortgage-based securities. By that time interest rates were rising, but it didn't seem to affect demand for the product (Lewis 2010, p. 23). CNNMoney reported that $640 billion in subprime loans were made in 2006.

The conventional mortgage denial rate in 1997 had been 29 percent. By 2003, the overall mortgage denial rate dropped to 14 percent. Hardly anybody was refused and, as we found out later, a lot of the buyers had no jobs, income, or credit rating. The market for subprimes consisted mostly of marginal borrowers, especially those who could not qualify for conventional fixed rate mortgages. Speculation was also a major factor in the mortgage market. In 2005 and 2006, purchases for investment and resale accounted for 28 and 22 percent of mortgages, respectively, and mortgages for vacation homes accounted for another 12 and 14 percent, respectively. It is said that up to 85 percent of Florida condominium properties were bought for investment and resale. By April 2007, 13 percent of subprime loans were delinquent, over five times the delinquency rate for home loans to borrowers with top credit. By the fourth quarter of 2007, foreclosure proceedings had started against more than 2 percent of subprime borrowers.

The property boom was not limited to the United States. The two most outstanding (if that is the right word) examples were spectacular US inspired, bank-led property booms in Iceland and Ireland (Lewis 2011). In the United States the boom was focused especially on the "sunbelt" states, Florida, Texas, New Mexico, Arizona, Nevada, and California. In mainland Europe, it was primarily centered in Spain and Portugal, with other hot spots in some Alpine ski resorts, Italy, Cyprus, and Greece. It is no accident that the European debt crisis that exploded after 2008, and the associated unemployment crisis, are centered in the same countries.

Fannie Mae and Freddie Mac were buyers as well as sellers, probably as their part in the regulatory arbitrage game being played by the banks to increase their leverage. (I mentioned this in connection with the introduction of Basel I, back in 1988.) Fannie and Freddie could also explain this behavior in terms of satisfying their CRA income obligations. At any rate, their combined purchases of subprime loans from mortgage originators increased from $38 billion in 2002 to $90 billion in 2006.

In October 2004 the SEC effectively lifted the capital requirements for five banks—Goldman Sachs, Lehman Brothers, Bear-Stearns, Merrill Lynch, and Morgan Stanley—to permit them to increase their leverage for the purpose of investing in CDOs themselves, not just selling the securities. Some banks (Lehman and Bear-Stearns come to mind) increased their leverage as high as 40:1 by exploiting the low (20 percent) risk-weighting allowed by Basel I for government-sponsored securities. (JPMorgan Chase, Deutsche, and Credit Suisse stayed aloof).

Speaking of Fannie Mae and Freddie Mac, there has been a concerted effort on the part of Republicans to lay the whole blame for the crisis on Bill Clinton's decision, back in 1992, to increase the fraction of Fannie and Freddy loans to lower income families. It is true that he did push things in that direction, and that it was not a good idea. It is also true that both entities were involved in influence peddling. (Newt Gingrich, ex-Speaker of the House, and recent Republican presidential hopeful, worked for Freddie Mac as an "historian," he says, during those years, and was paid $1.6 million for his efforts.) But it is not fair to blame the government-sponsored entities (GSEs) for the housing crisis. It was the non-GSEs that originated most of the worst mortgages and almost all of the ones written before 2004.

In keeping with its mandate to provide more housing opportunities for lower income groups, CEO Franklin Raines (Fannie Mae) had initiated a pilot program in 1999 to test the water by offering mortgage insurance to people whose credit ratings were a little below the prior cutoff. But those loans did not result in major losses. After 2004 Fannie and Freddie were more aggressive competitors, but they still tried to maintain reasonable standards. The following quotation is from testimony by the chairman of the Financial Crisis Inquiry Commission (FCIC), Philip Angelides:

... the FCIC analyzed the performance of roughly 25 million mortgages outstanding at the end of each year from 2006 to 2009 and found that delinquency rates for the loans that Fannie Mae and Freddie Mac purchased or guaranteed were substantially lower than for mortgages securitized by other financial firms. This holds true even for borrowers with similar credit scores or down payments. For example, data compiled by the FCIC for a subset of borrowers with scores below 660 shows that by the end of 2008 far fewer GSE mortgages were delinquent than non-GSE securitized mortgages: 6.2 percent versus 28.3 percent. (Angelides 2011)

Quite a difference! Evidently the mortgage-backed securities based on GSE loans were far safer than securities based on non-GSE loans, exactly as the authors of Basel I had assumed back in 1988.

It seems that the average new home loan made in 2007 was virtually 100 percent of the nominal value of the house, meaning that *recent borrowers had contributed almost zero in equity.*[4] They had nothing to lose, and there was no penalty apart from a bad credit rating for just walking away. Quite a few small investors bought more than one house on these terms, in the hope of renting them in the short run and cashing in after a few years as prices rose and before the ARM interest costs became unbearable. What analysts who looked closely saw was that the mortgage loans were being paid off surprisingly quickly by refinancing.

During the entire housing bubble, Basel I was still the standard for risk-weighting. Basel II was only adopted by the European Union in 2008 but not until 2009 in the United States. (Basel III is currently being discussed.) It is not clear what difference it would have made, in any case.

Why did nobody see the catastrophe coming? Well, of course, some did. Michael Lewis has chronicled several examples in his book *The Big Short* (Lewis 2010). Goldman Sachs started betting on both sides of the mortgage business in late 2006, both selling CDOs to clients and betting against them. It also bought the top tier of some CDOs and paired them with CDSs so that the package was theoretically risk free, and could be kept off the books. Deutsche Bank was also on both sides of the game, selling CDOs to a German bank in Düsseldorf at the same time that Greg Lipmann was shorting them with management approval.

JPMorgan Chase avoided the cliff at the last possible moment. In September 2006 Jamie Dimon, CEO at JPMorgan Chase, told his troops to reduce exposure to subprime securities. Commerzbank in Germany also started to cut its exposure in 2006. But the bosses of the other big banks, except for Goldman Sachs, all of which combined commercial banking with broking and investment banking by 2003, did not see it coming. This was partly because the bosses were all from the pre-quant era, and none of them really understood why or how they were making so much money, or how leveraged they really were.

Every time some pessimist like Nouriel Roubini of NYU warned about the dangers of excessive leverage and bonds based on subprime mortgages, the Wall Street pontiffs (including former Chairman Alan Greenspan and new Chairman Ben Bernanke at the Fed) shrugged and repeated the standard mantra: that mortgage-based securities were safe because the prices of houses had never (since WWII) declined everywhere in the United States at once. Even the failure of the hedge fund LTCM in the late 1990s taught no lessons, nor did the collapse of Bear-Stearns in 2007. *New York Magazine* recounts the story of the contretemps between Mike Gelband, head of commercial and residential real estate at Lehman Brothers, and his boss CEO Dick Fuld. Fuld criticized Gelband for not taking on enough risk, and fired him. Later, in 2008, he brought Gelband back to try to save the company, but it was too late (Rajan 2010, p. 145).

During 2005 and 2006 a few Cassandras warned against the oncoming crash, but they were ignored or shouted down. Probably the first to be heard by the top guns were Claudio Borio and William White from the Bank of International Settlements in Basel (BIS) at the Jackson Hole Economic Symposium in August 2003, with Greenspan present. They warned about the dangers of CDOs. They also warned about the conflict of interest of the rating agencies being paid by the banks. Raghuran Rajan, formerly chief economist at the IMF, delivered a paper at the same symposium, two years later, in 2005, again with Greenspan and Summers present. He too was shouted down. Robert Shiller of Yale warned of a bubble in talks at FDIC and the Comptroller of the Currency in 2003 and 2004 but was ignored. He wrote about it in the second edition of his book (Shiller 2006). Nouriel Roubini of NYU, nicknamed "Doctor Doom," was yet another; in September 2006 he warned the IMF about the dangers. Nobody in power listened, or acted on what he heard.

Within the financial industry, there were those who saw profit opportunities in betting against the CDOs. Greg Lipmann at Deutsche Bank has been mentioned. Mike Gelband and his team, and risk manager Madelyn Antoncic, at Lehman Brothers proposed going short, and were fired by CEO Dick Fuld for being too cautious. (Fuld and Dick Gregory went on to build up a huge position in real estate investments that were worthless a year later.) Commerzbank stopped accumulating CDOs early in the year, and AIG stopped writing CDS contracts in early 2006. But the municipal bond insurers, known as "monolines" continued to write them.[5] In May 2006 Merrill Lynch fired Jeff Kronthal and his team, previously hired away from Lewie Ranieri's group at Salomon Brothers, for making a presentation outlining the risks of the mortgage CDO market.

In January 2007 (according to the SEC) a hedge fund manager, John Paulson, asked Goldman Sachs to design and market some CDOs that were based on selections from a list of 123 particularly awful residential mortgage-backed securities selected by Paulson himself. Paulson may or may not have told the Goldman Sachs people that he intended to bet against those securities, but that was his intention. The prospectus for Abacus-2007-AC1 was written by a Goldman vice president, Fabrice Tourre. Later Tourre produced a 65-page "flip" book to explain the security, which was a synthetic CDO, to prospective buyers. Goldman hired an independent specialist in "portfolio selection," namely ACA Management, which was a subsidiary of the Dutch bank, ABN-Amro (now part of Royal Bank of Scotland, RBS). Goldman didn't tell ACA of Paulson's role in creating the list from which ACA made its selection. The synthetic CDOs were sold. Paulson shorted them and made about $20 billion for his investors and $4 billion for himself (Lewis 2010, p. xviii). But Goldman Sachs sold the Abacus securities to other clients, including the IKB bank in Düsseldorf, without telling them about who had selected the securities or why. Even so, it is important to note that synthetic CDOs are essentially gambles. There is always a winner and a loser. The only real question is whether the losers in this case were fully informed.

The most interesting tidbit of that history is an email sent by Tourre to an anonymous friend on January 27, 2007 as quoted in *The Telegraph* Business Section, April 10, 2010. In it he said "More and more leverage in the system. The whole building is about to collapse any time now . . . Only potential survivor, the fabulous Fab[rice] . . . standing in the midst of all these complex, highly leveraged, exotic trades he created without necessarily understanding all the implications of these monstrousities." On April 16, 2010, the SEC charged Goldman Sachs and Fabrice Tourre with fraud. (Paulson was not charged.) Goldman Sachs settled the complaint for $550 million, but the SEC sued Tourre again, over conversations he had with a representative of the German Bank, IKB, which bought some of the Abacus securities. Fabrice Tourre, who left Goldman in 2012, did what he was hired to do. His trial for fraud began in July 2013. He could go to jail.

The punishment for Goldman Sachs (which admitted no wrongdoing) was minimal compared to the profits they made selling synthetic CDOs. The SEC almost always settles out of court, with a fine and a promise from the company not to do it again. The company almost always does it again, and again. In any case, the fine was paid by the company (i.e., the shareholders), not by the nameless executives who did the deal with Paulson.

Another major player in the synthetic CDO game was Magnetar Capital, a hedge fund in Evanston, Illinois, founded by Alec Litowitz and Ross Laser. During 2006 Magnetar was buying a lot of the so-called equity tranches (supposedly the most risky) of CDOs. Their strategy, according to an investigative report by journalists for ProPublica/NPR was to create risky synthetic CDOs designed to fail, much as Goldman Sachs did for Paulson, by recombining the riskiest equity tranches of other CDOs, which they sold to other investors and then bet against.

Magnetar's explanation, in response to the ProPublica report, was that the firm's brain trust thought the equity tranches were underpriced as compared to the middle tranches, so they were buying the underpriced tranches and selling (shorting) the overpriced tranches. This is a perfectly reasonable (although somewhat implausible) strategy, similar in a way to the strategy of Long-Term Capital Management. The strategy was based on the assumption that there is a market and a basis for determining what is overpriced and what is underpriced. Magnetar's argument is that they assumed that all tranches would fail simultaneously, rather than the banker's assumption that the equity tranche would fail first. That is what happened.

But the ProPublica theory has not been disproved either. Greg Lippmann of Deutsche Bank believed that Magnetar's purchases kept the bubble going longer than it otherwise would have, on the ground that they created a market for equity tranches that otherwise would have been difficult to sell. That theory is also unprovable, but plausible (Senate Subcommittee on Investigations 2011).

There were in fact several other hedge funds that bet against the housing market and did very well out of it. Kyle Bass, the flamboyant Texan, who had left Bear-Stearns with $10 million of his own money, created a $500 million hedge fund called Hayman Capital in 2005 to bet against the housing market. Hayman was a big winner, and his fund is now betting that over-indebted countries in Europe (starting with Greece) will default. In effect he is betting against the survival of the eurozone (Lewis 2011, p. xi).

Why did Bear-Stearns, Lehman Brothers, Merrill Lynch, Morgan Stanley, CitiGroup, and AIG, who all had inside information, get hurt so badly? One possible explanation is that top executives of big firms really did not understand the business they had gotten into. There is probably some truth in this, given the extreme complexity of some of the securities, and the models, and the fact that the older men (there were no women) at the top generally had no mathematical qualifications but had been promoted mainly because of their family or school contacts, and sales ability (Ellis 2009). Another explanation is that they were all competing fiercely to be as profitable as Goldman Sachs (McGee 2010). This competition was real, and it undoubtedly contributed to the high degree of leverage employed by all of the key players on Wall Street.

The culture within the institutions contributed to this blindness. One academic analyst who was present at a meeting in 2007 between academics and bankers has recorded that the academics were surprised that the bankers were not worried about the risks. After the meeting, one of the bankers who was evidently out of step, with his bosses, spoke privately with the author during a break and said "You must understand that anyone who was worried was fired long ago and is not in this room" (Rajan 2010, p. 141).

The Bursting of the Biggest Bubble, 2007 to 2009

From 1998 to 2007 all of the big banks had more or less doubled their financial leverage. Based on "10K" reports to the SEC, in 2007 Citigroup, Bear-Stearns, and Morgan Stanley were leveraged at 33:1, Merrill Lynch was at 31:1, Lehman was at 29:1, and Goldman Sachs reported 25:1. During the eighteen months from the end of 2005 through the middle of 2007, those firms created at least $200 billion, and perhaps as much as $400 billion, in subprime mortgage-backed CDOs. (Nobody knows for sure.) Of those, something like 80 percent were AAA rated. (In an earlier section I explained what is known about how the banks persuaded the ratings agencies to award so many AAA ratings.) As such they were treated as risk free *and disclosure to the regulators (e.g., the SEC) was therefore not necessary by law.* Much or most of that triple A junk was held off-balance, meaning that actual leverage factors were significantly greater than the SEC numbers mentioned above (Lewis 2010, p. 234).

When the default rates rose above a few percent, the market value of those CDOs tanked. The ABX price index of the underlying bonds had already lost more than 30 percent by spring 2007 and was rapidly declining (Lewis 2010, pp.164–65). By March 2008 the ABX index was down (from 100) to a shocking 65.[6] The rising default rate had the unintended consequence that some CDOs became unsalable, if not actually worthless. The secondary market for mortgage-based bonds shrank in 2007, leaving many financial firms with unsalable securities in their vaults. And when this happened, the SEC's "mark-to-market" (MTM) rule became a kind of "Damocles sword" threatening the viability of the banks themselves. Incredibly, between February and June of 2007, well after the tea leaves had turned black, the banks led by Merrill Lynch and CitiGroup created and sold another $50 billion in new CDOs. They did it despite the clear warnings, to anybody who was paying attention, that subprime mortgage default rates were far above the levels assumed by the ratings agencies. The right hand didn't know what the left hand was doing.

In the third quarter of 2007, the rating agencies, Moody's, S&P, and Fitch, started downgrading CDOs for the first time: The first downgrade affected CDOs supposedly worth $85 billion. This was followed by another CDO downgrade of $237 billion in the fourth quarter of that year, then $739 billion in the first quarter of 2008 and $841 billion in the second quarter of that year. Thus during that year (July 2007–July 2008) the rating agencies belatedly downgraded $1.9 trillion of CDOs from "investment grade" to junk that could no longer be used as part of the capital base of financial institutions. The banks all needed to recapitalize in a hurry. This, of course, had a very bad effect on the value of the shares of the firms holding those securities. Michael Lewis commented that a share of Salomon Brothers, worth $42 in 1986 when he was working there, had been "converted" into 2.2 shares of CitiGroup worth a total of $7.48 at the beginning of 2010 (Lewis 2010, p. 258).

It was obvious by late 2007 that banks with large positions in CDOs were in trouble. Bear-Stearns was the first to go belly up. This happened in March 2008, during a rapid collapse of the share price, despite a $30 billion temporary loan from the New York Fed. Bear-Stearns was sold to JPMorgan Chase for $2 per share (although the price was later raised to $10 per share). The US Treasury guaranteed the most toxic loans. Only the bondholders were "made whole" in that deal. Shareholders lost almost everything.

The Bear-Stearns "rescue" was heavily criticized by people who were (and are) very unhappy with the notion that some banks are "too big to fail" (TBTF), meaning "too big to be allowed to fail." The phrase "moral hazard" kept being whispered in the wind. "Moral hazard" is the phrase economists use to say that if a big bank knows it will be bailed out, it may take excessive risks. Indeed the banks did take excessive risks, though almost certainly not because they knew they would be bailed out (Friedman and Kraus 2011, pp. 144–45, app.). (One of the ostensible reasons for letting Lehman Brothers fail was in fact to "send a message"—via the wind—to the effect that bailouts were not to be expected.)

When Lehman Brothers found itself in a situation similar to Bear-Stearns a few months later, with a pile of loans secured by unsalable CDOs, Treasury Secretary Henry Paulson and the new chairman of the FRB (Ben Bernanke) said—in perfect harmony—that in order to kill and bury "moral hazard" there would be no bailout. Lehman CEO Dick Fuld—who had fired all his top advisors for not taking enough risk—turned down more than one offer to buy the company (one was from Warren Buffet) on the ground that the price was too low. But on September 14, 2008, Lehman filed for bankruptcy protection and the shareholders got nothing. Even the bondholders lost $130 billion when the dust finally cleared. What was left of Lehman Brothers was sold to Barclay's Bank.

Starting in January 2007 there was a cascade of industry failures and big losses :

• Ownit Mortgage Solutions Inc. (bankrupt January 3)

• American Freedom Mortgage Inc. (bankrupt January 29)

• Mortgage Lenders Network USA Inc. (bankrupt February 5)

• Accredited Home Lenders Holding and DR Horton (filed for bankruptcy February–March)

• New Century Financial, the largest subprime lender in the United States (bankrupt April 2)

• Bear-Stearns halts redemptions in its two high leverage hedge funds (June 7)

• BNP Paribas (France) stops offering home equity loans; ditto Bank of China (August)

• American Home Mortgage Investment Corp. (August 6)

• Mortgage Guarantee Insurance Corp. suffers loss of $1 billion on its investment in Credit-Based Asset Servicing and Securitization, C-BASS, in New York (August)

• BNP Paribas suspends three investment funds that invested in CDOs (August 9)

• Country-Wide Financial announces big losses; avoids bankruptcy thanks to $11 billion emergency loan from a group of banks (August 16)

• Sentinel Management Group (bankrupt August 17)

• London interbank loan (LIBOR) rate is at 6.8 percent, far above the official B of E rate of 5.75 percent (August–September)

- CitiGroup borrows $3.375 billion from the Fed (September 12)
- Northern Rock asks for emergency financial support from Bank of England; next day depositors withdraw over $1.5 billion (September 13)
- Fed cuts its rate from 5.25 to 4.75 percent (September 18)
- UBS announces losses of $3.4 billion from subprime securities (October 1)
- CitiGroup announces $3.1 billion in subprime losses (October 1); two weeks later a further loss of $5 billion is announced. By April 1, 2008, CitiGroup losses add up to $40 billion.
- Merrill Lynch announces a loss of $5.5 billion (October 5); revised to $8.3 billion (October 24). At the end of October Merrill Lynch fires its CEO, Stan O'Neal for trying to sell the company. He is replaced by John Thain. (A year later it was sold to Bank of America for a much lower price.)
- Bank of England cuts interest rates to 5.5 percent (December 6)
- Fed auctions $20 billion (December 17)
- ECB lends $500 million to European banks to help over Christmas (December 18)
- S&P downgrades the "Monolines" (AMBAC, MBIA, ACA, etc.), municipal bond insurance companies (December 19). They start to collapse; by 2009 they were all gone.
- Fed cuts interest rates by 3/4 of a percent, to 4 percent (Jan. 22, 2008)
- Monoline insurer MBIA announces a loss of $2.3 billion for three months. (January 31, 2008)
- Bank of England cuts interest rate to 5.25 percent (February 7)
- Northern Rock is nationalized (February 17)
- Bear-Stearns is acquired by JPMorgan Chase for $240 million, backed by $30 billion in Fed loans (March 14). A year earlier Bear-Stearns had a market value of $38 billion.
- Abbey National withdraws the last 100 percent (no equity) mortgage from the market (April 7)
- Bank of England cuts interest rate to 5 percent (April 10)
- Bank of England announces a plan to allow banks to swap mortgage debts for government bonds (April 21)

• RBS announces a rights issue to raise $18 billion from its shareholders; also announces a write-down of $9 billion on its investments from April through June (April 22)

• UBS announces a rights issue of $15.5 billion to cover some of its $37 billion in losses on subprime mortgage debt (May 22)

• Barclays announces a $6.75 billion share offering to cover some of its losses. Qatar's sovereign investment buys $4 billion of that, giving it 7.7 percent of the shares. (July 7, 2008)

• US Treasury and the FRB start the process of nationalizing Fannie Mae and Freddie Mac, which together own $5 trillion in mortgages (July 14)

• Major banks and other financial institutions have cumulative losses of $435 billion (July 17). One trading desk at Morgan Stanley lost $9 billion; CitiGroup was down $60 billion; Merrill Lynch lost $55 billion, and (according to the Bankruptcy court) Lehman lost $130 billion, of which some was due to the "disorderly" windup, which could have been avoided by an earlier sale.

• Halifax (HBOS), the largest UK mortgage lender, offers rights to buy $6 billion in stock, but only 8 percent of shareholders accept, because the shares are selling at lower prices on the market. The underwriters have to buy the rest. (July 21)

• Fannie Mae and Freddie Mac are rescued in the biggest bailout ever (September 7). They were effectively nationalized and the shareholders lost most of their equity.

• Lehman Brothers posts a loss of $3.9 billion for the three months ending in August (September 10). Lehman files for bankruptcy, after failing to find a buyer (September 15). Barclays later takes over the UK branch (but not the debts).

• Merrill-Lynch sells itself to Bank of America for $50 billion, which is pennies on the shareholder dollar.

• Lloyds TSB takes over Halifax (HBOS) for $18 billion.

Soon after the Lehman bankruptcy Washington Mutual went bust, and was confiscated by the Treasury, leaving nothing for either bondholders or shareholders. This bankruptcy was followed by Wachovia Bank, also due to the downgrades by the rating agencies. In this case the NY Fed, under Timothy Geithner, encouraged CitiGroup to buy Wachovia at a very low price, with federal guarantees of the loans. Given the terrible financial condition of CitiGroup, this idea seems bizarre. Sheila Bair, head of the FDIC objected strongly, and the deal was held up (Bair 2012). In a surprising move, Wachovia was subsequently bought by Wells Fargo, a much healthier bank, at the end of December 2008, without any government help.

When large numbers of mortgages went sour in 2007 and 2008, the credit default swap (CDS) owners (including Goldman Sachs and several big European banks) aggressively demanded payment. AIG had made large profits by selling those derivatives, but at far too low a price. Worse, it had not created a reserve to pay off the counterparties (who thought they were insured.) In September 2007 the three credit rating agencies suddenly downgraded the American International Group's (AIG's) stock, causing a rapid withdrawal of $140 billion in a week. On September 15, AIG approached the New York Fed for help. Its potential liabilities were climbing day by day as the price of houses declined and more and more mortgages defaulted, resulting in a much sharper decline in the value of mortgage-backed securities. Suddenly AIG found itself with liabilities several times greater than its total assets and rising.

But AIG was also "too big to fail" (TBTF). The US Treasury took over all of AIG's CDS liabilities and paid off the counterparties the customers at 100 cents on the dollar. The Treasury took 80 percent of the ownership of AIG, although the stock was worth far less than the amount of the bailout. The fate of the other issuers of CDSs that were not TBTF, such as the "monolines" and their clients is probably still being determined by the courts. (The taxpayers did all right in this case. The US Treasury sold a lot of those shares in early September 2012, recouping its original $182 billion bailout at a profit for the Treasury of $12.4 billion, while retaining 22 percent of the common shares to be sold later.)

The first in line at AIG's CDS "window" in 2008 was none other than Goldman Sachs, which had bought CDSs (to short the mortgage bond market) and got $13 billion cash on the barrelhead for its foresight (Greider 2010). A strong case can be made that the New York Fed under Timothy Geithner, who later became Obama's Secretary of the Treasury, acted to protect the banks (like Goldman) in the AIG affair, and not in the public interest. William Greider has pointed out that the Fed could have provided short-term loans and threatened to let AIG file for bankruptcy.

In that case the government would have been a top creditor and could have forced all the parties to share the pain rather than let the biggest gorilla on the block get a better deal than the others.

The NY Fed's lawyers claim that it did not do this because it (the Fed) was too weak to make the threat credible. The lawyers said that Congress, in its deregulation frenzy had taken away the Fed's regulatory hickory stick and converted it to a balsawood baton (Greider 2010). In fairness, the risk probably was too great. The total collapse of AIG would have been much worse than the collapse of Lehman Brothers, which was bad enough. As the world's biggest insurer, it would have set off a chain reaction of failures around the world.

At this point the Secretary of the Treasury Henry Paulson (ex-CEO of Goldman Sachs) asked the US Congress for $700 billion, *supposedly to buy subprime mortgages*. Congress, under pressure, quickly agreed to the Troubled Asset Relief Program (TARP), which was signed by George Bush. What Paulson did with the money, however, was not to buy mortgages. Instead, he chose to give most of it to AIG and the banks, with no real strings attached in the banks' case. In fairness, Paulson really had to do it. The entire banking system was on the brink of collapse (and TBTF). Only a lot of public money could save it. Luckily that money was forthcoming, and the US banks are now much healthier, as a group, than their European counterparts. But the US taxpayers have had to take the haircut.

Don't be misled by my focus on a few big banks and AIG in the last few paragraphs. The truth is that after the rating agencies' sudden downgrade of mortgage-based securities in general, the whole financial system really was on the verge of collapse and the US Federal Reserve Bank system was the only possible savior. From mid-2007 through 2009, many US banks were seriously stressed (because of subprime mortgage based securities on their books), and during the second half of 2008, the fraction under "systemic financial stress" exceeded 60 percent several times. Only after those huge transfers of bank debt to the Fed, did the financial stress level decline to 10 percent, or less, where it remains (see figure 5.2).

It must be noted that many banks and other institutions that thought they were covered by credit default swaps (CDSs) from insurance companies other than AIG were deluded. When the issuer of the CDS didn't have the money to pay, the buyers of CDSs couldn't collect and their CDSs were worth a lot less than the buyers had assumed.

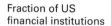

Fraction of US
financial institutions

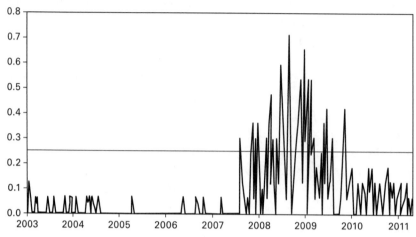

Figure 5.2
Systemic financial stress in the United States, 2003 to 2011. Data from *IMF Global Financial Stability Report,* Septermber 11, 2011.

The *notional* value of derivatives in existence in 2007 was $296 trillion. The *market value* of all the derivatives in existence in 2007, if they had been exercised at that time, was just $14.5 trillion about the size of the US GDP. That is a large number, to be sure, but a lot less than the *notional value*. And allowing for the fact that many of the options canceled each other out (e.g., puts and calls on the same stock), the *net* value of the derivatives was just $3.3 trillion. Obviously $3.3 trillion is a lot less than $596 trillion, but it is still a lot of money, as compared to the $14 trillion US GDP. It was far more than enough to catalyze an economic catastrophe.

To be fair, the derivatives, as such, cannot be blamed for the financial crash. They only helped to spread the risk, muddy the waters, and obscure what was really going on. To this day, it is hard to find even an accounting professor who can explain a synthetic CDO. However, the derivatives, taken as a whole, represented a large number of risky bets many of which were not, as it turned out, backed up by real collateral but only by other bets. The case for regulation of the derivatives market, at least to the extent of monitoring its composition and growth, is overwhelming. Fortunately, the Dodd–Frank law goes part way in that direction.

The Impact of the Financial Crash on Main Street

Apart from direct impacts of the price of oil, there are two principal ways in which the various financial bubbles initiated by Wall Street (for want of a better name) affect ordinary people on Main Street. The primary mechanism is asset price inflation and deflation, usually favoring the well-to-do on balance. The other is unemployment and lost growth.

When house prices rise faster than the rate of mortgage interest, homeowners benefit from rising prices by seeing increased home equity. This is, of course, the major historical incentive for homeownership. For most people the house is a savings account. Home equity accounts for a large fraction of personal wealth for the majority of middle-class Americans, whereas financial wealth (stocks, bonds) is restricted to a much smaller group (roughly the top income decile).

Farmers and blue-collar workers in the deteriorating central cities have lost ground. Homeowners have gained relative to renters (who generally belong to the lower income brackets) for most of the time since the end of WWII.[7] This differential was amplified during the period 2003 to 2007, when house prices were rising much faster than usual. The growing gap between owners and renters is one of the major reasons for the "ownership society" programs of both Presidents Clinton and Bush (II).

In mid-2005, single-family homes were selling at an annual rate of almost 1.4 million units. Yet about that time the banks began repossessing large numbers of houses due to defaults. In 2006, mortgage default rates were rising fast and home prices began to decline even faster in some overbuilt areas, such as the "sand states" (Arizona, California, Florida, Nevada) and the Mediterranean resort countries (Cyprus, Malta, Spain, and Portugal). Speculative investors with adjustable rate mortgages (ARMs) began to put their houses on the market. Borrowers who had subprime mortgages in that particular situation lost little or nothing (except a credit rating) when house prices started to decline. They could simply walk away. Some did just that.

As the supply of houses for sale increased, the demand for houses decreased, especially among potential buyers who were now inclined to wait in the hope that prices would drop still further. Prices did just that. By late 2008, the rate of mortgage default was sharply up, and the backlog of repossessed houses for sale by banks was rising fast. The demand for new houses fell by 40 percent in 2007 and still more in 2008. Sales declined until 2011, with annual sales hovering around 300,000 units, less than a quarter of the 2005 peak. There has been a small increase in sales since 2012

In the last quarter of 2005, US housing prices stalled and began to decline (figure 5.1). By the end of the first quarter of 2006, median home prices were down 3.3 percent nationwide. A brief rebound at the end of 2006 was followed by a precipitous decline. The S&P Case–Shiller index of home prices in twenty cities, which was 100 in 2000, peaked at 189.93 in the second quarter of 2006. Since then this index has fallen steadily until sometime in 2012. In the third quarter of 2010, it was 135.48, and by the end of September 2011, it was lower still. The average single-family house cost just over $260,000 in 2006 (the peak). By March 2012, it was down to about $158,000 (see figure 5.1). Rounding the loss to 55 points, home prices in 2006 were about 40 percent higher than they were in late September 2011.

On that basis the total value of homes in 2006 was close to $21 trillion, of which mortgage debt was less than $8.8 trillion (see below), leaving $12 trillion for home equity. From this calculation it seems that the change of home equity from 2006 to late 2011 was approximately $12 – $3.8 = $8.2 trillion, of which $2.4 trillion had been taken out as cash spent by homeowners who refinanced to convert higher home equity into spendable cash.[8] The rest (around $5.5 trillion) just disappeared when the bubble burst.

The subprime mortgage "bubble" of 2005 to 2008 created some undeserving winners, who got subprime mortgages with little or no equity and then refinanced or sold out before the bust. But most were losers. The biggest losers were homeowners whose equity suddenly vanished, leaving them "underwater." As of September 30, 2011, according to the *New York Times*, 10.7 million of the 48.5 million home mortgages in the United States (22 percent) were "underwater," and of those 1.3 million needed refinancing, restructuring, or faced default and repossession. The total mortgage debt in the United States at that time was $8,806 trillion, and total homeowner equity amounted to $3,817 trillion. Without the wave of refinancing on the way up, the homeowner's equity in 2011 would have been closer to $6.2 trillion and mortgage debt would have been less by $2.4 trillion.

This loss hit all homeowners, not just the fraction who bought new houses with subprimes. Looking at another way, it wiped out about 45 percent of the home equity portion of middle-class wealth in the United States as of 2006. Worse, as of the end of September 2011, 10.7 million homeowners about 22 percent of the total had *negative* equity amounting to $700 billion, or about $65,000 per household. *It is safe to assume that for most of those people the loss of home equity wealth exceeded 100 percent of their life savings.* They now find themselves deeply in debt thanks to financial games by others in which they had no part. (Remember, these are homeowners who believed in the American Dream and bought in good faith, usually several years before the crash. I am not referring to those who bought at the top, with adjustable rate mortgages and minimal or no equity.)

Since the beginning of 2007 about 4 million homeowners had already been evicted by January 2012 because of default. Some of these were improperly evicted by banks as a result of false or incomplete documentation, as revealed by investigations in 2010 by the US Attorney General. Their losses are not included in the negative equity figure cited in the paragraph above. Some of the foreclosures were houses bought for investment. But for others the loss is not just a financial gamble gone wrong. It also means that their credit ratings (and credit cards) are gone. For many years to come they will have to pay cash for everything they buy. Even finding a decent rental accommodation without a credit rating is difficult. For some of those people eviction actually means poverty and homelessness.

Major banks (including Bank of America, CitiGroup, JPMorgan Chase, and Wells Fargo) have agreed to compensation payments of $1,800 to $2,000 each for about 750,000 of those 4 million or so evictees (a total of less than $1.5 billion in outlays). Subsequently the banks agreed to provide an additional $32.3 billion to restructure existing mortgages, plus $3 billion to refinance existing mortgages and $2.7 billion to reimburse the states. This money would be applicable to only 10 percent of the underwater mortgages, not including any of the mortgages owned by Fannie Mae or Freddie Mac. The banks in question seem to be happy with the settlement because they expect to be free of any further liabilities. But they have been scandalously slow to make even the minimum effort to help the victims.

There were 3.5 million repossessed homes for sale in the United States as of October 15, 2011, and there will be more to come. In South Florida 200,000 homes were then in the hands of lenders or in the process of foreclosure, but only 30,000 homes were actually on the market at the time (*Miami Herald*, October 17, 2011). Many more were likely to be foreclosed in the following eighteen months as ARM floating rate adjustments went into effect. So the backlog in South Florida was still extremely large. This portends continuing long-term slump in the housing industry, at least in some overbuilt areas. This is consistent with data on new one-family houses sold in the United States (figure 5.3).

Construction of residential housing peaked in 2006. About 1 million workers were employed directly by builders and contractors. By 2010 the number was down to 550 thousand, a decline of 45 percent. Nonresidential construction peaked in 2007, with about 825 thousand workers directly employed. This number fell to 650 thousand in 2010, a decline of about 26 percent. Construction workers per se were not the only ones affected. Counting workers in all the supplier industries, the total number of lost jobs due to the collapse of the housing bubble was over 2 million, or more. *The job losses in the housing sector accounted for most of the increased unemployment in the United States after 2007.*

Thousands of units

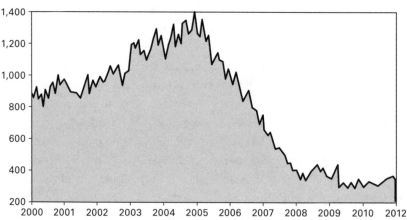

Figure 5.3
New one-family homes in the United States, 2000 to 2012. Data from US Census Bureau, March 12, 2012.

In 2008 there was huge loss on the US stock market. From the market high in 2007 to October 2008 the market lost no less than $8 trillion in paper value. True, the institutional losers had mostly been winners during the run-up before 2007 and (as of Spring 2013) all of those stock-market losses have been made up. However, the debt-to-income ratio for US households rose from 75 percent in 1990 to 125 percent by 2008. US household net worth declined from its peak of $66 trillion in 2007 to a low point of $51 billion in the winter of 2009, a net loss of $15 trillion, three times as great as the dot.com loss. As of the spring of 2012, US household net worth was back up to $60 trillion, but that is still at least $6 trillion below the 2007 peak, mainly due to reduced home equity (see figure 5.4).

As of midsummer 2013, US home prices are up about 12 percent year to year. That is certainly good news for some. About the same time, figures from the Federal Reserve Board suggest that aggregate US personal wealth is back up to the 2007 peak, in current dollars. Stocks and mutual funds are back at their 2007 levels. But net worth per household is still well below 2006 to 2007 levels (there are more households). And the extent of recovery is very different for different generations. Households

Trillion USD

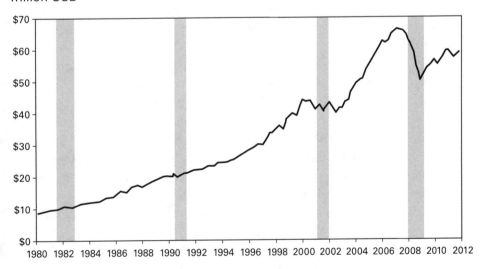

Figure 5.4
US household net worth, 2000 to 2012. Shaded areas indicate recessions.

headed by persons over 62 years of age have almost recovered completely, having average net worth in 2013 of $920K, close to the 2006 maximum. In the case of households headed by someone in the 40 to 61 age group, the average net worth in 2013 reached about $680K but still significantly less than the earlier peak of $750K. Younger households led by a person under 40 have scarcely recovered at all. Their 2013 net worth of roughly $100K is still much lower than the 2007 peak of about $160K. Evidently the wealth gap is still increasing.

As mentioned above, the home equity loss was about $5.5 trillion. In addition there were increases after 2008 in household and educational debt, though mortgage debt is down. Unemployed people added to consumer (credit card) debt, saved less or consumed past savings to survive. In some cases people had to sell things, including gold jewelry. All of these behavioral changes amounted to cutbacks in household net worth that will not be recovered for several more years, at best.

During the last three recessions (before 2008), unemployment reached a peak of 10.5 percent briefly in 1983 (due to the Iranian revolution and the Volker inflation killer), 7.5 percent in 1992 (due to the first Iraq war), and about 6 percent in 2003 after the dot.com bubble. The low unemployment levels reached after the low points were, respectively, 5 percent (1988 to 1989), nearly 4 percent (1999 to 2001), and about 4.5 percent in 2006. In these cases the economic and employment recovery after the peak was fairly prompt (two to three years), although the "peak to trough" was more like six years (see figure 5.5).

The financial crisis of 2008 was qualitatively as well as quantitatively different. Peak unemployment in 2009 was actually not as high as the Volker peak in 1983 (which briefly reached 10.5 percent). But the Volker peak was due to a credit crunch and extremely high short-term interest rates imposed by the Fed, but it didn't last long. This time, interest rates are near zero, and yet economic growth is barely enough to compensate for inflation (also very low). Also unemployment has stayed high. As of May 2013 it was still 7.5 percent. The real difference between 2008 and the earlier recessions is that the previous recessions were not accompanied by a financial collapse, together with a housing price crash and a continuing credit crunch.

Economists believe that the normal ("trend") for US economic growth is 3 to 3.5 percent above inflation, which is currently less than 2 percent

Percent of labor force

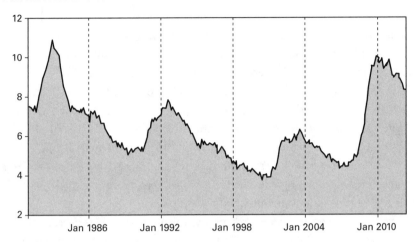

Figure 5.5
US unemployment rate, 2000 to 2012. Data from US Bureau of Labor Statistics.

per annum. It is generally assumed that "normal" unemployment would be about 5 percent (Taylor rule). Assuming the employment gap to be around 3.5 percent just during the four years (2009 to 2012), the lost GDP would have been in the neighborhood 3.5 percent of $14 trillion or about $500 billion per year, of which about $350 billion (70 percent) would have been wages and salaries. Over those four years alone, that loss approaches $1 trillion. And the bleeding is not over, since economic growth is still anemic, well below "trend." That is partly due to the budgetary cuts that have been forced by the deficit hawks.

It is hard to avoid the conclusion (see figure 5.5) that unemployment is a cyclic phenomenon with a periodicity of six years or so. Over longer periods the pattern is less clear, however. I think the cyclicity is human-made and primarily attributable to monetary and fiscal policies, confused by external events (e.g., oil price spikes).

The Impact of the Crash on the Macroeconomy

The impact of the financial crash on home equity and net worth was mentioned in the last chapter. A further consequence of the events since 1980 has been a dramatic increase in income inequality. In fact four-fifths of the US working population has actually lost ground since 1980. The upper middle class (top fifth) has gained modestly since 1980, but the top 5 percent got three-quarters of the total gain since 1980 and the top 1 percent, which includes many CEOs and a lot of bankers, has become much richer. The top 10 percent now gets half of all income and the top 1 percent gets a sixth of all income and holds more wealth than the bottom 90 percent. This redistribution of income and wealth accelerated after the dot.com bubble and accelerated again after the financial crisis of 2008 to 2009. Figure 5.6 (panels a and b) tells the story up through 2007.

The major beneficiaries of the decades since 1980 have been the top executives in big companies, investment bankers, and their spin-offs, such as hedge funds and "private equity" funds. It turns out that only the top 7 percent gained (in net worth terms) during the first two years of the "recovery, while the rest continued to lose (largely because of the continuing decline in house prices). The major losers have been the people who have lost their medical benefits, pensions or their jobs, thanks to weaker unions, outsourcing, and wage levels squeezed by competition from low-wage countries abroad. Beyond that, the nation as a whole (and the rest of the OECD countries, at least) has lost years of potential economic growth.

The tax policies that accelerated this increased inequality, especially preferential treatment for investment income, remain in effect as of 2013.

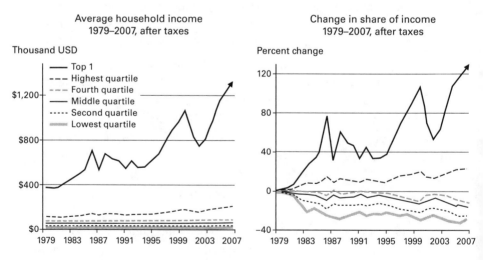

Figure 5.6
US after-tax income, 1979 to 2009

Those policies were advocated by conservatives, originally, on the basis that they would encourage economic growth. The argument, which has been widely accepted by all Republicans and much of the political and business elite in the United States for the last three decades, is that taxation should encourage saving, hard work, and risk-taking, whence economic success should be rewarded, not penalized. Most people would agree with that sentiment, so far as it goes. The problem is that there is no clear connection between tax cuts and hard work or business success. There is no clear evidence that increasing inequality is "pro-growth," notwithstanding some Republican claims.

On the contrary, the obsession with tax avoidance has created a worldwide network of tax shelters that siphon money away from the public sector while contributing little or nothing to economic growth in the countries where the money was earned. Moreover the use of corporate debt, rather than profits, to finance growth has also stifled innovation and created a culture of focusing management attention on the tax code and the legal ways of tax avoidance rather than on increasing energy efficiency, improving product quality, and conquering new markets.

On Main Street, too, the tax cuts have been more effective at encouraging tax avoidance or evasion than on encouraging people to work harder, save more, or become entrepreneurs. It is a fact that overall growth performance of the United States, since Reagan was elected (1980), has been worse than it was during the previous thirty years. There may be other reasons for this decline (e.g., foreign competition, military buildup, or market saturation), but while tax rates have been sharply reduced, growth has lagged. Recent research indicates that increasing inequality is actually a drag on growth.

Inequality may indeed be more important as a drag than the progrowth factors usually cited, such as "openness," free trade, foreign investment, exchange rate competitiveness, and institutions promoting political stability. Jonathan Ostry and Andrew Berg of the IMF suggest that the increased inequality in the United States since 1980 has cut potential growth by up to a third (*New York Times*, October 17, 2012). This is a shocking conclusion. But it is not difficult to understand, given the fact that much of the wealth "created" by the financial sector is used for acquisition and gambling, never re-invested in the real economy.

Of course, what we (on Main Street) notice is that the CEOs and other high-level financial executives are (still) making a lot more money than the rest of us. According to one recent AFL-CIO survey, the average American CEO earned 354 times as much as his employees in 2012, down from 380 the year before (because Tim Cook, the CEO of Apple, took a pay cut from $376 million in 2011 to $4.2 million in 2012. Examples of CEO overpayment are in the press every day. One wonders what exactly justifies such incredible rewards, especially given the fact that bankers and their fellows in Wall Street and in the "City" of London bear a major responsibility for causing the global financial mess. As yet the bosses have paid no penalty, and they continue to rake in the big bucks.

The question arises in some quarters: Don't banks serve a social purpose that justifies these outsize rewards? Is it unfair to blame individuals for doing what is legally permissible (or even required) to maximize the profits of their institutions? Don't the chief executives have a fiduciary responsibility to do exactly that? Isn't it the essence of capitalism? If so, why should successful capitalists be punished or reviled? A lot depends on what is meant by the word "success."

There is a somewhat abstract academic debate about the role of banks as institutions. A useful distinction can be made between two perspectives. The more academic perspective focuses on the financial architecture of banks and compares two "models": (1) the "specialized" banking model that existed in the United States from 1933 to 1998, and in Japan from 1948 to 2001, vis-à-vis (2) the "universal financial service" model that has evolved in most other countries. Great Britain had a third model before the "Big Bang" (of 1986), but it now resembles the Wall Street model.

The comparison among financial models is now based on a conceptual scheme involving entities characterized as "systemically important financial institutions" or SIFIs for short. Four benchmarks have been suggested (Saunders 2011):

• *Static efficiency* (as measured by the spread between interest paid by borrowers and interest received by savers

• *Dynamic efficiency* (as measured, in the last analysis, by economic growth, adjusted for other factors)

• *Stability* (in terms of avoiding shocks, whether exogenous or endogenous in origin)

- *Competitiveness and robustness* of the financial sector as a creator of income, employment, and trade

Without going into detail, it seems clear that the US "specialized" model worked as well as or better than the "universal banking" model by those benchmarks. This is demonstrable, even though the financial institutions, especially the chief executives and owners of SIFIs, in Europe, still strongly prefer the universal banking model. They usually cite "competitiveness" as justification. A less abstract argument for the deregulators might be the following: from 1928 to 1982, the US stock market (as measured by the Dow-Jones average) rose 300 percent, whereas from 1982 to 2005, it rose nearly five times as much.

In April 2008 Paul Volcker spoke at the Economic Club in New York. He said:

... today's financial crisis is the culmination, as I count them, of at least five serious breakdowns of systemic significance in the past twenty-five years on the average, one every five years. Warning enough that something rather basic is amiss.. . . Simply stated, the bright new financial system—for all its talented participants, for all its rich rewards has failed the test of the market place.... [A] demonstrably fragile financial system that has produced unimaginable wealth for some, while repeatedly risking a cascading breakdown of the system as a whole, needs repair and reform. (Saunders and Walter 2011, p. 7)

Which five near-breakdowns prior to April 2008 was Volcker referring to? It hardly matters. However, the shiny "new" (post-deregulation) model has failed other tests. In a review article published in 2011, the following paragraph appears in the conclusions of the same authors:

On the surface, functional separation in the United States from 1933 to 1999 may in fact have done little harm and a lot of good. Growth was respectable, financial efficiency and innovation eventually attracted imitators around the world, American firms dominated global financial markets and financial crises were largely avoided. The rapid emergence of financial conglomerates thereafter coincided with plenty of problems a spate of corporate scandals in which financial conglomerates were the leading facilitators, financial innovations aimed at thwarting regulation and redistributing wealth, market bubbles in tech stocks and real estate, slower growth, a financial bubble of massive size and long-lasting effects, and unprecedented tax-payer assumption of risks and losses. Circumstantial evidence? Perhaps. (Saunders and Walter 2011, pp. 21–22)

So much for the academic counterfactual ("what if?") perspective. The other perspective is that of the would-be reformers and regulators of the financial system. As noted in the last section, most banks in 2008 to 2009 held large inventories of subprime mortgage-based CDOs in their own accounts. In 2008 they rather suddenly lost value or even became illiquid, due to relatively small increases in the US home mortgage default rate. That was the immediate cause of the banking crisis of 2008 to 2009 and the European sovereign debt crisis that continues. It results from the fact that so many mortgage-backed securities of unknown value, and now belatedly downgraded by the rating agencies along with sovereign bonds also recently downgraded, were included as part of the capital base of many banks.

To be sure, the pain was not shared equally. Some banks survived the crisis much better than others. Among the world's largest universal banks, only a few managed to lose less than 50 percent of their asset value between spring 2007 and January 2009. Two were Santander, which lost (44.8 percent) of its asset value, and JPMorgan Chase, which lost (48.5 percent). HSBC came in third place with a loss of 54.9 percent of its asset value. Those three banks ended up much stronger in relative terms than pre-crisis. Another group (Morgan Stanley, Goldman Sachs, Crédit Suisse, UBS, Société Générale, and BP Paribas) managed to lose between 65 and 70 percent. Crédit Agricole and Unicredit (Italy) lost between 70 and 75 percent while Deutsche Bank (86.4 percent), Barclays (92 percent), CitiGroup (92.5 percent), and RBS (96.2 percent) were the biggest losers (Lietaer, Ulanowicz, and Goerner 2009). I have seen no data for Wells Fargo (which has grown stronger) or Bank of America (which was certainly a big loser).

From a somewhat more fundamental perspective, it is clear that economic growth also depends on the availability of credit to the producers of goods and services. Banks provide credit, and the creation of credit is effectively the creation of money. But, as Richard Werner has pointed out, credit money can be used for three purposes, namely (1) to finance ordinary activities contributing to productivity (GDP); (2) to finance excessive consumption, which also contributes to GDP; or (3) to finance financial transactions, mergers and acquisitions, leveraged buyouts (LBOs), hedge funds attempting to match puts and calls, credit default swaps, interest rate swaps, and other transactions not contributing to GDP (Werner 2005, 2010).

Yet the leveraged buyouts, mergers, and acquisitions that constitute a large fraction of financial activity today (and a larger share of both debt and profits) do little or nothing to increase production of goods and (non-financial) services. While driving stock prices higher (up 1,400 percent since 1982), these activities normally reduce employment, in the name of efficiency, and cut employee benefits, shifting the burden of health care and retirement as much as possible to the government. They have forced public companies to focus much more on short-term profits and much less on long-term growth. I suspect that a considerably lower level of corporate debt would be optimal for growth, but there is no way to prove it. The restructured LBO companies may or may not be a little more efficient at doing whatever they did before. There is very little credible evidence one way or the other. But in the majority of cases, I think they have also become less flexible and less innovative.

Adding up the bailouts to US banks already announced, through April 30, 2009, came to $12.2 trillion in commitments (a little less than one year's US GDP), of which $2.5 trillion had already been spent. The biggest chunk of that $12 trillion commitment ($9 trillion) was for purchases of corporate debt (e.g., Fannie Mae, Freddie Mac, GM, and AIG) and direct investments in financial institutions. Of that, $1.6 trillion had been spent in the first quarter (Q1) of 2009. These purchases essentially shifted private debt to the taxpayer. The next tranche of $1.7 trillion in commitments, of which $330 million had been spent in Q1 of 2009, was for insurance of bank deposits and mortgage debt held by the GSEs (Fannie Mae and Freddie Mac). The final tranche of $1.4 trillion in commitments, of which $528 billion had been spent in Q1 of 2009, was for liquidity loans, including overnight loans to banks. Meanwhile banks everywhere were (and are) being told to recapitalize, and the recapitalization has to be based on cash, or "investment grade" bonds. The mortgage-backed securities that were once rated AAA are no longer suitable (even if they have residual value.)

This is why so many banks bought sovereign government bonds after the crash. In the past government bonds issued by any Western European country were automatically rated AAA. But, due to the excessive debts of all the countries in southern Europe (plus Iceland and Ireland), the risk of default of many of the "sovereign" bonds is now significant. Their ratings are no longer sufficient for consideration as part of the capital base for the banks that bought the bonds. This in turn means that the European banks that bought those bonds must raise new capital by selling assets or issuing new shares (where possible) in order to justify existing lending. It is why the share prices of most banks are much lower now than they were a few years ago.

Notwithstanding the capital needs of banks, there is now a lot of capital out there looking for a place to go. Record corporate profits since 2010 have accumulated in corporate treasuries, or in stockpiles of US or German bonds. Three US firms alone (Apple, Microsoft, and Cisco Systems) sit on a hoard of around $250 billion, mostly held in offshore tax havens. The Norwegian sovereign wealth fund allegedly contains $700 billion. Yet people and companies with money are not spending it in ways that will increase economic productivity. They are saving it, using it for stock buybacks or acquisitions, many of which will fail, or spending it in more or less thinly disguised financial games. A few of those games are win-win when there is a real synergy to exploit, but the majority of the financial betting games are zero-sum or worse. Those games do not create financial wealth, they just move it around. *They do not increase the productivity of the nonfinancial economy from which those profits were originally generated.*

As I explained at the beginning of this book, the most fundamental unit of commerce is the exchange of goods or services for money. Person (or firm or player) A buys a "widget" from B, in exchange for an agreed price. This transaction will not take place unless both parties, A and B expect to be better off as a result. So, in the language of games, this transaction must be win-win. It follows that markets are socially beneficial and that commerce, in general, is win-win. Expansion of markets increases the benefits. That is why Adam Smith argued that trade is the "wealth of nations." It is why David Ricardo pointed out that international trade is most beneficial when each country sells what it can make most efficiently and buys from others what they can produce most efficiently (the rule of comparative advantage).

But gambling on cards, horse races, or currencies is not like buying and selling of goods. Some may argue that the gambling is entertainment, and that entertainment is a service worth paying for. This may be so, up to a point. But when the bets are in billions, with money not owned by the bettors, there is no entertainment value. More important, while both parties may gain from a real exchange deal, it is not true that both parties gain from a bet. One gains but the other loses. To be sure, there are professional poker players (and stock pickers) who win more than they lose. Those fellows would presumably attribute their winnings to skill. I suppose it took some time and practice to learn how to win at poker or stock picking on a regular basis. *But most of the losers do not expect to lose.* They lose because they are not as clever as they think they are or, more often, because they do not have all the facts. The key point is that poker is a zero-sum game. Every dollar of winnings came out of somebody else's pocket. It is an income transfer, not a source of new wealth.

Now consider savings banks. The short-term lenders (depositors) and the long-term borrowers (homeowners) are both like bettors in a game. The first group (depositors) is betting that the bank will return its money and pay the promised interest on time. The second group (bankers) is betting that it can use the depositor's money productively enough to stay in business. But to do so, the banks must also lend money to long-term borrowers, who are betting that they can use the money profitably enough to repay the bank when payment is due. So the bank in turn is betting that it will pay less to the short-term lenders than the present value of what it will get back (later) from the long-term borrowers. It is also betting that its liquid (cash) reserves are sufficient to keep it afloat in case of financial storms. (This is actually a major gamble in uncertain times, and one that many banks have lost. But it is not a zero-sum gamble.) Bankers and borrowers are not like bettors on horseracing, because for lenders the game is intended to be win-win: money borrowed by businesses is used productively to create something.

Insurance companies play a somewhat different game. Insurance companies are betting that they can make enough money from their investments (with clients money) to cover future outlays, calculated by actuaries or the equivalent. They collect money in the form of premiums from clients who are buying some security in an uncertain world. The clients don't see it as a bet, but they are nevertheless betting that if they or their loved ones do fall sick, or are involved in an accident, or if their house burns down, they will be reimbursed a lot more than they have paid into the pot. The premium income and profits thereon received by the insurer is ultimately redistributed to the widows and orphans, or to the sick and injured, at a later time. An ordinary insurance company, like the Prudential, is betting, like a savings bank, that it can use the money it receives from policy owners (depositors) productively enough to pay its future obligations and also make a profit for its owners. In this case it is the insurance companies that invest in productive nonfinancial enterprises. Traditional insurance is therefore potentially a win-win game because it pumps capital back into the real economy.

What about trading stocks and bonds? The buyers ("bulls") are betting that the market for his shares will rise, while the sellers ("bears") are betting that it will fall. Every trade has winners and losers, but altogether the losers lose more than the winners win. The banker-brokers take the difference. The broker's role is to "make a market" (provide liquidity), which means that any buyer or seller can buy or sell, "at the market," even if there is no "counterparty" at the moment. Effectively the broker is constantly buying and selling shares and skimming off a little from each trade. At the end of the day, trading stocks and shares is essentially another zero-sum game. That is how it looks under a microscope. But looking through a telescope (from Mars) the stock market does serve another purpose, namely to enable companies to raise money for investment in real activities, for example, via IPOs.

Finally, what about the hedge funds? The classic example is to find two financial assets that, in theory, should have the same price but that temporarily had slightly different prices, due to market imperfections. The fund makes a bet that the two assets will eventually converge (as per theory), and that the convergence will happen sooner than later. If the prices do converge, the hedge fund makes a profit at the expense of the owners of the mispriced assets. If the prices do not converge, as expected, the hedge fund, being heavily leveraged, can lose a lot (as LTCM did) and the owners of the mispriced assets will be a little richer. Nobody in this business creates jobs in the real economy. The hedge funds are playing zero-sum games, usually with other people's money. They have been big winners for a long time, because the losers didn't understand the games or didn't have all the facts. But it is still gambling. Gambling looks like economic activity because money moves, whence it adds to GDP, but it adds nothing to consumer welfare (Kubiszewski et al. 2013)

Just recently it has emerged that a certain financial product called a "constant proportion debt obligation," or CPDO, was created a few years ago (2006) by the Dutch bank ABN-Amro. It was rated AAA by the ratings agency S&P. Apparently the bank sold this product to investors, borrowed some more money to increase the leverage, and wrote credit default swaps (CDSs) on a "basket" of corporate bonds that were perceived (by the bank's analysts) to be either very safe or very unsafe. That was a wager, pure and simple. The innovative feature of this scheme was that if the initial bets turned sour (i.e., some of the bonds defaulted), the bank could increase its bet or "double down" in gambling lingo. The idea was that everything would work out in the end.

What actually happened was that the investors lost 90 percent of their money. An Australian judge recently decided that the ratings agency S&P should be liable for the losses because "no reasonably competent ratings agency" would have issued AAA ratings on such a risky financial product. S&P's defense was the usual, namely that their opinions are just constitutionally protected "free speech" (Floyd Norris, "Ruling dents legal shield for S&P," *New York Times*, November 9, 2012). But that argument is inconsistent with the SECs determination back in 1975 that the risk assessments of ratings agencies are something more than just opinions. This could be the opening wedge in a long overdue renovation of the ratings system that exists today.

In 2009 the Obama administration submitted several legislative proposals to the Congress. The process resulted in a very ambitious law, known as Dodd–Frank, with multiple objectives that may be quite hard to achieve. The stated purpose was:

To promote the financial stability of the United States by improving accountability and transparency in the financial system, to end "too big to fail," to protect the American taxpayer by ending bailouts, and to protect American consumers from abusive financial services and practices, and for other purposes.

As of 2013 the Dodd–Frank law (see box 5.2) is not yet fully in effect because the existing and new regulatory agencies need time to staff up and write new rules. The Republicans have made it as difficult as possible to implement the law by cutting administration budgets and refusing to approve senior appointments. And, above all, the anti-regulation lobbies have raised a firestorm of opposition, especially to the Volcker Rule. The problem, according to the banks and their lobbyists, is that there is no clear distinction between proprietary trading for profit, market-making and hedging.

The banking conglomerates and their lobbyists (Wall Street firms) are more or less unanimous in asserting that application of the Volcker Rule

Box 5.2
Restoring American Financial Stability Act of 2010, aka Dodd–Frank

This is a complicated piece of legislation that tries to accomplish a lot of things by revamping the whole regulatory framework. It is hard to summarize. The most important feature is arguably the Volcker Rule, which prohibits banks from "proprietary trading" without defining proprietary precisely. It creates new bodies, and re-organizes and re-combines others. It includes many rules (398), a number of major studies (67), and a number of new periodic reports (22), attempting to increase transparency. It regulates hedge funds and private equity funds mainly by reporting requirements, for example, on compensation plans and pay ratios. It also incentivizes banks to help consumers, especially in low-income groups, get better access to credit. And, it must be said, it adds significantly to the administrative burden, and associated costs, that financial institutions will have to bear in the future.

would sharply reduce liquidity in the system, and increase trading costs. But why do banks need so much liquidity? Jesse Eisinger of ProPublica says the liquidity objection is "bogus." He remarks "There is a surfeit of liquidity on Wall Street. Liquidity generates fees and short-term gains but little social worth. It is the opposite of useful" (Eisinger 2012). He points out that trading has increased in the past two decades, but that it has not resulted in cheaper capital for companies. (Credit for small and medium companies has in fact dried up.) I agree with him.

The chief point of contention has to do with how to draw a red line between making a market, which might mean "buying" a large block of securities from a client fund or company, which can't be resold all at once. So how long must such a block be held before it is "market-making" and not "proprietary trading"? The universal banks complain that they might not be able to provide that service to clients. But why should commercial banks be market makers for securities in the first place? The United States got along for sixty-six years without allowing commercial banks to be brokers or jobbers, or gamblers. In fact there is good reason not to allow it.

When the proposed language was published in the Federal Register for public comment, there were 13 substantive responses favoring an overhaul and 300 complaints from the financial industry. However, the lobbyists seem to have created a new strategy to emasculate the law. For the banks, unable to kill the law outright, death by "complexification" is a satisfactory second-best solution. According to some, they seem to have accomplished that already. The result is that, thanks to members of the Congress, SEC, and their staffs, all anxious to please the banks especially the most influential of them all, JPMorgan Chase CEO Jamie Dimon, the law as now rewritten, attempting to provide something for everyone, is a 530-page monstrosity. To put it into effect, federal agencies are required to write 398 rules. As of September, 2013, only 40 percent of these have been completed. Skeptics say that in this form it will achieve nothing (good) because the highly paid lawyers who work for the bankers will always be able to find language to justify whatever their clients want to do.

There is still a (remote) possibility that the regulators will "see the light," drastically simplify the language and strengthen the rules as well as incorporating clear and stiff penalties for violation of those rules. Fines and empty promises "not to do it again" are not enough. Not nearly enough.

The huge $5.8 billion speculative loss at JPMorgan Chase (spring 2012) was due to a hedging strategy involving complex derivatives that somehow misfired because the bank could not instantly "unwind" its huge positions. Why? Because its bank's positions were so large that they could not liquidate their positions by buying the derivatives that had been shorted. (In other words, there were not enough of the derivatives for sale to cover the shorts, probably because other banks or hedge funds had also been buying those same securities, perhaps to bet against or with JPMorgan Chase. There are hints that Morgan tried to "hedge the hedge" in some way. This has certainly reduced CEO Jamie Dimon's credibility. It may conceivably (and should) tilt the balance somewhat in favor of better rule-writing for the Dodd–Frank bill.

Quite apart from Dodd–Frank, the crucial fact that seems to have escaped many analysts and most of the politicians is that the huge financial losses in 2008 from the stock market and real estate (around $16 trillion in the United States) *were financial assets that literally disappeared.* The absence of those assets automatically reduces both borrowing and lending, in aggregate. This is one of the main reasons for the slow GDP recovery. Equally important, *when the real estate and stock-market assets disappeared, the corresponding debts did not.* Lenders expect to be repaid. Yet, shifting some of the US financial debt to the Federal Reserve

System—which was necessary to keep the banking system from collapse—did not increase the total national debt. It merely shifted the responsibility for repayment from the gamblers to the taxpayers.

One final point: the worries about imminent inflation due to "printing money" are completely unjustified (and mostly political). The actions of the US Federal Reserve Bank have kept the banking system alive but have not significantly increased their lending. *The real consequence of the destruction of financial assets in 2008 was deflation.* The fact that the financial crisis of 2008 to 2009 did not destroy the world's financial system is primarily due to the prompt actions of the US Treasury and the Federal Reserve Bank despite a barrage of criticism by libertarians.

But saving the banking system has not solved the larger economic problem. The financial wealth that was destroyed has been partly replaced since 2009. But the real estate losses are still not recovered, unemployment remains significantly higher than it was back in 2007, and the economic growth that might have occurred in five years did not happen. Is there a path to full recovery? I think so, but the story will have to wait.

6

The Role of Misbehavior

The Greek Crisis

When the eurozone was created in 2001, the Greek Public Debt Management Agency, headed by Christoforos Sardelis, had a problem. Greece needed to reduce its debt to GDP ratio to pacify financial markets. Like Enron and WorldCom, and others, Sardelis decided to do this using an off-balance-sheet gimmick concocted by Goldman Sachs. It was based on a complex set of interest rate swaps that would look like a net zero to an accountant, thus masking the real debt. In short, the numbers were concocted out of thin air to convey the appearance of near-conformation with the 3 percent per annum deficit benchmark specified in the Maastricht Treaty.

The actual Greek deficit in that year was 12.7 percent of GDP, and the public debt was $410 billion. Unemployment was then at 10 percent. This accounting trickery was apparently allowed under then-existing Eurostat accounting rules. In 2001 (when the euro was worth less than one dollar), Greece got a 2.8 billion euro loan from Goldman Sachs in exchange for corresponding debts in dollars and yen, at historical exchange rates. Then Goldman seems to have sold those debts to other institutions, probably without sharing all their information. It was a secret deal. Nobody is saying exactly how it worked, except that Goldman made a big profit (allegedly about 600 million euros in 2001 from fees and commissions).

When the existence of the deal was divulged in 2005, Greece's obligations in euros had somehow increased from 2.8 billion to 5 billion, according to Spyros Papanicolaou who took over the debt management agency from Sardelis. In transactions between economic agents with full information, both parties are supposed to be better off. Otherwise why deal? But somehow, when Goldman Sachs or the other Wall Street bankers are involved, there is usually only one winner, the bank. Greece lost twice over. When its statistical chicanery was revealed, the deal was restructured. It remained off the balance sheet until 2008 when Eurostat, the EEC statistical agency, ended the exemption loophole and forced restatement of the accounts. But then international bankers and investors naturally started to worry about the trustworthiness of Greece. Accordingly, Greek debt was downgraded step by step to junk, lowest in the European Union.

Georgio Papandreou, who was elected in 2009, responded with a harsh austerity program: to cut spending, higher taxes, a freeze on employment, tougher measures to collect unpaid taxes, and other measures. The public response was a wave of strikes and violent protests. On April 7, 2010, Papandreou appealed to the IMF for a stand-by arrangement and asked the EU partners to activate the support mechanism, for the first time. A month later, on May 8, the Greeks showed their dissatisfaction by giving him only a 22 percent vote of confidence in his handling of the situation and his policies. In June Papandreou barely survived a confidence vote in the Greek Parliament, but in October another poll reiterated the negative public view of him and his policies by the same percentage. On November 10, 2010, he resigned so that a new government of national unity could be formed under Lucas Papademos.

In the summer of 2011 the "wall of worry" quickly spread, helped by the rating agencies and their ill-timed downgrades. All the peripheral countries in the European Union (Ireland, Portugal, Spain, and most recently, Italy) faced higher interest payment for debt service until a bailout package finally was approved by the Greek government. For Germany, because of its "safe haven" reputation, interest rates have actually declined. Indeed, for Italy and Spain, sovereign bond interest rates, which peaked in the summer of 2011, have also declined recently from near 7 percent (regarded by some as a "red line") to the neighborhood of 5 percent by 2012. But now the situation has stabilized, at least temporarily. Merkel won the 2013 German election with 41 percent of the vote, implying a continuation of German policy in this regard.

The eurozone crisis can accurately be characterized as "subprime mortgage bubble, part II." The fundamental cause of the eurozone crisis was a combination of things. The first was globalization that permits easy capital flows, both into and out of countries, through the banking network, especially SWIFT (Society for Worldwide Interbank Financial Telecommunication). More recently, during 2002 to 2008 the US Federal Reserve Board (FRB) under Alan Greenspan, kept interest rates too low for too long. The low US interest rates were resisted by the European Central Bank (ECB) under deficit hawk Jean-Claude Trichet. But the spread between interest rates on loans from US banks vis-à-vis European banks led to a lot of inter-bank borrowing of dollars by European banks to take advantage of the lower US interest rates.

The globalization and easy money conditions of 2002 to 2008 permitted the unregulated banks in Iceland and Ireland to borrow enormous sums (in euros) from European banks for real estate projects, some real, some bogus. The Irish case was a spectacular land price boom driven almost entirely by a single bank, Anglo-Irish Bank (Carswell 2011). The bank collapsed in 2009. The bank's debts of about 70 billion euros were taken over by the nation (i.e., "socialized") after the failure. Ireland then received a bailout of 85 billion euros from the European Union and the IMF in 2010, subject to strict conditions, to cover the costs of national recapitalization (Carswell 2011, pp. 322–23).

Still another, more direct cause of the eurozone crisis was the collapse of the US subprime mortgage bubble in 2008 to 2009 which led to the destruction of a lot of (so-called) capital assets. As already mentioned, the ratings agencies, Moody's, S&P, and Fitch, belatedly downgraded a lot of the mortgage-based bonds and CDOs that had been created by US investment banks, especially after 2005, from AAA to "junk." That left a number of European countries and banks with huge paper losses.

Those losses triggered a consequent and urgent need on the part of the banks to rebuild their balance sheets. Remember that each 1 euro cut in risk-weighted capital reserves resulted in a 30 to 40 euro cut in bank lending capacity. On top of that, all the banks have been told by Basel III to increase their capital reserves to at least 8 percent risk-weighted, while the applicable risk weights have simultaneously been increased. (Under the old system, government bonds from any country were given risk weights of zero. After 2009 that is no longer the case.)

Under Basel III designated systemically important financial institutions (SIFIs) will also face a dual capital surcharge, partly for simply being systemic and partly for the riskiness of their business models (Saunders and Walter 2011). For the international majors the capital surcharge will be at least 9 percent. National regulators can go higher. Switzerland has announced a "Swiss finish" of 16 percent. These charges have meant that the banks are forced to cut back sharply on loans, *mostly to small and medium-size businesses*. This is one of the major "headwinds" that are reducing economic growth in Europe. Yet growth is exactly what is needed to reduce unsustainable levels of debt. In this context, it is noteworthy that the SME share of output in southern Europe is much larger than it is in the United States, the United Kingdom, or Germany. In France the SME share is 60 percent, in Spain it is 72 percent, while in Italy it is 80 percent.

Trade imbalances were (and are) another important contributor to the problem. It is the huge imbalance between the United States and China that partially drives that US federal budget deficit. There is an accounting balance which states, simply, that dollars sent to China (or any other country) to pay for imported goods must return to the United States in some form. Evidently, since China does not import goods or services in large amounts from the United States, the return flow *must* be used to purchase dollar assets. The Chinese have chosen Treasury bonds.

People who worry about China suddenly deciding to sell off its stockpile of US Treasury bonds are worrying unnecessarily. For China to do that on a large scale would require that the Chinese find other buyers for the bonds. And they would have to use the dollars to buy other US assets, such as minerals, stocks, buildings, or land. Or the balance of trade would have to be somehow magically reversed. That could not happen (in a free market) unless the yuan were to become much more valuable than the US dollar, which is highly unlikely to happen any time soon.[1] (If China were not manipulating its currency to favor its exporters, the yuan would rise automatically somewhat against the dollar, cutting Chinese exports and increasing imports. That revaluation is happening, but slowly.)

The German trade surplus corresponds to trade deficits elsewhere in Europe. That imbalance would, in "normal" circumstances, force Germany to buy goods or Treasury bonds from its neighbors, and it would cause the German deutschmark to rise with respect to the currencies of other euro member countries. That in turn would induce Germans to buy more oranges and olive oil, and take more vacations in the sun, while the Mediterranean countries would import fewer German cars (and probably work harder). But those things don't happen within the eurozone, at present, because of the fixed relationships embodied in the common currency.

The trade imbalances have allowed the countries with trade deficits to pay for their imports by borrowing (i.e., increasing debt), much as the United States has financed its overconsumption. Those days are over.

The final cause of the eurozone crisis was (and is) a fatal flaw in the original Treaty of Maastricht (see box 4.5) that created the common currency in the first place. The rule for entry into the eurozone was that national budgetary deficits should not exceed 3 percent of GDP. The flaw in the treaty was the absence of any realistic mechanism for central fiscal policy formation or coordination for the eurozone and the absence of any mechanism for enforcement of the 3 percent target. Member countries were treated as responsible sovereign decision makers.

Unfortunately, some countries chose to raise the salaries and pensions of public employees, as well as minimum wages and other entitlements to "European" (German) levels, without corresponding tax increases and labor market reforms to pay for the new benefits. Greece was the worst offender. But the flaw in the Maastricht Treaty (lack of central supervision of fiscal policy and budgets) is in the process of being fixed by the European Parliament and the European Commission, despite significant discomfort on the part of many governments. But it will take some time (one or two more years) to implement because it must be ratified by each national legislature. Meanwhile there is still a serious risk of cascading bank failures. The British are the most uncomfortable with the "fix," and it is possible that they will withdraw from the European Union after a referendum promised by the Cameron government for 2018.

It must be said that overall, the eurozone as a whole is in better shape than the United States in several ways. That is true for debt–GDP ratio, trade balance, and fiscal deficit. The main, and critical, difference is that the Federal Reserve Bank in the United States had the legal authority to rescue the banks by taking over a huge amount of their mortgage-related and other bank debt, and still hold interest rates down. That is why the United States is "recovering" at present, whereas the eurozone is still in a (thankfully mild) recession.

The Ratings Scandal

If there was a single most obvious cause of the subprime mortgage debacle of 2008, it was the fact that the rating agencies (Moody's, S&P, Fitch) gave triple A and double A ratings to a lot of mortgage-based bonds and derivatives, such as "collateralized debt obligations" (CDOs), that should have been rated as junk. It turns out that the AAA ratings were not based on mortgage quality at all, even though most people naturally assume the contrary. The ratings were automatic consequences of the tricky subordination structure of the mortgage-based securities and unrealistic assumptions about the probability of defaults.

In case that sounds too technical, let me remind you of the explanation given in chapter 4. The bankers divided a big pool of mortgage bonds into slices, or "tranches" (or floors of a tower, as Michael Lewis explains it). Then they ordered the tranches from 1 to N. The tranche with number 1 would get paid first, and the others were paid in order. (This scheme is called "subordination" in bank-speak.) So the first tranche in a CDO to be paid is almost automatically rated AAA, regardless of the quality of the individual mortgages in the tranche. About 80 percent of the mortgage-based bonds fell in fact into the AAA category, simply because it was unimaginable that the default rate would ever reach 20 percent. The AA tranche included the next 5 percent, while the A tranche accounted for 6.5 percent. The next 3.5 percent were BBB or BB, and the last 5 percent were unrated "equity" tranches. Everything less than AA is called "mezzanine."

Now, what happens if the mortgage default rate goes up? All defaults above the predicted 2 percent level cut the income available to pay the interest due to the lower rated tranches. If defaults exceed 2 percent, the income stream available to the equity or mezzanine tranches (15 percent of the total) will be reduced significantly, perhaps even to zero. This is a crucial point.[2]

Now suppose that a bank collects all the equity or mezzanine tranches of mortgage-based CDOs into a new pool to create a new "second-rank" CDO—a derivative of a derivative. Note that the underlying bonds (on average) are just as good (or bad) as the bonds in the original first-rank CDOs, since the order of payment of the tranches was random, not based on relative quality. So the issuing bank can play the same game and divide the new CDO constructed from the equity tranches of those first-rank CDOs into 100 new tranches, as before. They could then create a subordination ordering from 1 to 100, and pay the tranches in that order. However, the amount of money available to pay the tranches of one of these CDOs is not the same as it would be for the "first-rank" originals. It will be reduced by the amount of all of the defaults of the original CDOs. At first sight, these second-rank CDOs appear identical to the first-rank CDOs. But they are not identical because, if there are any excess defaults beyond the 2 percent level, the total flow of income to the second-rank CDO will be a lot less than the flow to the first-rank set. Evidently it would be highly unrealistic to rate any part of this group as AAA, but Michael Lewis suggests that it might have happened. Unfortunately, there is no published information on how the ratings agencies treated second- (or third-) rank CDOs, or whether they, or the customers, really understood the differences. Goldman Sachs and Morgan Stanley probably did. One suspects that the ratings agencies—and the clients—didn't.

One of the other false and dangerous assumptions made by all the ratings agencies (and the bankers) was that the financial circumstances of the individual homeowners whose mortgages were packaged into a single bond were absolutely uncorrelated. They made this assumption even if all the mortgages in a particular bond were from the same mortgage company in a single town (e.g., in Florida). This easy assumption was made by almost everyone involved in the system, from the top down (except for a few of the smartest "shorts"; see Lewis 2010).

Incidentally, the "zero correlation" assumption also nearly wrecked the insurance companies, starting with AIG, and the banks that sold credit default swaps (CDSs) on the bonds. Because of that assumption, the prices of the credit default swap derivatives were initially set much too low by the issuers. This led to an accumulation of liability risk to the insurers far beyond their reserves. One of the provisions of any new regulation (e.g., Dodd–Frank) must be to correct that problem.

There were almost certainly other model assumptions that should have been challenged by an outside auditing group with the responsibility for generating and testing "what if?" hypotheses. The rating agencies did not have the capability, nor did they ask for it, to "deconstruct" the complex securities and examine their contents (i.e., the individual mortgages). This was obviously not possible as a general practice, given the tens of millions of individual mortgages and tens of thousands of bonds the agencies were being asked to evaluate and rate. However, it would have been possible to randomly select some sample bonds for verification of the overall ratings methodology. This was not done. It was in fact actively discouraged by rating agency management, probably because of the cost involved.

One consequence of the rise of default rates in 2007 and 2008 was that the ratings agencies seem to have panicked. Lacking any systematic way to distinguish the inherent quality of different CDOs that they were being asked to rate, they suddenly downgraded all of them. This action weakened most of the banks and insurance companies in the world at a stroke. It was a major contributor to the financial crash of 2008.

During the golden age of the subprimes, the ratings oligopoly was—and still is—effectively working for the banks. The old golden rule, "he who has the gold makes the rules," seems to have been operational on Wall Street. Moody's, S&P, and Fitch were essentially employees of the banks that wanted to sell their bonds. The rating agencies did what their paymasters wanted to be done. They would deny that, of course.

Who's to Blame? What's to Blame?

On November 23, 2011, *Time Magazine* listed twenty-five "people to blame for the financial crisis." In previous drafts of this book I commented specifically on all of the people listed in the *Time* story. However, time has passed and it is increasingly clear that the bulk of the blame belongs to the system as a whole, not to individuals however greedy or short-sighted they were. (Some were.)

Several innocents were caught in the glare of bad publicity. Wen Jabao (*Time*'s proxy for China) was on the list, but neither he nor his country was directly involved and the only valid charge that can be leveled at China is that China keeps its currency exchange rate too low, encouraging its exports (and discouraging imports), resulting in the huge and intractable trade imbalance that keeps China buying US government bonds and arguably keeps US interest rates too low. This encourages excess consumption in the United States, which includes housing. But China had nothing directly to do with the creation of subprime mortgages and the real estate bubble per se. The "American consumer" is also on the list, but that seems like a case of blaming the victim. The only grain of truth in that is that some subprime consumers tried to "game" the mortgage system, but they did not create it.

Lewie Ranieri, formerly of Salomon Brothers, is on the list, because he was credited with "inventing" the mortgage-based security (in 1978, or so), which led to a very prosperous period for bond traders at Salomon (1982 to 1985). There is nothing wrong with securitizing mortgages and creating a market for those securities, as long as the mortgages underlying the bonds were legitimate (credit checked) and as long as the originator retains some responsibility. Ranieri was fired from Salomon in 1987 for disagreeing with the Salomon's CEO, John Gutfreund, about internal salary policy. Ranieri was not responsible for what happened later. In fact, since 2008, he created something called the *Selene Residential Mortgage Opportunity Fund* and helped raise $825 million for it. Selene buys delinquent mortgages at a deep discount and works with the homeowners to restructure the mortgage in such a way that the homeowner retains some positive equity. Then Selene resells the newly stable mortgages for a profit (he hopes; see Tully 2009).

Marion and Herb Sandler are on the list because back in 1963 they created one of the largest S&Ls in the country, Golden West Financial Corporation. By 2006 it had $60 billion in deposits, $125 billion in assets, and 12,000 employees. Then it was sold (for $24 billion) to Wachovia Bank. The Sandlers kept about 10 percent of the selling price, or $2.4 billion. In its last years Golden West originated huge numbers of subprime mortgages. When the mortgages began to default in large numbers in 2008, Wachovia collapsed and was sold to Wells Fargo. This happened, in part, due to the Golden West acquisition, termed "the deal from Hell" by one journalist. However, the Sandlers have personally given away $1.3 billion of their fortune to good works, including the *Center for Responsible Lending*, a nonprofit organization that fights predatory mortgage lending, payday loans, and other bad industry practices. They also support *ProPublica*, a nonprofit investigative reporting newsroom and other worthwhile causes (*New York Times Magazine* March 9, 2008).

Bill Clinton is being blamed by the Republicans, for obvious political reasons, but his "guilt" is that he failed to foresee the financial consequences of his homeownership policy based on reducing lending standards. That policy was well-intentioned but fundamentally ill-advised. The same policy was adopted by George Bush, who called it a "homeownership society." As explained previously, the homeownership policy was implemented by imposing a quota on the two federally sponsored home mortgage originating agencies, Fannie Mae and Freddie Mac. Prior to 1992 they had been required to reserve 30 percent of their loans for people with incomes below the median for their communities. During the Clinton and Bush administrations this quota was raised to 55 percent. It turned out there weren't enough qualified buyers without the ARMs and subprime loans being promoted most actively by the private mortgage-originating companies like Country-wide. Many of those mortgages, sold to unqualified people, were then bought by the government-sponsored agencies (Fannie and Freddie) to meet their quotas before being sold on to the banks and turned into mortgage-based securities and CDOs.

George Bush had much the same ideas as Clinton about homeowner-ship, but his tax cuts for the wealthy were not responsible for the sub-prime mess. He, too, was a pro-business deregulator and I think he was a terrible president, but as regards the subprime mess, I would blame him only for not seeing any problem, like lots of others, and most of all for nominating Alan Greenspan for a fourth disastrous term as Chairman of the FRB.

Curiously not on *Time's* list of people to blame was Goldman Sachs, which was selling toxic garbage to its clients and betting against those same securities. That is a crime, or should be. But the perps at Goldman have not been named or punished, and Goldman came out of the crisis unscathed. DeutscheBank played it both ways too, but more openly and less profitably.

I have left the most blameworthy (in my view) for last. They were the Gang of Four (or four plus one). One was Senator Phil Gramm, who crafted most of the deregulation bills, including the end of Glass–Steagall, while secretly helping Enron. Another was Arthur Levitt, Chairman of the SEC, who was in charge of a regulatory agency with considerable power but who declined to use it. He instead lent his weight and prestige to the deregulation party. Larry Summers and Robert Rubin both knew exactly what was going on, and not only chose to ignore it but to assist in the process of making it worse. I blame Summers, especially, because he was once a reputable economist. Rubin was the Secretary of the Treasury and Summers' boss. Like Paulson, he could never rid himself of his Wall Street bias against regulation. His attack on Brooksley Born was shameful.

Finally, there is Alan Greenspan, who was admired by British Chancel-lor of the Exchequer and later Prime Minister, Gordon Brown, as "the man who saved the world." That was back in 2002 when the Brits gave him (Greenspan) a knighthood. A critic has said that "to create one bubble may be seen as a misfortune. To create two looks like carelessness" (Blake 2008). That comment hits the nail on the head. Greenspan might not exactly have personally created the dot.com bubble, but in 1998 he knew it was happening and did nothing to stop it, *even though he acknowledged that doing something as simple as raising the margin rate would probably do the trick.*

Worse, in 1998 he effectively stopped the Commodity Futures Trading Commission from doing anything about regulating, or even monitoring, the derivatives market, though it was legally part of the CFTC's mandate. Then, a few years later, he was cheerleading the subprime mortgage boom. He repeatedly insisted that house prices could never go down, despite the contrary experience of the 1930s (which he lived through). Warned repeatedly by scholars that what was happening could only end in tears, he refused to listen. Instead, Alan Greenspan ignored all the evidence, and because he was probably the only one who could have stopped the madness, he deserves by far the most blame, at least among the living. (His mentor, Ayn Rand, deserves quite a bit of blame, too.)

So where, at last, does the blame lie? As I noted at the beginning of this chapter, human nature is part of it. Most people save too little and borrow too much, especially when encouraged to do so by hucksters like Lereah and Jablin. It is an interesting fact that Germans save more than Americans, and Chinese save more than Germans. This partially accounts for why Germany is in a better economic condition today than the United States and why China is growing so fast. That is undoubtedly a cultural difference.

Another aspect of human nature that is less culturally determined is what Greenspan memorably called "irrational exuberance" in 1998. Unfortunately, he only saw it as a harmless, mildly amusing, trait. But the Chairman of the FRB is supposed to be skeptical and critical. If the exuberance (about dot.com stocks) was irrational (it was), why did he do nothing? Worse, why did he choose to be a cheerleader? It is easy to misinterpret a bubble as a long-term trend. People who aren't trained to be skeptical find it all too easy to believe what they want to believe. The best evidence is religious belief. Every bubble in history illustrates the point, and I see no need to cite chapter and verse.

A more interesting point is that in the modern world of banks and central banks, bubbles tend to be self-reproducing. That is to say, every time a bubble collapses, it plants the seeds of the next bubble. The post-bubble recession triggers a "cheap money" response by the central bank. The cheap money (since 1982) is then used by banks to lend to hedge funds to gamble with high leverage and to private equity funds to make investments based on "financial engineering" or hiding profits in tax shelters rather than funding economic growth.

Speaking of financial engineering, which became a growth industry in the 1980s, the popularity of "shareholder value" thinking in business schools and executive suites needs to be included among the causal factors of the catastrophe. I pointed out in an earlier chapter that this doctrine, which originally grew out of a simplistic "principal–agent" model of the corporation (Jensen and Meckling 1976) spread like wildfire in the 1980s. It was an intellectual pseudo-justification for the sort of greed exemplified by the movie character Gordon Gekko who memorably said "greed . . . is good." The reason for its success, as doctrine, was that most economists believed (still believe) that it follows directly from Adam Smith's insight that self-interest is the driver of all economic activity and growth. The argument—that maximizing shareholder value is simply the legal duty of corporate boards of directors and CEOs—seems to follow from the assumption that they are agents of the shareholders, who are the real owners of the firm. But for public companies, that assumption is simply not true. When a public company goes bust, it is the bondholders who take over.

Then there is the problem of bad regulation and bad deregulation. Here the problem is unintended consequences. The FASB mark-to-market rule is a well-intentioned but bad regulation because it attempts to solve an essentially insoluble technical problem by bureaucratic means. (Recall previous discussion of the problems of estimating value in the absence of markets.) Basel I and Basel II were also examples of well-intentioned but bad regulations because the BIS risk weights effectively forced banks to shift away from corporate lending to lending to government-sponsored institutions (e.g., Fannie Mae and Freddie Mac), thus favoring real estate construction over business credit. The obvious example of bad deregulation was the slow dismantling of Glass–Steagall, starting when Greenspan's Fed began to allow banks to engage in non-bank activities (i.e., to underwrite securities), back in 1986, followed by a series of further and bigger exceptions to the rules. It was almost inevitable that the Congress, egged on by the "Gang of Four," finally put an official end to the Glass–Steagall Act in 1998 for no better reason than to allow "too big to fail" (TBTF) banks to get still bigger.

Finally, there is the persistent problem of how to accelerate economic growth to get out of debt. The world is already deeply in debt. The choice is default or accelerated growth. Yet the Republican ideologues like Dan Ryan insist on Andrew Mellon's famous recipe: "liquidate, liquidate, liquidate," which is another word for "laissez faire." Liquidation didn't drive growth in 1930 to 1932. Why should it work now? What is needed is a positive investment strategy. The only strategy that makes any sense to me is to invest in energy efficiency, decarbonization, and new sources of energy because the world needs to do that anyhow. I discuss that strategy in chapter 8.

To be sure, some blame must fall on ideology based on romantic fiction. Libertarianism is based largely on the ideas espoused by novelist Ayn Rand half a century ago. It is based on a set of ideas about markets and human behavior that are simply (and objectively) false. The most notable blind spot in her (their) view of the world is the notion that what unfettered capitalists will do is always good and progressive, while government regulators are invariably venal and self-serving. She (and her followers) blame the government for every problem. Meanwhile she (and they) fail to recognize that unfettered capitalism has frequently resulted in unintended disasters (e.g., toxic industrial pollution, climate change, and financial bubbles) that shift wealth to the few and harm the many.

7
Where Do We Stand Today?

Reprise on Debt and Moral Hazard

When Ronald Reagan was elected, the federal debt amounted to 26 percent of the GDP. After he took office with a Republican majority in1981, he (and Congress) cut taxes and increased military spending dramatically (and unnecessarily), resulting in significant growth of the federal debt. When he left office, it was 41 percent of the US GDP (figure 7.1). The supply-siders who advised Reagan that tax reductions would pay for

Percent of US GDP

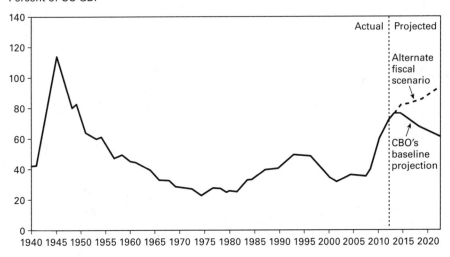

Figure 7.1
Federal debt held by the public projected in CBO's baseline and under an alternative fiscal scenario

themselves were evidently quite wrong, although none of them has yet apologized or conceded any error.

In 1986 Reagan signed a tax bill that cut the top income tax rate from 70 to 50 percent and later to 28 percent. He also equalized capital gains tax at 28 percent, almost double the current rate (figure 7.2). The federal deficit grew sharply during Reagan's time in office. It stayed higher under George Bush (senior). The deficit finally began to decline just before President Clinton took office at the beginning of 1993. However, while the tax cuts on high incomes were quite significant, tax rates for both ordinary income and capital gains remained at a much higher level than they are today.

In Clinton's first term the rate went up one point to 29 percent. But in 1997 Clinton allowed Congress to cut capital gains taxes to 20 percent in exchange for a children's health insurance program. Clinton's successor, George W. Bush, went much further in 2001, cutting the tax on dividends and the capital gains tax to 15 percent. That happens to be roughly the tax rate that people in the top 1 percent of the income range, such as Republican Presidential candidate Mitt Romney, pay today. Romney paid only 13.9 percent of his income in federal taxes in 2010. His strongest

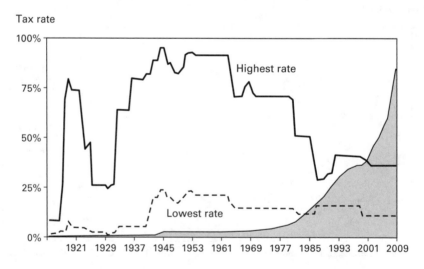

Figure 7.2
Income tax rates and national debt compared

primary opponent in the spring of 2012, former Senator Rick Santorum, paid more than twice as much (in percentage) on a much smaller income. The Reagan tax cuts and the Bush II tax cuts in 2002 did not increase revenues, despite vociferous claims by the "supply-siders." Figure 7.3 tells the story. The consequence, as most economists predicted, was reduced government revenues and increased federal debt. Lower taxes for the rich have not generated employment or jobs, despite claims by the "Club for Growth" and other lobby groups.

As figure 7.3 shows, there was a brief period at the end of the Clinton presidency and extending into the first year of George W. Bush's presidency, when federal revenues based on tax policies from the Clinton era exceeded outlays. In 2001 the Congressional Budget Office (CBO) projected average annual surpluses of roughly $850 billion from 2009 through 2012. But the second President Bush, winner of a disputed election against Al Gore that was decided by the Supreme Court in 2000,

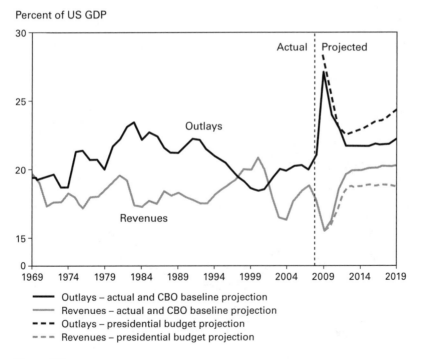

Percent of US GDP

Outlays – actual and CBO baseline projection
Revenues – actual and CBO baseline projection
Outlays – presidential budget projection
Revenues – presidential budget projection

Figure 7.3
Revenues compared with outlays as a percentage of GDP

used that surplus, and more, *not to reduce the debt* as Republicans always promise but to cut taxes for the wealthy even more and to fund the second war in Iraq. Actually the war was not paid for out of taxes but from borrowed money. Based on Bush's policies, the CBO foresaw an average deficit for the same years of $1,215 billion. The increased federal deficit s accounted for by the CBO as follows (Leonhardt 2009):

• Recessions of 2000 to 2001 and 2008 to 2009 and unemployment compensation (37 percent)

• Bush policies: tax cuts, Iraq war, Medicare drugs (33 percent)

Trillions of 2010 USD

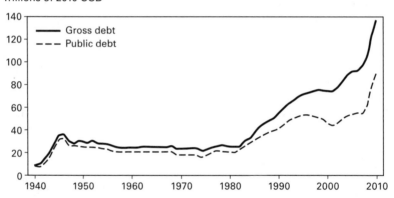

Fraction of GDP

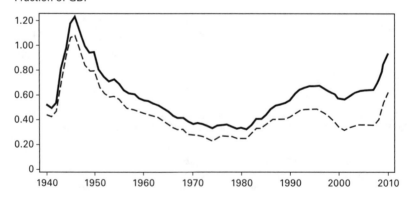

Figure 7.4
US public debt

- Bush policies extended by Obama, including bank bailouts (TARP), military (20 percent)
- New policies from Obama, stimulus and others (10 percent)

It is noteworthy that the economy added 11.5 million jobs (net) during Clinton's administration, as compared to a much smaller number added during the subsequent Bush II years.

The effect of "Reaganomics" on the national debt is shown in the two graphs (figure 7.4a, b). The low point was reached in 1975, just after the first "oil shock" and just before the second oil shock. It was almost the same in 1980 at the end of the Carter presidency. By the end of the Reagan–Bush (I) presidencies, the net federal debt had increased by $8.2 trillion (including interest). Since 2008 the Obama administration has added more than $5 trillion, but very little of that is attributable to social programs. Most of the new debt is due to a continuation of policies enacted by Bush (II). Some was the residue of George Bush's troubled assets relief program (TARP) the bank bailouts—and some was due to Obama's stimulus investment in early 2009. But mostly it was caused by federal takeovers of bank debts such as "toxic" CDOs comprised of mortgage-based bonds that were (but should not have been) rated AAA.

One may argue as to who is responsible for the Afghan war, which Obama upgraded but did not start. One may also argue that Obama's "stimulus" package in 2009 was really a response to the 2008 recession that was caused by the financial crisis that he did not create.

The composition of US debt is revealing (figure 7.5). At the end of WWII there was essentially no debt in the financial sector and very little in the state and local sector. Federal debt, which consisted of war bonds, amounted to about 105 percent of GDP, followed by non-bank corporate debt (about 30 percent of GDP) and private household debt (mortgages) amounting to about 15 percent of GDP. Until 1972 the federal debt declined as a fraction of GDP (to a little over 25 percent, as previously mentioned) while all other sectors increased their share, and the household sector increased the most (to 45 percent).

In 1972 total debt was just over 150 percent of the US GDP. After 1972 the major increase in debt has not been the Federal government. The big borrowers, by far, have been the financial sector, followed by households (mortgages, auto loans, credit cards, and educational loans). As of

Fraction of GDP

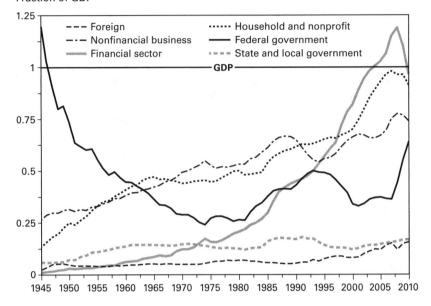

Figure 7.5
US debt as a fraction of US GDP

2008 the debt–GDP ratios by sector in percentage terms were roughly as follows: state and local government (10 percent), federal government (50 percent), households (110 percent), finance (120 percent), and nonfinancial industry (60 percent). Thus debt by financial institutions to each other accounted for 60 percent of the entire increase in national debt since 1972. Since this does not include credit card debt, household mortgage debt, corporate debt, or municipal debt, it consists entirely of debts between financial institutions or between regional banks and the Federal Reserve. It is evident that much of that debt was created for purposes of financing LBOs and other financial speculations that produced no visible goods or services outside of the financial sector itself.

US disposable income exceeded private consumption by a margin of 10 to 12 percent (the personal savings rate) from 1960 until 1982. But from 1983 on, the savings rate steadily decreased and consumption increased. By 2005, net saving had fallen to barely 2 percent of disposable income. In 2006 and 2007, the savings rate stayed at about 2.5 percent. Then, in 2008, it jumped back up to 5 percent, where it remained into 2012. That extra saving corresponds to reduced spending, of course, and is one of the reasons for the slow recovery after the recession of 2008 to 2009.

The three main causes of declining savings from 1980 to 2005 were (1) homeownership (mortgages), (2) credit card debt, and (3) educational debt. The number of people with credit cards increased from 82 million in 1990 to 144 million in 2003, a 75 percent increase. The total amount they charged in 1990 was $338 billion (*$533 billion*$_{2011}$); in 2003 that was up 350 percent to $1.5 trillion (*$1.8 trillion*$_{2011}$). The revolving balance in 1990 was $2,550 (*$4,000*$_{2011}$); in 2003 it was $7,520 ($9,000$_{2011}$). Yet personal income only increased from $4.9 trillion (*$7.7trillion*$_{2011}$) in 1990 to $9.2 trillion (*$11 trillion*$_{2011}$) in 2003. Household debt service payments to credit card companies, auto loans and education loans peaked at 14 percent of personal disposable income in 2007. Since then, thanks to the recession and other factors, household debt service has declined to 11 percent of disposable income. That is good news in terms of fiscal sanity, but not for spending our way back to prosperity. Unfortunately, educational debt is still increasing and will soon exceed $1 trillion. This is likely to be a major drag on the economy, especially as job creation for the young continues to lag.

The Hayek objection to debt finance was, and still is, that deficit spending on government projects, or private investments made possible by cheap (low-interest) money, tends to be very wasteful and a poor use of resources. This is really indisputable. The boom in common stocks purchased on margin in 1927 to 1929 was made possible by low-interest bank loans to brokers. The "financial engineering" and leveraged buyout bubble in the 1980s were financed by cheap money, and this continues on a much larger scale under the rubric "private equity." So were the real estate bubble in Japan in the 1980s and the dot.com bubble that ended in 2000. (That was when the federal budget was in surplus and the debt could have been reduced. But the Bush administration cut revenues and increased the debt instead.) The latest example is the US housing bubble that was created by ultra-cheap money and subprime mortgages after the recession of 2000.

The Hayek (anti-Keynes) prescription was to "liquidate" the banks that had made too many bad loans. Quite a few conservatives still claim that this was the right policy. But the inter-linkages between banks and the rest of the economy today are such that the consequences of letting several of the big ones fail would have been far worse than the current situation. Just letting Lehman Brothers fail nearly sank the system in 2008. Letting the others fail was never a practical possibility in an interconnected world. So the Hayek purists are somewhat short of practical advice about what to do now. That is why they talk so much about the importance of "confidence."

A logical response by the Hayek purists might be to propose a return to the gold standard, which looks better in retrospect than it did back then. The actual gold supply is far too small, of course, not to mention other problems like non-bank financing, wide private ownership, and industrial use. However, just as banks are able to create synthetic CDOs, one might speculate whether governments could create "synthetic gold." I return to this possibility later in a more serious vein.

In the interconnected world we live in, celebrated especially by Tom Friedman of the *New York Times*, some hedge funds (or "vulture funds") can bet against countries, as George Soros once did, by borrowing (Greek or other) government bonds from the big international banks and selling them at a discount. They then bet that the EU rescue effort will fail, in which case Greece (or Greek banks) will have to default. If that happens, the borrowed bonds become worthless, so the hedge funds collect on the credit default swaps they bought (at low prices) and make a huge profit at practically no cost to themselves. But, as always, somebody loses.

However, if the bailout comes through, there will be losses for the hedge funds. Nobody but their investors will cry for them. But needless to say the "shorts" will try every trick in their arsenal of tricks to prevent the rescue from succeeding, and never mind what happens in Greece if the bailout fails. It's just capitalism and the American way. Those hedge funds are like children playing with matches in a haystack. If they succeed, and the Greek bailout does not happen, the "daisy chain" of bank failures could drag the whole global banking system down. (Then again, it might not. But there is always Spain to bet against, or Italy. Counterfactual theorizing is always risky.)

The debts have indeed become a global problem, but they cannot be blamed on Keynes policy recommendations. Keynes in fact advocated balanced budgets, on average, but allowing for deficit spending to create demand during recessions, to be balanced by using surpluses to pay off debts during boom periods. What has actually happened, of course, is that politicians in most democracies have chosen the politically popular path to cut taxes and increase spending during booms as well as during recessions. (This was Bush II's choice in 2001 before 9/11.)

The conventional wisdom is that we must (and will) grow out of the present unsustainable debt burden. But the uncomfortable truth is that nobody in power has a clue as to how to make faster growth happen by means of government policy, if low interest rates do not suffice. (And, they don't.) Worse, the last few attempts to stimulate growth with cheap money have been counterproductive. Keynesians like Paul Krugman and some others think it can be done by investing in a much bigger stimulus (to be followed by an unspecified budget balancing effort later, by reducing entitlements and cutting military spending). In a rational world that might happen, but in the real world it seems unlikely in the extreme. Entitlement cuts are needed, to be sure, but they will not accelerate growth. If anything, they will slow it.

Is there hope? Yes. I think the policy wonks and the politicians are missing a key point, namely that the tools available to the Fed today are simply too crude. The FRB and other central banks now acknowledge that one of their mandates is to increase employment when times are bad. Their only tools for doing so are to cut interest rates and to buy debt from the banks. But, as hinted several times already in this book, consumer spending is not likely to increase enough to "kick-start" the US economy any time soon. Too many consumer product markets are approaching saturation, and too much of what consumers buy is now made in other countries. What needs further consideration is the critical role of energy in the economic system.

The Future of Oil

This book has emphasized the connection between fossil fuels and finance for two reasons. In the first place, the natural resource discoveries of the past (coal, oil, and gas) changed the nature of money. The shift from gold and silver coins to "faith and credit" took a long time; for some it is not yet over but it changed the nature and meaning of wealth, and thence of money itself. In the second place, as long as time series data have been available (since about 1850), there has been a very close correlation between global total primary energy requirements (TPER) and global GDP

Global TPER (Mtoe)

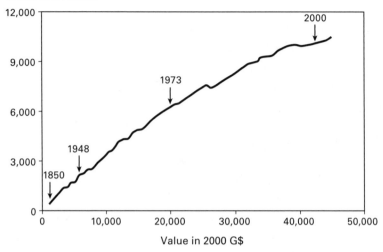

Figure 7.6
World primary energy and GDP, 1850 to 2002

in purchasing power parities (PPP), as can be seen in figure 7.6 (Bourdaire 2003). Up to between 1973 and 1975 the relationship was very nearly linear. That is to say, every index unit of primary energy consumed was accompanied by an index unit of GDP growth, and every index unit of growth was accompanied by a unit of energy (TPER).

Later I argue that the link between growth and primary energy is overshadowed by the link between economic activity and "useful work," which is the product of primary energy times the efficiency with which energy is converted to work. This relationship is intuitively reasonable, since "work" is what produces goods and services. However, the appropriate definition of "efficiency" is not immediately evident, and a detailed discussion must wait its turn.

The point is that after the date of the first "oil crisis" (1973 to 1974), there has been a gradual, but definite, "decoupling" of energy consumption and growth. Since then a unit of GDP growth has been accompanied by (or required) a little less energy consumption than before. Moreover the reduction in global "energy intensity" of the global economy (to use standard jargon) has continued. This is shown by the slight but clear indication of "saturation" in figure 7.6. This decoupling suggests that energy use has been getting more efficient. It might also logically imply that the growth mechanism is getting more efficient. Both may be true.

Before addressing the question of causation (does energy availability cause growth, or is it the other way around?), which is very important to theorists, I want to call attention to figure 7.7. It shows that there has been a succession of oil price shocks, starting in 1973, each of which has been followed by a recession. The latest example of an oil shock was 2008 when the price briefly reached $145/bbl and was followed by the global financial collapse in 2008 from which the Western countries, especially the United States, have not yet fully recovered. I don't claim that the recession in 2008 to 2009 was actually caused by the oil price spike of 2008. However, it is very likely that the price spike accelerated—or even triggered—the financial collapse that was coming (Hamilton 2009).

The history of events since 1970, shown in figure 7.7, also suggests that the state of the macroeconomy in the short term is tightly linked to the price of oil. Most economists still assume that increasing energy consumption is caused by growing GDP, *and not vice versa.* I think that the causal connection also works both ways: demand for energy creates demand for other goods and services that increase GDP.

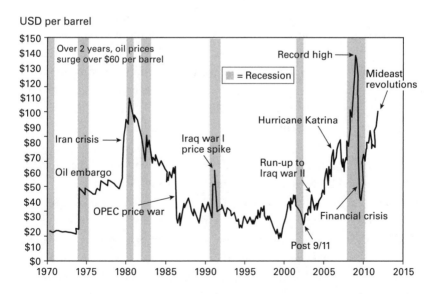

Figure 7.7
Oil prices and recessions

The magnitude and immediacy of the economic slowdowns after price spikes, especially the oil embargo in 1973 to 1974 and the Iranian revolution in 1979 to 1980, persuaded some economists such as Dale Jorgenson and his colleagues to try to recast the theory of economic growth so as to include energy as a "factor of production" (Hudson and Jorgenson 1974; Berndt and Jorgenson 1978; Allen 1979). I think they were on the right track. But their efforts did not succeed in persuading the majority of academic economists at the time (or since), probably for theoretical reasons explained at the end of chapter 1.

The post-spike recessions, in each case (except 1990) up to and including 2008 to 2009, have been partly caused by the extra burden of high oil prices on the economy. And, I think that burden is significantly greater than standard economic theory assumes. In the most recent case, the high oil price in 2008 coincided with (whether or not it caused) the collapse of housing prices. Most economists believe that the sharp rise in mortgage defaults that began in 2006 and accelerated in 2007 had little or nothing to do with the high price of oil. I disagree. The rising price of oil and other energy commodities from 2003 to 2008 absorbed an increasing share of household budgets, leaving less for other purposes, including mortgage payments. That may have been all it took to prick the bubble.

The oil price bubbles in 1973 to 1974, 1979 to 1980, and 2007 to 2008 had another unfortunate consequence. On the way up, they hurt the economy but encouraged some investment in energy efficiency or renewables. On the way down, they killed a lot of those investments. Now venture capital does not flow readily into new energy technology. The investors have been burned too often. For this reason, forward investments in alternative energy technologies will need to be hedged. I return to this point later in chapter 9.

The other major theory to explain oil price spikes is that they are due to speculation. There is no doubt that speculation affects prices. It tends to exaggerate both the rises and the falls. In a recession the demand for oil goes down by a few percent but the price goes down a lot more (Hamilton 2005). Some hedge funds bet on price changes on a daily basis. The presence of speculators in the market is a potential trap for long-term investors. Warren Buffet, the most successful of the "value investors" fell into that trap in the summer of 2008. In a letter to the shareholders of Hathaway (his fund) he apologized:

I bought a large amount of ConocoPhillips stock when oil and gas prices were near their peak. I in no way anticipated the dramatic fall in energy prices that occurred in the last half of the year. I still believe the odds are good that oil sells far higher in the future than the current $40–50 price. But so far I have been dead wrong. Even if prices should rise, moreover, the terrible timing of my purchase has cost Berkshire several billion dollars.

The reason Buffet bought ConocoPhillips shares in the first place was his recognition that demand for oil is rising everywhere, but especially in China, thanks to rapid economic growth in that country as well as India, Brazil, Russia and other developing countries. The correlation between economic growth rates and oil prices is *not* accidental (Ayres and Warr 2005). But I think Buffet was not wrong about the long-term trend, just the timing. By the winter of 2009, the price of oil had bottomed at $30/bbl (the low point), although it recovered quickly after that. In the spring of 2011, it was up to over $100/bbl again, despite a very weak economic recovery. The post-peak troughs are getting higher, and if Buffet had been patient, his investment would not have looked quite so bad.

The financial community, with most professional economists, tends to assume that there is no problem of shortage of natural resources. Until quite recently (2004) the International Energy Agency, the IMF, and the US Energy Information Agency (EIA) all assumed that coal reserves are too large to worry about for the next century or so, while petroleum and gas consumption would increase for many decades at no increase in price. Conversely, many geologists said that the annual supply of cheap liquid hydrocarbons (oil) was likely to peak and start to decline in the near future.[1]

The "peak oil" people were right, as regards the global output of conventional liquid petroleum. The main argument is quite simple and non-technical (figure 7.8). The peak year for global discoveries was 1948 and discoveries, including "unconventional oil," are way down from that level (see also figure 2.3)

Since 1980 annual consumption of petroleum has not been replaced by discoveries in the same year, with two exceptions. The last exception was 1991, and it was a fluke. For the past thirty-two years, oil has been consumed faster than new oil (including natural gas liquids) has been discovered, and the gap is growing. Some authors suggest that global output of terrestrial and offshore crude peaked around 2005.

Gigabarrels annually

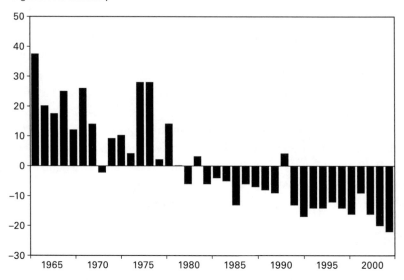

Figure 7.8
Global oil discoveries minus global oil consumption, 1965 to 2003

However, the reserve situation is less clear as regards "unconventional oil," meaning hydrocarbons that are not found in fluid form but that can be "fluidized" in a straightforward way (e.g., unlike coal). These resources include Venezuelan heavy oil and Canadian tar sands. But the big change in the last two decades is the demonstration of "fracking" to extract shale gas and "tight oil." Some of that oil is actually a liquid, trapped in shale (rock) where it doesn't flow naturally but can be extracted by horizontal drilling and "fracking."

There is little public information about the oil-from-shale process, except that it involves very high pressure water to fracture ("frack") the rock and release the bitumen. Then the oil, mixed with water and chemicals, must be pumped back to the surface from depths up to two kilometers. The shale-gas industry has been very reluctant to identify the chemicals in use, on the ground of proprietary secrecy. The oil and water must be separated, which is not so easy as experience with ocean spills has demonstrated, and the dirty saline water must be disposed of, probably in holding ponds, or recycled back into the shale (Hughes 2010). There is an obvious threat to aquifers and groundwater.

It is indeed true that the shale deposits that contain potentially recoverable oil are very large. The Bakken and Eagle Ford shales under Montana and North Dakota contain up to 700 billion barrels of fluid oil bound tightly into sandstone. Annual US consumption of petroleum is 7 billion barrels. According to the current wisdom of the US Geological Survey, 3 to 4.3 billion barrels of the shale oil will be recoverable, amounting to six months or so of current consumption. Even if the recovery rate is doubled or quadrupled, it would take care of perhaps two years of current US consumption. Interestingly, the Green River shale under Colorado, Wyoming and Utah, contains two trillion barrels of hydrocarbons (kerogen), but not in fluid form. It can only be recovered by means of a high-temperature "cooking" process. Despite many years of research, no practical means has yet been found to recover that resource, certainly not at current prices.

Shale gas (and tight oil) wells peak and decline much more rapidly than conventional wells. The longest experience in shale gas comes from the Barnett shale play under Dallas–Fort Worth, Texas. It peaked in 2009, when over 12,000 wells had been drilled costing $2 to $4 million each. Production rates were high at first, but declined rapidly, typically down 65 percent in the first year. The Haynesville shale play in east Texas and Louisiana experienced even faster declines, despite very high costs of $10 million per well (Hughes 2010). The Bakken shale play (North Dakota) exhibits similar decline rates (about 69 percent in the first year, 39 percent in the second year, 26 percent in the third year, etc.). Based on experience, if no new wells had been drilled after 2010, the Bakken shale oil output would have declined from the peak of just over 350,000 bbl/day in 2009 to 200,000 bbl/day two years later. Based on experience so far, the rate of decline for a field (as opposed to a single well) is between 30 and 35 percent a year. This is a much faster rate of decline than conventional oil fields exhibit (about 7 percent each year). Meanwhile the recovery is about 10 percent—as compared to 70 percent for a natural gas field.[2]

Water requirements in Texas were 2 to 5 million gallons (6 to 20 liters) per well. Moreover in much of the world there is simply not enough spare water, above and beyond agricultural, industrial, and municipal uses. Places where population density is very low (i.e., North Dakota) are also places where water is comparatively scarce. Water scarcity in several parts of the world, partly due to increased irrigation of agricultural lands, partly to competing industrial demands, partly due to pollution, and partly due to excessive use of "fossil" water from underground aquifers, are already pushing grain prices higher. Climate change will almost certainly make the water problem worse, and that will have a negative impact on shale "fracking" (as well as some other technologies, like Canadian tar sands)

Shale-gas (and oil) promoters have created a "mini-bubble" in shale gas. They insist that above $70 per barrel (well below the current price of oil (about $94/bbl) there is plenty of shale oil to be found. Investment in shale in 2010 and 2011 was apparently a trillion dollars, with another $600 billion scheduled for 2012. The publicity has been inspired partly by an advertising campaign financed by T. Boone Pickens ("The Pickens Plan").[3] Some the hype goes back to widely publicized report by Leonardo Maugeri, a former oil industry CEO, now at Harvard's Belfer Center.

The IEA and EIA gave shale their *imprimatur* of official acceptance in their respective Annual Energy Reviews/Outlooks of 2011. Both projected that the United States would be the world's biggest natural gas producer by 2015 and that the United States would produce 10 million bbl/day of oil or NGL from shale by 2020 before resuming the long-term decline. The *Wall Street Journal* editorialized about the coming of "Saudi America." Since then the media has converted it into a gusher with headlines like George Monbiot's article in the *Guardian*: "We were wrong on peak oil. There's enough to fry us all" (*The Guardian*, July 2, 2012). This year there is a lot of journalistic speculation about the geo-political consequences of future US energy independence/self-sufficiency. The big fact of the moment is that natural gas prices in the United States are currently well below European levels.

There is an odor of fish, however. The simultaneity and similarity of the IEA and EIA outlooks suggest a high degree of collaboration. It is important to remember that both organizations are political and their policies are strongly influenced by political (i.e., energy industry) rather than technical considerations.

I accept David Hughes's more cautious conclusion that the peak of US shale oil will occur around 2020 but that it will amount to only about one-third of the IEA-EIA's 10 million bbl/day estimate for oil and natural gas liquids (NGL). The gas forecasts are more realistic. But drilling for gas in the United States trebled from 2000 to 2009, with no increase in the quantity of gas recovered.

The cost of oil to the economy is virtually certain to rise in coming decades, despite fracking, if only because *the average energy return on energy invested (EROEI) has been declining for a long time.* The number of barrels of oil obtained on average per barrel of oil-equivalent needed to dig the wells and transport the product in east Texas in the 1930s was over 100. By 1980 the global average was down to 30 or so. Currently, as figure 7.9 shows, the global average is thought to be around 20, and the oil from tar sands and deep ocean probably has an EROEI of less than 10 (Hall 2008; Hall and Day 2009). This chart is not really authoritative. The EROEI for solar panels cited by Hall and Day is based on an old study and is too low. Modern PV panels are much better than the very low number suggested by figure 7.9. Also the EROEI for Canadian tar sands is now about 5:1 for open pit mines and 3:1 for underground steam extraction, both better than figure 7.9 suggests (Hughes 2010). In the case of ethanol from corn, the EROEI a few years ago was barely above unity by the most optimistic estimate (Pimentel 2003; Natural Resources Defense

Energy activity

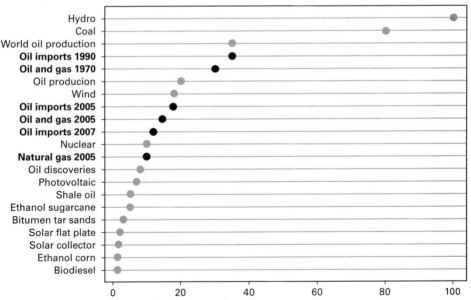

Figure 7.9
USA-2010 ratio of EROEI (energy returned on energy invested). Data from Murphy and Hall (2010).

Council 2006; Hammerschlag 2006). Due to higher productivity of corn per hectare, and dry rather than wet milling, the energy return today is somewhat higher than Pimentel calculated but not nearly high enough to justify diverting fertile land from food production to fuel production.

Apart from the geological evidence of coming scarcity there is another problem on the horizon that has not yet been recognized or incorporated into long term plans. That is the problem of climate change triggered by cumulative emissions of so-called greenhouse gases (GHGs), including carbon dioxide and methane (see the next chapter). The only way to cut these emissions is to stop burning fossil fuels and to depend instead on renewable alternatives. To do that will require a very large investment in alternative technology and new facilities. This is what economic policy should have been focusing on after the Iraq war, rather than providing cheap mortgages to increase home ownership. The need for investment in renewables and energy efficiency continues.

A standard response from economists who are skeptical about "peak oil" is that *everything, including petroleum, has a substitute.* Canadian tar sands and ethanol from corn or sugar cane are supposed to be substitutes for oil. "Clean coal" is an oxymoron. It really means coal gasification or liquefaction. Gasification produces a somewhat inferior substitute for natural gas, but if natural gas is not available, gasification may be a partial answer (e.g., in China or India). But coal gasification plants are complex, they take a long time to build, and each one is different. There is no standard design. Furthermore the gasification technology is very capital intensive, and it is also very energy intensive. In other words, it consumes a lot of the coal feedstock just to operate the conversion process. The useful energy content of the gas is only two-thirds of that in the coal, at best, and barely over half in existing plants. Apart from these points, coal gasification is only applicable to the electric power industry. It does not produce liquid fuels needed for transport systems.

Speaking of transport, over 60 percent of all petroleum is used to provide fuel for automobiles, while transportation as a whole takes 70 percent of production. Hybrids (a combination of rechargeable electric batteries, electric motors in the wheels, and a small gasoline or diesel engine to kick in for acceleration and hill climbing) are already mainstream. Toyota will produce over one million hybrids this year alone, and other manufacturers are following. Hybrids can replace all existing cars with half the fuel consumption. Advanced hybrids and lightweight all-electric vehicles, built from aluminum and composite materials, can cut fuel consumption by another 50 percent if not more, at costs that are currently higher than conventional vehicles but that promise to decline steadily. On top of that, bicycles—especially the electric bikes now available—can replace at least 40 percent of all urban passenger transport, as already demonstrated in the Netherlands and Denmark and increasingly throughout urban Europe and parts of the United States. Combining these changes, even without heavy investment in new rail-based public transport, can cut petroleum consumption for cars by around 80 percent (or 50 percent overall) without any special government intervention except at the local level (e.g., charging facilities for electric cars and reserved parking places for bicycles). This trend will cut demand for petroleum in the OECD countries by as much as 50 percent by 2035. That in turn will cut payments to the OPEC countries. It remains to be seen whether increasing demand by BRICs and other developing countries will compensate, and how much.

Economists make another point that is better grounded. Just as the "fracking" technology has brought down the price of gas, one can suppose that "green" technologies—as in the example above—will prove to be very successful in the near term, thereby reducing aggregate demand for petroleum and its tarry cousins. If lower demand led to lower prices, this would have the effect of reducing the profitability of projects like recovery from tar sands and fracking of shale. Shutting down high-cost projects like tar sand recovery and "fracking" would, of course, reduce the supply and drive the price of oil back up. It follows that the economics of unconventional oil is strongly dependent on the rate of increase of demand by developing countries, notably the BRICs.

A few other points need to be made here. First, and easiest, coal is not a substitute for liquid fuels, except insofar as it is used to make electricity for electrified trains or vehicles. It is also clear that "clean coal" is an advertising slogan, not even a theoretical possibility. All coal contains contaminants of sulfur, nitrogen, mercury, ash, and other pollutants. Most old coal-burning power plants do not do a very good job in capturing and sequestering all those pollutants before they get into the atmosphere. Improvements in that regard are possible and probable, but at a cost that increases as the treatment becomes more efficient.

Moreover carbon dioxide—the primary cause of climate change—is not captured and removed from the exhaust gas anywhere in the world yet. The highly touted carbon capture and storage (CCS) program, if it is ever implemented on a large scale, will be an undeserved welfare program for the coal industry. Why? Because it significantly increases the demand for energy to capture, compress, and pump the CO_2 back underground. Hence it would actually increase the consumption of coal. That is why the coal industry is so keen on the idea, especially if governments (i.e., taxpayers) can be induced to pay for it.

Coal liquefaction refers to a modern version of the Bergius or FischerTropsch hydrogenation processes used by Germany during WWII. The most plausible alternative for gasoline today is methanol, which can be made from natural gas and can be used in existing vehicles without modification (Olah, Goeppert, and Prakesh 2009). However, none of these alternatives is economically attractive today.

Nuclear power cannot be ruled out, much as many of its opponents would like. New design, based on so-called fourth-generation technology, may turn out to be much less vulnerable to meltdown than much of the public now believes. However, the waste storage problem and the proliferation problem remain unsolved. They may be insoluble. Moreover nuclear electricity cannot replace liquid fuels which are essential for all transportation except for electrified railways (and electric cars, eventually). Hence I do not consider the uranium-based nuclear option further. A thorium-based nuclear power technology may be a game-changer, however.

Crude oil production on land seems to have peaked already (in 2006) and the nonconventional substitutes, such as natural gas liquids or deep ocean drilling or oil from Canadian tar sands or from shale, are much more expensive than Middle Eastern oil is today. Nuclear power will also get more expensive due to increased safety controls and the future (yet unknown) costs of nuclear waste treatment and disposal that will have to be paid for.

As a matter of interest, a recent IMF working paper (Benes et al. 2012) presents a new nonlinear econometric model that encompasses both the technological and geological views (figure 7.10). The new model, which takes into account the unconventional oil technologies such as shale gas, fits past experience better than previous empirical models. The central model

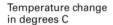

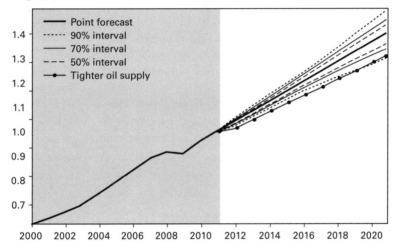

Figure 7.10
GDP forecast (logarithmic) with error bands

forecast for 2020 puts oil prices at $180/bbl, with a 90 percent probability of being in the range $122 to $240 per bbl. To be clear, this model result is not the "official" view at the IMF, but I think it will be, in time.

Climate Change

The current and continuing economic crisis has diverted the attention of politicians from the implications of climate change, but that cannot continue. The year 2012 was the warmest on record. Hurricane Sandy hit New York City and caused billions of dollars' worth of damage on Long Island, Staten Island, and the communities along the New Jersey shoreline. The New York subways were flooded and out of commission for days. All the bridges and tunnels across the Hudson River south of Westchester County were closed. Very few people died, to be sure, but the costs of recovery will be enormous and many people lost their homes and possessions. The impact on the insurance and re-insurance sector will be significant. The National Hurricane Center report issued in February 2013 estimates damage at $50 billion.

Hurricane Sandy was not a "black swan" or a one in a thousand years event, as some would like to believe. It is a symptom of climate change that has already begun. The storm that hit New York City was only one of several unusually large storms that occurred in 2012 (mostly in the western Pacific). An even bigger storm hit the Philippines in 2013. Other changes are occurring:

• Arctic warming twice as fast as the global average. The Arctic Ocean ice cover has been declining for years. The ice is also getting thinner. Between the end of 1979 and 2010 the September average (annual minimum) was 6.5 million square km. The latest IPCC Assessment Report (IPCC 2007) estimated that in seventy years the sea ice will disappear entirely. But the melting rate is accelerating. In 2012 ice coverage was below 4 million square km, the lowest ever by a significant margin. It is possible that much of the Arctic ocean will be ice free in the summer in as little as ten years.

• Greenland ice melting faster than previously projected. The Jakobshavn glacier, the most active in Greenland, has doubled its rate of discharge since 2002. Greenland lost 350 gigatonnes of ice in 2012, as compared to an average of 240 gigatonnes during 2003 to 2010. Earlier melt rates were much slower.

• Albedo effect. Warming rates increase as Arctic ice cover declines and more water surface is exposed because less sunlight is reflected. Thawing of frozen tundra in the far north of Siberia, Canada, and Alaska as anaerobic decay organisms become more active and convert organic material to carbon dioxide and methane. Methane is twenty times more potent than carbon dioxide as a greenhouse gas, so increasing the methane concentration in the atmosphere will speed up the warming.

The primary cause of climate change is atmospheric emissions of greenhouse gases (GHGs), named for their ability to absorb infrared radiation (low-temperature heat) from the earth's surface and re-radiate it back to the earth. Most of the GHGs are combustion products of fossil fuels; others are associated with synthetic fertilizers and a few industrial products (see figure 7.11). The climate change phenomenon is similar to what happens in a greenhouse, and it is why greenhouses are able to keep seedlings and tropical plants from freezing in the winter. Indeed the temperature of the earth is rising (figure 7.12). This global effect was once called "climate

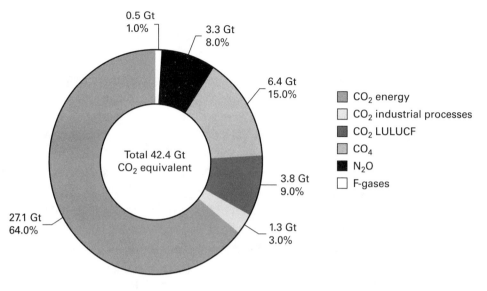

Figure 7.11
Global anthropogenic greenhouse gas emissions

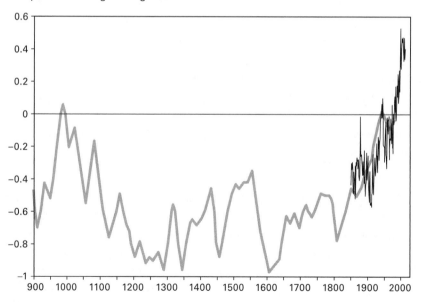

Figure 7.12
Surface temperatures over the last 1,100 years. Grey lines show data from tree ring analyses; black lines show data from instrumental records.

warming," which doesn't sound too threatening. It suggests that we may be able to grow wine grapes in Siberia. Who could object? Unfortunately, there are other serious consequences:

• The current rate of sea-level rise is about 3 mm per year, or 3 cm per decade. Part of this (about one-third) is due to thermal expansion of the water as the temperature rises. The rest is from the melting of mountain glaciers, Greenland and Antarctica. The rate of melting of mountain glaciers is quite well documented around the world. The main uncertainties concern Greenland and Antarctica. But melting is virtually certain to increase as global warming accelerates. The projections for the end of the twenty-first century range from 20 cm to 2 m, with a middle range of 0.4 to 1.0 m depending on the scenario and model. The sea-level rise will not stop in 2100. Nobody can say how high it will go.

• A "mere" one-meter sea-level rise means that some island countries like the Maldives will be uninhabitable. Coastal Bangladesh, Indonesia, Vietnam, the Philippines, Malaysia, and China, as well as Florida will be flooded regularly by storms. Many of the most productive agricultural (especially for rice cultivation) are river deltas where the land is only slightly above high tide (e.g., the Nile, the Mississippi, the Mekong, the Ganges-Brahmaputra, and the Indus). In those areas sea-level rise will cause salt penetration of groundwater and salt buildup in the soil, as well as more frequent flooding.

• Many big cities are on or near the seacoast, and much of the global population and productive capacity is at risk (as exemplified by the recent storm Sandy that hit New York City). Dikes are feasible in some cases, and dike-building is a source of employment, but at high cost. Dikes add nothing to economic productivity, however.

• Storm recovery efforts add to GDP but not to wealth.

If (when) all the ice on Greenland melts, the sea level will rise 7.1 meters. If the West Antarctic ice sheet also melts, it will add another 5 meters or so. If all of Antarctica melts, the sea level would rise 61 meters, but I think a mere 10 meters would be enough to end civilization as we know it. New York, London, Tokyo, Shanghai, Mumbai, Lagos, Buenos Aires, Rio de Janeiro, Caracas, and scores of other major cities would be under water. Huge territories that currently feed billions of people would be underwater, including much of the Nile valley, the Indus delta, the

Ganges–Brahmaputra delta, the lower Yangtze valley, the Yellow River delta, the lower Mekong, the Niger delta, the Mississippi delta (probably as far upstream as St. Louis), the whole of the Netherlands, and much of the Rhone and Loire valleys.

"Climate engineering" to reverse the effects of the GHGs is a theoretical possibility, but the various schemes that have been proposed are (obviously) untested and the potential for unanticipated consequences is great. Moreover, in my opinion, climate engineering would consume resources better spent on cutting GHG emissions drastically and sooner rather than later. This means cutting back on the use of coal, to begin with, and other hydrocarbons to follow. Substitution of nuclear power for coal-burning electric power plants is one alternative, but uranium-based nuclear power has well-known problems. Thorium-based nuclear power is theoretically feasible, and theoretically less risky, but untested.

The mandatory use of carbon capture and storage CCS technology is another theoretical possibility. It is the one favored by the energy industry because it actually requires fuel consumption to increase rather than decrease. The reason is that quite a lot of electric power is needed to extract, compress, and pump the carbon dioxide into storage caverns. The net effect of CCS will be extend the life of the fossil fuel based internal-combustion engine industries, while increasing the cost of fossil fuel based electric power vis-à-vis renewables.

This is not the place for a more detailed discussion of the options, except to note that they are limited. Unfortunately, outright denial of climate change in the face of overwhelming evidence has become part of Republican Party doctrine in the United States. The current wave of self-congratulation over the use of horizontal drilling and hydraulic fracturing ("fracking") technology is a case in point. Both the US government and the IEA are predicting significant increases in oil and gas production by the United States, resulting in energy independence or even exports, by 2030 (previous chapter). That is a major tragedy, from an environmental perspective, not only because climate change is real, and is being driven by fossil fuel combustion, but also because the denials are so utterly irrational. The origin of the denials appears to be directly motivated by the perceived financial interests of the fossil fuel industry and its adherents, filtered through pseudo-scientific reports publicized and given phony "legitimacy" by media organizations that pretend to present "both sides" of every issue.

A coming debate will be whether to get serious about reducing carbon and other GHG emissions or whether to try to compensate for the effects by some sort of engineering "fix" like carbon capture and storage (CCS). Meanwhile, as climate-related problems like big storms become more serious, public awareness and frustration will increase. The logical solution, which has been recognized by more and more economists (from the right as well as the left), is to cut emissions by means of a carbon tax or an equivalent "cap-and-trade" scheme.

Properly implemented, this will reduce GHG emissions. It will also provide needed government revenues. But cutting emissions is only possible when there are implementable efficiency gains or alternative noncarbon fuels. In the short run, efficiency is the obvious target. In the long run, the most attractive alternative is to increase the supply and cut the costs of alternatives that do not emit carbon dioxide or other GHGs. This is the logic that points to a major shift of investment toward efficiency and renewables (see chapter 8).

Austerity versus Stimulus: The "Confidence Fairy"

Austerity, meaning "balance the (government) budget," has been the watchword for government policy in many heavily indebted countries for several years since the size of the government debts in the United States and Europe began to get a lot of attention after 2008. The orthodox theory, promoted by defunct Austrian economists, wealthy hedge fund managers (e.g., Stanley Druckenmiller, Paul Singer, Kyle Bass, and David Einhorn) and German bankers, assumes that as a government's debt increases beyond a certain point traditionally said to be 90 percent of GDP interest rates will automatically rise, the government will "print" money and inflation will inevitably follow.

It is true that one of the theoretical ways of reducing the "real" value of debt is to inflate the currency deliberately by printing money. However, sophisticated creditors have become increasingly good at protecting themselves, such as by indexation. Besides, once inflationary expectations are "built in" as happened in the United States in the late 1960s and 1970s (and in Latin America during those years), it tends to accelerate. There is no easy exit strategy. What the US FRB did in 1980 to 1981 under Paul Volker was effective but extraordinarily painful, as I pointed out in an earlier chapter.

For reasons that are still not fully understood, the supposed (by conservatives) causal link between national debt and inflation has not been evident since 2009. The doomsters of debt have predicted over and over in recent years that the sky would fall, and they have demanded harsh cuts in (nonmilitary) government spending. Some of those cuts have been implemented, both in the United States and in Europe. But even though the US federal debt continues to rise, the rate of inflation remains low. How come?

There are several partial explanations. The simplest macroeconomic explanation is that demand for cars, houses, and other consumer goods is still lagging far behind production capacity. A more micro explanation is that much of the rise in US federal debt was a takeover of financial debt from the banking sector. Total debt did not change. Also, after 2009, many people have cut their personal credit card debt, while several million houses that had been mortgaged back in 2003 to 2007 are currently "un-owned" and delinquent or rented. Much of that mortgage debt of uncertain value has been sold by the banks to the Fed as an element of quantitative easing (QE). But, despite the cash influx from the Fed, the banks are not lending much, especially to small and medium-size businesses. The "cash mountain" from record corporate profits since 2009 (figure 7.13) is mostly sitting in tax havens as a target for "activist" investors and not creating jobs. In short, the actions of the Fed have not (yet) resulted in increased spending by the people who live in Main Street.

I cannot resist mentioning a recent academic farce. Two eminent Harvard Professors of Economics wrote a well-respected book *This Time It's Different: Eight Centuries of Financial Folly* (Reinhart and Rogoff 2009). A year later they collaborated on a paper entitled "Growth in a time of debt" based on data from their book (Reinhart and Rogoff 2010). The paper purported to confirm the existence of a "cutoff"—a sharp decline in growth in countries where the national debt–GDP ratio was above 90 percent. This was exactly what the austerians wanted to believe, so Reinhart and Rogoff were lionized by the financial conservatives. Their work was cited by such heavyweights as Paul Ryan, author of the GOP 2013 budget proposal, Ollie Rehn, EU Commissioner for Economic and Budgetary Affairs, and others, including the editorial board of the *Washington Post*. The believers took the R&R result as established fact, notwithstanding an obvious question about the direction of causation. (Does high debt cause slow growth or does slow growth contribute to high debt?)

Cash ratio

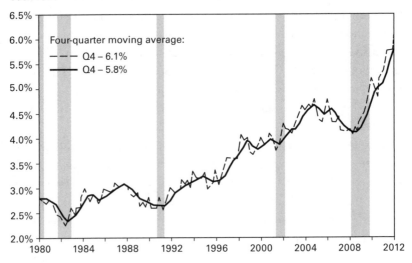

Figure 7.13
Corporate cash holdings

The denouement has been seriously embarrassing for the two authors: they made a silly coding error in their Excel spreadsheet, omitting five important countries (Australia, Austria, Belgium, Canada, and Denmark), not to mention some other questionable assumptions. When the data were re-run by the discoverer of the error (Michael Herndon, a grad student at University of Massachusetts and his teacher, Michael Ash), the 90 percent cutoff disappeared (Herndon et al. 2013). R&R have since acknowledged their coding mistake, but insist that their main message (that high debt has an adverse impact on growth) is "unaffected." Nobody quite believes that. Ollie Rehn, for one, disagrees. He, like Christine Lagarde of the IMF, now suggests that the eurozone should "pivot" away from budget cutting and back toward growth promotion.

So much for personalities. At a deeper level, the conservative ideology assumes that the economic system is inherently self-correcting. In practical terms their policy is not much changed since Andrew Mellon so vehemently espoused "liquidation" to get rid of "rotten-ness" in the economy (bad debts) in 1930. The theory is that the economy will automatically thrive when the government gets "out of the way." It is an article of conservative faith that job-creating private investment will emerge as soon as the "deadweight" regulatory burden is lifted and investors regain confidence in the fiscal and macroeconomic policies of the government (mainly lower taxes).

The assumption that austerity breeds business confidence, and that business confidence is the key to investment, deserves examination. After all, the welfare of billions of people on this planet is at stake. So far the "confidence fairy" (Paul Krugman's words) has been notably absent or ineffective. For instance, Japan has the greatest government debt of any industrialized country, and has experienced over twenty years of fiscal austerity, since 1990. The yen became stronger as a result. But a strong yen did not produce an economic recovery. Then, in 2013, a new Prime Minister, Shinzo Abe, threw the standard script away, pumped a lot of new money into the Japanese economy, encouraged the yen to weaken, and "voila!" the Japanese economy has finally resumed growth (3.5 percent is the current prediction). Pundits are still predicting disaster, but the early signs of a sustained recovery are good.

Anybody who tuned into business news on TV in the last couple of years since the Greek economy became famous—will have watched a number of interviews of prominent people from the financial world, conducted by interviewers who ask, sooner or later, "Corporations have been making record profits. Why don't they invest?" The size of the "cash mountain" (figure 7.13) has become a matter of some interest. Apple, MicroSoft, Amazon, Cisco Systems, and Google are all sitting on piles of cash (well, most of it is actually parked outside the United States to avoid taxes), and they don't know what to do with it. As the last section implies, there is actually a good place for that cash to go: renewable energy technologies.

The scripted answer from any prominent financier or CEO back in 2011 or 2012 was that lack of investment is entirely due to a "climate of uncertainty." He or she is never asked a key question: "Whose uncertainty and about what exactly?" If that question were asked on Main Street, where cash is fairly scarce, the honest answers would cover a wide range, such as "uncertainty about the price of milk or bread," or "uncertainty about the outcome of upcoming elections, or "Will I have a job next year?" If the TV interviewer persisted in asking s the guest guru or CEO, the answer would likely to be about taxes, Fed policy, the price of oil (or copper), or whether the Chinese market will continue to grow.

The CEO interviewee often answers with a rhetorical question: "Can we expect a small business owner to hire new employees in such an uncertain business climate?" He goes on to pronounce that uncertainty adversely affects business confidence. Without confidence, less uncertainty, he certainly won't invest. The interviewers working for Bloomberg TV or CNBC never ask what, exactly, the small business owner (who is supposed to be the source of all new jobs) is so uncertain about.

In reality the uncertainties worrying corporate CEOs being interviewed on Bloomberg or CNBC have very little to do with the problems of a small business owner. The tycoons privately worry about their compensation packages, the prices of their shares and options, and their own job security. In the boardroom they worry a lot about whether their quarterly profits will (or will not) exceed analyst's expectations. They worry about how to get a bigger foothold in the Chinese market and how to get their profits out of China. Being multinational, they worry about exchange rates, interest rates, and the prices of oil and other commodities. They worry about where in the world to claim profits and pay taxes and where to claim losses and get tax refunds. They also worry about how long they will be allowed to play that game. They worry about whether their corporate tax loopholes will be eliminated (or expanded), and now much they need to contribute to each political party to assure continued access and special treatment for their industry. They might also worry a bit about what to buy with their corporate cash.

But the small business owner is worried, mainly about whether the local bank will continue to provide the line of credit the business needs to continue operating. (That worry is, by far, the most pressing right now.) Labor costs have risen less in recent years than they did previously because wages have stagnated. The small business owner will in fact hire more workers and expand his business if, *and only if*, he sees actual growth in demand and an extended credit line. He faces uncertainties every day, but they are mostly familiar ones, except regarding his line of credit at the bank.

Back to the original question: Why don't big businesses with record profits re-invest? Is the reluctance really due to uncertainty about government monetary or fiscal policy? Probably it is, to some degree. But I conjecture that part of the problem is that most of the big companies in the world are in markets that are approaching saturation, at least in Europe and America, and they are all simultaneously trying to find opportunities for profitable investment in the developing (e.g., BRIC) countries. I think that market saturation is a real problem today for many industries, especially autos. (Peugeot-Citroen and Opel are the poster examples right now). I also think that there is at least one important area where saturation is not a problem and large-scale long-term investment could be very profitable. (See chapter 8.)

Having said these things, austerity is not just an abstraction. It means big cuts in government spending and, especially, in education, police, fire protection, and social services. It means lower wages, loss of benefits, and less job protection for unions. (That is what "labor market reform" means.) There are very few painless cuts available, except in the military budget, which is the one place conservatives are unwilling to cut. As government budgets are squeezed, more and more people (especially the young) become unemployed, stop paying taxes, commit crimes, and become wards of the state. The "black" (non–tax-paying) economy flourishes, but it won't support many families. Companies facing reduced demand because of government cutbacks lay off still more people and pay still less taxes on lower corporate incomes. The downward spiral makes the deficits still greater. It causes immense pain, exacerbates social stresses, but solves nothing. It is only too clear that if high unemployment of the young continues for too long, many of the best and brightest will emigrate, while others will be increasingly attracted to crime, vandalism, and political extremism. Greece, Portugal, and Spain are close to the tipping point into chaos right now.

If economic stimulus is needed, the question remains: What are the options? Central banks now have a mandate to combat a slowdown in employment (growth) as well as to guard against inflation. However, the primary tool at the disposal of the central banks today is to lower the short-term interest rates they charge to commercial banks and to purchase government or bank debt—quantitative easing—thus freeing up bank money for lending. But lending to whom and for what?

The QE method can be criticized. As of mid-summer 2012 the US Fed has pumped $2 trillion into the US economy through the banks, and yet the economy was barely growing. What the QE did was to drive up the price of bonds, thus lowering the interest rates they pay and increasing bank profits. This has also kept the cost of financing new borrowing (to cover the growing federal deficit) near zero in real (inflation-adjusted) terms. No doubt the banks needed recapitalization after the catastrophe of 2008. But the Fed is supposed to do more than save the banks. There is the other matter of creating jobs.

With lower interest rates on their credit cards, people do spend more on goods and services (much of it on credit), thus supposedly stimulating the economy. Every Christmas season one encounters this mantra. A big shopping day on "black Friday" (the day after Thanksgiving in the United States) is supposed to be a sure-fire portent of a big Christmas shopping season, which in turn tells the experts that Americans are back in a mood to spend. It means that Walmart will enjoy another season of increased sales. Never mind that most of the stuff the consumers carry home from Walmart was probably made in China or elsewhere in Asia. That's good for Asian exporters but doesn't do much for US or European employment.

Today more money in the hands of US consumers doesn't necessarily end up paying wages in Detroit or Chicago. A lot of it goes to pay wages in Mexico, Korea, China, or Malaysia. In theory, those people will turn around and buy goods from the United States. Or they will buy goods from other countries that in turn buy goods from the United States, thus balancing the system. In reality, however, Americans produce very little that developing economies need at prices they can afford. Consequently most of the exporters have been buying US government bonds instead of American-made products. That keeps US interest rates low, allowing people to borrow and spend still more, and allowing the unstable and unsustainable trade system to continue for a while longer.

Europe as a whole has a more balanced trade with the rest of the world. Domestic stimulus would be more effective than in the United States. The problems in the southern tier countries are much more directly related to the local real estate and banking sectors. Those problems could be solved fairly easily with help from the rest of Europe, once the necessary centralization of monetary and fiscal authority is accomplished, if it is accomplished. In fact, just as the "sunbelt" states of the United States have attracted both residents and business from the colder northern states, the same southward migration pattern will eventually re-emerge in Europe.

The notion that low interest rates will stimulate investment and job creation in general is also not supported by the evidence of past experience. Japan has had near-zero interest rates for over twenty years (since

1990) with no corresponding job creation boom. In the United States, the lower interest rates after Paul Volcker's inflation-killer in 1981–82 had completely different consequences: the Reagan Administration unnecessarily increased spending on the military, cut taxes on capital gains (and tripled the deficit) while the banks financed hundreds of leveraged buyouts (LBOs). The mortgage-based securities business boomed in the 1980s, providing financing for a lot of near-insolvent S&Ls. Much of that new capital went into commercial real-estate projects such as shopping malls and office buildings. Yet US economic growth in the 1980s was significantly slower than it had been in the 1960s.

Back to the virtues and vices of stimulus, I lean toward Keynes, but with reservations. On the one hand, austerity is not generating growth and there is little reason to believe in Paul Krugman's "confidence fairy." On the contrary, austerity is evidently driving deflation. Putting it another way, there is very little reason to believe in the benefits of "liquidation" (Andrew Mellon's prosperity potion) or the power of pain to create prosperity. Past history (summarized in chapters 3 through 5) suggests that the most likely outcome of lower interest rates per se will be increased financial speculation, asset bubbles, and greater income disparity between the richest few who can manipulate the system and everyone else, between Wall Street and Main Street.

An advertisement from a Luxembourg broker-dealer on the Bloomberg TV station in Europe (2013) starts by noting that central banks around the world are "flooding the world" with cheap money. It goes on to offer loans of 1 million euros at 2.4 percent interest, to anyone with a 200,000 euro margin account. Are we seeing a repetition of 1928 to 1929?

Spreading the Risk

As was pointed out earlier, *spreading risk* does not mean *reducing risk*. In practice, on Wall Street it means reducing the risk for JPMorgan Chase or Goldman Sachs by increasing the risk for others, mainly their clients. One of the consequences of the unregulated derivatives market is that all trades are private contracts between parties who are supposedly "sophisticated," and there is no public record of the prices paid.

At first the risks thus avoided by the banks were passed on to insurance companies such as American International Group (AIG), which had to be bailed out by the Fed in 2008 for $180 billion. A number of smaller insurers, such as the municipal bond insurance companies known as "monolines" (AMBAC, MBIA, ACA, etc.) were not too big to fail, and did not get bailed out. Clearly, the folks at AIG didn't understand exactly what they were doing or the risks they were taking on. Meanwhile the clever people back at JPMorgan Chase and Goldman Sachs, having "spread" the risk to unwitting clients, were able to take on still more risk themselves (using clients' money). There can be no doubt that spreading the risk increased risk-seeking behavior by the banks at the expense of insurance companies and taxpayers.

A standard argument used by Alan Greenspan, Larry Summers, et al. has been that complex derivatives are beneficial because they make the markets work better and "spread risk." Who could object to that? An anecdote is worth recording. When Greenspan was in England in 2002 to pick up his knighthood, he was invited to address a meeting of the Monetary Policy Committee of the Bank of England. In his talk he said that even though US share prices had lost half of their value during the collapse of the dot.com bubble (to that point), and there had been massive bond defaults, the US system was "resilient" *and no major bank had failed* (my italics.) Asked to explain how this could be, he said that the risks had been spread out, thanks to the use of complex derivative instruments (meaning credit default swaps).

Then a member of the audience noted that while the risk had been spread, somebody must have suffered the losses, "so who was it?" Someone who was present reported later that "a look of quiet satisfaction came across Mr. Greenspan's face as he answered 'European insurance companies'" (Blake 2008). Like his hosts, and like Rupert Murdoch's newspapers, Alan Greenspan apparently didn't think Great Britain was part of Europe, or that there was anything wrong or unethical with "spreading the risk" in that way. To Greenspan (and the Brits) it seems that European banks and insurance companies are the "gudgeons" of today, the ignorant fools who still believe that bankers can be trusted. The unspoken justification was *caveat emptor*. But in 2008, six years later, it was an insurance company, American International Group (AIG) that would have failed, thanks to those credit default swaps, if not for the mother of all government bailouts.

What the European insurance companies (and all the other "gud-geons" that shared those risks) knew was that the ratings agencies said that the bonds insured by those credit default swaps were AAA in quality. That rating supposedly meant that the chance of default was one in ten thousand per year. Another thing the European "gudgeons" didn't know was that they could no longer trust the Wall Street firms, or their employees, to tell them the truth. That was a major change in an industry that was originally based on trust. It started in the 1970s when the old investment banking partnerships turned themselves into corporations, which meant that nobody was personally liable. As the corporations grew in size, they became ever more impersonal. Moreover they started dividing responsibilities into different departments. For example, trading (where the profits are made) is one department and risk management is another. The traders get big bonuses, but the risk managers do not. Such a division of responsibilities is a recipe for disaster, and disaster has duly occurred.

Another source of increased risky behavior by banks and other financial organizations was the elimination of the investment-banking partnerships, where partners risked their own money. Since 1970 investment banking partnerships have all been converted into public corporations where the executives are exempt from personal liability. This was another way of spreading the risk, in this case to shareholders. The corporatization trend started with the "boutique" investment bank Donaldson, Lufkin & Jenrette (DLJ) in 1971 and spread to all the investment banks and brokers by 1999 (Goldman Sachs was the last partnership). Not only did the ex-partners cease to be liable for their own bad judgments, they also received huge amounts of money personally, which was no longer used or needed as a part of the business. Since corporatization and the end of Glass–Steagall, bankers are able to gamble with depositor's money without taking personal responsibility. This practice is supposed to be prohibited by the Volcker Rule in the Dodd–Frank law, but somehow I can't believe that the regulators will be able to stop it.

As for the use of complex derivatives making the market "work better," one wonders "better than what"? And better for whom? And as for spreading risk, what the financial industry has really done (quite successfully) is to transfer most of the formerly private risk to the public sector and the taxpayers, while retaining all of the benefits.

There is nothing wrong with risk-taking. It is essential to innovation. Venture capitalists do it all the time, with investor's money, and sometimes they win big. Those big wins are a major element of economic growth today. Meanwhile the investors in venture capital firms know the odds, and they don't complain when they lose. But there is a lot wrong with bank employees betting billions of dollars of depositor's money in order to earn large bonuses for themselves. Like the managers of LTCM, they may make a lot of money most of the time. But they can lose it all and a lot more when things go wrong. As they do.

I think the Volcker Rule is well intentioned, but that the gamblers who run very big banks will find ways to get around it. The best answer would be to separate lending from gambling: go back to Glass–Steagall.

Too Big to Fail? Too Big to Bail?

Debt is a core problem in finance. After the bursting of the subprime bubble in 2008, a lot of private-sector financial debt was taken over by governments, in the form of "bailouts." Apart from outright default, or a partial default called a "haircut" (to make it sound less painful), economic growth is the only way to reduce the burden of government debt. If the debt load is too great, growth becomes impossible and default is unavoidable. This has already happened many times in history. Reinhart and Rogoff counted 250 sovereign defaults from 1800 to 2007 (Reinhart and Rogoff 2009). In this case the debt, or part of it, must be written off. Needless to say, bankers hate that idea.

One of the most famous defaults was the decree of December 1917, by the newly empowered Bolsheviks under Lenin, repudiating all Tsarist Russian government debts. This prompted the British to intervene militarily with the White Russians. The Treaty of Versailles, which attempted to force Germany to repay British and French debts, as well as reparations for war damage (in gold), had the unanticipated consequence of propelling the Nazi party to power in Germany.

The world has survived hundreds of sovereign defaults, not always kindly. Some regimes, like France and Spain in the sixteenth and seventeenth centuries, defaulted multiple times. But a big default at the national level in the interconnected modern world would be a kind of financial bomb, with incalculable but very costly and destabilizing consequences that could be worldwide in scope. Meanwhile the central banks still use their main tool, which is to create more credit (cheap money). The purpose is to stimulate a new round of growth, which is all too likely to create another asset bubble. In economic terminology, the economywide growth "kick" from cheap money is a *positive externality* while the bursting of the resulting asset bubble leaving more debt in its wake is a *negative externality*. Increasingly, in mega-finance the negative has outweighed the positive. In plain English, the downside of cheap money has increasingly swamped the growth upside. The tool is no longer working well.

It may seem strange in the light of recent events that some libertarians (e.g., recent US presidential candidate Ron Paul) advocate outright elimination of the central bank. The justification for that position is known as "moral hazard." In simple English, if the central bank is ready to provide emergency loans often at favorable interest rates, the member banks ("too big to fail") are likely to take excessive risks with depositor's (and their own) money. The libertarian theory is that some banks may fail due to risky behavior and the other banks will learn to be more prudent.

One counterargument is that many small banks failed in the past, not because of their own risk-taking but because of events beyond their control. Banks, like other enterprises, can fail for reasons beyond their manager's control, such as the failure of a major borrower. There have also been a number of notable examples of bank failures or near failures due to unauthorized or illegal behavior on the part of "rogue" employees. The failure of Baring's Bank was one such case. Moreover it is not at all clear that even the biggest bankers really behave as though they know that they will be bailed out. Actually the evidence says otherwise (Friedman and Kraus 2011, pp. 43–46, 145).

As regards debt, there is some interesting background on this topic in a new book entitled *Debt: The first 5000 years* (Graeber 2011). The historical research is massive and fascinating and the stories of punishments for nonpayment of debts by poor people are horrifying. (It seems the rich rarely suffer and the powerful do not pay at all, if it is inconvenient, which is why the banks get so tough on lesser folk.) But the major lesson of the book is that the Calvinist notion that all debts must be repaid is essentially a moral statement. A consequence of this morality, it seems, is that creditors (banks) are protected much better than debtors (e.g., homeowners) by the existing legal system. When too many debtors are suffering because of misdeeds by the creditors, you may hear the sound of distant drums.

Apart from the asymmetry mentioned in the last paragraph, the primary problem of the financial system is excessive leverage. Most of the big banks were "officially" leveraged by a factor of 30 (or more) in 2008, as mentioned in chapter 5. This meant that about 97 percent of every loan was made with money borrowed from depositors or clients, and only 3 percent was made with the bank's own money. When bank assets—from company shares to mortgage-based bonds—lost value in 2008, the banks were nearly bankrupted. They had to be "bailed out" by central banks or taxpayers. It made them very vulnerable. Now the Basel III rules have formalized the 3 percent capital base rule (leverage of 33:1). Many economists (including me) believe that 3 percent is too low, and that 6 percent or even more is desirable. The bankers complain (as they always have) that such restrictions would cut lending and therefore economic growth. I, for one, think that the large share of lending that goes into gambling (zero-sum) activities could be dispensed with advantageously.

Perhaps the second most important factor in the financial collapse of 2008, not to mention a series of earlier crises, is the sheer size of the biggest banks. Central banks were originally created to provide liquidity to local banks threatened by "runs" that would, if not stopped, quickly lead to failure, even if the bank were fundamentally sound. Runs on the bank were often started by rumors. (In some cases those rumors may have been deliberately started by competitors or larger banks hoping to pick up the pieces at a favorable price.) The consequences of a run on the bank undoubtedly caused financial harm to many homeowners, neighborhood businesses, and farmers, as well as some larger businesses. In short, bank failures constituted a significant negative externality, in that they caused great harm to people who had nothing to do with the actions that caused the failure.

The Bank of England was originally privately owned, albeit the official bank of the English government. It became the trusted "Old Lady of Threadneedle Street" because it stepped in to rescue the shareholders of the fraudulent South Sea Company in 1720. The system worked pretty well for the next two centuries. The bank-run on Northern Rock in 2007 was the first for a British bank in 150 years. In the nineteenth century the US banking system was still the "wild west" by comparison. The frequency of bank failures in nineteenth-century America was the main justification for the creation of the Federal Reserve Bank, a consortium of twelve regional banks. It was finally approved by the Congress and signed into law by President Theodore Roosevelt in 1913. The central bank system is, of course, a government intervention in the marketplace explicitly intended prevent a particular type of negative financial externality.

However, the central banks have taken on other responsibilities, also related to externalities. They control the national money supply (aggregate financial credit) by fixing the required deposits from local and regional banks, and fixing the interest rate they charge for loans to those banks. But central banks do not control government, private spending, or government revenues. Hence they have no control over government deficits or debt. Still central banks do have the ability to *devalue* debt by "printing money" and keeping interest rates very low. Japan has exemplified this policy over the past two decades (Werner 2003).

The other way to devalue debt is to allow monetary inflation. This has been the historical solution of most bankrupt governments. Unfortunately, once inflation has been "turned on," so to speak, it is extraordinarily difficult to "turn off." The method adopted by Paul Volcker in 1981 to 1982 was effective but extremely costly to vulnerable borrowers (e.g., Latin American countries) that had no part in causing the US inflationary spiral: another example of a financial externality.

Inflation per se (by "printing money") is also a kind of externality that can be caused by the central bank. Inflation at the rate of a few percent per year may seem tolerable, and even desirable (according to some economists), because it allows the central bank some room to compensate for too frequent recessions by cutting interest rates. But higher rates of inflation, such as was experienced by Latin America for a long time (and by the United States during the late 1960s and 1970s), are very harmful both to savers and people with fixed incomes, and to small and medium-size businesses. In an inflationary situation, creditors (i.e., banks) are naturally unwilling to make long-term loans, which are essential for some kinds of investments. So central banks have been given explicit responsibility to control inflation by raising interest rates when "irrational exuberance" begins to show itself. They have, for the most part, done this reasonably well (albeit not well enough in 2004 to 2006).

However, central banks have no control over private spending, or private debt, including the debts created by transactions between private banks. The near collapse of Continental Illinois National Bank (CINB) in 1984, due to the nonperformance of its enormous loans to the defaulting Penn Square Bank in Oklahoma, exemplifies this problem. Penn Square failed due to its nonperforming loans to oil and gas wildcatters, resulting from the sharp decline in oil prices after the Iranian crisis in 1980. One thing led to another. The Federal Reserve had no influence over oil prices, or over bank lending policies, but the Fed, together with the Federal Deposit Insurance Corporation (FDIC), ended up "holding the bag" because Continental Illinois National Bank was deemed to be "too big to fail." That is to say, if that bank had been allowed to fail, a large number of its depositors and creditors would have failed also. So the government had to step in to prevent a run on CINB by compensating all its depositors, even the uninsured ones.

Some purists believe that government intervention is wrong in general, and wrong for saving banks in particular. They cite the "moral hazard" of bailouts, which is another way of saying that bankers who count on being rescued will do riskier things than those who know that they must be responsible for their own actions. In principle, this is a very legitimate concern. In practice, it is exactly the reason why "too big to fail" is potentially dangerous. However, to be fair, there is no evidence that the bank chiefs on Wall Street knew or expected that they would be bailed out in 2008. (Remember, Lehmann didn't get bailed out.)

Nevertheless, the banks that are "too big to fail" are also oligopolies and some are already essentially too big to bail out. Consider the three largest banks in each country and compare their assets with the GDP of the country: Germany 130 percent, Italy 142 percent, Portugal, 147 percent, Spain 218 percent, France 257 percent, United Kingdom, 317 percent, the Netherlands 409 percent (only 2 banks), Belgium-Luxembourg 528 percent, Switzerland 773 percent (2 banks), and Iceland 1,070 percent. Those numbers were computed from a *Financial Times* map of September 30, 2008, cited in (Lietaer, Ulanowicz, and Goerner 2009). It is not clear at what date the bank assets were calculated, but the numbers are shocking. I think it is clear that these mega-banks are already much too big to bail out. I think that they should be broken up into much smaller, more localized pieces.

The usual excuse that big commercial banks are necessary "to allocate capital in a global market" is not very convincing. In the first place, there are international organizations, such as the World Bank and the regional development banks for Asia, Africa, and Latin America, that were explicitly created to perform this task, and they do it reasonably well. In the second place, the big multinational companies have no need of big banks. They can borrow from mid-size local banks for mid-size local projects or finance themselves out of profits. Bigger projects can (and do) obtain financing from non-bank sources (e.g., bond issues).

The other excuse for giant banks is even less convincing: namely that they are necessary to compete with giant foreign banks. I remember when, back in the later 1980s, there was a lot of semi-hysteria in the US financial press about the size of the Japanese banks compared to US banks. Of course, the assets of those Japanese banks were mainly Tokyo real estate and shares of Japanese companies, all of which were vastly inflated at the time. All of those assets have since fallen dramatically in value to more realistic levels. The real argument for very large banks is that they can make very large short-term loans to hedge funds and private equity funds for the purpose of financing large LBOs. The social value of this activity, however, is far from proved.

Not surprisingly, big banks have learned that the best way to protect themselves from the consequences of risky behavior is to get bigger, thus forcing the Fed (and the counterparts in other countries) to act as an effective guarantor (moral hazard again). This has allowed them to make riskier loans and to operate with even more (and riskier) leverage. I accept the likelihood that the bankers in 2008 were not actually counting on being bailed out (Lehman Brothers wasn't). But the financial collapse of 2008 was unquestionably a consequence of too much leverage, as well as deceptive bond ratings and fraudulent mortgages.

A straightforward way to attack the problem of "too big to fail" would be to apply the antitrust laws already on the books. The Standard Oil monopoly was broken up in 1911, with significant benefits to the shareholders. Similarly the telephone monopoly AT&T was sued by the Antitrust division in 1974 and agreed to break itself up in 1983. Again, the pieces turned out to be much more valuable than the original giant. So why not simply break up JPMorgan Chase, Bank of America, Citigroup, Barclays, RBS, DeutscheBank, and others into smaller pieces? Those smaller banks should be restricted to operate within a geopolitical subdivision such as a single US or German state (e.g., California or Bavaria), a French department, or a smaller European country or province. The point of the breakup should be to restrict the size of banks, partly so that they are not individually "too big to fail" but partly to induce them to concentrate more on ordinary business lending and less on lending to hedge funds and buyout specialists. I suspect that once again, the pieces would be more valuable, collectively, than the goliaths are today, and the financial world would be considerably safer.

It is interesting that Sanford Weill, who led the charge to repeal Glass–Steagall in 1998 (in order to legalize a *fait accompli*, the merger of CitiBank with Travelers Insurance Company to create Citi-Group) has now changed his mind. In an interview on CNBC-TV he said: "What we should probably do is go and split up investment banking and banking." One of his reasons was that the pieces would be more valuable separately than the whole. He still thinks, however, that the Glass–Steagall repeal was "the right thing to do at the time." Why it was right then and wrong now is hard to fathom. But every convert to common sense, however late, is welcome.

It seems that the *New York Times* has also changed its editorial mind. In 1988, it printed an editorial that said: "Few economic historians now find the logic behind Glass–Steagall persuasive." Again in 1990, it printed another editorial to the effect that the idea that mixing stocks and banks creates a "dangerous mixture . . . makes little sense now." However, in the editorial where it noted Sanford Weill's conversion, it also published a *mea culpa*: "Having seen the results of this sweeping deregulation, we now think we were wrong to have supported it" (*New York Times*, Editorial, July 28–29, 2012). I agree.

8

A Policy Agenda for Stabilization

Recapitulation of the Theses of This Book So Far

The first two industrial revolutions, in the eighteenth and nineteenth centuries, were based largely on extraction and transformation technologies that were introduced to exploit pockets of high quality natural resources, notably fossil fuels (coal and petroleum) but also metal ores and other minerals. The finite stores of high-quality natural resources in the earth, from freshwater, virgin forests, and fertile soil, to fossil fuels, are unevenly distributed. Some are fast being exhausted, while the renewable resources (like sunlight and wind) are generally much lower in quality and much more costly to exploit.[1] When petroleum, in particular, was first discovered in large quantities (in Pennsylvania, Azerbaijan, and Texas), it was nearly all "surplus" from an energy (exergy) perspective, and also from a financial perspective. That financial surplus financed most of the industrial development that has occurred since then.

The age of resource discovery is past. By the end of the present century, resource (exergy) extractive activities will consume a large fraction of their own output. In the absence of renewable exergy sources, more and more economic activity and a rising share of GDP will be required to provide material and energy inputs for the economy. Efficiency gains (absent a major program of focused R&D will not keep up with demand growth from developing countries. It follows that the price of useful energy (especially fossil fuels such as oil) will rise over time. The world is becoming more crowded; population has more than tripled since 1940. It is rapidly urbanizing, and production is increasingly mechanized and automated. Economic-financial activity is far more global and more complex. The highest quality resources are being used up fast. The trade-off between efficiency (in finance) and resiliency has gone too far. It must be reversed. Greenhouse gases, mainly from fossil fuel combustion but also from land use and some industrial activities, are modifying the composition of the atmosphere. These modifications are essentially irreversible (in terms of human time scales), and they are driving irreversible climate changes. Those changes, such as increased storminess, ocean and atmospheric warming, increased ocean acidification, glacier melting, and sea level rise, are capable of triggering a massive socioeconomic disaster. (The vast majority of the scientific community agrees with this assessment, even though most governments and industry leaders still ignore the implications.)

In contradiction to conventional economic theory, the global economy is not driven simply by capital accumulation and human labor. The economy cannot function without an ample supply of useful energy (exergy), both in the "condensed" form embodied in capital equipment and as an "activator" (fuel) for both human labor per se and the machines that augment (and increasingly replace) human labor. Without a supply of useful energy to feed muscle and brain workers and to activate machines, there can be no economic output, no production. Useful energy (exergy), or useful work, is as much a "factor of production" as labor or capital.

The world economy is especially dependent on petroleum today because liquid fuels from petroleum are essential for internal combustion engines. Such engines power almost every sort of vehicle in the transport system from jet aircraft to diesel trucks and buses, to private cars, not to mention off-road construction machinery and farm machinery. Coal and gas are also primary fuels for the electric power sector. The whole economic system is overly dependent on fossil fuels.

The existing global economic system is functioning very badly, in several ways. Financial (pecuniary) externalities like "bubbles" result from an unstable and out-of-control financial system and an ineffective political system. Financial externalities (crashes) have a long history. However, a series of political and institutional changes, starting in 1933 but accelerating after 1975, has made the global financial system, mainly in the United States, increasingly unstable. These changes include the end of the gold standard (1933), the collapse of the Bretton Woods system (1971), the end of partnership-based investment banks (1975–1999), the designation of "official" credit ratings agencies by the SEC—with a built-in conflict of interest (1975), securitization of mortgage-based bonds (1977–1978), the crude Basel I and Basel II risk-weighting rules (1988), the FASB mark-to-market (MTM) rule (1993), the Maastrich Treaty that created the eurozone without central supervision over fiscal policy (2001), and, finally, the demolition of the Glass–Steagall Act (1999). Glass–Steagall kept the lid on unbridled bank speculation for sixty-six years. Banks are overleveraged and "brittle." Almost nothing has been done to prevent a recurrence of the crash of 2008. The negative externalities caused by purely financial activities such as asset "bubbles," credit collapse, debt default, austerity, and its economic-social consequences have vastly increased in scale and scope since the days of Adam Smith and his successors, who were concerned mainly with trade.

The ultra-low interest rates that averted bank failures after the dot.com bubble of 1999 to 2000 also encouraged excessive borrowing and spending. Securitization of mortgage debt into bonds that could be packaged by the banks and then sold on to long-term investors was a contributing factor, as was the homeownership policy of Presidents Clinton and Bush (II). Borrowing by underqualified homeowners was the most obvious result. That story has been told in detail in chapters 3 to 5 of this book.

The consequences for marginal homebuyers, when the prices of homes (and land) stopped rising and began to fall (in parts of Europe as well as the United States) were devastating and unprecedented. The losses of home equity, combined with lost jobs and lower incomes due to austerity policies, have resulted in a collapse in demand for new home construction. This alone accounts for a big part of the slow economic recovery. Negative externalities from bubbles already outweigh the efficiency gains from business mergers and mega-finance. They indeed constitute a real challenge to the future of capitalism.

The recession that followed the crisis of 2008 was not only deeper than the usual business-cycle recession but very different. The subprime mortgage driven real estate bubble was much bigger than any previous bubble. When the bubble burst in 2007 to 2008, the global financial system nearly collapsed. It was a "near-death" experience. The banking system survived in a very weakened state, thanks to the intervention of the US Federal Reserve Bank and the US Congress' approval of the Troubled Asset Relief Program (TARP). However, many of the borrowers (homeowners with mortgages) have not yet recovered, even five years later (2013).

The primary cause of unemployment is sharply reduced lending by banks, especially to small and medium-size businesses (SMEs), which create most of the new jobs. This cutback in lending is partly due to losses of bank capital, attributable to their widespread use of mortgage bonds (in the form of CDOs) for that purpose. The sudden downgrading of most of those securities by the ratings agencies after 2008 meant that CDOs could no longer be counted as risk-free investment-grade securities. At the same time sovereign bonds of heavily indebted European countries suddenly became targets of the ratings agencies. Many of those bonds lost their previous AAA classification, and some (e.g., Greek debt) lost their investment-grade and could no longer be counted as part of a bank's core capital.

Virtually all the big banks have been forced to recapitalize, either by selling more shares, for cash, or by selling other assets. (Some banks in Spain fraudulently persuaded depositors to convert their deposits into "preferred" shares in the bank, resulting in losses of life-savings by unwitting savers when the bank failed). This illustrates one of the risks. Under Basel I and II risk-weighting rules, banks are allowed to lend more (in the form of mortgages and other collateralized loans) to less risky clients like governments and government-sponsored institutions than to ordinary businesses. The small and medium-size businesses (SMEs) that need bank financing the most are being financially starved. This is another part of the explanation for slow economic recovery.

The last reason for the slow economic recovery, and the crucial headwind affecting future growth, is the prospect of continuing and rising costs of petroleum. This is due, in part, to geological scarcity. The scarcity has a consequence: the global energy return on invested energy (EROEI) is declining, notwithstanding technological improvements (e.g., "fracking"). Economists generally assume that technology will always trump geological scarcity, but I think they are wrong. There are limits to what technology can do. I think the tycoons at Davos need to consider the possibility that the energy efficiency gains from technological progress will not reduce demand as much as the growth of developing countries (especially China and India) increases demand.

The importance of useful energy,[2] and energy costs, in the real economy has been discussed at the end of chapter 1 and need not be recapitulated here. The future prospects are considered next.

A New Debt-Ratings System

The existing debt-ratings system is based on a legal oligopoly of three for-profit companies (Moody's, S&P, Fitch). The system reeks of conflict of interest because the work these companies do is mostly for the banks. That urgently needs to be changed. One idea would be to create one or more new independent, not-for-profit ratings agencies from scratch, with the mandate to work for (and be paid by) the purchasers of the bonds, namely pension funds, insurance companies, endowment funds, and charities. Or they could be paid by risk insurers (e.g., of CDSs).

I also think that every major central bank in the world should create an internal risk-rating department, for national debt, if only to verify the methodologies used by the commercial agencies. There is progress on this front. The Bertelsmann Foundation has financed a pilot project called the International Nonprofit Credit-Rating Agency (INCRA) to show how it could be done. It recently made a splash by publishing an independent critique of the French government's credit within hours of the 2012 downgrade by Moody's.

In this context it is encouraging that the European Parliament has recommended that the EEC should create a new independent rating agency for the European Union. The German environmental organization, Deutsche Umweltsiftung, has been supporting the creation of a European Rating Agency (ENRA) with a strict mandate to incorporate sustainability criteria in the ratings. I'm told that the idea is not going anywhere, but it should.

Tax Reform

As regards taxes, I agree with President Obama and Warren Buffet that the rich need to pay more: a lot more than Mitt Romney pays and certainly more than their secretaries as a percentage of income. (Even though I do not live in the United States and receive no services from the US government, I pay about 20 percent of my small retirement income to the US government, *in addition* to French taxes, all for the privilege of having a US passport.) It is perfectly true that taxing the rich will not alone solve the deficit problem.

Speaking of taxes, remember, that under the Clinton administration the US government had a surplus, and in 2001 the Congressional Budget

Office (CBO) projected that it would continue indefinitely. Clinton's successor, George Bush, decided to use that surplus to cut taxes for the wealthy (and to finance a war). Both Bush and Clinton, as well as the CBO, failed to notice that the surplus coincided with the lowest oil price in two decades, and that it was unlikely to be permanent. Meanwhile the US government debt has increased a lot, thanks to the rising cost of servicing existing debt, not to mention taking over financial debt by means of bank bailouts. So Clinton era tax policies can no longer produce a surplus. But the annual deficit should be much lower than it is now.

One example: Republicans since Clinton have succeeded in cutting the US federal estate tax to a very low level, largely by calling it a "death tax." Those cuts should be reversed. There is no valid social purpose in putting large amounts of unearned wealth in the hands of young people who did nothing to create that wealth. Large estates should be broken up and largely distributed before death. This is one of the few available mechanisms for compensating for inequality. There may be a case for exempting certain transfers (e.g., family farms) but only by allowing explicit untaxed gifts to successors.

From a broader perspective, it can be argued that it is a proper and necessary role of taxes to compensate for, and correct, distortions in the economy resulting from market imperfections. In particular, I refer to the tendency of a competitive capitalist economic system to favor large and centralized financial interests (e.g., Wall Street) over smaller, much more decentralized interests (Main Street). I think governments need to "tilt" against the forces that cause adverse redistribution of income in favor of the wealthy few. Other things being equal, the big get bigger, the rich get richer, and the least educated and the least skilled fall off the ladder unless the whole system is growing. In the end, without such a regulatory tilt, the winner—someone like Rupert Murdoch—takes it all.

Income inequality leads to poverty, unemployment, homelessness, and other social maladies. The end result is a breakdown of the social order. Peaceful strikes become riots. Homeless people become squatters. Young boys (especially) turn to crime in the absence of jobs. Young girls are sold into slavery or forced into prostitution. The jails are overcrowded. (But services to help prisoners re-enter society are cut back or eliminated because of budgetary constraints.) Thus inequality is one of the things that need to be addressed by government, via the tax system.

Let's face it: the 15 percent capital gains tax is the biggest single cause of wealth redistribution in the United States today, since it favors people with large investments in stocks and bonds or commercial real estate. I think there is a strong case for treating capital gains from (say) land speculation, commodity speculation, or investing in hedge funds or "private equity" differently from capital gains from bringing a start-up in the garage to its first IPO.[3] A minimum holding period of three years would cool speculative fever. I would advocate a 25 percent alternative minimum tax that everyone with a high income must pay. I would also eliminate the tax loopholes that permit multinationals to keep their profits outside the United States in tax haven countries like the Cayman Islands that exist only for that purpose. (This would probably require an international agreement, at least within the OECD.)

The fairest (but probably too radical) scheme would be to scrap the profits tax entirely and impose a value-added tax on the turnover of every company on business conducted in each country. This would work best if the other OECD countries agree to do the same. An alternative scheme would be to tax the profits of each multinational company (as reported to shareholders) on the same basis, that is, in proportion to turnover in each country where it does business. I think something along these lines is inevitable.

A lot of the tax gimmicks in current law, such as the exemption for "carried interest" (the gimmick that makes private equity so profitable), need to be changed. I agree that the top rate for corporate income taxes in France, Germany, and the United States may be a little too high. But none of the multinationals actually pay it because of other loopholes and gimmicks. The fact that profitable corporate giants like Apple, Google, and GE pay virtually no federal taxes makes the point. A flat tax of 20 percent for corporations (and partnerships) based on revenues earned in a country, with no deduction for interest payments on loans, would make a lot of sense. This would discourage some debt-financed mergers and acquisitions (M&A), but I think that would be a good idea anyhow for other reasons. I use the word "discourage" advisedly. When a merger makes solid economic sense, it will go forward even if the cost of the temporary loan is not deductible from income tax. But financing M&A by adding to the debt burden on target companies (and depriving the Treasury of tax revenue), in order to enable corporate raiders or private equity firms to make enormous private profits, is not economically or socially justifiable.

We should also eliminate tax loopholes that encourage manufacturing job outsourcing to countries where there is child labor or employees get no health or retirement benefits. There is one other loophole I would close, namely allowing banks to treat the bundling of securities into CDOs as "sales" for accounting purposes but as "debt" for tax purposes. (This means that the money banks pay to the purchasers of CDOs are counted as "debt repayment" and are thus tax exempt.) This gimmick has played a significant role in inflating bank profits and in the buildup to the subprime mortgage crisis of 2008.

The mortgage interest deduction for individuals for second homes and vacation homes needs to be cut to zero, in my opinion. It should be phased out gradually for primary residences, and limited to a maximum of perhaps $250,000 for primary residences to start with. (In Europe there is no mortgage interest exemption.) Mortgage interest deduction is arguably justifiable for young people moving from rental accommodations into their first homes. Beyond that, it has been, in effect, a subsidy for the building industry.

The so-called Tobin tax on international money transfers would make a lot of sense, in my opinion. Currently the rate of money transfers is literally in the trillions of dollars per day. Banks charge their individual clients minimum fees that amount to as much as 10 percent on small transfers, but they object vehemently to any tax at all on large money flows. There should be a small tax, perhaps 0.01 percent on such flows, including the overnight loans that many banks keep rolling over to get cheap money from the Fed or the ECB.

A tax on use of the Internet (if only to curb its abuse for junk mail) would also be a good idea. If the cost of a stamp for sending a physical letter is approaching $0.50 a virtual "stamp" costing, perhaps, $0.001 or even $0.01 per kilobyte sent to an email address would raise some needed revenue while discouraging mass junk mailers, who mostly operate from offshore. Admittedly there is a problem of collection and allocation, but in this era of digital miracles, such a problem should be solvable.

The kind of taxes that are needed, above all, are taxes on activities resulting in large negative externalities. Taxes on liquor and tobacco are in this category, and taxes on relatively harmless drugs like cannabis ought to be. But by far the most obvious example (at present) is the proposed tax on carbon (e.g., von Weizsaecker and Jesinghaus 1992) or the tricky alternative known as "cap and trade."[4] Since every ton of coal, gallon of motor fuel, or cubic meter of natural gas produces carbon dioxide when burned, why not impose a tax on the carbon content of fuels that cause those emissions? This increases the immediate cost to other industries and consumers. Such a tax would automatically increase the profitability of alternative "renewables." The tax rate should to be increased gradually over time according to a published schedule. It would be applicable only to the firms extracting or importing fossil fuels, such as coal companies, oil and gas companies, not the users who pay indirectly.

That simplification should compensate to some degree for the theoretical advantages of "cap and trade" over the carbon tax. The fossil energy companies in turn would pass on most of those added costs to their customers. But the customers would, of course, push back. Coal users such as electric power generating companies would try much harder to use less coal and more natural gas or even solar power. Auto companies would try harder to design more fuel-efficient vehicles. The downstream impact on the economy would be gradual but, ultimately, radical.

I should mention that while the carbon tax (or cap and trade) has run into strong headwinds, there is a precedent that worked well: the sulfur tax in the United States. Sulfur is a contaminant of fossil fuels, especially coal, and sulfur dioxide is a pollutant responsible for (among other things) acid rain. There was a major dispute about the costs of reducing sulfur emissions, with estimates ranging from $1,500 per ton (industry) to $350 per ton (environmentalists). To induce the users (mainly power companies) to get rid of the sulfur, by the cheapest means, a cap-and-trade system was introduced in 1992. The opening price for a permit was $250 per ton. By 1966 it was down to $66/ton, and sulfur emissions were down, too (Lovins 2011, p. 240).

My most radical suggestion would be to tax wasted energy by industry, that is, the heat and chemical energy embodied in air and waterborne emissions. This would require some moderately—but not overwhelmingly—complex record-keeping, together with some standards for measurement. Continuous monitoring would be required for all industrial smokestacks and wastewater outfalls, with random checks to discourage cheating. But allowing for some "shakedown" for debugging, the data requirements would probably be no greater than the environmental protection agency (US EPA) already demands (or should demand).

Independently of the carbon tax, I would increase the US gasoline tax to European levels (but gradually over a ten-year period). I know this is regarded as a political impossibility (like gun control), but it would go a long way toward eliminating the federal deficit. The losers would be the people living in suburbs and rural towns and the US auto companies that still obtain a large fraction of their revenues by selling gas-guzzling SUVs and small "pickup" trucks that are misleadingly classified as private automobiles by EPA. Apart from history, the main difference between the United States and Europe here is that public transportation in Europe is much better, even in rural areas, whereas large metropolitan areas in Europe are served by a dense network of railways and tramways (plus buses), making cars much less necessary, or even superfluous.

Among the benefits of carbon taxes and motor fuel taxes, the rate of technological innovation in energy efficiency would accelerate. GHG emissions would certainly decline (as compared to the current trend). The health costs associated with air pollution due to fossil fuel especially coal combustion would be reduced. And the federal budget deficit would be cut because of the reduced need for oil imports and reduced health costs. These benefits should, in a rational political system, easily outweigh the costs to the owners of the fossil resources and those employed in the extractive industry. Will it happen? I don't know. The odds don't look good right now.

Entitlements

To solve the deficit problems, it may be necessary to cut some "entitlements," notably retirement benefits, and health care benefits. In the US context these programs are Social Security, Medicare, and Medicaid. Such programs need to be securely financed by a defined (and nonincreasing) share of government tax revenues, whereas the benefits themselves may be variable. As regards Social Security, I agree that the retirement age at which pensions start should be increased beyond 65 (eventually up to 70) for most white-collar jobs, allowing earlier retirement for (some) physically demanding jobs. It should be done gradually, as life expectancy increases.

As regards health care, it is true that health costs are rising faster than GDP in all countries, and that this has to stop. I also agree with the Democrats in the United States and everybody else in Europe that health care should be universal, as it is in most OECD countries already. It is demonstrably not true that private insurance will keep costs lower than "single-pay" systems such as we have in France. The evidence is clearly otherwise. The overhead costs of most private health maintenance organizations (HMOs) in the United States range from 10 to 15 percent of revenues, compared to 1 percent for Medicare. Incidentally, it is very hard to explain why the US system costs over 18 percent of GDP, whereas the European countries do a better job by spending only 12 percent of smaller GDPs.

One problem is that the HMOs in the United States are in business to make a profit, and when reimbursements are limited (as they must be), the managers have a clear incentive to cut back on the quality of treatment or to carry out unnecessary procedures (especially tests) for which reimbursement is rarely challenged. In the United States there is an additional problem arising from litigation. Lawsuits for medical malpractice are quite commonplace in the United States, whence doctors and surgeons need insurance, which is very expensive and gets added to the overall cost of treatment. Lawsuits in Europe are much rarer, for various reasons that need not be elaborated here.

How to square the circle? I think the health care system needs to distinguish three functions, namely reproductive care (obstetrics and gynecology), health maintenance of active adults, and public health. Of course, maintenance becomes more complex (and costly) for incapacitated patients, people with long-term illnesses, and geriatric patients. The first function does not require elaborate facilities except for fairly rare (but expensive) problems, notably premature birth. A system of local clinics, staffed by nurses and midwives, supervised by doctors, would suffice for most of the workload. The second function (maintenance) can also be taken care of partly by local GPs, with local clinics for ambulatory treatment. Hospitals would be needed only for the emergencies, accidents, infections and difficult diagnoses (using costly equipment), and surgeries. The third function, public health, is responsible for preventive measures like education, routine examinations, vaccinations, and inspection of restaurant kitchens.

Geriatric care is the most expensive. It is probably fair to say that the last two years of life, on average, require medical treatment costing as much, or more, than all the rest. Here is where cost savings resulting from effective preventive measures during earlier times, can pay off in terms of fewer lung cancers, less obesity, less osteoporosis, and so forth. But, inevitably, choices will have to be made with regard to levels of treatment, costs, and probabilities of success. Patients in the future may need to pay for supplemental private insurance, for instance, to cover certain very expensive procedures like organ transplants. Genetic testing will increasingly be available to guide such choices.

There are a number of short-term adjustments that would cut health care costs and increase efficiency. One would be put a limit on costly testing that is done mainly to protect doctors and hospitals from lawsuits. I would propose a mandatory arbitration system to deal with malpractice lawsuits. By the same token, the incentives that encourage class action lawsuits (which are not a problem outside the United States) should be reduced by limiting legal fees on such lawsuits.

But the biggest single change for the better, I think, would be to impose stiff pollution taxes on dirty industries, especially those that burn coal, in proportion to the health care costs caused by those pollutants. (Those health-related costs cannot be determined exactly, but the bipartisan Congressional Budget Office (CBO) or even the Census Bureau might undertake the task.) The tax receipts should be used to help finance the national health care system.

The Eurozone: What Next?

In the preface of this book I expressed some annoyance that British and American commentators seem unaware of the primary justification of the euro, despite its obvious faults. Here I quote one British pundit, Simon Jenkins, who writes for the *Manchester Guardian*. On June 8, 2012, he wrote:

A currency fashioned to enrich German exporters and ensnare Mediterranean nations in German credit was never going to work. Single currency zones are fragile, short-lived constructs. Their supra-national governors must enforce equalization of labor costs, or tax and cross-subsidize on a massive scale.

Well, the United States of America is just such a construct. When I was a boy, the average wage in the southern state of Mississippi was not much above a third of the average wage in New York City. New Yorkers paid much more than their share into the federal government, while the southern states got most of the movable goodies, such as new military bases, NASA installations, and aircraft factories. Since then, New York's once potent garment industry has moved south (or overseas), while wages in the south have risen to near New York City levels. Today, New York City no longer has any manufacturing industry—most of it has moved south—and very little shipping. Yet it survives quite well, and the United States is not about to fall apart.

Just twenty-three years ago East Germany rejoined West Germany. The easterners were not nearly productive enough to be competitive. Most East German industries have since closed down. Yet Germany did adopt a common currency, and there has been massive taxation and cross-subsidization, just as Mr. Jenkins says. Surprise! Today Germany is again one country and its currency is the euro.

Here is another bit of Mr. Jenkins's prose:

From the moment the Euro entered circulation in 2002, the Eurozone's collapse was only a matter of time. Yet its authors still deny its faults, intoning the need for more austerity and more indebtedness through new Eurobonds. At its core remains the heaving ghost of an undervalued deutschmark. The German financial-industrial complex is as dependent on the euro as the US military industrial complex is on war.

The last sentence is near the mark (not the deutschmark), but completely beside the point. It is perfectly true that German industry (and German banks) depend a lot on exports to the periphery. It is also true (though not mentioned by Jenkins) that the financial cost of unwinding the euro would be horrendous for those same banks and exporters. It is also perfectly true that austerity is falling out of favor in the eurozone, largely because it doesn't create jobs. Since the election of Francois Hollande in France, economic growth is on the agenda. It is possible that growth policies will increase the deficits still more, for a while, though it is also possible that economic stimulus will decrease the deficits

So I agree that economic growth is the only way to reduce the unemployment in Greece, Spain, Italy, Portugal, and Ireland. I do not agree that currency devaluation, after the presumed departure of Greece and others from the Eurozone, is the "right" solution to the competitiveness differential. There are other approaches to the growth problem (see chapter 9). What the Anglo-American economic pundits fail to understand, in my opinion, is that economic rationality is not always in charge. I think Germany (and the rest of the northern tier) will continue to subsidize the periphery (while also demanding structural reforms) because the age of competitive nationalism in Europe is really over. It is Chancellor Merkel and her Minister of Finance, Wolfgang Schauble, who keep insisting on a long-term roadmap leading to some form of federal structure. It is the French, for the moment, who are holding back on the long-term vision and asking for quicker fixes. It is the British who can't get over their loss of global hegemony. But the countries that suffered under Nazi occupation in the 1940s and Russian occupation beyond the "iron curtain" for the next forty years, do not want a Europe of competing nation-states to happen again. The political unification of Europe, possibly without Britain, is a slow process, but it is coming. There is simply no appetite for leaving the eurozone.[5]

In February 2012, 25 out of 27 members of the European Union (all but the United Kingdom and the Czech Republic) did finally agree, in principle, on a new and much more effective mechanism for preventing excessive future budgetary deficits.[6] To make it happen the Germans, led by Angela Merkel, have played "hardball" (and will continue to do so) to persuade the Greeks (and others) that they must get serious about reform and pay their taxes. Angela Merkel is a physicist with solid grasp of numbers, but she is also the daughter of a Lutheran pastor. Germany's focus on austerity and hard work is largely Lutheran based. But Merkel's austerity, while beginning to show real progress, is also showing signs of fatigue. A year or two down the road, I think that there will have to be a "Marshall Plan" (a "Merkel Plan"?) based on investment, not charity, to help the periphery countries to get back on their feet.

There is an obvious similarity between the German reunification after 1990 and the current situation in Europe. When East Germany joined West Germany there was a huge gap in *per capita* productivity, as everybody knows. But East Germany had been a police state. All the government institutions associated with that state and much of the social infrastructure had to be eliminated and replaced. Even the universities had to be reconstructed. There is no such problem in Greece, Ireland, Portugal, or any of the others. Low productivity due to unaffordable state welfare and labor market protectionism is the key problem of the periphery.[7]

Moreover Chancellor Kohl set the ost-mark equal to the west-mark. This was a "welcome home" bonanza for the easterners and, to some, an electoral bribe to secure Kohl's re-election. To others, it was a recognition that the rational solution, to allow the ost-mark to "float," would have resulted in deep resentment that would have lasted for generations. True, the East Germans quickly spent their newly augmented savings accounts on bananas, oranges, TVs, new VWs, and other things. And the common currency made the industries in eastern Germany even more uncompetitive by raising wages without raising productivity. (The southern tier of the eurozone now has the same problem.) Yet the population of West Germany at the time of the reunification was barely twice that of the east, so the financial burden on the West Germans was truly painful. The reunification process, paid for by a7.5 percent income surtax, has taken over twenty years and is not yet complete. But the unification is not questioned.

Allowing Greece, Ireland, Portugal, and other peripheral countries to join the eurozone without central fiscal controls (and reliable data) was truly a bad mistake in terms of rational economics. It was, in effect, the same "mistake" that Chancellor Kohl made in 1990 (although Kohl probably knew what would happen and made a deliberate choice only partly for his own political benefit). However, that "mistake" is now being rectified, a step at a time. The downstream burden of Greek, Irish, Portuguese, and Spanish redevelopment on the northern countries of Europe will be far less, in relative terms, than the cost of German reunification was to the West Germans.

That is the optimistic view, admittedly. The debate among central bankers and economists today is mostly between those who fear inflation and those who fear deflation, namely the end of growth. The evidence of the markets increasingly supports the latter view. Yet, as I write in late 2013, the euro is at $1.38. There is no inflation problem today. There is a growth problem. This book seeks to identify the source of the growth problem and what can be done about it.

It may be true, as some pundits keep saying, that competitive devaluation/inflation would be the most efficient and quickest way for Greece, Portugal, Spain, and Ireland to resolve the currency crisis. Some others suggest the reverse, that Germany should withdraw. However, I think the centripetal forces holding the eurozone together are less visible, but much stronger, than the centrifugal forces that appear to be dominant. The Greeks are a possible special case, for historical reasons, but I think the European Union will administer artificial respiration to Greece because of the second reason why the euro will survive. That reason is that the Germans, not just the politicians, understand very well that they will be blamed if even one country (except Greece) is forced out of the eurozone. Germany and France can afford to pay a little bit more, and they will pay.

It won't be easy. Germany may be the industrial locomotive of Europe, but it is still paying for the unification, and it has not profited from the eurozone nearly as much as most people think. A lot of German capital moved into the periphery (some of it into bad real estate investments, to be sure). In fact German growth lagged behind virtually all of its trading partners, including the eurozone periphery for many years. Germany's public debt (82 percent of GDP) is higher than many of its neighbors. Germany's exposure to losses due to guarantees and loans is about 700 billion euros, equivalent to a third of current debt. If that were accounted for, the German debt would approach Irish, Italian, and Portuguese levels. So Angela Merkel can't throw money around, even if she wanted to. Still the German economy is strong and Germany will muddle through. As will France, Italy, and even Spain.

Multiple and Alternative Currencies

I have already commented on the desirability of increasing stability (at some cost in efficiency) by breaking up and decentralizing the big banks. In times of crisis, which are far too frequent, governments have repeatedly made matters worse by encouraging big banks to swallow up smaller banks, thus getting bigger all the time. "Too big to fail" is in the process of becoming "too big to bail" (Lietaer, Ulanowicz, and Goerner 2009). I think that is a big mistake.

A further idea worth serious consideration is to revisit the notion of multiple currencies. A full explanation of how this might work would take me far outside the scope of this book. But it must be said that there is no good case for enforcing a monopoly national currency. Hayek proposed to denationalize currency (allowing each bank to issue its own) back in 1976 (Hayek 1976). There were in fact a number of local currencies in the past. The Bank of England only got its monopoly on issuing banknotes (in England) when it was nationalized in 1946. A number of communities in France and England have adopted the idea for local commerce and local taxes. A group of European cities (Amsterdam, Bremen, Bristol, Brussels, and Dublin) hasapplied to the European Commission for funding to create carbon-reduction currencies. In some locations (e.g., Bank of Ithaca in New York, GLS Bank with Chiemgauer in Bavaria, Germany, and Raffeissenbank in Vorarlberg, Austria) banks offer accounts and payment services in both standard and complementary currencies (Lietaer, Ulanowicz, and Goerner 2009).

Switzerland has had a secondary complementary currency called WIR since 1934 (Lietaer, Ulanowicz, and Goerner 2009). It started in Zurich during a banking crisis. Each company in the original group of sixteen had received notice that its line of credit at the bank was to be reduced or cut off. However, much of the bank credit they needed was to pay each other or their suppliers. They invited their suppliers to join in a business-to-business arrangement. Whenever a deal is made between the members, one gets a debit and the other a credit, in their private currency. Originally they did not charge interest. Later, as the system grew, they formed a cooperative, which lends to its members at 1 to 1.5 percent per annum.

The WIR system was not allowed to grow without fierce opposition from the conventional banks. However, it survived. Currently somewhere in the neighborhood of 25 percent of all the businesses in Switzerland use the B-to-B system, which does annual business of about $2 billion. There is some evidence that the WIR currency has had a stabilizing role in the Swiss economy (Stodder 1998, 2000). The WIR system now accepts deposits and makes loans also in Swiss francs (Studer 1998). Certainly, the Swiss economy has been remarkably free from the kinds of banking crisis that other economies around the world (and around Switzerland) have suffered in the past fifty years. And then came the "bitcoin."

The main requirements for a complementary currency are scale, and a mechanism for buying and selling, to determine exchange rates. With modern computer technology that problem is not insuperable. The real argument for a single European currency is that it is more efficient, in that there is less need for buying and selling national currencies and hence lower costs for international transactions. But there is also a disadvantage, as is becoming increasingly obvious in the eurozone. The disadvantage is precisely that the traditional mechanism of exchange rate adjustment to compensate for structural imbalances is not available. On reflection, there is really no good reason (other than efficiency) to insist that New York and California should have the same currency for all purposes, and even less reason why everybody in the eurozone should use the same currency for all local as well as cross-national exchanges. I wonder why nobody in the power centers of the European Union seems to be thinking about encouraging supplementary alternative currencies as a (partial) way out of the eurozone crisis.

The advantage of multiple currencies, in exchange for less efficiency, would be greater resilience. That much can be said with confidence. The primary argument for encouraging complementary currencies is the amount of taxpayer money that has gone into bailouts, just for the big banks. However, the magnitude of the cost differential among different schemes would require a major study and analysis. I think that such analysis would be worthwhile. I also think the big banks need to get on board, rather than opposing all innovation that they do not control.

9
Economic Growth

Reconcentrating Risk?

How can risk-spreading from the bankers to their customers or the tax-payers be reversed? Part of the answer must be to change the incentives. Two recent EU decisions may point the way forward. One is to allow the European Central Bank to deal directly with troubled banks, as the US Federal Reserve has been doing since 2009 (as illustrated by the monthly purchases of bonds, known as "qualitative easing" or QE). This transfers bank debt to the central bank, but not to the taxpayers, at least not directly.

The other important EU decision was the agreement to "bail-in" bank creditors (bondholders), namely to make them share up to 8 percent of liabilities in the event of major losses that would otherwise require taxpayer or IMF bailouts. In an extreme case, the "haircut" could go as high as 20 percent. The case of Cyprus, where offshore depositors took most of the cost of the bailout is a bad example that will (hopefully) not be repeated. The most promising alternative under consideration is a special bail-in reserve. Some of the risk takers with very high incomes should probably be forced to cough up bonus money based on risks that turn sour. Some banker compensation could be in the form of so-called bail-in bonds, for instance.

As mentioned previously, banks (especially in Europe) also need to be recapitalized to increase reserves, especially in the biggest banks that would cause the greatest economic damage in case of failure. The current 3 percent requirement is too low. It should almost certainly be doubled, or more. The arguments used by banks to defend their high leverage risk-taking are essentially self-serving, not based on economic theory or evidence (Admati and Hellwig 2013). Here there are two problems. The Basel rules properly demand that reserves be risk-weighted so that the riskiest loans require more capital in reserve than less risky loans. But currently big banks are given too much freedom to define their own risk-weighting rules. Not surprisingly, they tend give themselves more leeway than smaller competitors are allowed. This special treatment needs to be eliminated.

The other problem is that the Basel rules favor loans to governments, government-sponsored institutions, financial institutions, and real estate, in preference to loans to business, especially small and medium-size enterprises (SMEs). But it is the SMEs that employ the most people and account for most of the new jobs that are created. This is particularly true in the case in southern Europe where there are few large multinational employers. The present slow recovery in the United States and the long recession in Europe is largely due to the fact that SMEs—even some with long records of prompt repayment—are unable to get loans.

As a partial answer to this problem, I suggest that something like the Federal Deposit Insurance Corporation (FDIC) could be created to insure small business loans. The banks need not be bailed out completely in the event of a default by the borrower, but a recovery by the bank of perhaps 90 percent of the loan value in case of default (perhaps more for smaller loans) would be very helpful in that domain.

There is a good argument for stronger regulation of the derivatives market. That market, which is 90 percent controlled by five banks,[1] involves derivatives with nominal values in the hundreds of trillions of dollars. It is now officially regulated by the Commodity Futures Trading Commission (CFTC), once briefly chaired by Brooksley Born. It was still entirely unsupervised and invisible throughout the remainder of Greenspan's tenure at the FRB, thanks to the anti-Born conspiracy by Greenspan-Rubin-Summers back in 1998 to 1999. The Dodd–Frank law is supposed to correct this problem, but it has no effective monitoring or control mechanisms in place, as yet. Needless to say, the five banks are still resisting all regulation, despite the terrible consequences of deregulation after 1982

It is tempting to recall a system that worked very well for the insurance pioneer Lloyds of London for over two centuries. When a ship sank or some other disaster occurred, the members of the consortium (called "names") that had insured that project were personally liable for the loss to the extent of their capital contribution, *without limit*. Even though every consortium spread its risk among many projects a number of English families that had enjoyed a high income from Lloyds for many years found themselves penniless overnight.

Something similar but slightly less draconian might still be possible. I think the executives of banks or other financial firms should be made individually responsible for losses, at least to the same extent that they are now qualified for bonuses. This would work best at the departmental level. Thus government bond traders (for instance) should be responsible, to some extent at least, for losses in the government bond trading department. Similarly traders of corporates, or derivatives should be at least partially responsible for losses.

By the same token, banks that sell complex financial products should also provide some sort of guarantee, much as any reliable merchant will guarantee its merchandise. A "take-back" law, similar to the law that is now in effect for many merchandise sales, except for a longer trial period, could be the answer.

The Economic Growth Dilemma

The question confronting political and business leaders with ever greater urgency is: what will drive future economic growth? Of course, stabilizing global financial system is a necessary condition for long-term economic growth. In my opinion, separating the functions of investment banks and commercial banks—back to Glass–Steagall—would be the biggest single step in that direction. Breaking up some of the oversized "universal banks" would be another step. Opening the spigot of bank lending to small and medium-size businesses (SMEs), however it is done, would be a third step.

As to the latter, it is not realistic to think in terms of top-down lending controls (except perhaps in China). Nor is it realistic to think in terms of changing the risk-weighting criteria as determined by the Bank of International Settlements in Basel. It is an undoubted fact that loans to small business are riskier than collateralized mortgage loans or even loans to finance large LBOs, for instance. Governments are not completely powerless, however. What they—or the EEC—could do, for instance, is to offer credit default insurance, somewhat like deposit insurance, for small loans up to, say, 25 percent of turnover. The borrower would have to put up some cash or collateral, say 10 percent of the loan. To minimize the "moral hazard" problem, the banks would also have to take some risk, perhaps equivalent to one or two years of interest. Thus the bank would get back something between 90 and 95 percent of the loan value, in the event of default. The defaulting borrower would lose its cash deposit.

The backing for this insurance could be the Treasury, or it could be a fund created for the purpose by a special tax on loans to finance LBOs or mergers. Or it could be financed by a Tobin tax on financial transactions. Then again, once the credit insurance system is in place, the BIS risk weights would (or should) change for small business loans. It is fair to mention that the existing market for credit default swaps (CDSs) would shrink, or even dry up, in the face of government sponsored credit insurance. The five banks that control 90 percent of the market for these derivatives would doubtless object to the creation of a competitor. However, something needs to be done to revive the SME sector.

While the banks play an essential role in recovery, they cannot drive growth. It was the discovery of enormous new energy resources and the new technologies that were developed to utilize those resources that drove economic growth during the first two industrial revolutions. The third industrial revolution, driven by information transmission and processing technologies, arguably began with the electric telegraph. But by the middle of the twentieth century, progress was constrained by the electric power supply. This led to the invention of the transistor, followed by the integrated circuit, the microprocessor and finally the Internet, now just twenty-one years old. Since then, the Internet has been the engine of global economic growth.

The explosive growth of the information age exemplifies an economic phenomenon that has been dubbed "the rebound effect" with a special case known (in the literature) as "backfire." The rebound effect is what happens when an energy efficiency improvement results in lower costs that, in turn, stimulate greater demand. For example, if cars become more fuel efficient, people may drive more, thus negating some of the energy savings that might have been expected from the efficiency improvement (Khazzoom 1980; Brookes 1990; Saunders 1992). In general, the greater demand stimulated by greater efficiency can be counted as economic growth (Ayres and Warr 2009).

There are in fact a few cases in history where the rebound effect of an efficiency improvement did not just negate part of the energy savings but sharply increased energy use by cutting costs to the point where new markets for the product opened up. (This situation has been characterized by "backfire.") The invention of the Bessemer process in the steel industry saved energy per ton of steel, but the cost savings created vast new markets for steel. And so it has been with solid-state electronics since the transistor. The original application was to telephone switchboards, but the new applications were the electronic computer and the transistor radio. The first has led, by stages, to the Internet, while the second has led to the cellphone. Today those developments are in the process of converging and combining.

Contrary to the impression created by some journalists, information technology is by no means immaterial or "dematerialized." Material/ energy conversion technologies are not only essential now; they are become more essential (if that makes sense) every day. Think for a moment about the technology of an Intel computer chip. A device that weights a few grams can do calculations in microseconds that would have ten the early computers like ENIAC thousands if not millions of years to do. Yet ENIAC, based on old-fashioned wires, resistors, capacitors, and vacuum tubes, weighed hundreds of kilograms. The microprocessor chip that weighed 10 grams a few years ago required 1.7 kilograms of raw materials, mostly (99.4 percent) converted into wastes (Williams, Heller, and Ayres 2003). Of course, this is an extreme case, but it also makes the point that miniaturization of end-use products does not eliminate material or energy consumption. In fact, this is another case of "backfire" thanks to mass production of cellphones, tablets, and laptop and desktop PCs.

So efficiency improvement, thanks to the rebound effect (and backfire), is economic growth under another name. The question is: How far can it take us? The good news is that responding to the global need for practical alternatives to fossil fuels also provides the *only* plausible hope for OECD governments to accelerate economic growth and escape from the unending cycle of financial bubbles and increasing debt. Global political and business leaders need to recognize that if the economy grows and the automobile market grows with it, hydrocarbon fuels will, sooner or later, become unaffordable because the energy costs of extraction are rising irreversibly. Shale oil and gas may ease the pain for a few years, but that only delays the evil day. Moreover the greenhouse gases from fossil fuel combustion are rapidly accumulating in the atmosphere and driving climate change. Hence increasing dependence on fuels from shale can only make that problem worse.

The rising price of useful energy from fossil fuels, especially petroleum, implies that renewable energy technologies—abbreviated as RETs—will be increasingly viable competitors to fossil fuels, *without government subsidies*. Government intervention will be needed mainly to counteract the pressures brought to bear by the energy industries to protect the status quo. I believe that rising concern about climate change must eventually tip the balance. Consequently there is a reasonable financial bet that investments in carbon-based resources will be increasingly less profitable, while renewables will be increasingly more profitable over time. To be sure, there are skeptics out there who will bet that costs will never get low enough (despite that rapid declines we have observed in the past) and besides (they argue) "there is an ocean of oil (or gas) out there" just waiting for drillers and pipelines. But most skepticism is financial.

Those are the two scenarios that the financial world will have to choose between. It strikes me that my first bet is a lot safer than the bet that drove the madness of 2003 to 2007, that real estate prices would continue to rise indefinitely. I think that governments can (and should) redirect global finance away from other goals (e.g., roadworks or home-ownership) to one primary goal: to break the global "addiction" to oil and to the internal combustion engine. The need to break out of this box has been evident to many scientists for some time. However, the politicians and financiers still don't seem to get the message.

There is a pot of gold out there in the economic fog. The good news is that money spent on "green" (nonnuclear, nonfossil energy) technologies should be very profitable in the long run if oil (liquid hydrocarbon) prices continue to increase as I believe they will. The next chapter discusses the potential in some detail.

Energy-Efficient Technologies (EETs)

Energy-efficient technologies (EETs) come in all sizes and shapes, but they have a common feature: they save energy and (consequently) cut emissions of GHGs. Once the investments are made the savings per unit of activity are permanent. The EETs, in general, are not new, although some of the older technologies have been improved significantly in recent years. (LED lighting is the best example.) Otherwise, EETs are mainly just applications of existing technologies—such as combined heat and power (CHP) insulation, double-glazed windows, back-pressure turbines, heat pumps, and heat exchangers—to existing systems as well as new ones.

The surprising thing is that the cost-effective opportunities are so large, whereas the rate of application is so low. For noneconomists the explanations range from ignorance, to high "discount rates" on the part of users, to growth rather than cost-oriented corporate strategies, and to conservative lending practices by banks. The latter constraint is particularly critical. Most mainstream economists believe that the economy is always at or near equilibrium, whence "double dividends" (or "free lunches") opportunities to cut emissions, while cutting costs, are too rare to base a strategy on.

However, there is a large and well-known heterodox literature on the subject, especially by Amory Lovins and colleagues at the Rocky Mountain Institute (Lovins 1978, 1996, 1998; Lovins et al. 1981; Lovins and Lovins 1987, 1991, 1992).

The prestigious management consultancy McKinsey and Co. recently undertook a major survey of opportunities for conserving energy in the US called Unlocking Energy Efficiency in the US Economy (Granade et al. 2009). McKinsey's summary results are shown in figure 9.1. Its central conclusion was that opportunities exist that could save $1.2 trillion from 2010 to 2020, well above the front-end cost of $520 billion. Those opportunities would result in savings of 23 percent of estimated energy demand and reduce GHG emissions by an average of 1.1 gigatons annually (less at first, more later). The McKinsey studies have largely settled the "double-dividend" issue by identifying and quantifying a great many of them.

Several other studies have focused more on the long-term goal than on the economics. One of the first was the Carnoules Declaration (of which I was one of the signatories), based on the very radical idea that fast economic growth in the developing world can only be tolerated by our finite planet if the industrialized world cuts resource use (and emissions) by 90 percent (Factor Ten Club 1994, 1997). This study was followed by a 1996 book, taking a slightly less radical position, entitled *Factor Four:*

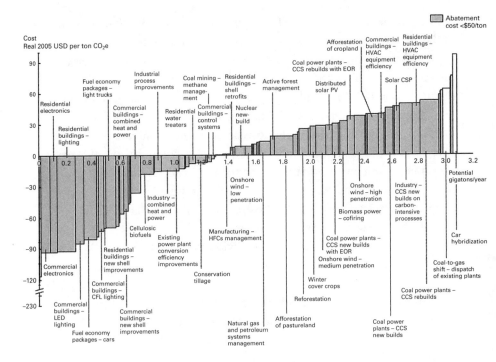

Figure 9.1
US mid-range abatement cost curve

Doubling Wealth, Halving Resource Use (von Weizsaecker, Lovins, and Lovins 1998). Since the possibility of such enormous changes evidently depends on the existence of many potential "double dividends" (which most mainstream economists deny), I became interested in that issue from a theoretical perspective (Ayres and Van Leynseele 1997). Since then, von Weizsaecker et al. have written another book entitled *Factor Five: Transforming the Global Economy through 80 Percent Improvements in Resource Productivity* (von Weizsaecker et al. 2009).

A recent study by the American Council for an Energy-Efficient Economy (ACEEE) sets the savings potential at 40 to 60 percent of the standard BAU projection of energy use in the year 2050. The necessary investments would create 2 million jobs, with an enormous double dividend of $400 billion per year (net), or $2,600 per household every year (Laitner et al. 2012). The cumulative saving of energy from 2012 to 2050 would be 250 billion barrels of oil equivalent.

However, the most readable authoritative analysis that I have seen yet asserts, with a great deal of backup analysis, that the "double-dividend" potential is huge (Lovins 2011): by 2050 the US economy could be 158 percent bigger, consuming no coal, no oil, no nuclear energy, and one-third less natural gas than now. In that scenario total energy-equivalent consumption—counting efficiency savings as if it were consumption—would be about 50 percent higher than today. In percentage terms, two-thirds of the total would be due to efficiency gains ("negawatts") and one-third would be fuel consumption, dominated by renewables.

In Lovins's scenario 1.3 gigatons of CO_2 emissions could be eliminated at negative cost (savings) of $5 trillion, in round numbers. (The upfront investment needed would be $4.5 trillion, but the gross savings would be $9.5 trillion, resulting in $5 trillion in net savings.) Needless to say, that is only one scenario. But I think there is little doubt that it is technically feasible. The economics remain to be demonstrated. However, most mainstream economists and business leaders do not yet take the issue seriously.

Given the number and availability of previous studies, I do not attempt to discuss the pros and cons of all of the EETs in detail. For readers who want more, David Mackay's book *Sustainable Energy without the Hot Air* (free on the Internet) is technically very authoritative (Mackay 2008). The International Energy Agency has tackled the question from a climate change standpoint (Worrell et al. 2009; IEA 2009). Here I mention only a few of the major efficiency technologies that are already well developed, although not widely enough applied.

The first example of an EET is decentralized combined heat and power (CHP). The industrial economy needs a lot of electrical power, of course, but it also needs heat. It needs medium temperature heat for purposes such as cooking, laundry, steam cleaning, and some chemical processes. The economy also needs low-temperature heat for buildings. Most of the medium- and low-temperature heat that is needed is currently supplied by fuel, mainly natural gas. Yet electric power is mostly produced by large centralized "electricity-only" power plants that discard huge amounts of low-temperature heat into the atmosphere. That waste heat could be used if the users were located near the producers. The problem is distribution.

One idea behind decentralized CHP is to utilize high-temperature heat from industrial waste streams and convert it into electric power. High temperature waste heat is available from a number of industries, including metal smelters and refiners, petroleum refineries, petrochemical plants, cement plants, silicon refiners, brickworks, ceramics, and glassworks. High-temperature heat can make steam, which can be used to generate electric power. Since the "fuel" is free (being waste heat), the resulting electricity can be cheaper than electric power from the grid for a nearby user. In 2010 the power from CHP generated 78 GW in the United States. The IEA expects this to increase to 123 GW by 2050, However, Lovins sets the potential for 2050 at 187 GW, or 60 percent of the 2010 output of electricity from coal-fired plants (Lovins 2011, p. 137). In fact 240 GW by 2050 is technically possible. Apart from producing electric power, decentralized CHP can generate industrial steam (now 35 percent of total industrial energy use).

However, under present law in most countries, the regulated public utilities have a monopoly on distribution. So all would-be CHP producers are forced to sell to the "grid," which is controlled by the incumbent utilities. Other producers of electricity must accept whatever price the utility wants to pay. That price is typically too low to justify the capital cost of a CHP project, unless the surplus power can be used within the same plant. A change in utility regulation would open up the CHP market for industrial waste heat significantly. The electric power utilities could use the same technology in reverse: sell heat to residential and commercial buildings. District heating was a fairly widespread system in Eastern Europe and Russia, where it was imposed by central government authority. It requires a large network of insulated pipes and a long-term commitment by users to pay for the heat, regardless of how much they need. Hence large-scale district heating is inconsistent with the motivations of centralized electric power generators. But small-scale decentralized CHP could save a considerable amount of energy and simultaneously cut emissions (USDOE 1999; Casten and Collins 2002; Tanaka 2008; IEA 2008).

Industrial efficiency can also be increased in several other ways apart from CHP. Figure 9.2 shows where energy is used in manufacturing. One major source of inefficiency is pumping systems, which are very important for steam distribution, as well as water, gas, and other fluids. Pumps use electric power, which is only 33 percent efficient, at present, with further losses due to transmission and distribution, inefficient motors, drive trains, pumps valves, and internal friction in the pipes. The overall efficiency of pumping systems is less than 10 percent (40 percent if electricity is regarded

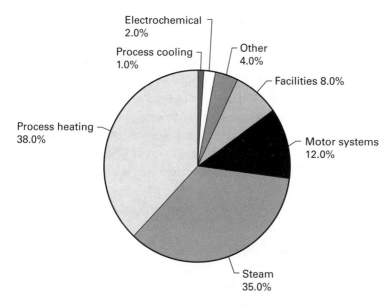

Figure 9.2
Manufacturing use by type of US system, 2007. Data from US Department of Energy, 2009.

as free). Redesigning the system without any new technology can save as much as 75 percent of the pumping energy (Lovins 2011, pp. 141–43).

Motor systems to drive machinery account for about 12 percent of global final manufacturing energy use, and another 3 percent is consumed by refrigeration and air-conditioning. The IEA estimates that global potential from motor system energy efficiency is about 2.6 EJ annually of final energy use (2007). Motor systems now lose on average approximately 55 percent of their input energy, before reaching the process or end-use work thanks to oversizing, failure to adapt to variable loads, and failure to turn off motors that are not in use (US DOE 2004d). Some of these losses are inherent in the energy conversion process; for example, a compressor typically loses 80 percent of its input energy to low-grade waste heat as the incoming air is converted from atmospheric pressure to the desired system pressure (Compressed Air Challenge™ 2003). Other losses can be avoided through the application of commercially available technology combined with good engineering practices. These improvements are cost effective, with costs typically recovered in two years or less. More details can be found in the GEA report (Johansson et al. 2012).

Another category of efficiency improvements arises from integrated systems design (or redesign). A good example of a very inefficient process design is a metal refinery where molten metal is quenched to solid ingots with water, then dried with electrically heated air, before being moved to a rolling facility where the metal ingots are re-heated before rolling, drawing, molding, or other forming processes. After rolling the same quenching and drying procedure is repeated. Why not design a facility where the two processes are located next to each other? This is an example to make the point. There are numerous situations where better facility design could save energy vis-à-vis standard industrial practice. Taking all the opportunities for increased efficiency into account, I think that "negawatts" can do more, for less, than alternative fuels.

There is a little-known industry consisting of so-called energy service companies (ESCOs) that offers energy engineering services to municipalities and firms. The industry was "invented" in the late 1970s when a Texas company called Time-Energy, which made switches that automatically turned off unused lights, offered to install the devices in exchange for a share of the savings. In the 1980s the industry expanded, often specializing on particular client groups (e.g., hospitals) or particular technologies, such as heating, ventilation, and air-conditioning (HVAC) systems.

Today ESCOs deliver advisory, engineering, procurement, financing, and related services. They often set themselves apart from other energy services' providers (utilities) by their ability to engage in energy performance contracting (EPC). EPC aims at, "developing, installing and financing comprehensive, performance-based energy projects" (Vine 2005). ESCOs and the end-user (their customer) usually stipulate an energy performance contract (EPC), in which the two parties set the terms of risk- and finance-sharing for a program of energy efficiency investments. Depending on the type of contract stipulated, the ESCO guarantees a minimum level of energy savings, provides or arranges financing for the project, and receives a payment based on energy services provided by the project. It may or may not take credit risks. (If not, it finds a partner to do that.) Revenue for ESCOs is thus associated with the energy performance of the facilities of customers. The economics are illustrated schematically in figure 9.3.

The industry prospered in the 1990s, partly due to a US government program called. "Super-ESPC," which still exists. (ESPC stands for energy service performance contracting.) It was responsible for over $2.9 billion

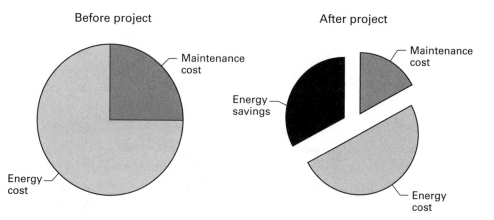

Figure 9.3
Effects of ESCO projects based on World Bank data.

in contracts since being created. It was re-authorized in 2008. But in the aftermath of the dot.com bubble and the collapse of Enron (2002 and 2003), many of the utilities closed or sold their energy service subsidiaries, while smaller firms disappeared or merged. However, growth resumed and in 2006 the industry grew by 22 percent and generated total revenues of $3.6 billion in the United States alone (Hopper et al 2007).

Perhaps the most important single example of EET is in the electrification of passenger transportation. I discussed this point briefly in connection with the earlier chapter on the future of oil. Demand for petroleum in the industrialized (OECD) countries is tightly tied to demand for automobiles and light trucks. But the increased market for hybrid electric vehicles (HEVs) and plug-in electric vehicles (EVs) —trends already well under way in the OECD—may cut demand for petroleum products significantly in the next twenty years, all other factors remaining the same. This set of changes can be characterized as an EET. The major change driving factor here is the rate at which costs, such as lithium batteries, decline, bringing EV and HEV costs closer to the costs of conventional cars.

A recent analysis by McKinsey and Co. based on research at Argonne National Laboratories suggests that costs for the battery pack used for electric cars will probably decline from the current level of $500 to $600 per kwh to $200 per kwh by 2020 and to $160 per kwh by 2025 (Hensley, Newman, and Rogers 2012). About a third of the reduction would come from economies of scale in manufacturing and another quarter from lower costs from component suppliers (also due in part to scale and standardization, and in part to technological improvements). The other 40 to 45 percent of the cost reduction would be from technological improvements in the battery, as are already foreseen and in progress. Putting it all together, the McKinsey analysis says that assuming that gasoline prices at the pump stay at $3.50 a gallon or above (compared to an average of $3.50 to $4.00 a gallon in 2011), hybrid electric vehicles (HEVs) will become cost competitive (based on total cost of ownership) when battery pack costs fall to $350 per kwh or less, and plug-in electric vehicles will be competitive at $250 per kwh, roughly half of today's level but probably achievable within a decade. Given this prospect, the market for HEVs and EVs can only go up. By 2035 conventional gasoline and diesel vehicles will probably be obsolete.

Nevertheless, the need for fuels will not go away entirely and the climate challenge means that renewables *must* replace coal and oil in coming decades. The most advanced renewables apart from ethanol (wind and solar) also suffer from two main drawbacks. The first is intermittent supply of energy due to natural fluctuations. The second drawback is high initial capital costs, given the reluctance of banks to lend on "risky" projects at any scale regarded as depending on "unproven" technologies. This is especially problematic where coal or natural gas is readily available. Unfortunately, for most situations, fossil-fuel solutions still offer the lowest upfront costs. A diesel generator costs about $1,000/kW of capacity, as compared to $3,000/kW to $6,000/kW for low-head hydropower. Capital costs in 2005 averaged about $6,500/kW capacity for solar PV, although costs have been falling quickly in recent years; $5,500 has been estimated for 2013. This figure is likely to be even lower in the future. Costs in 2005 for wind averaged $4,850/kW, but also in this case, costs have also been falling (ESMAP 2007). But the gap is still great.

Renewable Energy Technologies (RETs)

In 2008 renewable energy sources (including large hydro) provided 12.9 percent of global primary energy supply. The bulk of global energy was supplied by fossil fuels An estimated 20,700 TWh of electricity was generated in 2008 (REN21 2010, p. 69). Of this amount, RE contributed 18 percent of the total (see figure 9.4), but most of this was from large

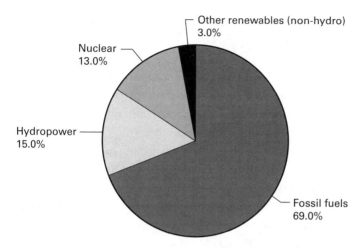

Figure 9.4
Share of global electricity by energy source, 2008

hydroelectric installations. Only 3 percent came from all other renewable sources, although that was up from 0.8 percent in 2004.

This section provides a brief overview of the most promising renewable energy technologies (hereafter RETs). Unlike EETs, RETs are new or previously unused sources of energy.. The major examples are biofuels, wind, and solar PV. I also discuss storage, briefly. I have decided, rather reluctantly, to include one nuclear technology that has very attractive features. Other examples not discussed here include low-head hydro, solar heat, geothermal, and tidal and wind energy. This is not to suggest that such sources, or some of them, will not be important in the more distant future.

Biofuels are liquid fuels made from plant material that can be used as a substitute for or additive to petroleum-derived fuels. They generate CO_2 when burned, but they are derived from photosynthetic plants that take CO_2 out of the air in the first place. There are two types, namely alcohols (ethanol, methanol, or butanol) and biodiesel. Ethanol, which is made from grain (corn, soya) or sugar beets or sugar cane, is currently by far the most important of the alcohols. The sugar is converted to ethanol by a process of fermentation followed by distillation (much like the process used to make rum or vodka). Because alcohols are based on edible biomass, there is a direct competition between their use as food or fuel. This has led to controversy over food security and food crises (e.g., Runge and

Senauer 2007). Other problems include low net energy (EROEI) as well as concerns related to the need for fertilizer and water usage on a large scale.

Ethanol is typically added to gasoline in a ratio of about one part in ten. Biodiesel, which is made from oilseeds (rape, sunflower), can be mixed with conventional petroleum-based diesel oil, or in some cases it can replace petroleum-based diesel fuel altogether.

Second-generation biofuels derived from nonedible biomass (e.g., cellulose) would eliminate the competition between food and fuel, although there could still be competition over land and water usage. Annual global production of biomass is estimated at 146 billion metric tons. Of course, only a small fraction of this would be available for conversion to liquid biofuel. However, a more detailed study by the US Department of Agriculture in 2005 noted that US agricultural land produced 75 million dry tons of crop wastes: 37 million tons of corn stover (stalks), 11 million tons of wheat straw, and 27 million tons of other crop residues. Of the total available, only 20 percent was actually used for biomass energy or biofuels.

Forest products residues in the United States were estimated to be 6.7 billion tons per year, or 31 percent of the total harvested wood for lumber and pulp (Perlack et al. 2005). Global figures are probably comparable, in percentages, except that remaining tropical rainforests may not be regarded as harvestable in the future. All in all, the total tonnage of biomass produced from existing harvestable land has increased significantly due to advancing genetic technology.

The economics are still very unclear. If it were only a question of converting rice straw or cornstalks (stover) into ethanol, the organisms in the rumens of cows, sheep, and goats (and termites) would provide a straightforward solution. The problem is that simple cellulose, a long chain of sugar molecules, constitutes only half of the mass of wood. The remainder consists of more complex carbohydrates, hemicellulose, and lignin, which the most familiar ruminants cannot digest. Therefore a future industrial wood-to-ethanol process will have to start with a chemical process to break down the complex molecules that "glue" the cellulose chains together in wood and woody plants into component sugar molecules.

Unfortunately, this is easier said than done because the separation step (enzymatic hydrolysis) yields a lot of 5-carbon sugars that commercial brewer's yeast cannot convert into alcohol. The unconverted carbohydrate residue can only be dried and burned for fuel, just as the "black liquor" from paper pulping cannot be utilized (as yet) for any purpose other than burning for heat content. This is why the current yield of ethanol from wood is so low, and why it is still noneconomic. Also the high cost is partly because the synthetic enzymes used in the hydrolysis are still very expensive. Progress in biotechnology may change this situation in time, of course.

Like ethanol, methanol can be burned in a slightly modified gasoline engine, although to take advantage of the high octane number a higher compression ratio is needed. (Race cars have used methanol for a long time.) Methanol is more toxic than ethanol and more corrosive. It also has slightly less energy content per unit volume. Nevertheless, methanol is a possible future substitute for, or additive to, gasoline. It can be produced from cellulosic biomass, including municipal wastes, agricultural wastes, and/or woody materials, which have to be transported to a gasifier. Feedstock, whether from agriculture or forestry, should be considerably cheaper per ton than corn or soybeans. In the case of municipal wastes (consisting mostly of paper and plastics), feedstock would be free and the bigger cities might even pay to get rid of it. So if (or when) the hydrolysis problem can be solved economically, both capital and operating costs will drop. Thus, under reasonable assumptions, cellulosic ethanol or methanol could be cheaper than gasoline or diesel oil in twenty or thirty years, or even less if petroleum prices keep increasing.

A possible breakthrough of major importance has recently been reported. It is known as the "carabao paradigm." The carabao is a ruminant (a domesticated subspecies of water buffalo) common in the Philippines, Malaysia and southern China. It not only digests grass as cattle and sheep do, but it also consumes and digests woody shrubs. It was discovered recently that the microorganisms in the carabao rumen can hydrolyze complex carbohydrates, *including hemicellulose and lignin*, and can convert 5-carbon sugars into the 6-carbon sugars (glucose) that support life processes. In short, the microorganisms in the carabao rumen convert woody materials into stuff that brewer's yeast can subsequently ferment into ethanol. The research on this process has barely begun and nobody can predict the outcome. If all goes well, the carabao paradigm (as it is called) could be of great importance, at least in the Philippines, Indonesia, and South Asia where those animals thrive.

A potentially promising new approach starts from algae, grown either in freshwater ponds or in saltwater. In contrast to agricultural crops, algal ponds can, in principle, produce as much as 40,000 to 80,000 liters of biodiesel per acre (Briggs 2004). The process would start by harvesting the dead algae, extracting the oil by pressing, and then process the solid residue into ethanol. Practice is another story. Enclosed ultra-clean climate controlled ponds would be needed. Such closed ponds are expensive to construct and cost a lot to maintain, while open ponds are subject to invasion by other species. Up to now it has also been difficult to control the algae growth process adequately to produce a continuous output of feedstock for a refinery.

Another approach has been developed by Solazyme Corp. Its system does not require ponds or external sunlight. Instead, micro-algae are fed with biomass (switchgrass), similar to the use of yeasts to convert carbohydrates into ethanol. In the Solazyme process algae convert the carbohydrates into oil. The company claims the oil is equivalent to number 2 diesel fuel and can be burned in pure form without blending, year round.

Joule Biotechnologies of Bedford, Massachusetts, has patented a more advanced process, based on genetically engineered microorganisms working in flat plastic bioreactors consuming CO_2, sunlight, and some nutrients. Since the process utilizes pure CO_2, it might replace the highly touted carbon dioxide capture and storage (CCS) technology currently regarded as the best hope of cutting GHG emissions to tolerable levels. The bioproduct, either ethanol or biodiesel, is secreted continuously. A pilot plant for ethanol is already producing 50 percent of the theoretical limit and the target is 90 percent, equivalent to 25,000 gallons per acre, which is ten times the potential productivity of cellulosic ethanol and a thousand times greater than the corn ethanol produced today. This target may be reached in a few years. The process now appears to be very near commercialization (perhaps in 2014). Joule was named "2013 New Energy Pioneer" by Bloomberg, with Solazyme as a close second in the rankings.

It is evident that ethanol, methanol, and biodiesel do not yet qualify as negative cost solutions ("free lunches"), although the long-term potential is reasonably favorable. The prospects for second generation biofuels will be clearer in two or three years, perhaps by 2016.

Wind energy technologies are the most mature of the RETs. The wind power capacity installed by the end of 2009 was capable of meeting roughly 1.8 percent of worldwide electricity demand. According to IPCC (2011), that contribution could grow to over 20 percent by 2050 under some scenarios. A number of global wind resource assessments have demonstrated that global technical potential exceeds current global electricity production. The great advantage of wind power is that, once built, the cost of operating a wind turbine is nearly zero (except for maintenance). It is likely that a lot of the maintenance can be automated, necessitating personal inspections only when something breaks.

Solar thermal heating for buildings is an old technology. However, it is increasingly important for new buildings, especially the German "passive house" designs, which rely entirely on solar heat, combined with insulation, double- (or triple-)glazed windows, and countercurrent heat exchangers to heat incoming ventilation air. In the summer this procedure can be reversed to conserve air-conditioning (Elswijk and Kaan 2008). In new construction, this technology cuts energy consumption by 90 to 95 percent, although there is a penalty insofar as capital costs are roughly 10 percent higher than conventional designs. The major challenge is to find ways to achieve some of these efficiency gains in existing buildings, at reasonable costs. Unfortunately, the benefits that can be achieved from fairly obvious leak reductions like insulating cavity walls and roofs, and double-glazing windows, are far less than can be achieved by new construction with air exchange. The improvement from insulation add-ons and LED lighting would probably be in the neighborhood of 25 percent (Mackay 2008, p. 295). It would take many years to pay off.

PV is a semiconductor technology that converts the energy of sunlight (photons) directly into electricity. The phenomenon has been known for a long time, but the first commercial applications utilized ultra-pure scrap silicon from computer "chip" manufacturing. However, the purity requirements for silicon PV cells are much less than for chips, and by 2000 the demand for PV justified investment in specialized dedicated fabrication facilities. Many have been built in Japan, China, the United States, Spain, and Germany. Costs per kwh are still much higher than for coal-based electricity, but PV costs continue to decline, especially since China recently began exporting panels on a large scale (see figure 9.5).

Several PV technologies have been developed in parallel. The three major types that are commercially available now include multicrystalline silicon, amorphous silicon, and thin films on a glass or plastic sheet.

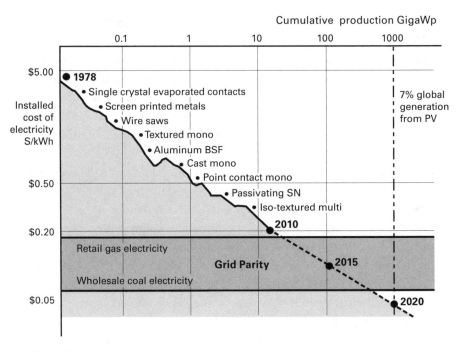

Figure 9.5
Cumulative PV production

Thin film PV compounds in use today include copper indium gallium disulfide(di)selenide (CIGS), cadmium telluride (CdTe), and amorphous silicon. The panels can be utilized on virtually any scale from a single panel on a rooftop to a multitude of panels organized in arrays that comprise solar farms. Solar PV power systems can be either off-grid or grid-connected into mini grids or larger national grids.

Intermittency is a major problem for solar PV, which operates only when the sun is shining. As with wind, storage for off-grid applications is possible with storage batteries, but the economics is unattractive, so intermittency remains a problem that has not yet been resolved and requires further technological progress. In contrast, thermal storage is possible with centralized solar power (CSP), although there is a cost penalty.

Even for grid-connected solar PV, local output varies not only predictably according to the diurnal (night and day) cycle, but unpredictably according to weather conditions. This variability can in some instances have a significant impact on the management and control of local transmission and distribution systems and may constrain integration into the power system. Predictability also varies with location; although in many locations where there is a high level of solar insolation, there is a reasonably high level of weather predictability as well. In any case, solar PV applications are expanding rapidly, even though the technology is still undergoing rapid development.

It is true that the most familiar "renewables," solar heat, solar electricity, and wind, do not promise significant (if any) cost savings at present prices as compared to old coal-fired power plants, *as long as the latter are exempt from paying the costs of environmental and health damages.* But unit costs are declining rapidly thanks to increasing experience and scale.

Evidently, while renewables are gaining ground in the energy markets, the penetration of RETs would be much greater if the problem of intermittency, for both wind and solar energy, could be solved. Wind gusts can increase wind speeds very sharply in a few seconds, with dangerous consequences for both turbines and for the grid. The electrical output of wind turbines varies with fluctuating wind speeds. Predictability of fluctuations in wind speed is an issue because gusts are very difficult to predict, even a few seconds in advance. But storage is the key problem for both wind power and PV because it is the only way to match demand with supply.

The only large-scale storage technology now available is pumped storage, using artificial reservoirs on hilltops to store surplus energy when demand is low and have it available during periods when demand is high. For utilities, several rechargeable battery technologies are now approaching commercialization by utilities. One is a variant of the lead-acid battery, from Xtreme Power. It is being tested by Duke Energy for a wind farm. Another is a sodium-sulfur battery, based on a concept developed originally at Ford (for cars) but never implemented. The modern version, now being tested by Pacific Gas and Electric Co (PG&E), is capable of storing six hours of energy. Another type of battery is the zinc-air cell, which has a great advantage of using cheap and nontoxic materials but has suffered for a long time from problems with the recharge stage. There are at least two modern versions now being tested by utilities, one from Urban Electric Power and the other from Eos Energy Storage. The latter is being tested by several utilities, including Consolidated Edison of New York, Nationalgrid, Enel (Italy), and GDF Suez (France). Eos expects that its battery will cost $160 per kwh, as compared to other battery technologies costing upward of $400 per kwh. This would be a significant breakthrough.

For the household rooftop PV, lead-acid batteries can perform a similar function, but for the grid as a whole, they are too slow to recharge after a discharge. One possibility now under consideration would utilize the electric vehicle (EV) fleet as a whole (it gets large enough) as a storage battery to stabilize the grid. The idea would depend on individual owners being paid to allow their car batteries to feed back into the grid up to 2 kwh per car (and subsequently be recharged) during short periods when the car is not in use. EVs have a storage capacity ranging from 10 to 50 kwh each. A fleet of 3 million EVs could be regarded as a single-storage battery with a capacity of the order of 6 million kwh, enough to stabilize most short-term supply swings (Mackay 2008).

There are several technical storage possibilities that have not yet been evaluated in this context. "Supercapacitors" are one. Typical supercapacitors now available can store 6 watt-hours per kg of weight. A more advanced system promises 280 watt-hours per kg. Another possibility is flywheels, made of advanced superstrong composite materials. Flywheels now available can store 4.6 watt-hours per kg of weight. There is no published information on present or future costs.

The most practical scheme for matching demand and supply is to extend the grid by interconnections. This will enable wind or solar producers to export surplus power to regions where there is pumped storage or where hydropower can be turned off, and to import from the same regions during times of high local demand and low production. Denmark is already doing this; it has 3.1 GW of wind capacity, with interconnections to Germany, Norway, and Sweden capable of carrying up to 2.8 GW (Mackay 2008).

The rate of penetration of RETs will be even greater than figure 9.3 suggests if (or when) future governments are able to summon the political will to confront the fossil energy lobbies and impose appropriate pollution taxes. (Those taxes could, incidentally, go a long way to pay for public health programs and health-related entitlements that are currently facing increasing deficits.) The increasing rates of return and low risk (due to government guarantees) would make the green energy bonds attractive to insurance companies, pension funds, and university endowments—the same customers that bought CDOs created from subprime mortgages because of their (unjustified) AAA ratings.

As mentioned at the beginning of this chapter, there is a "different" nuclear technology that could overcome some of the current objections to solid fuel uranium-based power. I refer to the liquid fluoride thorium reactor or LFTR (Hargraves 2012; Hargraves and Moir 2010). The key feature, as the name suggests, is that the fuel element (thorium or uranium) is dissolved in a liquefied salt (a fluoride for preference) at a high temperature (800°C) but at atmospheric pressure. The thorium 232 is not fissionable, but when it absorbs a neutron from a chain reaction, it emits an electron (beta decay) and becomes uranium 233, which is fissionable. Other fission products are generated as the reactions continue, all the way up to plutonium, but in comparatively tiny amounts compared to the uranium chain.

The liquid salt circulates in normal operation. The fluoride is essentially immune to radiation damage, in contrast to the fuel rods used in uranium-based power plants.[2] The design includes a "freeze plug" that has to be cooled by a fan. If the power goes off, the fan stops and the liquid salt flows out into a catch basin where it cools and solidifies. No explosion or "meltdown" such as occurred at Chernobyl or Fukushima is possible. This means that the containment system is far more compact, which means that the LFTR can be made much smaller, probably small enough to power a jet engine, for example. The high operating temperature permits an electric power plant to achieve 45 percent efficiency, as compared to 33 percent for a conventional nuclear plant.

Moreover the quantity of material to be mined and processed and the quantity of waste that must be stored safely for hundreds of generations is far less than with uranium-based reactors with solid fuel rods. The comparison is roughly as follows: 1 ton of thorium is equivalent in terms of power output to 250 tons of uranium containing 1.75 tons of U-235. There are no highly radioactive "spent" fuel rods to store. The fission products decay to stability in 300 years, not hundreds of centuries. The fission products, overall, are approximately 10,000 times less toxic than the fission products from uranium-based power plants.

The technology was actually under development at Oak Ridge National Laboratory (ORNL) from 1965 to 1970, when the program was stopped. It could be re-started. The Indian government is currently doing so. There is a thorium research program in France. The economics of the LFTR appear attractive, since the enormous containment system and much of the waste storage needed for today's nuclear power plants would be unnecessary. However, more research is needed.

On Private Sector Financing

Let me start with my dream scenario. Imagine that the tycoons, bankers, and heads of state who meet every year at the World Economic Forum, at Davos, in Switzerland, agree on several simple propositions, propositions that I believe to be true and demonstrable. Here is a short list:

• That the world is too heavily indebted and that faster economic growth is the only way to avoid massive financial defaults and social chaos.
• That austerity isn't creating jobs or growth.
• That cheap money isn't the panacea.
• That climate change is real and probably accelerating.
• That the world is "hooked" on oil (meaning petroleum) as the one form of fossil fuel that is a liquid and has no practical substitute for fueling internal combustion engines—hence all forms of transportation as well as agricultural machinery and construction machinery. Oil is also consequently a proxy for "useful energy" in general.
• That the global energy return on energy investment (EROEI) is declining and will decline faster as the cheap and easy-to-extract oil is used up. "Peak oil" from land would have happened already. This means hydrocarbon prices will rise, unless alternatives are developed fast enough to cut demand for oil. The cost/price increase of fossil energy will not be smooth; there may be a temporary decline due to the boom in shale gas, for instance, but the rising cost will be unstoppable if growth continues.
• That the internal combustion engine whether depending on gasoline, diesel, or jet fuel must be replaced, sooner or later.
• That due to conflict with food production for a growing global population, liquid biofuels from grain or sugar cannot be produced in large enough quantities. Hence electrification of most ground transportation is inevitable, and it is also well under way.

Taken together, these propositions clearly imply that—if nothing changes—an increasing fraction of the global economy will be devoted to producing the energy needed to provide services—from lighting to heating and air conditioning to transportation and communication—that we take for granted now.

Why should the tycoons and bankers of the world care about these issues? The reasons are quite simple. When oil (i.e., energy) prices rise, the economy slows down. This reduces profits. The central banks usually respond with cheap money. Cheap money is less effective at "kick-starting" growth than the Keynesians like to think, because it enables speculators to make bad or unwise investments (e.g., real estate bubbles).

One of the unwise investments that may already be encouraged by low-interest loans may be to invest in more highways, bridges and other infrastructure that supports the growth of the automobile industry. Yet it is perfectly clear that highways in China and India pave over productive land that is now devoted to growing food crops. This displaces the farmers and raises food prices. It is also perfectly clear that highway construction competes with investment in rail-based public transport systems that are far more efficient, both as "people movers" and in terms of energy consumption. Low-interest loans also encourage utilities and heavy industries in developing countries (e.g., China and India) to overinvest in new coal-based electric power plants, steel mills, and cement plants with long lives, using current inefficient technologies. This will have the effect of "locking in" long-term demand for coal, in particular. It is said that China is building one new coal-based electric power plant every week.

A further concern for the tycoons and bankers at Davos is that unwise investments in fossil-fuel based technology during the current decade (2010 to 2019) may become "stranded assets" in twenty or thirty years, long before their useful life is exhausted. This would have a negative effect on markets and on economic growth. I think the points made above should be persuasive.

Contrary to what most of the folks on Main Street may think, the tycoons at Davos know perfectly well that there is no shortage of capital for long-term investment. On the contrary, they are sitting on a great deal of idle cash while looking for better returns. It is the government(s) of the democracies that have no spare money to spend because those same governments have allowed wealthy individuals and multinational companies like Apple and Google (and hundreds of others) to divert their profits away from the countries where they earn money into "tax havens" where the money accumulates doing very little good to anybody.

Another important fact, well known to the people at Davos, is that the problem of providing pensions for retirees is becoming acute. Dependency ratios are climbing in all Western countries. By 2050 they will double in most Western countries. In Japan the number of retirees, now 35 percent of active workers, will reach 80 percent. Most European countries will have dependency ratios greater than 50 percent. The United States, now about 20 percent, lags a little because of continued immigration (mainly from Latin America), but the ratio will rise to 40 percent by 2050. So there is no way retirement incomes for ever more elderly people can be paid for by taxing currently active workers in the future. Increasing the retirement age will be necessary, but it is only part of the solution, at most, because life expectancy is increasing rapidly. Cutting benefits is considered to be politically impossible (with the possible exception of de-linking benefits from inflation).

So-called defined benefit pension funds were already in a difficult spot by 2007 because of aging populations. The ratio of assets to liabilities for such pension plans declined by 25 percent from 2007 to 2010. The financial crisis of 2008 made this shortfall much worse because the ratings agencies (which helped create the problem) have been forced to downgrade many mortgage-based securities to point where they are no longer "investment grade." Now these pension funds are faced with the task of producing higher returns for a growing class of beneficiaries.

Companies have been replacing "defined benefit" retirement plans with "defined contribution" plans, leaving the problem for individual retirees to solve for themselves (presumably by investing in the stock market). But, while brokers love the idea, stock markets do not always rise as predicted. The only way out of the bind is to increase the returns on long-term investments. That is where renewable energy investments can contribute.

It would be tempting to conclude this book with a strong critique of the tax system and those that have created and manipulated it in their own interest. However, others have already done this better than I could. My real point is that there is plenty of money to invest long term if suitable investment vehicles can be created. Apart from the uncomfortable facts noted above, there is another fact, namely that among the supposedly safe investments the pension funds and insurance companies depend on for future dividends are large blocks of shares in the oil companies and electric utilities that are going to be hurt by the coming de-carbonization. The need for alternatives is clear.

Suppose, then, that "de-carbonization" bonds are the order of the day. What conditions are necessary? One condition is that they should have an "investment grade" rating, preferably AAA, but anything above BBB. This means that they must be secured by assets that will hold or increase their value over time. On the one hand, hydrocarbon reserves might satisfy this criterion, especially in the price of petroleum continues to rise. On the other hand, if the demand for liquid fuels should decline, for instance, because of a massive shift to electrification, the value of those oil reserves (and the shares of the firms that own those reserves) will also decline. In that case, the smart money would "short" those same stocks. (How to do this profitably when the time frame may be anywhere from a few years to a few decades is a challenge for the hedge funds.)

The lady or the tiger? It is evident that one of the primary conditions for the creation of long-term investment grade assets is the existence of a convincing predictive theory for energy commodities in general, and oil prices in particular. Or, failing that, investors would need access to a statistical tool capable of extracting the underlying trends and the corresponding abnormal ("fat-tailed") distribution functions from volatile time series data. To put it another way, investors will need statistical tools significantly better than the ones used by the unfortunate founders of Long-Term Capital Management (LTCM) back in 1997. As it happens, such tools are currently under development.

Another absolute requirement for the hypothetical de-carbonization bonds is liquidity. Owners must be able to sell the bonds at any time. This means that whoever makes the market—when it is mature—must have access to very deep pockets. This need is in fact the only convincing argument I can think of for universal banks like JPMorgan Chase, or Citi-Group, or Bank-of-America–Merrill Lynch to continue to exist.

A collateralized debt obligation (CDO) is essentially a large "bundle" of asset-based bonds, preferably representing a diverse collection of underlying assets that are not closely correlated with each other. The first requirement for a bond issue is a predictable and stable revenue stream. Government entities can issue bonds based on future tax revenues. Other examples of (relatively) risk-free revenue streams include tolls for roads, bridges, and tunnels or bonds for the construction of power lines, water and sewer treatment plants, and electric power plants. Mortgage payments on conventional home loans where the owner has significant equity are also comparatively risk free. So to (perhaps) lesser degrees are credit card payments, auto loan payments, and education loan payments. The question arises: Are there any such examples in the energy-saving domain?

The answer is certainly yes. The obvious example is payments to utilities for electricity, gas, water and sewage. However the utilities have no incentive to save energy. They want to increase sales, not the contrary. This opportunity has been apparent for several decades, but individual homeowners rarely choose to invest spare money in energy saving that will only pay off in the future vis-à-vis immediate consumption, like a new i-phone or plasma HDTV. But if major savings can be achieved with relatively modest investment, there is still a profit opportunity for an investor with access to capital and a longer term horizon. This is where energy service companies (ESCOs) enter the picture. Bonds have been issued in the past for particular ESCO energy-saving projects.

This brings me to the core question: What assets should the "de-carb" bonds be predicated on? In the distant past those assets would have had to be real and physical (e.g., oil in the ground), but today that is no longer necessary. Bonds can be constructed from any kind of asset, even derivatives of other assets, so long as a reliable stream of revenue exists. For instance, the electricity produced by wind turbines has a value when it is sold to the grid. This is also true for electricity sold to the grid by PV panel owners, whether large or small. Energy service contracts (ESCO) create revenue streams. Some of the biggest ones are already funded by bond issues. One such company is about to take over the utility system for Kodak Park in Rochester, New York. Dividends of biofuel companies constitute a revenue stream. Loans to small start-up companies can also create a revenue stream. The main requirement for creating long-term bonds is that the components of the revenue stream be very diverse, and not closely correlated with each other. It is indeed important that a variety of different EETs and RETs be represented.

Incidentally, some of the uncertainties and risks associated with de-carbonization can be minimized through the use of insurance and/or derivatives analogous to the credit default swaps (CDS). There is a large market for insurance against exchange rate changes and even changes in government policy, for instance. So if the current market for wind turbines and rooftop PV) depends in part on government incentives or subsidies that could be withdrawn by a different political regime, it is possible to hedge against those changes. Lloyds of London still specializes in hedging against unusual risks. The cost of the hedge would have to be set against the potential profit for the fund, of course.

Luckily some of the sophisticated financial techniques (notably "securitization") that have been used in pursuance of a well-intentioned, but poorly implemented, housing policy ("the ownership society" can be better employed to pursue a different and necessary objective: *energy security*). In summary, the financial system (with some government help in the form of regulation) can create energy-based securities analogous to the mortgage-based securities that drove the "subprime" bubble. The customers for those securities would be the same institutions (insurance companies, pension funds, university endowments, and banks) that so eagerly bought securities based on subprime mortgages that were mistakenly rated as ultra-safe (AAA). The financial sector needs to design long-term energy-based securities (either bonds or equities) that can be bought by institutional investors. This will encourage real and energy-efficient economic growth and increased employment. Some of the challenges that need to be overcome to make this happen are discussed in the next chapter.

10
Concluding Thoughts on Bubbles and Energy

The View from a Tall Ivory Tower

This book started from two sets of facts and several propositions. The first set of undoubted facts relates to the state of the world economic and financial system. The second set of facts relates to material and energy resources.

As regards the first set of facts, I believe the global economy is increasingly unstable. The scope and magnitude of the potential instabilities is growing, partly due to economies of scale and partly to globalization. The negative externalities caused by asset bubbles, credit collapse, and debt defaults have increased enormously in scale and scope. Furthermore Wall Street has discovered that it is more profitable—under existing rules—to make money from money by trading and gambling (thanks to information asymmetries) than by investing in the "real' economy. This has deprived small and medium-size businesses of access to capital. It has resulted in slower economic growth, as well as increasing inequality. The underlying causes are attributable in part to "design flaws" in the system and partly to pressures originating outside the economy itself, including globalization, demographics, and geological resource scarcities.

The negative externalities are growing in parallel (if not faster than) the scale of ordinary economic activities, as the world is becoming more urbanized, more densely populated, more productive, and more complex. This book argues that these negatives already outweigh the efficiency benefits of real-time mega-finance. These negatives in fact constitute a serious challenge to the future of capitalism. One disturbing trend is that economic inequality has been worsening, at the same time as the financial sector of the economy has been increasing its share of the GDP. The existence of a causal connection is hard to deny, still less to ignore.

The problems of financial instability have a long history, summarized in chapter 3. These problems got a lot worse in 2007 to 2008, thanks to the collapse of the subprime real estate bubble in the United States and its financial "ripple" effects. Some cosmetic changes have been made to correct the most obvious flaws in the system (Dodd–Frank), but the deeper problems—resulting in rising income inequality, for instance—have not been addressed. A similar or even bigger financial bubble can, and may, occur in the future. If it does, the global economy could suffer a massive deflation and depression.

The Financial Facts

The current financial troubles have many aspects, but the one that is most obvious to the politicians and the public is the sovereign debt crisis. Whether the situation is as dire as some conservatives insist is open to question. But the fact that increasing debt is not sustainable in the long term is not in doubt. The current debate among economists concerns growth and growth stimulus policies. Related problems arising from income inequality and free trade without free movement of labor are not yet being seriously addressed.

The second important fact, following from the first, is that economic growth has become even more imperative than it was in the past. The reasons for the slower growth in Europe and the United States are multifold. But the key point is that the financial crisis that began in 2008 to 2009 is not over. The loss of home equity has cut demand for new homes drastically and the construction industry, which usually leads recoveries, continues in the doldrums, notwithstanding year-to-year gains starting in 2012. Moreover the European debt crisis still continues in 2014. It is a direct consequence of bank losses stemming from 2007 to 2008 (exacerbated by the overreaction of the ratings agencies). It is also one of the excuses for the austerity policies that are currently in effect. Those austerity policies have increased unemployment and decreased government revenues, causing a downward spiral that shows no signs of ending.

The third fact is that there are three ways for governments to escape from debt. One is to stop payment to foreign creditors unilaterally. That option worked for some countries in the past (most recently by the USSR in 1917 and Nazi Germany in 1933), but if any big country tried it today, the global contagion would be unimaginable. The second alternative is to "inflate" the debt away (by devaluing it). Hyperinflation as in Germany in 1922 to 1924, or in some Latin American countries since WWII devalued government debt by impoverishing the middle class. This is also unimaginable today. In Germany's case, the social consequences led to the rise of Hitler. "Moderate" rates of inflation have not worked well either, as in Latin America and the United States during the 1960s and 1970s. The very low (2 percent or so) rate of inflation currently regarded as optimal, by some economists, would not wipe out the debt. Hence renewed (and accelerated) economic growth is the only acceptable way to escape from the existing sovereign debt burden, much of which arises from overlavish "entitlements" that were originally predicated on automatic future economic growth. That growth can no longer be seen as automatic, but it is no less important. Meanwhile those entitlements are driving government deficits deeper into the red and adding to the government debt burden.

Fact four is that cutting entitlements like pensions and health care is politically very difficult in a democracy. There is now a seemingly irreconcilable dispute between two groups of policy makers. One consists of political conservatives supported by "free market" economists, who believe in low taxes, less regulation, and the supposed regenerative power of budget balancing, even during recessions. The other group consists of liberal and quasi-socialist politicians, supported by Keynesian economists, who believe that the government needs to lean against the wind by deficit spending during recessions while maintaining a budgetary surplus during boom times. The counterargument, of course, is that politicians always spend the surplus. At least, they always have done that.

Fact five is that the current policy of austerity in Europe, enforced by financial conservatives, has *not* brought forth a flood of private sector investment and is not generating growth or jobs. There is no sign of any economic boom to come soon. On the contrary, austerity is making government deficits worse. Meanwhile the central banks are trying to overcome the fiscal austerity headwind by cutting interest rates to stimulate growth. But the low interest rates in the United States, Japan, and Europe have not had a significant positive effect so far (although "Abe-nomics" in Japan could be a game-changer). That is the current economic situation in a nutshell. I have merely summarized in these paragraphs what is quite well-known to readers of the *New York Times*, *Wall Street Journal*, *Financial Times*, and *The Economist* as well as other news media.

The second set of facts concerns the energy-economy relationship. The first fact, in a word, is that energy is essential to all economic activity. Few would doubt this fact, as simply stated. Less well understood is the high degree of importance of energy availability as a driver of past economic growth and as a source of current wealth.

But the second fact, (though most neoclassical economists dispute it) is that economic theory underrates the importance of energy. Chapter 1 very briefly explained why energy has been neglected in economic theory (the explanation could have fallen between two stools—too technical for some and too simplified for experts). This is important because energy services have been declining in cost (and price) from the eighteenth century to the twentieth century, but the decline seems to have stopped and even reversed. This has enabled a huge degree of substitution of mechanical and electrical machines for human and animal labor. That substitution has been a primary driver of past economic growth. A related crucial fact is that fossil fuels (coal, petroleum, and natural gas) count for a large fraction (around 70 percent) of global energy use.

The primary reason for this book emerges from two more clusters of facts both disputed but true nevertheless. One is that cheap high-quality liquid hydrocarbons are essential for almost all surface and water transportation systems (not to mention petrochemistry, construction, and agriculture). Without those services the rest of the urban economy cannot function. But the liquid fuels are obtained exclusively from crude petroleum with a very small contribution from natural gas liquids. Shale oil and tar sands can be converted to liquid fuel but at much higher cost. The shale gas receiving so much publicity may make electricity cheaper, but it has little relevance to the liquid fuel problem. The introduction of carbon capture and storage (CCS) technology for electric power plants would have the opposite effect, making electricity much more expensive.

Moreover there is still another "elephant in the room." It is a fact that climate change is already happening, and all signs point to acceleration. Global temperatures are increasing, storms are becoming more violent, floods are more common, arctic and glacier ice are melting, and the sea level is rising. Climate change is due to the so-called greenhouse effect, which in turn is due mainly to the atmospheric accumulation of combustion products (e.g., CO_2) of fossil fuels. It is a human-made phenomenon. The possible responses to climate change cannot be summarized and compared in a few words. But the bottom line, is that, to prevent "runaway" global temperatures from rising more than 2 degrees Celsius—which climate scientists now regard the "tipping point" where the process becomes irreversible—fossil fuel combustion must be cut rather sharply in the coming decades.

Whether due to natural scarcity (of cheap petroleum) or due to legal restrictions on fossil fuel use, or both, I think it is highly probable that carbon prices will rise in the future, albeit not smoothly, especially if the economy grows. Scarcity of liquid fuels is one factor. Economic growth is the other. A research group at the IMF has recently published a forecast confirming this conclusion (Benes et al. 2012). According to their model, oil prices are likely to double by 2020, due mainly to increasing demand from China and other developing countries, regardless of what happens with shale. The negative consequences for economic growth would be dire.

One last fact, as I count it, is that while the costs of liquid hydrocarbons will rise, the costs of efficiency technologies (EETs) and renewable technologies (RETs) will almost certainly decline. This decline is a natural consequence of R&D, economies of scale, learning-by-doing (Arrow 1962), and the so-called experience curve (Wene 2000). In brief, the cost of any manufactured product tends to decline as a function of the total cumulative quantity produced. This phenomenon is, of course, the major reason why computer chips, flash drives, and cell phones are now so cheap.

Having summarized the main facts, I come to the implications. They are as follows. First, given that the financial system is inherently unstable, managing the global financial system requires constant "tweaking" by regulators. One type of tweak (cheap money) tends to create asset "bubbles," and the collapse of every major bubble causes a recession and creates the conditions for another bubble. The bursting of many bubbles also causes a major externality: heavy losses to people not involved directly with the bubble creation mechanism. This process also tends to shift wealth and power from the poor and middle class to the rich. That is a tendency governments will need to counteract (and soon) if major social disturbances are to be avoided.

But, as noted already, the low interest rates are not working to trigger new economic growth, at least not well enough. Another approach to stimulate growth is needed. The rising price of energy from fossil fuels suggests that renewables will be increasingly profitable. Hence governments should redirect private savings (and global finance) away from home ownership toward "de-carbonization" or "re-inventing fire" (Lovins 2011). By that, I mean breaking the "addiction" to carbon-based fossil fuels in general, and to oil in particular. The need to break that addiction is gradually becoming evident, even to the oil industry.

It is not necessary to "pick winners" at this stage. What is necessary is to create a financial "cradle" within which the inventors and innovators can perform their wonders without requiring direct subsidies from the taxpayer. The role of financial innovation, in a word, must be to direct private investment toward energy independence. (Essentially what President Jimmy Carter tried unsuccessfully to initiate in the 1970s.)

Luckily some of the financial techniques that have been used in pursuance of a well-intentioned but poorly executed policy of increasing home-ownership by two presidents can now be employed to pursue a different and necessary objective. Large-scale investing in renewables may in fact be the way to achieve a triple-win ("trifecta"): (1) cut greenhouse gas emissions, (2) stimulate innovation-based economic growth and employment, and (3) offer long-term investment opportunities for the insurance companies and pensions funds that were so eager a decade ago to buy mortgage-based CDOs with AAA ratings from Wall Street.

To make this happen sooner than later, one financial innovation from the 1980s seems relevant: *securitization.* I can imagine that a farsighted Wall Street investment bank may see advantages in creating CDOs based on revenue streams from a wide variety of EET and RET projects, some of which will fail while others will succeed spectacularly. *But it will be driven by rising energy (oil) prices rather than rising real estate prices.*

There are some barriers to overcome. Skeptics are not in short supply. They will argue, among other things, that the debt crisis really is the most important challenge facing the world economy and that the only solution is to liquidate all the unprofitable investments, don't bail out the losers, let the free market work its magic. (Look how well that worked in 1929!) Oh yes, and cut taxes still more on the rich "who are the job creators." Others will say that there is no climate crisis, so nothing should stop us from exploiting that ocean of oil (and gas) locked in shale that can and will be extracted profitably.

Some others will argue that renewables like wind power and rooftop PV or solar concentrators, or tidal power, or oil from algae are not profitable now, that they need to be subsidized to make it in the marketplace. Others (trained in economics) will argue that the economy doesn't really depend much on energy because energy has (has had) such a small cost share in the GDP. It follows from that line of argument that we don't need to change anything because "the economy wants to grow" and it will grow automatically. It also follows from that assumption that economic growth can continue indefinitely and that our grandchildren will be a lot richer than we are.

This book argues that all these skeptics are betting on the wrong horse. They assume that the future will be like the past, even though the game has changed. When the majority of punters are betting on the favorite, the opportunities for betting on underrated outsiders can be very good. That is exactly the right time to bet.

Appendix: Two More Digressions

On Models of Human Behavior, Rationality, and "Physics Envy"

In a recent speech Mario Draghi, the Chairman of the European Central Bank, commented that, according to traditional aerodynamic theory the bumblebee should not be able to fly. But the bumblebee doesn't know that, so it flies anyway. By the same token (he said) in theory the euro should not work, but in practice it does work fairly well. Well, almost. My point is that a lot of what is happening in financial markets is not rational. The role of irrationality in economics needs to be explored (and taken into account) more intelligently.

In 1961 a mathematician named Ed Thorp presented a paper to the American Mathematical Society entitled "Fortune's Formula: A Winning Strategy for Blackjack." This paper was a pathbreaking contribution to the broader problem of calculating the probabilities of so-called random events. Thorp expanded this paper into a book, *Beat the Dealer*, that became a *New York Times* best seller (Thorp 1962). A few years later he joined with Sheen Kassouf, a finance professor at New York University, to develop a practical method of forecasting the prices of warrants (Thorp and Kassouf 1967). Some of the basic ideas came from a 1964 book edited by Paul Cootner entitled *The Random Character of Stock Market Prices*.

In 1965 a graduate student named Eugene Fama, at the University of Chicago's Booth School of Business, published his PhD dissertation, entitled "An Efficient Market Hypothesis." It built on earlier work by French engineer Louis Bachelier in his PhD thesis "A Theory of Specu-lation" (1900), which proposed a random-walk model of stock-market prices. It was later supported by Alfred Cowles in the 1930s and 1940s, who argued that professional money managers rarely outperformed the markets.

Economists had neglected Bachelier's work until Paul Samuelson promoted it in the early 1960s. Fama took it further and provided theoretical underpinnings. It created a sensation among investors and financial economists because the efficient market hypothesis (EMH) implies that *investors cannot beat the markets* (i.e., the averages) in the long run (Fama and French 1965; Fama 1965, 1970; Fama et al. 1969). As it happens, EMH has been much more accepted by financial economists (especially before 1998) than it ever was by bankers and traders, most of whom (like Warren Buffet) believe that it is possible to beat the market. Some of the reasons are discussed below. The truth seems to be that Fama is right about the impossibility of consistently guessing right about short-term fluctuations, but not about long-term investment strategies where information is not equally available to all parties.

Thorp's first application of statistics to making money was to warrants (or call options) to purchase stock at some future time at a given price. Meanwhile market prices fluctuate, and if the market price never exceeds the option price plus the cost of the warrant before the option expires, the warrant is worthless. If, on the contrary, one of the fluctuations takes the market price above that point, there is a potential profit and the warrant has value. The value can be realized by an automated trading system.

What Thorp did was to apply Fama's EMH to option pricing by assuming that the individual market fluctuations are random, and that these random events constitute a "normal" (Gaussian) distribution whose parameters can be determined from historical volatility data. This assumption about the shape of the distribution function is where physics intersects economics. It is usually called "random walk," or "drunkard's walk." But it is based on a phenomenon called "Brownian motion" that was explained for the first time, long ago, by Albert Einstein. It assumes, in effect, that people or stock prices behave like microscopic particles bouncing off each other. However, the random-walk theory worked well enough, often enough, in the stock market context to enable Thorp (and many since) to determine whether the option was overpriced or underpriced. By buying underpriced options and selling (or shorting) overpriced options, he could make money (i.e., beat the market on average), and he did so.

At any rate, based on the assumption above (random walk), the probabilities of the next price movement of a stock or bond can be calculated from historical data on *volatility* if the "right" price is known. Volatility information is routinely utilized by traders and modelers today to determine whether a brief fluctuation from the "right" price is more likely to reverse and move back toward the "right" price or move further away. If the "right" price has changed (due to new information), the model will give the wrong answer. But if the fluctuation is truly random, the model will detect a buying or selling opportunity. However, price changes due to new information (available to some but not all traders), panics, or other irrational behavior are unpredictable. The fact that real market behavior sometimes deviates from the random-walk model is largely responsible for some huge financial market disasters, notably the collapse of the Long-Term Capital Management (LTCM) hedge fund in 1998, as well as recent losses by JPMorgan Chase.

Thorp and Kassouf's work undoubtedly influenced the work of Fischer Black and Myron Scholes at MIT, a few years later. In 1973 the Black–Scholes–Merton option-pricing model, mentioned earlier, was published in an academic journal (Black and Scholes 1973) and later developed into a practical working tool by Merton. Finance professors in business schools quickly adopted it. By 1975 it was being used as the method of pricing options traded on the floor of the Chicago Board of Options Trading (CBOT). Soon after that it was adopted by most of the Wall Street "quants" (Patterson 2010).

The first major use of the model by the "quants" was to identify mispricing of options as compared to the component stocks. Then, as mentioned, the trader's strategy would be to short the overpriced component and long the underpriced component. The most famous example of mispricing (which did not depend on the Black–Scholes–Merton model) was the Value Line Futures index, which was always overpriced as compared to the underlying stocks because it used a geometric average instead of an arithmetic average. This simple discovery by Black (together with the automated direct order trading system initiated by Goldman Sachs) resulted in a $20 million profit for the firm with no risk exposure at all (Ellis 2009, p. 414).

The Black–Scholes–Merton option pricing model made options trading into a major market. The International Monetary Market opened in

Chicago in 1972. Robert Rubin of Goldman Sachs was a member of the Options Exchange Board from 1973 on. The ban on commodity options was lifted by Congress in 1976. By the early 1980s, S&P futures contracts also began trading at the Chicago Mercantile exchange. All of this activity was based on the Black–Scholes–Merton asset-pricing model. (In 1983 Rubin hired Fischer Black away from MIT to organize the "quantitative strategies group" at Goldman Sachs.)

The LTCM hedge fund was created in 1994. It utilized the Black–Scholes–Merton (BSM) asset-pricing model for arbitraging. It was based on identifying two assets that were theoretically equal, such as government bonds with the same redemption date but issued in different years or traded in different markets. Such bonds were often priced differently (usually by tiny amounts). The BSM model allowed LTCM to calculate the "right" price and to make bets that the asset prices would converge in the long run. The overpriced asset would be "shorted," while the underpriced asset was held "long," with shorts and longs as nearly as possible in balance. LTCM was incredibly successful for several years, before collapsing very suddenly in 1998 due to nonrandom behavior in the markets. More specifically, it collapsed because of a Russian currency bet that went awry that summer. By a strange twist of fate, Scholes and Merton (Black had died) received the Nobel Prize in economics in 1999, just a year after the collapse of LTCM.

In principle, LTCM couldn't lose if the cost of borrowing were zero and there was time to let every asset pair reach the convergence point. In reality, the fund was betting that the rate of convergence would be fast enough to compensate for the borrowing costs. For several years the fund was amazingly successful. By the end of 1997 its capital base had grown to over $7 billion (*$9.3 billion*$_{2011}$) and it allegedly had a leverage ratio of 16 to 1. To make more money, the fund needed more leverage, so over $2 billion (*$2.7 billion*$_{2011}$) was returned to the outside investors in order to increase the fund's leverage to 125:1 (Kirk 2009). Time ran out for them. Notwithstanding the collapse of LTCM, the 1990s was really the era of the "quants," as reflected by the creation of hundreds, if not thousands, of hedge funds, most of them using some variant of the Black–Scholes–Merton capital asset-pricing model (Patterson 2010).

What went wrong was that in times of panic, there can be irrational behavior in the markets, whence the "normal" distribution of fluctuations is no longer valid. Or, in ordinary language, other players in the game (e.g., of poker) may notice that "someone" is betting against the trend, and that the bets are increasing in size. This situation can resemble a game of poker in which a player with a weak hand is bluffing and betting heavily to drive the other players out of the game. The poker game can become a contest between two players where the one with the deepest pocket can sometimes win just by betting heavily.

Incidentally, according to the efficient market hypothesis, there is no such thing as a "bubble" in the stock market because markets always reflect the total of all available information, and therefore prices are always "correct," even from moment to moment. To put it simply, EMH does not allow for irrationality. It is probably needless to say that if bubbles are real, the simple EMH is not valid. There are other theories, such as "behavioral finance" and the "managed market hypothesis," that give government policy much of the blame. But this is not the place to explain where and how those theories differ.

It is interesting that Warren Buffet, the world's most successful "value investor" took issue with Fama and EMH in a 1984 article for *Hermes*, the magazine of Columbia Business School. The article was entitled "The Super-investors of Graham-and-Doddsville" (Buffet 1984). In the article he named a number of investors, apart from himself, all from the value-investing camp, who had in fact beaten "the market" by large margins. Fama tries to explain this as luck. He says that given a large number of bettors and two choices, say, red or black, there will always be a small number who win many times in succession (as well as a similar number who lose as frequently as the winners win). Buffet disagrees with this explanation. After all, he is not playing with dice.

A recent book by Pablo Triana, a former derivatives trader who is also an academic, entitled *Lecturing Birds on Flying* makes similar points about models. His target is mathematical models of human behavior in markets that depend too much on notions borrowed from physics (e.g., Brownian motion). I can agree with his comment, "Make no mistake, quantitative finance had a very large hand in what could well be the worst financial crisis in the history of mankind" (Triana 2012, p. xxix). That much is true, since it was the use, and misuse of mathematical models, especially BSM (discussed earlier) and another one called Value at Risk (VaR), that encouraged hedge funds, in particular, to increase their leverage so much. There is little doubt that dependence on the BSM model was primarily responsible for the collapse of Long-Term Capital Management in 1998. And it was the excessive leverage operating in reverse that caused the economic crisis of 2008 to 2009. But it was not the risk models that created ARMs and the subprime mortgage market per se.

I am reminded of an episode in *The Big Short* where Michael Lewis recounts a disagreement between senior executives in Deutsche Bank and senior executives at Morgan Stanley. The conversation was initially between Greg Lipmann at Deutsche Bank, who had bought a lot of credit default swaps ($4 billion of them) on subprime CDOs from Howie Hubler at Morgan Stanley. Up to that time, Hubler's bets that the CDOs would not lose their value seemed to have been very profitable, since Deutsche Bank was paying his group millions of dollars in premiums. But early in July 2007 Lipmann phoned Hubler and said (as quoted by Michael Lewis) "Dude, you owe us one point two billion." Lipmann went on to say that the CDOs were "down to 70," meaning 70 cents on the original dollar of purchase price (Lewis 2010, pp 212–13).

This amounted to a partial default, and it was supposed to trigger a transfer of collateral. At 70, the CDOs were down 30 percent, and 30 percent of 4 billion is roughly equal to $1.2 billion Lipmann wanted Morgan Stanley to pay. A Morgan Stanley person on the phone replied "What do you mean 70? Our model says they are worth 95." The Deutsche modeler answered "Our model says they are worth 70." The Morgan Stanley person asserted once again that his model said they were worth 95, and the argument between modelers went on. It turned out that they were making different assumptions about the degree of correlation between the default rates of mortgages in the bonds. Morgan Stanley assumed, like the ratings agencies, that the mortgages were not correlated whereas Deutsche Bank assumed (correctly) that they were highly correlated. Eventually Morgan Stanley compromised by sending $600 million following that conversation, although that was only the beginning. They had to pay the full amount a few months later.

Obviously the two financial models had different assumptions, and the assumptions made the difference. There is a lesson in this, but it is not that "quants" are superfluous (if not dangerous) or that mathematical models are inappropriate. On the contrary, in *Lecturing Birds on Flying* Triana says that before mathematical finance, traders had "working models" for things such as option pricing and that those models were "effective and accurate" whereas the later, more sophisticated models were not. Maybe they were, and maybe they weren't. The option trading activities at the Chicago Board of Trade used and depended on the BSM option-pricing model for many years, and probably still does.

But Triana's complaint is really about specific models (developed by academic theorists) that were used for making huge bets with other people's money, by people who did not understand their (real) limitations. One of those limitations was identified by none other than Alan Greenspan, in testimony before Congress (October 23, 2008). He said: "The whole intellectual edifice . . . collapsed . . . because the data inputted into the risk management models generally covered only the past two decades, a period of euphoria." He was partially right about that, although he acknowledged none of his own responsibility for the euphoria.

In 1995 the Barings Bank, the oldest merchant bank in the United Kingdom (founded in the eighteenth century) collapsed with $1.4 billion (*$2 billion*$_{2011}$) of debt, due to bad bets by Nick Leeson, their chief trader in the Singapore office. Leeson had gambled on the rate at which the Japanese stock market would recover from the Kobe earthquake, which occurred earlier in that year. His bets did not succeed. Leeson was trying to recover from losses due to earlier bad bets on derivatives, which he disguised in the bank's "error account" (famously designated 88888). His bad bets destroyed Baring's Bank, and he went to jail.

The (very) recent loss of at least $5.8 billion at JPMorgan Chase illustrates another way in which irrational behavior can trump a rational strategy. A single trader named Bruno Iksil, known as "the London Whale" because of the size of his bets, reacted unwisely to the discovery that his short position on a certain derivative was "under water." (It turns out that he or his modelers had made a human error: they divided by a sum instead of an average.) Instead of unwinding his position and taking his losses, he "doubled down" as the saying goes, depending on the unlimited reserves of his employer (the bank) to frighten off any investors who had the temerity to bet against him. It was an expensive version of the poker player's bluff an attempt to scare an opponent into dropping out by increasing the size of the bet. As it happens, the players (hedge funds) on the other side of the "Whale's" bets were not bluffed out. One of them, a hedge fund manager named Boaz Weinstein, has allegedly made $600 million on the bet, and (as this is written) it may not be over yet. My point is that in this case, as in others, winning and losing are not necessarily attributable to rational market behavior. Sometimes it comes down to contests between individuals with enormous egos and deep pockets.[1] But that strategy can go wrong if other players guess what is happening and combine to "call" the bet.

Measurement and quantification, or models, are not the real problem. The uncomfortable truth is that valuation is impossible without quantification, and quantification is actually the primary advantage of markets over primeval barter. We just need to recognize that all models are imperfect representations of reality, all markets are imperfect thanks to externalities, and the imperfections can be crucial. When the models depart from reality, the models have to be changed. Unfortunately, it happens all too often that people who have invested too much in their models sometimes behave as though reality is wrong.

A new trend in the markets that is not explicitly a model, but uses simple models (algorithms), is known as "high-frequency trading" (HFT) by ultra-fast computers. These "robot" traders operate independently of human intervention or judgment. IBM and Hewlett-Packard independently developed such algorithms in 1996 and 1997 (MGD and ZOP, respectively). In 2001 an IBM group showed that the HFT outperformed human traders and estimated the overall benefits at several billions of dollars per year. That triggered a race. Deutsche Bank developed its "Stealth" algorithm. Credit Suisse now uses "Sniper " and "Guerilla." The champion of all the hedge funds using HFT is James Simon's Renaissance Technologies, which develops its own algorithms and does it better than anybody else. By 2006 a third of all market transactions in the United States and Europe were done by HFTs. By 2009 the HFT share in the United States was up to 79 percent, and it seems likely that the current share is even higher, in that HFT is now *de rigueur* for all major financial institutions on both the buy side and the sell side. This fact is very bad news for individual traders or small brokerage firms that cannot compete.

The benefits overall cannot be easily measured, but there are several market strategies that utilize HFT, especially arbitrage—tracking prices for the same security in several different markets and profiting from differences by buying one long and shorting the other. This was the original LTCM strategy. Evidently prices can change quickly, so it becomes important to carry out both sides of these transactions simultaneously so as to minimize the potential for loss due to price changes during the order execution (known as "execution risk"). Immediacy of execution is less important for other strategies, such as trend-following, which is based on utilizing all possible market data on relationships between pairs of indicators in order to predict long-term trends and to profit from short-term departures one way or the other.

But robot traders are fundamentally stupid: they do only what they are told to do in specific circumstances. On May 6, 2010, an event occurred that demonstrated this point dramatically. A major trader (alleged to be Kansas-based Waddell and Reed, a mutual fund) decided to sell a large number ($4.1 billion worth) of E-mini futures contracts for the Standard & Poor 500 index fund. The sale was executed by an algorithm-driven robot. What happened was that the Dow Jones Industrial Average (DJIA) dropped 481 points in six minutes and then recovered by 502 points ten minutes later. From an overall market-watcher's perspective, it was a "blip" of no particular significance. However, as the later report by the SEC and the Commodity Futures Trading Commission (CFTC) noted, "over 20,000 trades across more than 300 securities were executed at prices more than 60% away from their values just moments before" (SEC and CTFC 2010). . In fact during one period of just 14 seconds 27,000 automated orders were executed between HFTs, but only 200 E-minis were bought "to keep," so to speak.

In essence the HFTs were selling to each other during those seconds because there was not enough cash (liquidity) in the system to absorb all the sell orders. So robot traders were buying E-minis because they were programmed to do so whenever the price fell below a certain level. But every time such a purchase of E-minis brought the allowed inventory for that fund above a preset level, the robot trader proceeded to re-sell them to other robot traders programmed to buy that security. The ownership of those orphan E-minis was passed round and round the merry-go-round, until enough liquidity (cash) became available. This behavior became known as the "hot potato effect." Luckily it didn't do much damage, on that occasion.

Other unanticipated chain effects were far more important. For instance, an automated purchase of one security (e.g., an E-mini) would force a buyer to sell some another security, to maintain the cash value of the fund. Of course, this could (and did) result in a chain of still other forced transactions. It was the chain effect that pushed the DJIA down so fast. Luckily the market re-equilibrated in a short time, and the DJIA rose back up to its earlier level. In this case the faulty assumption behind the "flash crash" was that there would always be enough liquidity in the system to absorb the securities being offered for sale. Regulators are still wondering whether this kind of (unintended) behavior constitutes a major hazard to the markets and, if so, what to do about it. (An obvious remedy would be to put an upper limit on the size of the sell or buy order that can be executed at one time, in relation to the total trading activity in that market over some previous time period measured in hours or days, not milliseconds.)

To summarize, there was a time, roughly from 1985 to 2005, when the smartest hedge fund managers made money with algorithms that identified market inefficiencies of the sort discovered by Thorp and Kassouf back in the 1960s. There were always losers as well as winners, but in the five golden years 2003 to 2007, the winners won a great deal from a large number of losers who hardly noticed because each loss was so small. Naturally those winners attracted a lot of investors: assets under management tripled from about $600 billion to $1.8 trillion. The hedge fund industry now (2014) has over $2 trillion in assets under management.

Yet the average hedge fund lost money in 2011, and even the top 10 percent of funds only made returns of 19.5 percent. Not bad, but less than half of the returns made by the top 10 percent in every single year from 2000 through 2010 (Dan McCrum, *Financial Times*, September 11, 2012). McCrum attributes this decline to the fact that statistical information from Bloomberg and other sources is now so easy to tap into that the number of money-making opportunities from inefficiency-fishing have declined significantly. He calls it "the end of alpha," meaning that it is getting much harder to beat the market using computers. Let's hope that the plot of the novel (and movie) *The Fear Index* by Robert Harris was just imaginative fiction.

Digression Continued: Economic Models

Now I need to mention another kind of model, known as a computable general equilibrium (CGE) model. While the models are incredibly complex and difficult to change—they are based on a set of assumptions that are much too simplistic. (They in fact largely reflect insights from the nineteenth and early twentieth centuries without much modification to reflect changes in the economy.) The models used by governments and international institutions are still based on axioms and theorems based on idealized situations. To begin with, they assume equilibrium, and economic growth in equilibrium, despite the fact that growth is inherently a disequilibrium process, as Schumpeter explained more than a century ago (Schumpeter [1911] 1961). Hence, to put it bluntly, the CGE models are incapable of predicting (or explaining) bubbles, which are inherently nonequilibrium phenomena.

But deep inside the CGE models, every one of them, is a set of other assumptions. One of those assumptions (actually based on a very simple model of the economy) is that the only two "factors of production" are capital and labor. To say it slightly differently for emphasis, the standard theory of economic growth assumes that only labor supply, capital, and "multifactor productivity" (MFP) are the responsible drivers. MFP was formerly called "technological progress" or the "Solow residual," named after Robert Solow, the economist who first formulated growth theory in terms of production functions (Solow 1956, 1957). MFP is determined empirically by looking at past economic growth, comparing it with what can be explained by capital and labor, and extrapolating the difference. When short-term fluctuations are averaged out, it turns out that the effect of MFP can be expressed as a certain average percentage increase in GDP per year (of the order of 2 percent "real" per annum).

The theory economic growth embedded in the CGE models does not allow for the energy input as a primary "factor of production." The models treat energy as an intermediate good, namely something that is produced by the economy itself, that is, by some combination of capital and human labor. But, as I discussed in an earlier chapter, neither labor nor capital goods are productive without energy inputs. Moreover it was the discovery and utilization of natural resources (coal, then petroleum, and finally natural gas) that enabled our ancestors to escape from bondage to the land, got us to the motorized and computerized world where we live today, and financed the transition.

There is a large body of economic literature, much of it sponsored by the World Bank, attempting to explain the different growth rates in developing countries, hence MFP, in terms of socioeconomic variables. These variables include literacy, monetary policy, debt, tax rates, barriers to trade, "rule of law," corruption, and "ease of doing business." Some theorists have suggested that MFP may be explained as the consequence of increasing "knowledge" (e.g., Machlup 1962; Schmookler 1962). But knowledge in the aggregate is typically assumed to increase gradually and automatically, with no mechanism to focus knowledge on an urgent specific problem, such as war or rising oil prices.

I have to say it again (I said it earlier in chapter 1 in my discussion of energy in economics): *The conventional neoclassical theory of economic growth overestimates the importance of labor and underestimates the importance of energy.* Needless to say, the CGE models reflect that theory. As a consequence the models cannot predict the consequences of resource scarcity, climate changes, major technological changes (e.g., the Internet) that affect energy requirements, or societal changes (e.g., the "Arab Spring") for which there is no historical experience. As regards the current economic situation, by not including energy as a factor of production, the CGE models are unable to predict the consequences of a historic shift (as I see it) from declining to increasing fossil energy prices. Hence the models tend to assume that energy prices will remain stable and that growth will continue at historic rates. (Interestingly, the IMF is just beginning to experiment with alternative model assumptions; see Benes et al. 2012.)

Incidentally, I think the overweighting of labor in the standard growth models means that routine human labor is now overpriced (in the West) in strictly economic terms, whereas (useful) energy is underweighted because it is underpriced. The high price of routine labor is partly a leftover from the time several decades ago when the West had an effective monopoly on advanced technology and the production of sophisticated capital goods and consumer goods for sale to the rest of the world, in exchange for their raw materials (provided by very cheap labor). It is also partly due to bargaining by labor unions in the past with political support due to fear of communism and partly due to purely political interventions ranging from minimum-wage laws to civil service salaries and unemployment benefits. The expectation of rising standards of living is now so deeply entrenched that the sociopolitical consequences of any significant reduction in labor (wage) costs in Europe or the United States would be politically devastating. We see hints of this devastation in Greece today.

If the previous paragraph is on target, then the economic optimum would be a situation using less overpriced labor and more underpriced energy. That doesn't happen because the political system can't and won't allow it. We all know what central banks do after each bubble collapses: they "print" cheap money to stimulate the economy by increasing demand. The idea goes back to Keynes. *What they should do, is to "print" barrels of oil or solar panels—instead of dollars.* Of course, that possibility isn't included in the government's current bag of tricks. Cheap money made available through the banking system has in fact little or no effect on energy prices and produces less sustainable economic growth than conventional wisdom suggests, partly because it does *not* increase the energy supply or reduce the cost of energy.

Better economic models are badly needed because the world economy needs growth that doesn't increase demand for fossil fuels, and leaders must first understand the drivers of growth better than they do now. Supply-side orthodoxy—shared by the vast majority of economists and bankers—assumes that growth must and will be driven by private sector investment and that investment will follow deregulation and fiscal austerity, as the dawn follows the night. Minority Keynesians, like Paul Krugman, doubt this assumption and propose to reverse the downward spiral by artificially increasing demand ("stimulus") to "kick-start" the economy. In the Keynesian worldview the extra spending by consumers is what induces producers to increase output and investors to invest. That translates into increased employment and more tax revenue for the government. But if the growth is not fast enough, the debt will still grow, and almost everyone in the senior financial community has now accepted the German doctrine that growth driven by increasing debt is not acceptable, whence fiscal reform and labor market reform must come first.

The problem is that the Keynesian mechanism for growth stimulation may not be working any more, thanks to near-saturation of many goods markets, as well as the fact that much of the increased consumer demand nowadays generates employment in other countries. A pro-growth policy in the United States must attack the trade deficit, and the fossil fuel problem, as well as the government budget deficit. If there is a way to get economic growth without increasing the debt burden unacceptably, it will be somewhat akin to squeezing through the proverbial "eye of the needle." I discussed this issue in chapter 8.

Notes

Preface

1. The Department of Engineering and Public Policy at Carnegie-Mellon University, in Pittsburgh.

2. Useful energy, which is technically called "exergy" is energy that can do work. Not all energy is useful.

3. The reasons for this undervaluation are too technical to be explained in this book. Details can be found in academic journal articles and books cited later.

Chapter 1

1. McAfee was general counsel of the Federal Reserve Bank of Richmond and has been associate secretary of the Federal Reserve Board. The views "Senator Glass" expressed in the fictitious interview may not fully or strictly represent the views of Senator Glass.

2. In the first edition of *Atlas Shrugged*, she named Branden her "intellectual heir." Later she broke with him. In the 1970 edition of *Capitalism: The Unknown Ideal*, she says that "Nathaniel Branden is no longer associated with me, with my philosophy, or with The Objectivist." She interpreted any disagreement with her views as a personal betrayal.

3. But not including Smith's *Theory of Moral Sentiments*.

4. The Sherman Anti–Trust Act was passed 51–1 in the Senate and 242–0 in the House. It was signed by President Benjamin Harrison.

5. Capitalism is defined in dictionaries in terms of associated characteristics, including private ownership of the "means of production," profit-seeking behavior, property rights, accumulation of capital, competition, "free markets," and wage labor.

6. The fact that bad bargains are not infrequent on Wall Street makes the point. The recent $8.8 billion write-down by Hewlett-Packard of its $10 billion purchase of a software company called Autonomy is an illustration.

7. The price elasticity is not really a fixed number, since it varies along the whole demand curve. However, in practice, it is defined at or near the point where the demand curve meets the increasing supply curve.

8. This topic is discussed in the last chapter of the book.

9. There are several other more powerful greenhouse gases, such as fluorocarbons and sulfur hexafluoride (SF_6), that are released in very small quantities. Altogether they account for about 2 percent of total emissions, in terms of carbon equivalent. Carbon dioxide accounts for 84 percent of the GHGs and all but 2 percent of that is from fossil fuel combustion.

10. Solow's original model assumed an exogenous driver called "technical progress," now called "total factor productivity," that was not explained by increases in capital or labor. The explanation of "total factor productivity" is still controversial. I comment on this point later.

11. The technical term for "importance" as applied to energy is "output elasticity," which is the logarithmic derivative of output (GDP) with respect to the energy input.

12. See, for instance, the popular macroeconomic textbook by Mankiw (1997).

13. The social consequences of zero or negative growth are not explained by the economic theory. In reality these consequences are likely to be so de-stabilizing that economic theory becomes irrelevant to what will follow.

Chapter 2

1. In the 1970s nuclear power plants were being built at a rapid pace by the utility industry, and the "nuclear future"—when electric power would be "too cheap to measure"—was still widely anticipated. It was also widely expected by the nuclear community, that fusion power would be available relatively soon, certainly before the year 2000. That rosy future turned dark after the Three Mile Island accident in 1979 and the Chernobyl accident a few years later. Those events were good news for the oil exporters, of course.

Chapter 3

1. Charles Ponzi was a Boston-based "developer" who sold building lots (23 to the acre) in a largely fictitious real estate development "near Jacksonville" in Florida—but actually 65 miles west of the city—during the Florida land boom of 1925 to 1926 (Galbraith 1954, pp. 9–10).

2. Ironically, Jefferson barely won the election of 1800. He was able by a narrow vote (the 36th ballot) in the House of Representatives, after a tie in the Electoral College, and with Hamilton's help, to defeat Aaron Burr. The enmity between Hamilton and Burr ended with a fatal duel in 1804 that killed Hamilton and ended Burr's political career.

3. The underwriters routinely retained a large fraction of the funds raised from the sale of stock, as payments for their services. This practice was called "watering" of the stock. For example, J. P. Morgan's creation of the steel trust (US Steel Co.) resulted in instant profits for the syndicate organized by the Morgan bank of roughly $62.5 million (*$1.6 billion*$_{2011}$), not including profits from the later sale of shares awarded to themselves (Myers [1909] 1936, p. 603). These shares could be added to the bank reserves, thus increasing their lending capacity. It was a win-win strategy for the bankers.

4. Dollar values before 2005 are shown also in constant 2011 dollars, converted using the US GDP deflator. Dollar values from 2005 are "current," although one 2005 dollar was $1.13 by this measure in 2011 and $1.16 at the end of 2013.

5. Calcium carbide is a convenient and safe way to carry energy safely. Adding water makes acetylene, which can be used for lamps, as every Boy Scout knows.

6. The Bell system was originally financed by Boston bankers who invested as venture capitalists in the original invention. However, during the life of the patents the system was not only self-financed but was extremely profitable, paying as much as 50 percent of gross receipts as dividends. The most rapid growth occurred after 1894.

7. The names of some of the "malefactors of great wealth" who made their fortunes from railroads are familiar: Astor, Vanderbilt, Gould, Cooke, Sage, Harriman, and Stanford (Myers [1909] 1936).

8. A client could purchase 100 shares of XYZ Corp for the price of (say) 25 shares, the remainder being financed by the brokerage (using money from the banks) and held as security. If the value of the shares went up, the customer kept the profits on all the shares. However, if prices went down, the broker would make a "margin call" asking for more security. If the client could not find more money, the broker would sell shares.

9. Senator Glass said of him, after the 1929 crash "Mitchell, more than any 50 men, is responsible for this crash."

10. Harrison Williams was reputed to be the richest man in the United States in 1929 having made his fortune by organizing Central States Electric Co. He had a partnership with Wadill Catchings.

11. For a detailed description of the disaster, which nearly destroyed Goldman Sachs, see Ellis (2009, ch. 2).

12. Richard Whitney was later arrested (1938) and convicted of embezzlement. (He had stolen from the NYSE gratuity fund, from his brother George, and from his father-in-law's estate, besides from others.) He served three years and four months in Sing-Sing prison.

Chapter 4

1. "Commercial paper" is short-term debt, usually three months, used for a variety of temporary purposes. It is funded by firms with excess cash, insurance companies, or private investors.

2. Warren Buffet appeared on the scene in the 1950s. He became the most successful investor in history. When he started investing in Berkshire Hathaway (a Massachusetts shirt company) in the early 1960s, he was paying $7.60 per share. By 1965 Buffet was buying aggressively and paying $14.86 per share, for a company with $19 per share of working capital not to mention land, factory, and equipment. He took over the company at a board meeting, became chairman, and named a new president. The rest, as they say, is history.

3. A CDO is a "collateralized debt obligation," which is a package of mortgage-based securities. The term "mezzanine" refers to the fact that these securities had been "sliced and diced" into little pieces and then reconstructed into "tranches" that were supposed to be differentiated according to inherent risk, the "mezzanine" class being the highest rated and least risky. Unfortunately, the rating agencies, which worked for the banks, had been thoroughly deceived—or deceived themselves—into awarding AAA ratings for bonds that should have been regarded as "junk."

4. The main reason seems to be that whereas in Germany there were no preexisting inflationary expectations in 1922 to 1923, in Latin America inflation had become habitual. Countries like Brazil planned for it, and even the United States introduced automatic inflation-adjustments into social security. See Kiguel and Liviatan (1995).

5. Speaking of "flight capital," the cumulative total of unreported wealth stored in offshore repositories, or private banks in Switzerland and elsewhere, as of late 2010 seems to have amounted to at least $9.7 trillion, and perhaps $21 trillion, owned by fewer than 100,000 people (Henry 2011). Of this, at least $775 billion had disappeared from the Russian economy, $305 billion came from Saudi Arabia, and $303 billion came from Nigeria. In those cases (and probably others) the source of the money was oil or gas. And most of it ended up being managed by private banks, such as UBS, Credit Suisse, and Goldman Sachs.

6. To pull this off, it was necessary for the target company to take over responsibility for the raider's costs (i.e., redeeming the junk bonds) as part of the LBO. This was the trickiest part of the operation.

7. A report written by Steve Eisman, of Oppenheimer and Co., pointed out that these companies were only profitable if given credit for future earnings from mortgage-based securities that they retained in their treasuries, assuming that none of the underlying mortgages would default, even though the actual default rates in subprime mortgages were high and rising. Most of those mortgage companies went bust (Lewis 2010, pp. 17–18).

8. Under new (Basel III) rules, starting in January 2013, gold is treated as a tier 1 asset, essentially doubling its value for lending purposes. Anticipation of this change resulted in a rising gold price, which has now reversed.

9. A bank's capital is effectively its net worth, meaning whatever is left when liabilities are subtracted from assets. The measurement of asset value became a major accounting issue when "mark to market" (MTM) was adopted by the Financial Accounting Standards Board (FASB Rule 115). That was a few years later, in 1992.

10. The notional value is the amount on which payments to the counterparties are based. The amount at risk is generally much smaller. The market value was estimated by the GAO at 3 percent of the notional value.

11. The term "deadweight" is econo-speak for the notion that regulation reduces the "option space" for firms. Of course, that is what it is supposed to do. But conservatives opposed to regulation tend to assume that the options thereby ruled out would be harmless to society and beneficial to the firms. That assumption is indefensible.

Chapter 5

1. However, the Mozilla Project, originally from Netscape, gave birth to the open-source nonprofit Mozilla Foundation and a wholly owned subsidiary, Mozilla Firefox.

2. The rule was simultaneously issued by the Federal Deposit Insurance Corporation (FDIC), the FRB, the Office of Thrift Supervision, and the Office of the Comptroller of the Currency, on November 29, 2001.

3. HFC was sold to HFSC in 2003; The Money Store was bought by First Union that later merged with Wachovia, bought by Wells-Fargo (2008), while Country-Wide was bought by Bank of America in 2008.

4. This figure was shown in the movie "Margin Call," which was a relatively accurate portrayal of the collapse of Lehman Brothers. I suspect the number 99.9 percent is also accurate but I don't know the source.

5. The first bond insurance company, American Municipal Bond Assurance Corporation (AMBAC), was created in 1971. This was followed by Municipal Bond Insurance Association (MBIA) in 1973. Several other companies entered the business later, notably Financial Guarantee Insurance Company (FGIC) in 1983 and Financial Security Assurance, Inc. (FSA) in 1985. These insurance companies only insured municipal bonds that were rated "investment grade." Because of their narrow focus they were called "monolines." They all maintained very low profiles until the housing bubble after 2002 when they sold a lot of credit default swaps (CDSs). In 2009 they all crashed.

6. The ABX index created by CDSindexco and Markit, was published starting in January 2006 (06-1), with three subsequent publications at six month intervals (06-2, 07-1, and 07-2). The index was based on credit default swaps (CDSs) on subprime mortgage-based bonds.

7. The rising real estate prices were mainly a suburban and "sunbelt" phenomenon, not enjoyed by central cities, especially in the industrial heartland. Home prices lagged or declined in central cities like Boston and New York (except for Manhattan); Philadelphia, Pittsburgh, Cleveland, Detroit, Chicago, and St. Louis; Washington, DC, and Los Angeles were exceptions.

8. That money helped accelerate GDP growth, which averaged 4.1 percent per annum during the years 2003 to 2007, as compared to a mere 2 percent per annum in Europe at the same time.

Chapter 6

1. It remains true that the Chinese stockpile of Treasury bonds is also part of the US public debt. However, it is important to realize that Chinese purchases of US Treasury bonds are fixed by the trade imbalance. They are independent of the interest rate paid by the US government. In economic jargon, the price elasticity of Chinese demand for US debt is close to zero. But the United States is approaching a limit in its ability to absorb Chinese exports and pay for them with borrowed money. This is leading the Chinese government to move toward a more consumption-driven economy.

2. Some defaults are allowed for in the construction of the bonds, based on historical averages. Excess defaults are defaults beyond that base rate.

Chapter 7

1. A small selection of these authors would include Hubbert (1962), Campbell (1997), Campbell and Laherrère (1998), Deffeyes (2001), Heinberg (2007), Strahan (2007), and Aleklett (2010).

2. Some of the material in this paragraph was taken from a guest posting by James Hamilton on *Econbrowser*, of data taken from J. David Hughes's presentation at the American Geophysical Union (AGU) annual meeting in December, 2012, available at: http://www.econbrowser.com/archives/2012/12/future_producti.html.

3. Pickens was the corporate raider who made a lot of money in the 1980s by a tactic known as "green-mail," using money from junk bonds to invest in low priced shares in big oil companies with large reserves, thus driving the share prices up. His major target was Gulf Oil Company, which eventually sold itself to Chevron. I suspect he is a player in the shale industry.

Chapter 8

1. The net energy return on energy investment (EROEI) for petroleum has declined from more than 100:1 in 1930 to around 25:1 today. The EROEI for biofuels, solar power, wind turbines, tar sands, or shale is far less.

2. Not all energy is useful; for example, high temperature heat can be **used**. Heat at room temperature is not useful.

3. The difficulty in making this distinction is easier in principle than in practice. Would a spin-off from a conglomerate be treated as a start-up? You can see the problem.

4. The idea is to auction permits to emit a certain amount of carbon dioxide. In principle, all firms that need to burn fossil fuels must bid for the permits. This bidding process should establish a market price that will increase gradually over time as the maximum total carbon emissions (the "cap") is increased. The system

was established in Europe several years ago, but the big German utilities, which got their permits free because of "grandfathering," sold their permits, driving the price down. Then they apparently bought what they needed at a cheaper price (and claimed the cost as a business expense). This "gaming" has given the whole scheme a black eye.

5. If the Scottish independence movement succeeds, Scotland might choose to join the eurozone, leaving "little Britain" (England, Wales, and Northern Ireland) out in the cold.

6. It has yet to be ratified by the member countries.

7. The other problem, especially for Spain, Ireland, Cyprus, and Iceland, is (or was) losses by out-of-control banks.

Chapter 9

1. Goldman Sachs, JPMorgan Chase, Morgan Stanley, CitiGroup, and Deutsche Bank.

2. Conventional fuel rods have to be removed after four to five years of operation, with only 5 percent of the energy extracted. Storing the radioactive fuel rods safely is the major unsolved problem for U-based nuclear power technology.

Appendix

1. The role of deliberate obfuscation by the use of jargon cannot be ignored. As reported by Floyd Norris (*New York Times* Business Section, March 21, 2013) Bruno Iksil ("The Whale") made a presentation of his intentions to his bosses on January 26, 2012. He proposed to "sell the forward spread and buy protection on the tightening move," "go long risk on some belly tranches especially where defaults may realize," and "buy protection on HY and Xover in rallies and turn the position over to monetize volatility." None of his superiors seem to have known what he was talking about. One wonders whether he knew himself. (And in proofing this book, I thought I had garbled the word-processing and thrown words together at random!)

References

Admati, Anat, and Martin Hellwig. 2013. *The Bankers' New Clothes*. Princeton: Princeton University Press.

Ahamed, Liaquat. 2009. *Lords of Finance: The Bankers Who Broke the World*. London: Penguin.

Aleklett, Kjell. 2010. Peak fossil and the human well-being equation. The Stockholm Seminars, 9 June. Stockholm Resilience Centre. http://www4.tsl.uu.se/~aleklett/powerpoint/20100609_Aleklett_kva.pdf.

Allen, Edward L. 1979. *Energy and Economic Growth in the United States: Perspectives in Energy*. Cambridge: MIT Press.

Angelides, Philip. 2011. *Financial Crisis Inquiry Report: Final Report of the National* Commission *on the Causes of the Financial and Economic Crisis in the United States*. Washington, DC: Financial Crisis Inquiry Commission.

Anonymous. The dismantling of the Standard Oil Trust. LINUX INFO 2004. Available at: http://www.linfo.org/standarddoil.http.

Arnold, Bruce. 2000. *Causes and Consequences of the Trade Deficit: An Overview*. Washington: Congressional Budget Office.

Arrow, Kenneth J. 1962. The economic implications of learning by doing. *Review of Economic Studies* 29: 155–73.

Arrow, Kenneth J., and Gerard Debreu. 1954. Existence of an equilibrium for a competitive economy. *Econometrica* 22 (3): 265–90.

Ashcraft, Adam B., and Til Scheuermann. 2008. *Understanding the Securitization of Sub-prime Mortgage Credit*. New York: Federal Reserve Bank of New York.

Ayres, Robert U., and Allen V. Kneese. 1969. Production, consumption and externalities. *American Economic Review* 59: 282–97.

Ayres, Robert U., and Katalin Martinás. 2006. *On the Reappraisal of Microeconomics: Economic Growth and Change in a Material World*. Cheltenham, UK: Edward Elgar.

Ayres, Robert U., and Tania Van Leynseele. 1997. *Eco-efficiency, Double Dividends and the Sustainable Firm*. Fontainebleau, France: INSEAD.

Ayres, Robert U., and Benjamin S. Warr. 2005. Accounting for growth: The role of physical work. *Structural Change and Economic Dynamics* 16 (2): 181–209.

Ayres, Robert U., and Benjamin S. Warr. 2009. Energy efficiency and economic growth: The "rebound effect" as a driver. In Horace Herring and Steve Sorrell, eds., *Energy Efficiency and Sustainable Consumption*. London: Palgrave Macmillan, 121–37.

Bair, Sheila C. 2012. *Bull by the Horns: Fighting to save Main Street from Wall Street and Wall Street from Itself*. New York: Free Press.

Bank for International Settlements. 1988. *International Convergence of Capital Measurement and Capital Standards (Basel I)*. Basel: BIS.

Bank for International Settlements. 1998. *International Convergence of Capital Measurement and Capital Standards, Basel I Update to Reflect Several Textual Changes Made since Basel Accords of July 1988*. Basel: BIS.

Bank for International Settlements. 2006. *International Convergence of Capital Measurement and Capital Standards: A Revised Framework, Comprehensive Version (Basel II)*. Basel: BIS.

Baumol, William J. 1967. *Welfare Economics and the Theory of the State*. Cambridge: Harvard University Press.

BBC. 2012. Timeline: Credit crunch to downturn. bbc.com/future 20122012]. Available at: http://news.bbc.co.uk/2/hi/7521250.stm.

Benes, Jaromir, Marcelle Chauvet, Ondra Kamenik, Michael Kumhof, Douglas Laxton, Susanna Marsala, and Jack Selody. 2012. *The Future of Oil: Geology versus Technology*. Washington, DC: IMF.

Bergh, Jeroen C. J. M. van den, and Harmen Verbruggen. 1999. Spatial sustainability, trade and indicators: An evaluation of the ecological footprint. *Ecological Economics* 29 (1): 61–72.

Bernanke, Benjamin. 2000. *Essays on the Great Depression*. Princeton: Princeton University Press.

Berndt, Ernst R., and Dale W. Jorgenson. 1978. How energy and its cost enter the productivity equation. *IEEE Spectrum* 15: 50–52.

Black, Fischer, and Myron Scholes. 1973. The pricing of options and corporate liabilities. *Journal of Political Economy* 81 (3): 637–54.

Blake, David. 2008. The sins of Greenspan have come back to haunt us. *Financial Times*, December 15, p. 2.

Bourdaire, Jean-Charles, et al. 2003. *Drivers of the Energy Scene*. London: World Energy Council (WEC).

Branden, Barbara. 1986. *The Passion of Ayn Rand*. New York: Anchor Books.

Briggs, Michael. Widescale biodiesel production from algae. UNH Biodiesel Group. 2004. Available at: http://www.unh.edu/p2/biodiesel/research_index.html.

Brookes, Len. 1990. Energy efficiency and economic fallacies. *Energy Policy* 18 (2): 199–201.

Buffet, Warren. 1984. The superinvestors of Graham-and-Doddsville. *Hermes* (fall).

Buffet, Warren. 2002. *Berkshire Hathaway Annual Report*. Omaha, NE: Berkshire Hathaway.

Burns, Jennifer. 1997. *Goddess of the Market: Ayn Rand and the American Right*. Oxford: Oxford University Press.

Butkiewicz, James. Reconstruction Finance Corp., Economic History (EH).net 2002. Available at: http://eh.net/encyclopedia/article/butkiewicz/finance.corp.reconstruction.

Campbell, Colin J. 1997. *The Coming Oil Crisis*. Brentwood, UK: Multi-Science Publishing and Petro-consultants.

Campbell, Colin J., and Jean H. Laherrère. 1998. The end of cheap oil. *Scientific American* 278 (3): 60–65.

Carson, Rachel. 1962. *Silent Spring*. Boston: Houghton Mifflin Company.

Carswell, Simon. 2011. *Inside the Bank That Broke Ireland*. Dublin: Penguin.

Casten, Thomas R., and Martin J. Collins. 2002. Co-generation and on-site power production: Optimizing future heat and power generation. *Technological Forecasting and Social Change* 6 (3): 71–77.

Coase, Ronald. 1960. The problem of social costs. *Journal of Law and Economics* 3 (October): 1–44.

Cohan, William D. 2010. The art of the deal: Bruce Wasserstein's last surprise. *Vanity Fair* (May).

Cootner, Paul, ed. 1964. *The Random Character of Stock Market Prices*. Cambridge: MIT Press.

Deffeyes, Kenneth S. 2001. *Hubbert's Peak*. Princeton: Princeton University Press.

Dodd, Randall. 2004. Derivatives markets: Sources of vulnerability in U.S. financial markets. Financial Policy Forum. Derivatives Study Center, Washington, DC.

Eisinger, Jesse. 2012. Killing the Volcker Rule with complexity. *International Herald Tribune* (*New York Times*), February 24, p. 20.

Ellis, Charles D. 2009. *The Partnership: The Making of Goldman-Sachs*. New York: Penguin.

Elswijk, Marcel, and Henk Kaan. 2009. European embedding of passive houses. PEP project, 2008. Available at: www.aee-intec.at/0uploads/dateien578.pdf, accessed January 15, 2009.

Enos, J. L. 1962. *Petroleum Progress and Profits: A History of Process Innovation*. Cambridge: MIT Press.

Epstein, Edward Jay. 1983. The BIS—Ruling the world of money. *Harper's* 248: 112–23.

Epstein, Paul, Jonathan J. Buonocore, Kevin Eckerle, Michael Hendrix, Benjamin M. Stout III, Richard Heinberg, Richard W. Clapp, Beverly May, Nancy L. Reinhart, Melissa M. Ahern, Samir K. Doshi, and Leslie Glustrom. 2012. The full cost of accounting for the life cycle of coal. *Annals of the New York Academy of Sciences* 1219 (Ecological Economics Reviews): 73–98. doi: 10.1111/j.1749-6632.2010.05890.

ESMAP. 2007. *Technical and Economic Assessment of Off-grid, Mini-grid and Grid Electrification Technologies.* Washington, DC: World Bank.

Factor Ten Club. 1994 and 1997. Carnoules declaration. Carnoules, France.

Fama, Eugene F. 1965. Random walks in stock market prices. *Financial Analysts Journal* 21 (September–October): 55–59.

Fama, Eugene F. 1970. Efficient capital markets: A review of theory and empirical work. *Journal of Finance* 25 (2): 383–417.

Fama, Eugene F., Lawrence Fisher, Michael Jensen, and Richard Roll. 1969. The adjustment of stock prices to new information. *International Economic Review* 10 (1): 1–21.

Fama, Eugene F., and K. R. French. 2004. The capital asset pricing model: Theory and evidence. *Journal of Economic Perspectives* 18 (3): 25–46.

Fama, Eugene F., and Kenneth R. French. 1965. The behavior of stock market prices. *Journal of Business* 38 (1): 34–105.

Federal Insurance Deposit Corp. 1997. *History of the '80s: Lessons for the Future*, vol. 1. Washington DC: FDIC Public Information Office. www.fdic.gov/bank/historical/history/.

Friedman, Jeffrey, and Wladimir Kraus. 2011. *Engineering the Financial Crisis.* Philadelphia: University of Pennsylvania Press.

Friedman, Milton. 1962. *Capitalism and Freedom.* Chicago: University of Chicago Press.

Friedman, Milton, and Anna Schwartz. 1963. *A Monetary History of the United States, 1867–1960.* Princeton: Princeton University Press.

Friedman, Milton. 1970. The social responsibility of business is to increase its profits. *New York Times Magazine*, September 13, p. 32.

Friedman, Milton, and Anna Jacobson Schwartz. 2008. *The Great Contraction: 1929–1933.* Princeton: Princeton University Press.

Fukuyama, Francis. 1992. *The End of History and the Last Man.* London: Penguin Books.

Galbraith, John Kenneth. 1954. *The Great Crash 1929.* Boston: Houghton Mifflin.

General Accounting Office (GAO). 1997. *OTC Derivatives: Additional Oversight Could Reduce Costly Sales Practice Disputes.* Washington, DC: General Accounting Office.

Goodman, Peter S. 2008. The reckoning: Taking a hard new look at the Greenspan legacy. *New York Times*, October 9.

Gordon, Robert J. 2012. Is US economic growth over? Faltering innovation confronts the six headwinds. CEPR 63. Centre for Economic Policy Research, Washington, DC. Available at: www.cepr.org.

Graeber, David. 2011. *Debt: The First 5000 Years.* New York: Melville.

Granade, Hannah Choi, Jon Creyts, Anton Derkach, Philip Farese, Scott Nyquist, and Ken Ostrowski. 2009. *Unlocking Energy Efficiency in the US Economy*. New York: McKinsey.

Greenspan, Alan. 2005. Consumer Finance. In *Federal Reserve System's Fourth Annual Community Affairs Research Conference*. Washington, DC: Federal Reserve Board.

Greider, William. 2010. The AIG bailout. [Available at: www.thenation.com.] *Nation* (August):6.

Hall, Charles A. S. 2008. Why EROI matters (part 1 of 6). *The Oil Drum*. Available at: www.theoildrum.com.

Hall, Charles A. S., and J. W. Day. 2009. Revisiting the limits to growth after peak oil. *American Scientist* 97: 230–37.

Hamilton, James D. 2005. Oil and the macroeconomy. In J. Eatwell, M. Millgate, and P. Newman, eds., *The New Palgrave: A Dictionary of Economics*. London: Macmillan.

Hamilton, James D. 2009. Causes and consequences of the oil shock of 2007–08. *Brookings Papers on Economic Activity*.

Hammerschlag, Roel. 2006. Ethanol's energy return on investment; A survey of the literature 1990. *Environmental Science and Technology* 40 (6): 1744–50.

Hansmann, Henry, and Reiner Kraakman. 2001. The end of history for corporate law. *Georgetown Law Review* 89:439–468.

Hardin, Garett. 1968. The tragedy of the commons. *Science* 162: 1243–48.

Hargraves, Robert. 2012. *Thorium: Energy Cheaper Than Coal*. Hanover, NH: Robert Hargraves.

Hargraves, Robert, and Ralph Moir. 2010. Liquid fluoride thorium reactors. *American Scientist* 98: 304–13.

Hayek, Friedrich A. 1976. *The Denationalization of Money: An Analysis of the Theory and Practice of Concurrent Currencies*. London: Coronet Books.

Hayek, Friedrich August. 1931. *Prices and Production*. London: Routledge.

Hayek, Friedrich August. 1944. *The Road to Serfdom*. Chicago: University of Chicago Press.

Hayek, Friedrich August. 1960. *The Constitution of Liberty*. Chicago: University of Chicago Press.

Heinberg, Richard. 2007. *Peak Everything: Waking up to a Century of Decline*. Santa Rosa, CA: New Society Publishers.

Heinberg, Richard. 2009. *Blackout: Coal, Climate and the Last Energy Crisis*. Santa Rosa, CA: New Society Publishers.

Henderson, Dean. 2012. The Federal Reserve cartel: The eight families. Globalization Research.ca 20122012]. Available at: http://www.global.research.ca.

Henry, James. 2011. *The Price of Offshore, Revisited*. London: Tax Justice Network.

Hensley, Russell, John Newman, and Matt Rogers. 2012. Battery technology charges ahead. *McKinsey Quarterly* (July).

Herndon, Thomas. 2013. Does high public debt consistently stifle economic growth? A critique of Reinhart and Rogoff. Political Economy Research Institute, University of Massachusetts, Amherst.

Higham, Charles. 1983. A bank for all reasons. In *Trading with the Enemy: How the Allied Multinationals Supplied Nazi Germany throughout World War Two*. London: Robert Hale, ch. 3.

Hoover, Herbert. 1951. *The Memoirs of Herbert Hoover*. vol. 3. *The Great Depression 1929–1941*. New York: Macmillan.

Hopper, Nicole, Charles Goldman, Donald Gilligan, Terry Singer, and Dave Birr. 2007. *A survey of the U.S. ESCO industry: Market growth and development from 2000 to 2006*. Berkeley, CA: Lawrence Berkeley National Laboratory.

Hubbert, M. King. 1962. Energy resources. A report to the Committee on Natural Resources of the National Academy of Sciences–National Research Council, Washington, DC.

Hudson, Edward, and Dale W. Jorgenson. 1974. US energy policy and economic growth, 1975–2000. *Bell Journal of Economics and Management Science* 5 (2): 461–514.

Hughes, J. David. 2010. *Hydrocarbons in North America*. Santa Rosa, CA: Post Carbon Institute.

International Energy Agency. 2008. *Combined Heat and Power: Evaluating the Benefits of Greater Global Investment*, Tom Kerr, ed. Paris: IEA.

International Energy Agency. 2009. *Energy Technology Transitions for Industry: Strategies for the Next Industrial Revolution*. Paris: OECD/IEA.

IPCC. 2007. *IPCC Fourth Assessment Report: Climate Change 2007 (AR4)*. 4 vols. Geneva: Intergovernmental Panel on Climate Change.

Jensen, Michael C., and William H. Meckling. 1976. Theory of the firm: Managerial behavior, agency costs and ownership structures. *Journal of Financial Economics* 3 (4):305.

Jevons, William Stanley. [1865] 1974. The coal question: Can Britain survive? *Environment and Change* (February). Extracts from 1865 original.

Johansson, Thomas B., Anand Padwardha, Nebojsa Nakicenovic, and Luis Gomez-Echeverri, eds. 2012. *Global Energy Assessment (GEA)*. Cambridge: Cambridge University Press.

Kapp, K. W. 1950. *The Social Costs of Private Enterprise*. Cambridge: Harvard University Press.

Keen, Steve. 2011. A monetary Minsky model of the Great Moderation and the Great Depression. *Journal of Economic Behavior and Organization*. Available at: www.journals.elsevier.com/journal-of-economic-behavior-and-organization/.

Keen, Steve. 2012. Instability in financial markets: Sources and remedies. Paper read at INET Conference, April 12–14, Berlin.

Kennedy, Paul. 1989. *The Rise and Fall of the Great Powers.* New York: Vintage Books.

Keynes, John Maynard. 1920. *Economic Consequences of the Peace.* New York: Harcourt Brace.

Keynes, John Maynard. 1935. *The General Theory of Employment, Interest and Money.* London: Macmillan.

Khazzoom, J. Daniel. 1980. Economic implications of mandated efficiency standards for household appliances. *Energy Journal* 1 (4): 21–39.

Kiguel, Miguel A., and Nissan Liviatan. 1995. Stopping three big inflations: Argentina, Brazil and Peru. In Rudiger Dornbusch and Sebastien Edwards, eds., *Reform, Recovery and Growth: Latin America and the Middle East.* Chicago: University of Chicago Press, 369–414.

Kindleberger, Charles P. 1989. *Manias, Panics and Crashes: A History of Financial Crises,* rev. ed. New York: Basic Books.

Kirk, Michael. 2009. The warning. In *PBS Public Affairs Program,* WGBH/PBS, Boston.

Kneese, Allen V. 1977. *Economics and the Environment.* New York: Penguin Books.

Kneese, Allen V., Robert U. Ayres, and Ralph C. d'Arge. 1970. *Economics and the Environment: A Materials Balance Approach.* Baltimore: RFF Press/Johns Hopkins University Press.

Kolko, Gabriel. 1963. *The Triumph of Conservatism.* New York: Macmillan.

Kubiszewski, Ida, Robert Costanze, Carol Franco, Philip Lawn, John Talberth, Tim Jackson, and Camille Aylmerm. 2013. Beyond GDP: Measuring and achieving global genuine progress. *Ecological Economics* 93 (September): 57–68.

Kuemmel, Reiner, Robert U. Ayres, and Dietmar Lindenberger. 2010. Thermodynamic laws, economic methods and the productive power of energy. *Journal of Non-equilibrium Thermodynamics* 35: 145–81.

Laitner, John A. ("Skip"), Steve Nadel, Neil Elliott, H. Sachs, and Subik Khan. 2012. The long-term energy efficiency potential: What the evidence suggests. American Council for an Energy-Efficient Economy (ACEEE), Washington, DC.

Leonhardt, David. 2009. America's sea of red ink was years in the making. *New York Times,* June 9.

Lewis, Michael. 1989. *Liar's Poker.* London: Hodder and Stoughton.

Lewis, Michael. 1999. *The New New Thing: A Silicon Valley Story.* London: Hodder and Stoughton.

Lewis, Michael. 2010. *The Big Short.* New York: Norton Penguin.

Lewis, Michael. 2011. *Boomerang: The Melt-down Tour.* New York: Norton Penguin.

Lietaer, Bernard, Robert E. Ulanowicz, and Sally Goerner. 2009. Options for managing a systemic bank crisis. Surveys and Perspectives Integrating Environment and Society (SAPIENS) 2 (1). Available at: www.sapiens.revues.org/747.

Lloyd-George, David. 1932. *The Truth about Reparations and War Debts*. London: Heinemann.

Lovelock, James E. 1979. *Gaia: A New Look at Life on Earth*. London: Oxford University Press.

Lovins, Amory. 1998. Energy efficiencies resulting from the adoption of more efficient appliances: Another view. *Energy Journal* 9 (2):155–62.

Lovins, Amory. 2011. *Reinventing Fire*. White River Junction, VT: Chelsea Green.

Lovins, Amory B. 1978. Soft energy technologies. *Annual Review of Energy* 3: 477–517.

Lovins, Amory B. 1996. Hypercars: The next industrial revolution. Paper read at 13th International Electric Vehicle Symposium (EVS 13), October 14, Osaka, Japan.

Lovins, Amory B., and L. Hunter Lovins. 1987. Energy: The avoidable oil crisis. *Atlantic Monthly* 260 (6): 22–29.

Lovins, Amory B., and L. Hunter Lovins. 1991. Least-cost climatic stabilization. *Annual Review of Energy* 16: 433–531.

Lovins, Amory B., and L. Hunter Lovins. 1992. Profitability stabilizing global climate. *Climatic Change* 22 (2): 89–94.

Lovins, Amory B., L. Hunter Lovins, Florentin Krause, and Wilfred Bach. 1981. *Least-Cost Energy: Solving the CO_2 Problem*. Andover, MA: Brickhouse.

Lundberg, Ferdinand. 1968. *The Rich and the Super-Rich*. New York: Bantam.

Machlup, Fritz. 1962. *The Production and Distribution of Knowledge in the US*. Princeton: Princeton University Press.

Mackay, David J. C. 2008. *Sustainable Energy—Without the Hot Air*. Cambridge, UK: UIT Cambridge.

Makin, John H. 1984. *The Global Debt Crisis: America's Growing Involvement*. New York: Basic Books.

Malkin, Lawrence. 1988. *The National Debt*. New York: New American Library, Mentor.

Mankiw, N. Gregory. 1997. *Macroeconomics*. London: Worth Publishing.

Markham, Jerry A. 1997. *Commodities Regulation: Fraud, Manipulation and Other Claims*. Washington, DC: General Accounting Office.

Marshall, Alfred. 1930. *Principles of Economics*, 8th ed. London: Macmillan.

McAdoo, William G. 1931. *The Crowded Years: The Reminiscences of William G. McAdoo*. New York: Houghton Mifflin.

McAfee, James. 1997. A Conversation with Senator Carter Glass. *The Region: Banking and Policy Issues* (December).

McGee, Suzanne. 2010. *Chasing Goldman Sachs*. New York: Crown Business.

McKenzie, Lionel W. 1954. On equilibrium in Graham's model of world trade and other competitive systems. *Econometrica* 22: 147–161.

McLean, Bethany, and Joe Nocera. 2010. *All the Devils Are Here: The Hidden History of the Financial Crisis*. New York: Portfolio.

Mendez, Alfred. 2001. The network. Paper read at The World Central Bank: The Bank for International Settlements, at Manchester, UK.

Menger, Carl. [1871] 1994. *Grundsaetze der Volkswirtschaftslehre* [Principles of economics]. Vienna: Institute for Humane Studies Series in Economic Theory/ Libertarian Press.

Mill, John Stuart. 1848. *Principles of Political Economy with Some of Their Applications to Social Philosophy*. London: Little Brown.

Mill, John Stuart. 1869. *On Liberty*, 4th ed. London: Parker.

Minsky, Hyman. 1982. *Can "It" Happen Again? Essays on Instability and Finance*. Armonk, NY: Sharpe.

Morgan, Tim. 2013. The perfect storm: Energy, finance and the end of growth. Strategic insights 9. Tullett Prebon, New York.

Mullins, Eustace. 1983. *The Secrets of the Federal Reserve*. Staunton, VA: Bankers Research Institute.

Myers, Gustavus. [1909] 1936. *History of the Great American Fortunes*. New York: Modern Library.

New York Times. 2012. Adding up the government's total bailout tab. *New York Times*. Available at: http://www.nytimes.com/interactive/2009/02/04/ business/20090205-bailout-totals-graphic.

NAS/NRC. 2005. *The Hidden Costs of Energy*. Washington, DC: National Academy of Sciences, National Research Council.

Natural Resources Defense Council. 2006. *Ethanol: Energy Well Spent: A Survey of Studies Published since 1990*. New York: NRDC.

Nocera, Joe. 2011. Who could blame GE? *New York Times*, April 4.

Olah, George A., Alain Goeppert, and G. K. Surya Prakesh. 2009. *Beyond Oil and Gas: The Methanol Economy*, 2nd ed. Hoboken, NJ: Wiley-VCH.

Pareto, Vilfredo. 1906. *Manuale di economica politica*. Rome: n.p.

Parker, Sean. 2000. Burning up. *Barron's National Business and Financial Weekly* 20 (March).

Patterson, Scott. 2010. *The Quants*. New York: Crown.

Perlack, Robert D., Lynn L. Wright, Anthony F. Turhollow, Robin L. Graham, Bryce J. Stokes, and Donald C. Erbach. 2005. Biomass as feedstock for a bioenergy and bioproducts industry: The technical feasibility of a billion-ton annual supply. Technical report. Oak Ridge National Labs, Oak Ridge, TN.

Pigou, A. C. 1920. *The Economics of Welfare*. London: Macmillan.

Pimentel, David. 2003. Ethanol Fuels: Energy Balance, Economics and Environmental Impacts Are Negative. *Natural Resources Research* 12 (2): 127–34.

Pollock, Alex J. 2012. Yet another sovereign debt crisis. American Enterprise Institute. Available at: http://www.aei.org/print/yet-another-sovereign-debt-crisis. Accessed April 1, 2012.

Rajan, Raghuram G. 2010. *Fault Lines*. Princeton: Princeton University Press.

Rand, Ayn. 1943. *The Fountainhead*. New York: Bobbs Merrill.

Rand, Ayn. 1957. *Atlas Shrugged*. New York: Random House.

Rand, Ayn. 1964. *The Virtue of Selfishness*. New York: New American Library, Signet.

Rand, Ayn. 1967. *Capitalism: The Unknown Ideal*. New York: New American Library.

Reinhart, Carmen M., and Kenneth S. Rogoff. 2009. *This Time Is Different: Eight Centuries of Financial Folly*. Princeton: Princeton University Press.

Reinhart, Carmen M., and Kenneth S. Rogoff. 2010. *Growth in a time of debt*. Cambridge, MA: National Bureau of Economic Research.

REN21. *Renewables 2010 Global Status Report*. REN21, Renewable Energy Policy Network for the 21st Century 2010. Available at: http://www.ren21.net/Portals/97/documents/GSR/REN21_GSR_2010_full_revised%20Sept2010.pdf.

Reynolds, Douglas B., and Marek Kolodziej. 2008. Former Soviet Union oil production and GDP decline: Granger causality and the multi-cycle Hubbert curve. *Energy Economics* 30 (2): 271–89.

Ritschl, Albrecht. 2012. Reparations, deficits and debt default: The Great Depression in Germany. In Nicholas Crafts and Peter Fearon, eds., *The Great Depression of the 1930s: Lessons for Today*. Oxford: Oxford University Press, 110–39.

Runge, C. Ford, and Benjamin Senauer. 2007. How biofuels could starve the poor. *Foreign Affairs* (May/June).

Saunders, Anthony, and Ingo Walter. 1994. *Universal Banking in the United States*. New York: Oxford University Press.

Saunders, Anthony, and Ingo Walter. 2011. *Financial Architecture, Systemic Risk, and Universal Banking*. Social Science Electronic Publishing Inc. Available at: http://ssm.com/sol3/papers.cfm.

Saunders, Harry. 1992. The Khazzoom–Brookes postulate and neoclassical growth. *Energy Journal* 13 (4): 131–48.

Say, Jean Baptiste. [1803] 1821. *A Treatise on Political Economy*, 4th ed. Translated by Prinsep. Paris.

Schmookler, Jacob. 1962. Changes in industry and in the state of knowledge as determinants of industrial invention. In Harold M. Groved, ed. *The Rate and Direction of Inventive Activity*. Cambridge, MA: National Bureau of Economic Research, 195–232.

Schumpeter, Joseph A. 1912. *Theorie der Wirtschaftlichen Entwicklungen*. Leipzig: Duncker and Humboldt.

Schumpeter, Joseph A. 1928. The instability of capitalism. *Economic Journal* 38: 361–86.

Schumpeter, Joseph A. 1934. *Theory of Economic Development*. Cambridge: Harvard University Press.

Schumpeter, Joseph A. 1943. *Capitalism, Socialism and Democracy*. New York: Harper and Row.

Schumpeter, Joseph A. 1911. *The Theory of Economic Development*. New York: Oxford University Press.

Securities and Exchange Commission, and the Commodities Futures Exchange Commission. 2010. *Findings regarding the market events of May 6, 2010. Report of the Staffs of the CFTC and SEC to the Joint Advisory Committee on Emerging Regulatory Issues*. Washington, DC: Securities and Exchange Commission and the Commodities Futures Exchange Commission.

SEMP. 2011. *Carter Glass and the Banking Act of 1933 (Glass–Steagall Act)*. Suburban Emergency Management Project, Inc. Available at: http://www.semp.us/publications/biot_reader.php?BiotD=606.

Senate Subcommittee on Investigations. 2011. *Wall Street and the financial crisis: Anatomy of a financial collapse*. Cosimo Reports.

Shiller, Robert J. 2006. *Irrational Exuberance*, 2nd ed. Crown Business.

Smith, Adam. [1776] 1976. An inquiry into the nature and causes of the wealth of nations. In *Collected works of Adam Smith*. Oxford, UK: Clarendon.

Smith, Adam. [1790] 2013. *The Theory of Moral Sentiments*. New York: Empire Books.

Solow, Robert M. 1956. A contribution to the theory of economic growth. *Quarterly Journal of Economics* 70: 65–94.

Solow, Robert M. 1957. Technical change and the aggregate production function. *Review of Economics and Statistics* 39: 312–20.

Solow, Robert M. 1970. Foreword. In Edwin Burmeister and A. Rodney Dobell, eds., *Mathematical Theories of Economic Growth*. New York: Macmillan, vii–ix.

Soros, George. 1988. *The Alchemy of Finance*. London: Weidenfeld and Nicolson.

Stodder, James. 1998. Corporate barter and economic stabilization. *International Journal of Community Currency Research* 2.

Stodder, James. 2000. Reciprocal exchange networks: Implications for macroeconomic stability. Paper read at International Electronic and Electrical Engineering (IEEE), Engineering Management Society (EMS), Albuquerque, NM.

Stout, Lynn. 2012. *The Shareholder Value Myth: How Putting Shareholders First Harms Investors, Corporations, and the Public*. San Francisco: Barrett-Koehler.

Strahan, David. 2007. *The Last Oil Shock*. London: Murray.

Studer, T. 2012. *WIR in unsere Volkswirtschaft—WIR and the Swiss National Economy (in English)*. Available at: http://www.lulu.com/content/268895.

Tanaka, Nobuo. 2008. *Today's Energy Challenges: The Role of CHP*. Paris: IEA.

Tarbell, Ida. 1904. *The History of the Standard Oil Company*. New York: McLure, Phillips.

Taylor, F. Sherwood. 1942. *The Century of Science: 1840–1940.* London: Heinemann.

Taylor, John B. 1993. Discretion vs. public policy rules in practice. *Carnegie-Rochester Conference Series on Public Policy* 39: 195–214.

Temin, Peter. 1976. *Did Monetary Policy Cause the Great Depression?* New York: Norton.

Thorp, Edward O. 1962. *Beat the Dealer: A Winning Strategy for the Game of Twenty-One.* New York: Vintage.

Thorp, Edward O., and Sheen Kassouf. 1967. *Beat the Market: A Scientific Stock Market System.* New York: Random House.

Triana, Pablo. 2012. *Lecturing Birds on Flying.* New York: Wiley.

Tuchman, Barbara W. 1962. *The Guns of August.* New York: MacMillan.

Tully, Shawn. 2009. Lewie Ranieri wants to fix the mortgage mess. *Fortune,* December, p. 9.

US Department of Energy. 1999. *Review of Combined Heat and Power Technologies.* ONSITE SYCOM Energy Corporation for the California Energy Commission with the US Department of Energy. Washington, DC: Office of Energy Efficiency and Renewable Energy.

Vine, Edward. 2005. An international survey of the energy service company (ESCO) industry. *Energy Policy* 33 (5): 691–704.

von Neumann, John, and Oskar Morgenstern. 1944. *Theory of Games and Economic Behavior.* Princeton: Princeton University Press.

von Weizsaecker, Ernst Ulrich, Karlson Hargroves, Michael H. Smith, Cheryl Desha, and Peter Stasinopoulos. 2009. *Factor Five:Transforming the Global Economy through 80% Improvements in Resource Productivity.* London: Earthscan.

von Weizsaecker, Ernst Ulrich, and Jochen Jesinghaus. 1992. *Ecological Tax Reform: A Policy Proposal for Sustained Development.* London: Zed Books.

von Weizsaecker, Ernst Ulrich, Amory B. Lovins, and L. Hunter Lovins. 1998. *Factor Four: Doubling Wealth, Halving Resource Use.* London: Earthscan.

Wald, Abraham. 1936. Uber einige Gleichungssysteme der mathematischen Oekonomie. *Zeitschrift fur Nationalkonomie* 7: 637–70.

Walras, Leon. [1874] 1954. *Elements of Pure Economics or the Theory of Social Wealth,* trans. by Jaffe. London: Allen and Unwin.

Walter, Ingo. 1985. *Secret Money.* Lexington, MA: Heath.

Warr, Benjamin S., and Robert U. Ayres. 2006. The MEET-REXS model. *Structural Change and Economic Dynamics* 17: 329–78.

Watkins, Thayer. 2013. Options, forward contracts, swaps and other derivative securities. San Jose State University. Available at: http://www.sjsu.edu/faculty/watkins/deriv.htm.

Wene, Clas-Otto. 2000. *Experience Curves for Energy Technology Policy.* Paris: OECD.

Werner, Richard A. 2003. *Princes of the Yen: Japan's Central Bankers and the Transformation of the Economy*. Armonk, NY: Sharpe/Eastgate Books.

Werner, Richard A. 2005. *New Paradigm in Macro-Economics*. Basingstoke: Palgrave-Macmillan.

Werner, Richard A. 2010. Towards stable and competitive banking in the U.K.—Evidence for the ICB. Centre for Banking, Finance and Sustainable Development (CBFSD), University of Southampton.

Williams, Eric, Miriam Heller, and Robert U. Ayres. 2003. The 1.7 kg microchip: Energy and material use in the production of semiconductor devices. *Environmental Science and Technology* 36 (24): 5504–10.

Worrell, Ernst, Lenny Bernstein, Joyashree Roy, Lynn Price, and Jochen Harnisch. 2009. Industrial energy efficiency and climate change migration. *Energy Efficiency* 2: 109–23.

Yergin, Daniel. 1991. *The Prize: The Epic Quest for Oil, Money and Power*. New York: Simon and Schuster.

Index